Reading About the World

Volume 1 Third Edition

Edited by Brians, Gallwey, Hughes, Hussain, Law, Myers, Neville, Schlesinger, Spitzer, Swain

CENGAGE
Learning™

Australia • Brazil • Japan • Korea • Mexico • Singapore • Spain • United Kingdom • United States

CENGAGE
Learning

Reading About the World: Volume 1 Third Edition

Edited by Brians, Gallwey, Hughes, Hussain, Law, Myers, Neville, Schlesinger, Spitzer, Swain

Executive Editors:
Michele Baird
Maureen Staudt
Michael Stranz

Project Development Manager:
Linda deStefano

Senior Marketing Coordinators:
Sara Mercurio
Lindsay Shapiro

Senior Production / Manufacturing Manager:
Donna M. Brown

PreMedia Services Supervisor:
Rebecca A. Walker

Rights & Permissions Specialist:
Kalina Hintz

Cover Image:
Getty Images*

For product information and technology assistance, contact us at
Cengage Learning Customer & Sales Support, 1-800-354-9706

For permission to use material from this text or product, submit all requests online at **cengage.com/permissions**
Further permissions questions can be emailed to
permissionrequest@cengage.com

ISBN-13: 978-0-15-567425-7

ISBN-10: 0-15-567425-0

Cengage Learning
5191 Natorp Boulevard
Mason, Ohio 45040
USA

Cengage Learning is a leading provider of customized learning solutions with office locations around the globe, including Singapore, the United Kingdom, Australia, Mexico, Brazil, and Japan. Locate your local office at: **international.cengage.com/region**

Cengage Learning products are represented in Canada by Nelson Education, Ltd.

For your lifelong learning solutions, visit **custom.cengage.com**

Visit our corporate website at **cengage.com**

Printed in the United States of America

Contributors and Consultants

from Washington State University:
Donald Bushaw
Roger Chan
Paula Elliot
Shelli Fowler
Lydia Gerber
Richard Hooker
John Kicza
Katherine Meyer
Richard Law
Marina Tolmacheva

Others:
Salman Azhar, Duke University
Jon LaCure, University of Tennessee, Knoxville
Nicholas Heer, University of Washington
Izumi Koide, International House of Japan, Tokyo
Tom Lamont, American University in Cairo

This publication made possible with support from the Office of General Education
Richard Law, Director.

Introduction

Why read these texts?

As students, you have likely been told that we can learn something about the world by studying literary and philosophical texts. One strong benefit of reading texts from a variety of periods and cultures, such as those found in this book, is that it can contribute to a deeper understanding of the past, of history. When reading about history in conventional textbooks, it is easy to assume that what is written down are "the facts" without really thinking about where those ideas came from. Although historians—people whose job it is to write down "what has happened"—have existed in many cultures, much of our information about the past has actually come, not from professional historians, but from such diverse people as lawmakers and dramatists, politicians and poets. These people, through the texts they have written, convey to us from a variety of perspectives fundamental information about their cultures. For example, if a lawmaker makes a law punishing people who aid escaped slaves, as in *The Code of Hammurabi*, we can conclude that the lawmaker's society included the class of "slave." If a dramatist writes about a woman who braves death in order to bury her brother, as in *Antigone*, we can conclude that burial of the dead was an important part of Greek society. Also, because these accounts of society come from a such a wide range of perspectives (instead of just the perspective of one historian), we can hope to achieve a broader understanding of what a society was really like. This broader understanding of the past, of culture, can in turn give us a greater appreciation of the literature that helped contribute to that culture's creation and history—including one's own culture.

But writings do not only help explain the past; the past can be used to explain writings. Conventional history courses have traditionally asked of the past, "What has happened?" Literature courses, on the other hand, have traditionally asked "What has lasted?" In a literature course the political and social events may be studied in order to explain a work whose main value is that it is still stimulating and enjoyable to read today, regardless of whether it illustrates important historical points. Greek tragedies are important as the world's first written dramas quite apart from what they tell us about Greek history. Their very existence is an important item of literary history. This reader is designed to combine both approaches to texts: "sources" used to understand history and texts valuable in themselves.

Readings chosen because they are original sources for the writing of history include legal documents, travel books, and speeches. Other readings illustrate the past in a way that brings them vividly to life: comic stories, tragic dramas, or songs of devotion to a loved one or even a god. Some selections are literary works which are generally considered "classics." Finally, many of the readings have profoundly influenced the course of thought—philosophical, religious, social, and so on—of various cultures; China's Confucian *Analects*, Islam's *Qur'an*, and the Hebrew Bible are some examples. Although the extreme variety of the selections gathered here may seem bewildering, you will find many common themes running through them: religion, social customs, love and sex, death. Many of the readings illustrate contacts or conflicts between cultures or the influences of one culture on another. We have tried especially to illustrate the lives of two groups of people who are often neglected in more traditional histories: those of women and the poor. Finally, as you read the selections in this book, keep in mind that these readings are not merely sources for writing about history; they *are* history—a history that allows a variety of voices to speak, to tell us their stories.

What do these texts "mean"?

One difficulty in learning about the past and about cultures through reading a variety of literature is that it seems a less "straightforward" method than simply reading a history textbook. Furthermore, although you may have studied literature before, your experience with texts may not be as wide-ranging as the selections in this book; perhaps you had to read some fairly contemporary poetry in an introductory English class, but you have no idea how to approach the second-century Hindu religious poem, the *Bhagavad Gita*. Although reading strategies vary for different types of literary works, we would like to offer a few suggestions on how to get started when you examine a text. We should also note that because much of what is considered the world's great literature is poetry, this volume contains a great deal of poetry. Many students are convinced that poetry is a deliberately obscure form of writing that one needs special training to read, but we hope that you will find that this is not the case with the poetic selections in this book. We have selected many of these poems on the basis of how readable and enjoyable we hope they are for a typical student reader. Few of these poems are really difficult, and the editors have tried to provide detailed notes to help you through those few, as we understand that there is often not time to do the kind of detailed study of a poem that is common in literature classes. Also for this reason, we have provided some additional reading strategies for poetry at the end of this section.

Finally, most selections in this book (both poetry and prose), besides having the usual introductory note and footnotes, are also prefaced by one or more study questions. These questions may be used as the basis for discussions, quizzes, or exams by your instructor, but even if they are not, you should pay attention to them. Although they may take the form of questions, introductory sections are designed to guide you toward significant points in the reading and to provide valuable information. As you become more comfortable with a variety of literary texts, you may also find that you are able to create study questions for yourself, for example by deciding to compare a text you are reading with another text you have read about a similar theme. Feel free to be creative as you consider new ways to engage with the readings.

Getting Started: Prose Non-Fiction Texts

There are a variety of prose non-fiction texts collected here, including excerpts from philosophical treatises and legal documents. Before you get started with the actual text, be sure to look at the orienting information you are given about the work: identify the culture out of which the piece came and in what period it was written so you get an idea of the "setting" of the piece. Next, skim the introductory notes to get a sense of what's ahead (you can read the notes in more detail later). Now you are ready to read the text itself. One of the first things to do when approaching these sometimes difficult texts is to try to determine what a text means on a literal, sentence-by-sentence level. Unless you understand what the different thoughts conveyed in a text are, you will not be able to form strong ideas about the work as a whole. For this reason, we recommend that you keep a dictionary handy as you read, and that you look up words you are unfamiliar with. Also, if you see a familiar word but cannot make sense of how it is being used, check to see if there are other definitions or connotations of the word that the writer may be employing. Keep in mind that many of the selections in this book are presented in translation, and wherever possible, the translators have tried to choose the English words that most closely approach the meanings and connotations of the words in the text's original language. Because of this, it is important to understand these words as clearly as you can.

Once you have an idea of what the sentences literally mean, try to paraphrase the text (put it into your own words). You might jot down your ideas, or perhaps try to explain what you've read to a friend. You may need to read the text and/or specific passages in it several times in order to do this. When you have a general idea of what the text is "about," you can ask yourself a series of questions. What seems to be the purpose of the text? Is it meant to inform? Persuade? Entertain? (You may find that there is a combination of these purposes). Also, what is the writer's tone? This can help you determine a writer's attitude toward her or his subject; for example, does the writer seem serious? Nostalgic? Angry? Ironic?. Finally, look again at the study questions and try to answer them using specific examples from the text to support your answers.

Getting Started: "Literary" Texts

Along with the prose non-fiction texts discussed above, there are a variety of more specifically "literary" texts in this collection, including fictional prose (such as stories and drama) and different types of poetry (such as epics, hymns, and haiku). The following comments apply especially to the poems. As with the prose non-fiction texts, be sure to identify the culture and period in which the poem was written and skim the introductory notes to get oriented to the poem. Then try skimming the poem to get general sense of it, even if you don't yet have any idea of what the poem might mean. If you sense that it is, for example, a poem about love, how is it different from reading a prose statement about love? One important distinction between poetry and prose literature is the idea that poetry is both (a) somehow more concise than prose; and (b) somehow more rhythmic than prose. This is not to say that prose texts cannot be poetic (parts of the "prose" Hebrew Bible, for example, have been set to music); however, in general, poetry is generally considered to be its own special form of literature. It may also help to remember that much poetry is oral. Early poetry, especially poetry written before the invention of writing (such as Homer's *Odyssey*), was usually performed aloud, often to instrumental accompaniment. In fact, some of the poems in this book are actually songs, such as those poems that are called "hymns." For this reason, you might try reading the poem aloud to see how it sounds. For example, lines in a poem which contain a series of long words might seem to be asking you to slow down as you speak them, perhaps to create a sense of dreaminess or languor, while a series of short, quick words might be asking you to speed up, perhaps to create a sense of cheerfulness or urgency.

After you get a general sense of the poem, go ahead and look at its language. Poets are usually extremely careful in their choice of words, using fewer words to convey an idea than one would in prose. Because each word counts for so much, it especially important to look up those you don't know. Also, when looking at words and phrases in a poem, you will often notice the poet's use of "figurative language," or language that means something beyond its literal definition. You may have learned about "similes," "metaphors," and "personification" in your literature classes; all of these are types of figurative language. For example, in the Sufi poem "There's hidden sweetness," the poet Rumi writes, "if you've lost all will and control,/they come back when you fast, like soldiers appearing/out of the ground, pennants flying above them." Here Rumi uses simile: he makes a comparison between returning will and control and soldiers. When he states "We are lutes, no more, no less," naturally, Rumi does not mean to say that people are actually lutes; he is using metaphor: he makes an implicit comparison between human beings and musical instruments. When you read poetry, then, look closely at the type of figurative language the poets use to convey their ideas, and try to imagine why they chose those particular images. For example, comparing love with "sweet soothing oil to the limbs of the restless," as in an anonymous New Kingdom Egyptian poem, gives a very different sense than describing love as Lady Kasa does in this Japanese poem: "The breakers of the Ise Sea/roar like thunder on the shore,/as fierce as they, as proud as they,/Is he who pounds my heart." Poets may also make use of symbols, or words that somehow stand for "more" than what they are. For example, in Rumi's poem "I was, on the day that the heavens were not," the speaker searches for traces of the Prophet Muhammad while he traverses "the Cross" and ascends "to the summit of Mount Qaf." This search is symbolic, as the speaker of the poem could not actually do these things; instead, he is describing his inner search for a particular type of faith. When the speaker discovers that "He [Muhammad] was not in the Cross," he is using "the Cross" as a symbol for Christianity. Learning to understand the use of figurative language is very helpful when approaching poetry (and some prose as well), as it allows you to gain a deeper experience of the poem, along with poets' possible feelings or attitudes toward their subjects when they were writing. (At the end of this introduction you will find a glossary that will help explain some of the types of figurative language you may encounter when you read the poetry in this collection, along with some other definitions of literary terms that may be helpful to you).

Once you get a sense of what the poem means on a literal and figurative level (you may even try to paraphrase it, as with prose selections), try to decide what the poet's purpose is. A poem may try to do many things: tell a story, capture a memory, express a certain mood or feeling, convey a particular idea, or even teach a moral lesson; it is your task to consider how and why a poem's "work" is done. Guided by the introductions and study questions, consider how effectively the poets have accomplished their purposes by the choices they have made. Finally, it is important to try to be receptive to all types of experience, even if they are unfamiliar to you, or differ from what you think or believe. You don't have to agree with the ideas in a poem to be able to appreciate it as a piece of literature, and this is true of the other readings in this collection as well. Overall, we hope that *Reading About the World* will help you find ways to grow as a reader of texts and of history, and will guide you toward a deeper appreciation and understanding of the past and of culture.

Glossary

Allegory. A story or description that has both its literal meaning as well as another meaning beneath its surface. Example: in Plato's "The Allegory of the Cave," the description of shadows in the cave is used to suggest that the prisoners in the cave only think they are seeing reality.

Allusion. A reference to something in previous literary or other works. Example: the use of the phrase "slaves of drunkenness, wine, and Dionysus" in Anna Comnena's *The Alexiad* is an allusion to the idea in Greek mythology that Dionysus is (among other things) the god of wine.

Connotation. The "shade" of a word, or what it suggests beyond its literal meaning. Example: the word "soft" can mean several things, but the use of the word "soft" to describe the Buddha's glance in Ratnakirti's "Hymn to the Buddha" has the connotation of a glance that is "gentle."

Denotation. The literal or dictionary definition of a word.

Hymn. A song of praise or devotion, generally to a deity. In this reader, hymns are often the same thing as prayers. Example: the Egyptian "Hymn to Osiris."

Metaphor. An implied comparison between two things. Example: "we'll be clay for Fate to make pitchers of" from Hafiz of Shiraz's Sufi poem "The dawn is breaking." Compare with *simile*, below.

Paraphrase. Use of one's own words to state what another person has said.

Personification. To give human qualities to something that is not human. Example: in the line "lightning flirts with the sky" from an Indian love poem by Vatoka, lightning is treated as if it had a mannerism that a person might have.

Satire. A type of literature that ridicules someone or something. Example: in Juvenal's *On the City of Rome*, the speaker describes in an exaggerated fashion some of the problems of his own time, presumably with a hope for change. Most ancient satire is conservative in purpose: the author is criticizing his or her own time by contrasting it with an idealized past.

Simile. An explicit comparison between two things, using such words as "like" or "as." Example: "my thoughts/Are as disordered/As my black hair" from Lady Horikawa's poem "Will he always love me?"

Symbol. A word or phrase that means more than what it literally is. Example: when, in *The Song of Roland*, Roland offers his glove to God, he is offering more than just an article of clothing; the glove is a symbol of feudal obedience in Medieval Europe.

Theme. The central idea (or one of the central ideas) in a text. Example: in the Chinese story "Allowing Mosquitoes to Feast on His Blood," the theme is the importance of the Chinese concept of filial piety, which requires strict devotion to one's parents.

Tone. A writer's apparent attitude toward her or his subject, audience, or self. Example: when Sei Shonagon describes the qualities of a bad lover in *The Pillow Book*, her tone is one of aggravation.

Contents

China

Japan

The Islamic World

The European Middle Ages

Mesopotamia

Enuma Elish: The Babylonian Creation Epic (2nd Millennium BCE)

Most ancient cultures developed stories to explain how the world came to be. Frequently these stories follow the analogy of biological reproduction, with a series of gods giving birth to each other and to the universe itself. Often, as here and in Greco-Roman myth, one generation of gods destroys or overthrows another so that the creator god is not in the end the supreme god. Another common pattern in the creation myths of the ancient Middle East is the emergence of land from an original watery chaos. The world is not so much called into being as it is organized out of a primordial chaos. This excerpt from the Old Babylonian Enuma Elish *follows this pattern, associating this chaos with the female principal represented by the goddess Tiamat. Many male-dominated societies viewed the subjection of women as an essential precondition for order. Thus the supreme sky-god, Marduk, ensures the order of the universe by slaying and dismembering the sea goddess Tiamat. One way to read this section of the epic is as a metaphor of the triumph of state power over the affectional ties of the family represented by motherhood.*

How does the younger generation of gods annoy Tiamat and Apsu? How does Apsu's plot to destroy them backfire? What is Tiamat's reaction to Apsu's plan? Why is she later so enraged that the younger gods decide she must be destroyed? How are the various parts of the universe created out of Tiamat's dismembered body? Why do you think the sea might be viewed as a chaotic element threatening order, needing to be penned in?

When skies above were not yet named.[1]
Nor earth below pronounced by name,
Apsu, the first one, their begetter
And maker Tiamat, who bore them all,[2]
Had mixed their waters together,
But had not formed pastures, nor discovered reed-beds;
When yet no gods were manifest,
Nor names pronounced, nor destinies decreed,
Then gods were born within them.
Lahmu and Lahamu[3] emerged, their names pronounced.
As soon as they matured, were fully formed.
Anshar and Kishar[4] were born, surpassing them.
They passed the days at length, they added to the years.
Anu[5] their first-born son rivaled his forefathers:
Anshar made his son Anu like himself,

---

[1]The Babylonians called the epic by its opening words, *Enuma Elish,* "When skies above."

[2]Apsu, father of the primeval gods, is the personification of the body of fresh water beneath the earth. Tiamat, "Ocean," is the primordial mother of the gods.

[3]Primeval heroes, controllers of water and fishing.

[4]"Whole Sky" and "Whole Earth."

[5]"Sky," patron god of Uruk, head of the older generation of gods.

And Anu begot Nudimmud[6] in his likeness.
He, Nudimmud, was superior to his forefathers:
Profound of understanding, he was wise, was very strong at arms.
Mightier by far than Anshar his father's begetter,
He had no rival among the gods his peers.
The gods of that generation would meet together
And disturb Tiamat, and their clamor reverberated.
They stirred up Tiamat's belly,
They were annoying her by playing inside Anduruna.[7]
Apsu could not quell their noise
And Tiamat became mute before them;
However grievous their behavior to her,
However bad their ways, she would indulge them.
Finally Apsu, begetter of the great gods,
Called out and addressed his vizier Mummu,
    "O Mummu, vizier who pleases me!
    Come, let us go to Tiamat!"
They went and sat in front of Tiamat,
And discussed affairs concerning the gods their sons.
Apsu made his voice heard
And spoke to Tiamat in a loud voice,
    "Their ways have become very grievous to me,
    By day I cannot rest, by night I cannot sleep.
    I shall abolish their ways and disperse them!
    Let peace prevail, so that we can sleep."
When Tiamat heard this,
She was furious and shouted at her lover;
She shouted dreadfully and was beside herself with rage,
But then suppressed the evil in her belly.
    "How could we allow what we ourselves created to perish?
    Even though their ways are so grievous, we should bear it patiently."
Mummu replied and counseled Apsu:
The vizier did not agree with the counsel of his earth mother.
    "O father, put an end to their troublesome ways,
    So that she may be allowed to rest by day and sleep at night."
Apsu was pleased with him, his face lit up
At the evil he was planning for the gods his sons.
Mummu hugged him,
Sat on his lap and kissed him rapturously.
But everything they plotted between them
Was relayed to the gods their sons.
The gods listened and wandered about restlessly,
They fell silent, they sat mute.

---

[6]A name for Ea or Enki, god of wisdom and incantations, who sent the Seven Sages to teach the arts and skills of civilization to humanity.
[7]Name of the god's dwelling.

Superior in understanding, wise and capable,
Ea[8] who knows everything found out their plot,
Made for himself a design of everything,
and laid it out correctly.
Made it cleverly, his pure spell was superb.
He recited it and it stilled the waters.
He poured sleep upon him so that he was sleeping soundly,
Put Apsu to sleep, drenched with sleep.
Vizier Mummu the counselor was in a sleepless daze.
Ea unfastened his belt, took off his crown,
Took away his mantle of radiance and put it on himself.
He held Apsu down and slew him;
Tied up Mummu and laid him across him.
He set up his dwelling on top of Apsu,
And grasped Mummu, held him by a nose-rope.
When he had overcome and slain his enemies,
Ea set up his triumphal cry over his foes,
Then he rested very quietly inside his private quarters
And named them Apsu and assigned chapels,
His own residence there. . . .

[In the ensuing 350 lines, omitted here, Qingu and other gods urge Tiamat to avenge the death of her husband. She assembles an army, which Ea and his allies hesitate to oppose, until Ea's son Marduk agrees to lead the defending forces.]

They founded a princely shrine for him,
And he took up residence as ruler before his fathers, who proclaimed
  "You are honored among the great gods.
  Your destiny is unequaled, your word has the power of Anu!
  O Marduk, you are honored among the great gods.
  Your destiny is unequaled, your word has the power of Anu!
  From this day onwards your command shall not be altered.
  Yours is the power to exalt and abase.
  May your utterance be law, your word never be falsified.
  None of the gods shall transgress your limits.
  May endowment, required for the gods' shrines
  Wherever they have temples, be established for your place.
  O Marduk, you are our champion!
  We hereby give you sovereignty over all of the whole universe.
  Sit in the assembly and your word shall be pre-eminent!
  May your weapons never miss, may they smash your enemies!
  O lord, spare the life of him who trusts in you,
  But drain the life of the god who has espoused evil!"
They set up in their midst one constellation,
And then they addressed Marduk their son,

---

[8]God of Wisdom.

"May your decree, O lord, impress the gods!
Command to destroy and to recreate, and let it be so!
Speak and let the constellation vanish!
Speak to it again and let the constellation reappear."
He spoke, and at his word the constellation vanished.
He spoke to it again and the constellation was recreated.
When the gods his fathers saw how effective his utterance was,
They rejoiced, they proclaimed: "Marduk is King."
They invested him with scepter, throne, and staff-of-office.
They gave him an unfaceable weapon to crush the foe.
"Go, and cut off the life of Tiamat!
Let the winds bear her blood to us as good news!"
The gods his fathers thus decreed the destiny of the lord
And set him on the path of peace and obedience.
He fashioned a bow, designated it as his weapon,
Feathered the arrow, set it in the string.
He lifted up a mace and carried it in his right hand,
Slung the bow and quiver at his side,
Put lightning in front of him,[9]
His body was filled with an ever-blazing flame.
He made a net to encircle Tiamat within it,
Marshaled the four winds so that no part of her could escape.
South Wind, North Wind, East Wind, West Wind,
The gift of his father Anu, he kept them close to the net at his side.
He created the evil wind, the tempest, the whirlwind,
The Four Winds, the Seven Winds, the tornado, the unfaceable facing wind.
He released the winds which he had created, seven of them.
They advanced behind him to make turmoil inside Tiamat.
The lord raised the flood-weapon, his great weapon,
And mounted the frightful, unfaceable storm-chariot.
He had yoked to it a team of four and had harnessed to its side
"Slayer," "Pitiless," "Racer," and "Flyer'"
Their lips were drawn back, their teeth carried poison.
They know not exhaustion, they can only devastate.
He stationed on his right "Fiercesome Fight" and "Conflict."
On the left "Battle" to knock down every contender.
Clothed in a cloak of awesome armor,
His head was crowned with a terrible radiance.
The Lord set out and took the road,
And set his face towards Tiamat who raged out of control.
In his lips he gripped a spell,
In his hand he grasped an herb to counter poison.
Then they thronged about him, the gods thronged about him;
The gods his fathers thronged about him, the gods thronged about him.
The Lord drew near and looked into the middle of Tiamat:
He was trying to find out the strategy of Qingu her lover.

---

[9]Marduk's usual weapon is the lightning bolt, like that of the later gods, Baal and Zeus.

As he looked, Qingu's mind became confused,
His will crumbled and his actions were muddled.
As for the gods his helpers, who marched at his side,
When they saw the warrior, the leader, their looks were strained.
Tiamat cast her spell. She did not even turn her neck.
In her lips she was holding falsehood, lies, wheedling.
    "How powerful is your attacking force, O lord of the gods!
    The whole assembly of them has gathered to your place!"
The Lord lifted up the flood-weapon, his great weapon
And sent a message to Tiamat who feigned goodwill, saying:
    "Why are you so friendly on the surface
    When your depths conspire to muster a battle force?
    Just because the sons were noisy and disrespectful to their fathers,
    Should you, who gave them birth, reject compassion?
    You named Qingu as your lover,
    You appointed him to rites of Anu-power, wrongfully his.
    You sought out evil for Anshar, king of the gods,
    So you have compounded your wickedness against the gods my fathers!
    Let your host prepare! Let them gird themselves with your weapons!
    Stand forth, and you and I shall do single combat!"
When Tiamat heard this,
She went wild, she lost her temper.
Tiamat screamed aloud in a passion,
Her lower parts shook together from the depths.
She recited the incantation and kept casting her spell.
Meanwhile the gods of battle were sharpening their weapons.
Face to face they came, Tiamat and Marduk, sage of the gods.
They engaged in combat, they closed for battle.
The Lord spread his net and made it encircle her,
To her face he dispatched the evil wind, which had been behind:
Tiamat opened her mouth to swallow it,
And he forced in the evil wind so that she could not close her lips.
Fierce winds distended her belly;
Her insides were constipated and she stretched her mouth wide.
He shot an arrow which pierced her belly,
Split her down the middle and slit her heart,
Vanquished her and extinguished her life.
He threw down her corpse and stood on top of her.
When he had slain Tiamat, the leader,
He broke up her regiments, her assembly was scattered.
Then the gods her helpers, who had marched at her side,
Began to tremble, panicked, and turned tail.
Although he allowed them to come out and spared their lives.
They were surrounded, they could not flee.
Then he tied them up and smashed their weapons.
They were thrown into the net and sat there ensnared.
They cowered back, filled with woe.
They had to bear his punishment, confined to prison.

And as for the dozens of creatures, covered in fearsome rays,
The gang of demons who all marched on her right,
He fixed them with nose-ropes and tied their arms.
He trampled their battle-filth beneath him.
As for Qingu, who had once been the greatest among them,
He defeated him and counted him among the dead gods,
Wrested from him the Tablet of Destinies,[10] wrongfully his,
Sealed it with his own seal and pressed it to his breast.
When he had defeated and killed his enemies
And had proclaimed the submissive foe his slave,
And had set up the triumphal cry of Anshar over all the enemy,
And had achieved the desire of Nudimmud, Marduk the warrior
Strengthened his hold over the captive gods,
And to Tiamat, whom he had ensnared, he turned back.
The Lord trampled the lower part of Tiamat,
With his unsparing mace smashed her skull,
Severed the arteries of her blood,
And made the North Wind carry it off as good news.
His fathers saw it and were jubilant: they rejoiced,
Arranged to greet him with presents, greetings gifts.
The Lord rested, and inspected her corpse.
He divided the monstrous shape and created marvels from it.
He sliced her in half like a fish for drying:
Half of her he put up to roof the sky,
Drew a bolt across and made a guard hold it.
Her waters he arranged so that they could not escape.
He crossed the heavens and sought out a shrine;
He leveled Apsu, dwelling of Nudimmud.
The Lord measured the dimensions of Apsu
And the large temple which he built in its image was Esharra:
In the great shrine Esharra, which he had created as the sky
He founded cult centers for Anu, Enlil, and Ea.

Translated by Stephanie Dalley

---

[10]A book recording everyone's fate.

The Epic of Gilgamesh: The Flood Myth (3rd Millennium BCE)

About 4700 years ago there was a powerful king who ruled over the Mesopotamian city of Uruk, named Gilgamesh. Whatever his real biography, he seems to have impressed people so powerfully that a number of legends came to be told about him. Among other things, it is said that he could strangle lions with his bare hands. These tales remained popular for over a thousand years, and became gradually woven into the narrative which we now call The Epic of Gilgamesh. *When it was first rediscovered in 1872 scholars found to their astonishment that it contained an account of a universal flood which was demonstrably earlier than but clearly related to that narrated in the Hebrew Bible (Genesis 6–9). The Tigris and Euphrates Rivers are noted for their floods, and evidence remains of some which would clearly have inundated cities which had been built along its banks (very few people in arid Mesopotamia lived far from the river banks. One theory argues that the Mediterranean flood myths may have been inspired by distant memories of the catastrophic filling of the Black Sea in the mid-6th millennium BCE which would have inundated settlements around its shores in an extremely spectacular manner (see Bill Ryan and Walter Pitman:* Noah's Flood). *Whatever its origin, the sstory was passed from one culture to another around the Mediterranean, probably eventually influencing the Greco-Roman myth of Deucalion and Pyrrha. However, the flood tale told here seems to bear no relation to the cataclysmic flood stories found in some non-Mediterranean cultures (except, of course, where such stories have developed in response to missionary contact). The point of the story in its original context has little to do with apocalyptic thinking and much to do with the fear of death. Gilgamesh, grieving over the loss of his friend and companion Enkidu, goes on a quest in search of the secret of immortality. In this story he learns from Ut-napishtim (the Sumerian Noah, whose nickname is "the far-away") that only he and his wife have been spared death. Great as he is, Gilgamesh can expect no such special favor. At the end of the story Ut-napishtim challenges him to remain awake for a week, knowing full well that he cannot. If a man cannot stay awake for so short a time, how can he hope to live forever? The Sumerians had rather gloomy ideas about the afterlife, like the Greeks, and both peoples told stories designed to reconcile the hearers to the inevitable necessity of death. Despite its discouraging message, the story retains the fascination which has caused it to be retold in one form or another longer than any other story in human history.*

What would be the advantages of living forever? Can you think of disadvantages? Compare this story with the flood narrative in Genesis. What sorts of things are similar? What do the differences tell us about the beliefs of the two different cultures that produced them?

Ut-napishtim spoke to him, to Gilgamesh,
"Let me reveal to you a closely guarded matter, Gilgamesh,
And let me tell you the secret of the gods.
Shuruppak is a city that you yourself know,
Situated on the bank of the Euphrates.
That city was already old when the gods within it
Decided that the great gods should make a flood.
There was Anu their father,
Warrior Enil their counselor,
Ninurta was their chamberlain,

Ennugi their canal-controller.[1]
Far-sighted Ea swore the oath of secrecy with them,
So he repeated their speech to a reed hut,[2]
'Reed hut, reed hut, brick wall, brick wall,
Listen, reed hut, and pay attention, brick wall:
(This is the message:)
Man of Shuruppak, son of Ubara-Tutu,[3]
Dismantle your house, build a boat.
Leave possessions, search out living things.
Reject chattels and save lives!
Put aboard the seed of all living things, into the boat.
The boat that you are to build
Shall have her dimensions in proportion,
Her width and length shall be in harmony,
Roof her like the Apsu.'[4]
I realized and spoke to my master Ea,
'I have paid attention to the words that you spoke in this way,
My master, and I shall act upon them.
But how can I explain myself to the city, the men and the elders?'
Ea made his voice heard and spoke,
He said to me, his servant,
'You shall speak to them thus:
"I think that Enlil has rejected me,
And so I cannot stay in your city,
And I cannot set foot on Enlil's land again.
I must go down to the Apsu and stay with my master Ea.[5]
Then he will shower abundance upon you,
A wealth of fowl, a treasure of fish.
. . . prosperity, a harvest,[6]
In the morning cakes/"darkness,"
In the evening a rain of wheat/"heaviness" he will shower upon you."'
When the first light of dawn appeared
The country gathered about me.

---

[1]The Sumerians had many gods, but since they were a people utterly dependent on artificial irrigation, one would naturally be the keeper of canals.
[2]Ea technically keeps his oath by speaking to no human, but rather to the inanimate hut; of course he intends that Ut-napishtim should overhear him.
[3]Titles of Ut-napishtim.
[4]The sky (not literally, of course; the idea is that this will be the biggest boat ever built).
[5]Note that gods are conceived as being attached to specific geographical locations. Ut-napishtim is to tell his fellow citizens that he is leaving the city because Enlil has rejected him; but in fact he is seeking refuge under the protection of Ea.
[6]From this point on, there are various missing words (indicated by ellipses) or passages that are difficult to interpret; but the general sense is clear.

The carpenter brought his ax,
The reed-worker brought his stone,
The young men [brought?] oakum,
Children carried the bitumen,
The poor fetched what was needed.
On the fifth day I laid down her form.
One acre was her circumference, ten poles each the height of her walls,
Her top edge was likewise ten poles all round.
I laid down her structure, drew it out,
Gave her six decks,
Divided her into seven.
Her middle I divided into nine,
Drove the water pegs into her middle.
I saw to the paddles and put down what was needed.
Three *sar* of bitumen I poured into the kiln,
Three *sar* of pitch I poured into the inside.
Three *sar* of oil they fetched, the workmen who carried the baskets.
Not counting the sar of oil which the dust soaked up,
The boatman stowed away two more *sar* of oil.
At the . . . I slaughtered oxen.
I sacrificed sheep every day.
I gave the workmen ale and beer to drink,
Oil and wine as if they were river water
They made a feast, like the New Year's Day festival.
When the sun rose, I provided hand oil.
When the sun went down the boat was complete.
The launching was very difficult;
Launching rollers had to be fetched from above to below.
Two-thirds of it stood clear of the water line.
I loaded her with everything there was,
Loaded her with all the silver,
Loaded her with all the gold
Loaded her with all the seed of living things, all of them.
I put on board the boat all my kith and kin.
Put on board cattle from open country, wild
beasts from open country, all kinds of craftsmen.
Shamash had fixed the hour:
"In the morning cakes/"darkness,"
In the evening a rain of wheat/"heaviness"[7]
I shall shower down:
Enter into the boat and shut your door!"
That hour arrived;
In the morning cakes/"darkness", in the evening
a rain of wheat/"heaviness" showered down.
I saw the shape of the storm,

---

[7]These two lines translate puns in the original. Instead of the promised shower of cakes and wheat comes a heavy darkness in the form of a downpour.

Mesopotamia

The storm was terrifying to see.
I went aboard the boat and closed the door.
To seal the boat I handed over the floating palace with her cargo to Puzur-Amurru the
    boatman.
When the first light of dawn appeared,
A black cloud came up from the base of the sky.
Adad kept rumbling inside it.
Shullat and Hanish were marching ahead,
Marched as chamberlains over mountain and country.
Erakal pulled out the mooring poles,
Ninurta marched on and made the weirs overflow.
The Anunnaki had to carry torches,
They lit up the land with their brightness.[8]
The calm before the Storm-god came over the sky,
Everything light turned to darkness.
On the first day the tempest rose up,
Blew swiftly and brought the flood-weapon,
Like a battle force the destructive *kasusu*-weapon passed over the people
No man could see his fellow,
Nor could people be distinguished from the sky.
Even the gods were afraid of the flood-weapon.
They withdrew; they went up to the heaven of Anu.
The gods cowered, like dogs crouched by an outside wall.
Ishtar screamed like a woman giving birth;[9]
The Mistress of the Gods, sweet of voice, was wailing,
'Has that time really returned to clay,
Because I spoke evil in the gods' assembly?
How could I have spoken such evil in the gods' assembly?
I should have ordered a battle to destroy my people;
I myself gave birth to them, they are my own people,
Yet they fill the sea like fish spawn!'
The gods of the Anunnaki were weeping with her.
The gods, humbled, sat there weeping.
Their lips were closed and covered with scab.
For six days and seven nights
The wind blew, flood and tempest overwhelmed the land;
When the seventh day arrived, the tempest, flood and onslaught
Which had struggled like a woman in labor, blew themselves out.
The sea became calm, the *imhullu*-wind grew quiet, the flood held back.
I looked at the weather; silence reigned.
For all mankind had returned to clay.
The flood-plain was flat as a roof.

---

[8]Lightning.
[9]Ishtar (later known as Ashtoreth, Astarte and related to some forms of the Greek goddess Aphrodite) is the Mesopotamian goddess of sexuality and fertility, and is here depicted as being a compassionate creator, though she could also be fierce.

10

I opened a porthole and light fell on my cheeks.
I bent down, then sat. I wept.
My tears ran down my cheeks.
I looked for banks, for limits to the sea.
Areas of land were emerging everywhere.
The boat had come to rest on Mount Nimush.
The mountain Nimush held the boat fast and did not let it budge.
The first and second day the mountain Nimush held the boat fast and did not let it budge.
The third and fourth day the mountain Nimush held the boat fast and did not let it budge.
The fifth and sixth day the mountain Nimush held the boat fast and did not let it budge.
When the seventh day arrived,
I put out and released a dove.[10]
The dove went; it came back,
For no perching place was visible to it, and it turned round.
I put out and released a swallow.
The swallow went; it came back,
For no perching place was visible to it, and it turned round.
I put out and released a raven.
The raven went, and saw the waters receding.
And it ate, preened, lifted its tail and did not turn round.
Then I put everything out to the four winds, and I made a sacrifice,
Set out a *surqinnu*-offering upon the mountain peak,
Arranged the jars seven and seven;
Into the bottom of them I poured essences of reeds, pine, and myrtle.
The gods smelt the fragrance,
The gods smelt the pleasant fragrance,
The gods like flies gathered over the sacrifice.[11]
As soon as the Mistress of the Gods arrived
She raised the great flies which Anu had made to please her:
'Behold, O gods, I shall never forget the significance of my lapis lazuli necklace,
I shall remember these times, and I shall never forget.
Let other gods come to the *surqinnu*-offering
But let Enlil not come to the *surqinnu*-offering,
Because he did not consult before imposing the flood,
And consigned my people to destruction!'
As soon as Enlil arrived
He saw the boat. Enlil was furious,
Filled with anger at the Igigi gods.
'What sort of life survived? No man should have lived through the destruction!'

---

[10]Utnapishtim releases these birds in hopes that their failure to return to the boat will prove that other dry land has emerged from the flood.
[11]In the *Odyssey* Homer also compares the Gods flocking to a sacrifice as greedy flies, which was probably not meant impiously but strikes modern readers oddly.

Ninurta made his voice heard and spoke,
He said to the warrior Enlil,
'Who other than Ea would have done such a thing?
For Ea can do everything!'
Ea made his voice heard and spoke,
He said to the warrior Enlil,
'You are the sage of the gods, warrior,
So how, O how, could you fail to consult, and impose the flood?
Punish the sinner for his sin, punish the criminal for his crime,
But ease off, let work not cease; be patient. . . .
Instead of your imposing a flood, let a lion come up and diminish the people.
Instead of your imposing a flood, let a wolf come up and diminish the people.
Instead of your imposing a flood, let famine be imposed and [lessen] the land.
Instead of your imposing a flood, let Erra rise up and savage the people.
I did not disclose the secret of the great gods,
I just showed Atrahasis a dream, and thus he heard the secret of the gods."
Now the advice that prevailed was his advice.
Enlil came up into the boat,
And seized my hand and led me up.
He led up my woman and made her kneel down at my side.
He touched our foreheads, stood between us, blessed us:
'Until now Ut-napishtim was mortal,
But henceforth Ut-napishtim and his woman shall be as we gods are.
Ut-napishtim shall dwell far off at the mouth of the rivers.'[12]
They took me and made me dwell far off, at the mouth of the rivers.
So now, who can gather the gods on your behalf, Gilgamesh,
That you too may find eternal life which you seek?
For a start, you must not sleep for six days and seven nights."
As soon as he was sitting, his head between his knees,
Sleep breathed over him like a fog.
Ut-napishtim spoke to her, to his wife,
"Look at the young man who wants eternal life!
Sleep breathes over him like a fog!"
His wife spoke to him, to Ut-napishtim the far-distant,
"Touch him, and let the man wake up.
Let him go back in peace the way he came,
Go back to his country through the great gate, through which he once left."
Ut-napishtim spoke to her, to his wife,
"Man behaves badly: he will behave badly towards you.
For a start, bake a daily portion for him, put it each time by his head,
And mark on the wall the days that he sleeps."
She baked a daily portion for him, put it each time by his head,
And marked on the wall for him the days that he slept.

---

[12]Ut-napishtim and his wife are blessed not because of any apparent virtue, but simply because Ea favors them: a common theme in classical mythology, but very different from the moral cast which the Hebrews gave to the story of Noah.

His first day's portion was dried out,
The second was going bad, the third was soggy,
The fourth had white mold. . . .
The fifth had discolored,
The sixth was stinking,
The seventh—at that moment he touched him and the man woke up.
Gilgamesh spoke to him, to Ut-napishtim the far-distant,
"No sooner had sleep come upon me
Than you touched me, straight away, and roused me!"
Ut-napishtim spoke to him, to Gilgamesh,
"Look Gilgamesh, count your daily portions,
That the number of days you slept may be proved to you.
Your first day's ration is dried out,
The second is going bad, the third is soggy,
The fourth has white mold. . . ,
The fifth has discolored, the sixth is stinking, . . .[13]
At that moment [on the seventh day] you woke up."
Gilgamesh spoke to him, to Ut-napishtim the far-distant,
"How, O how could I have done it, Ut-napishtim?
Wherever can I go?
The Snatchers have blocked my routes:
Death is waiting in my bedroom,
And wherever I set my foot, Death is there too."

Translated by Stephanie Dalley

---

[13]This series of bread loaves in various states of decay acts as a calendar to prove to Gilgamesh that, far from staying awake for a week, he has in fact slept for a week.

Fragments describing Sumerian evil spirits

The Sumerians are notable for the pessimism of their views of the afterlife. Though they had an enormous pantheon of gods they were also haunted by thoughts of demons who would plague them in this life and the next.

They are gloomy, their shadows dark,
   no light is in their bodies,
ever they slink along covertly,
   walk not upright,
from their claws dripping bitter gall,
   their footprints are full of venom.
Neither males are they, nor females,
they are winds ever sweeping along,
they have not wives, engender not children,
know not how to show mercy,
hear not prayer and supplication.

The shivers and chills of death
   that fritter the sum of things,
   spawn of the god of heaven,
   spawned on an evil spirit,
the death warrants, beloved sons of the storm god,
   born of the queen of the netherworld,
who were torn out of heaven and hurled from the earth as castoffs,
   are creatures of the underworld, all.

Up above they roar, down below they cheep,
they are the bitter venom of the gods,
they are the great storms let loose from heaven,
they are the owl of ill omen that hoots in the town,
spawn spawned by the god of heaven, sons born by earth are they.

Over high roofs, over broad roofs like a floodwave they surge,
from house to house they climb over,
Doors do not hold them, locks do not restrain them,
through the doors they glide like snakes,
through the hinge boxes they blow like wind.

From the man's embrace they lead off the wife,
from the man's knee they make the child get up,
and the youth they fetch out of the house of his in-laws,
they are the numbness, the daze,
that tread on the heels of man.

Translated by Thorkild Jacobsen

Sumer-Akkadian Hymn to Ishtar (c. 1600 BCE)

In Mesopotamian culture—and in those cultures which it influenced, including ancient Europe—sexuality was associated consistently with a powerful goddess, both charming and fearsome. Passion could bring ecstasy or horror. In her various forms as Ishtar, Astarte, Ashtoreth, Aphrodite, Venus, et al., she drew widespread adoration. She is not the voluptuous pin-up of the Renaissance, and she is most emphatically not, as she is often called, "the goddess of love" in the modern romantic sense. She was often associated with women because her blessings included the ability to attract a mate and bear children. In this hymn from the Sumerian city of Akkad, she is also depicted as wise, unlike the sometimes reckless and foolish Greek Aphrodite. The king of Akkad, Ammiditana, is said to draw much of his power from her. The history of the image of this goddess is one of a long, gradual decline from the awesome stature of her earliest origins.

What effects do you think it might have on a culture to have a goddess who is specifically worshipped for her encouragement of sexuality and reproduction?

Praise the goddess, the most awesome of the goddesses.
Let one revere the mistress of the peoples, the greatest of the Igigi[1]
Praise Ishtar, the most awesome of the goddesses.
Let one revere the queen of women, the greatest of the Igigi.

She is clothed with pleasure and love.
She is laden with vitality, charm, and voluptuousness.
Ishtar is clothed with pleasure and love.
She is laden with vitality, charm, and voluptuousness.

In lips she is sweet; life is in her mouth.
At her appearance rejoicing becomes full.
She is glorious; veils are thrown over her head.
Her figure is beautiful; her eyes are brilliant.

The goddess—with her there is counsel.
The fate of everything she holds in her hand.
At her glance there is created joy,
Power, magnificence, the protecting deity and guardian spirit.

She dwells in, she pays heed to compassion and friendliness.
Besides, agreeableness she truly possesses.
Be it slave, unattached girl, or mother, she preserves her.
One calls on her; among women one names her name.

Who—to her greatness who can be equal?
Strong, exalted, splendid are her decrees.

---

[1]A collective name for the great gods of heaven.

Ishtar—to her greatness who can be equal?
Strong, exalted, splendid are her decrees.

She is sought after among the gods; extraordinary is her station.
Respected is her word; it is *supreme* over them.
Ishtar among the gods, extraordinary is her station.
Respected is her word; it is *supreme* over them.

She is their queen; they continually cause her commands to be executed.
All of them bow down before her.
They receive her light before her.
Women and men indeed revere her.

In their assembly her word is powerful; it is dominating.
Before Anum their king she fully supports them.
She rests in intelligence, cleverness, and wisdom.
They take counsel together, she and her lord.

Indeed they occupy the throne room together.
In the divine chamber, the dwelling of joy,
Before them the gods take their places.
To their utterances their attention is turned.

The king their favorite, beloved of their hearts,
Magnificently offers to them his pure sacrifices.
Ammiditana, as the pure offering of his hands,
Brings before them fat oxen and gazelles.

From Anum, her consort, she has been pleased to ask for him
An enduring, a long life.
Many years of living, to Ammiditana
She has granted, Ishtar has decided to give.

By her orders she has subjected to him
The four world regions at his feet;
And the total of all peoples
She has decided to attach them to his yoke.

Translated by Ferris J. Stephens

Hymn to the Moon God, Nanna

Ancient Sumer was unusual in regarding the moon god as male.

How are the different phases of the moon reflected in this poem? Why do you think most cultures consider the moon as female?

Father Nanna, lord, conspicuously crowned,
    prince of the gods,
Father Nanna, grandly perfect in majesty,
    prince of the gods;
Father Nanna measuredly proceed in noble raiment,
    prince of the gods;
fierce young bull, thick of horns, perfect of limbs,
    with lapis lazuli beard, full of beauty;
fruit, created of itself, grown to full size,
    good to look at, with whose beauty one is never sated;
womb, giving birth to all, who has settled down
    in a holy abode;
merciful forgiving father, who holds in his hand
    the life of all the land;
Lord! the compass of your divine providence,
    vast as the far-off heavens, the wide sea,
    is awesome to behold.

Translated by Thorkild Jacobsen

The Code of Hammurabi (18th Century BCE)

Of the several law codes surviving from the ancient Middle East, the most famous after the Hebrew Torah is the Code of Hammurabi, sixth king of the Amorite Dynasty of Old Babylon. It is best known from a beautifully engraved diorite stela now in the Louvre Museum which depicts the king receiving the law from Shamash, the god of justice. This copy was made long after Hammurabi's time, and it is clear that his was a long-lasting contribution to Mesopotamian civilization. It is interesting to the general reader because of what it tells us about the attitudes and daily lives of the ancient Babylonians. In the following selection, most of the long prologue praising Hammurabi's power and wisdom is omitted.

What do these laws tell us about attitudes toward slavery? Toward women? Which laws deviate from the egalitarian standard of "an eye for an eye and a tooth for a tooth?" What qualities does this text say a ruler should have to enable him to write new laws?

. . . Anu and Bel called by name me, Hammurabi, the exalted prince, who feared God, to bring about the rule of righteousness in the land, to destroy the wicked and the evil-doers; so that the strong should not harm the weak; so that I should rule over the black-headed people like Shamash, and enlighten the land, to further the well-being of mankind.

15: If any one take a male or female slave of the court, or a male or female slave of a freed man, outside the city gates [to escape], he shall be put to death.

16: If any one receive into his house a runaway male or female slave of the court, or of a freedman, and does not bring it out at the public proclamation of the police, the master of the house shall be put to death.

53: If any one be too lazy to keep his dam in proper condition, and does not so keep it; if then the dam break and all the fields be flooded, then shall he in whose dam the break occurred be sold for money, and the money shall replace the grain which he has caused to be ruined.

54: If he be not able to replace the grain, then he and his possessions shall be divided among the farmers whose corn he has flooded.

108: If a woman wine-seller does not accept grain according to gross weight in payment of drink, but takes money, and the price of the drink is less than that of the corn, she shall be convicted and thrown into the water.[1]

109: If conspirators meet in the house of a woman wine-seller, and these conspirators are not captured and delivered to the court, the [wine-seller] shall be put to death.

110: If a "sister of a god" [nun] open a tavern, or enter a tavern to drink, then shall this woman be burned to death.

129: If a man's wife be surprised having intercourse with another man, both shall be tied

---

[1]This refers to a practice known as "trial by ordeal" which has been commonplace in many cultures, including Medieval Europe. It was believed that the Euphrates River could act as judge of people accused of various crimes. If, when thrown into the river, the accused floated, she was considered innocent; but if she sank, the river had found her guilty. For an interesting instance of a different trial by ordeal in ancient Hebrew law, see Numbers 5:11–31.

and thrown into the water, but the husband may pardon his wife and the king his slaves.

130: If a man violate the wife (betrothed or child-wife) of another man, who has never known a man, and still lives in her father's house, and sleep with her and be surprised [caught], this man shall be put to death, but the wife is blameless.

131: If a man bring a charge against [his] wife, but she is not surprised with another man, she must take an oath and then may return to her house.

132: If the "finger is pointed" at a man's wife about another man, but she is not caught sleeping with the other man, she shall jump into the river for the sake of her husband.[2]

138: If a man wishes to separate from his wife who has borne him no children, he shall give her the amount of her purchase money and the dowry which she brought from her father's house, and let her go.

141: If a man's wife, who lives in his house, wishes to leave it, plunges into debt [to go into business], tries to ruin her house, neglects her husband, and is judicially convicted: if her husband offers her release, she may go on her way, and he gives her nothing as a gift of release. If her husband does not wish to release her, and if he takes another wife, she shall remain as servant in her husband's house.

142: If a woman quarrel with her husband, and say: "You are not congenial to me," the reasons for her prejudice must be presented. If she is guiltless, and there is no fault on her part, but he leaves and neglects her, then no guilt attaches to this woman, she shall take her dowry and go back to her father's house.[3]

143: If she is not innocent, but leaves her husband, and ruins her house, neglecting her husband, this woman shall be cast into the water.

195: If a son strike his father, his hands shall be cut off.[4]

196: If a [noble-]man put out the eye of another nobleman, his eye shall be put out.[5]

197: If he break another nobleman's bone, his bone shall be broken.

198: If he put out the eye of a commoner, or break the bone of a [commoner], he shall pay one silver mina.

199: If he put out the eye of a man's slave, or break the bone of a man's slave, he shall pay one-half of its value.

200: If a man knock out the teeth of his equal, his teeth shall be knocked out.

201: If he knock out the teeth of a commoner, he shall pay one-third of a [silver] mina.

In future time, through all coming generations, let the king, who may be in the land, observe the words of righteousness which I have written on my monument; let him not alter the law of the land which I have given, the edicts which I have enacted; my monument let him not mar. If such a ruler have wisdom, and be able to keep his land in order, he shall observe the words which I have written in this inscription; the rule, statute, and law of the land which I have given; the decisions which I have made will this inscription show him; let him rule his subjects accordingly, speak justice to them, give right decisions, root out the miscreants and criminals from this land, and grant prosperity to his subjects.

---

[2] I. e., to prove her innocence.

[3] The right of women to initiate divorce proceedings is extremely rare in ancient civilizations.

[4] Cf. Hebrew law, which prescribes the death penalty for such an act (Exodus 21:15) and extends its scope to mothers.

[5] Note how punishments are administered according to the social status of the attacker and the victim. "Equality before the law" is a rare concept in ancient times.

Hammurabi, the king of righteousness, on whom Shamash has conferred right (or law) am I. My words are well considered; my deeds are not equaled; to bring low those that were high; to humble the proud, to expel insolence.

Translated by L. W. King

Sumerian Proverbs

Many ancient Middle Eastern cultures left behind bodies of wise sayings, often borrowing from each other. Some are almost universal commonplaces; but others give interesting glimpses into the cultures which produced them.

Which proverbs express sympathy for men? For women? What two qualities are especially prized in a singer?

He who does not support either a wife or a child, his nose has not borne a leash.

For his pleasure—married! On his thinking it over—divorced!

A rebellious male may be permitted a reconciliation;
A rebellious female will be dragged in the mud.[1]

A sick person is [relatively] well; it is the woman in childbirth who is really ill!

When a singer knows the hymns and performs well the trills, he is indeed a singer!

Translated by W. G. Lambert

---

[1]This proverb reads like a protest against the unequal treatment of women, but it may in fact have been intended as a stern warning to women that expectations were higher for them than for men.

Babylonian Proverbs (17th Century BCE?)

Why is a person who informs on another compared to a scorpion? Which proverb seems to urge moderation in the use of wealth? What social custom is referred to in the final proverb of this group?

Do no evil, and then you will not experience lasting misfortune.

A scorpion stung a man. What did he get for it? A common informer caused a man's death. What good did it do him?

Has she become pregnant without intercourse? Has she become fat without eating?

If I store up things, they will be robbed. If I use them up too fast, who will give anything to me?

The strong man makes his living by the work of his arms, but the weak man by selling his children.

Translated by Robert H. Pfeiffer

Egypt

Hymn to Sekhmet-Bast

Despite the extravagant terms in which she is praised, Sekhmet or Bast was far from the most prominent god in ancient Egypt. Yet this hymn is interesting in the way it seeks motherly divine mercy, much as do prayers to the Christian Virgin Mary and the Buddhist Kuan-Yin (Kannon in Japanese). Notice how the hymn links the daily cycle of dark and light to death and resurrection.

In what ways in Sekhmet seen as kindly? As fearsome?

Mother of the gods, the One, the Only,
   Mistress of the Crowns, thou rulest all;
Sekhmet is thy name when thou art wrathful,
   Bast, belovèd, when thy people call.

Daughter of the Sun, with flame and fury
   Flashing from the prow upon the foe;
Safely sails the Boat[1] with thy protection
   Passing scatheless where thy fires glow.

Daughter of the Sun, the burial chamber
   Lies in the darkness till thy light appears.
From thy Throne of Silence send us comfort,
   Bast, belovèd, banish all our fears.

Mother of the gods, no gods existed
   Till thou camest there and gave them life.
Sekhmet of the Boat, the wicked fear thee
   Trampling down all evil and all strife.

Mother of the gods, the great, the loved one,
   Winged and mighty, unto thee we call,
Naming thee the Comforter, the Ruler,
   Bast, belovèd, Mother of us all.

Translated by Margaret Murray

---

[1]The celestial boat in which the sun daily sails across the sky.

Hymn to Osiris

Osiris was one of the supreme gods of ancient Egypt, long worshipped throughout much of the Mediterranean world. Bringer of agriculture and civilization, he was also a classic dying god, having been slain and dismembered by his evil brother Set. His sister-wife Isis' act of reuniting the parts of his corpse symbolizes the resurrection-like process of sowing, growing, and reaping crops. Out of death, Osiris brings life.

What pairs of opposites are used to describe various aspects of Osiris? Why do you think the worship of Osiris was popular?

O Lord of Time, the Lord of Life Eternal,
O holy Child, O God the self-created,
Fear in our hearts, we humbly fall before Him.
Praise we the Lord whose glory shines from heaven.

The Son of God, we fear and we adore Him.
Though still His heart, He is not dead but living.
Lord God of Terror, come to Thy own city.
Beloved one of God, Thy temple now awaits Thee.

O Lord of Night, illumining dark places.
Ancient of days yet young in every aspect,
O Hidden One, of men unknown aforetime,
The living Soul of God, He shines above us.

Within the Secret Place there lies His sacred body,
Within that holy shrine is now His quiet sleeping.
O Hidden God, O Judge of dead and living,
In humblest wise we worship and adore Thee.

Translated by Margaret A. Murray

Three Love Poems from the New Kingdom

During the long twilight of Egyptian civilization before it fell to Alexander the Great, it produced numerous writings with a movingly personal and intimate tone which strike modern readers as reflecting emotions familiar to themselves. Among these some of the most charming are many love poems.

Your love, dear man, is as lovely to me

It is impossible to know whether this poem, narrated in the voice of a young woman, actually had a female author; but it is clearly meant to reflect female attitudes. Ancient Egypt, while being male-dominated like all civilizations, nevertheless granted far more freedom and independence to women than most. The singer (like almost all ancient poetry, this would probably have been sung) forthrightly tells of her passion for her beloved and asks him to marry her. Of course her heart's desire is to devote herself entirely to her spouse. It would be anachronistic to expect her to want anything else. But the fact that she feels free to make her own choice and articulate it marks her as unusual. The sensual food metaphors she uses have been compared to those found in the Hebrew Song of Solomon (see, for instance, 2:3–5) which is sometimes argued to have been influenced in a general way by Egyptian love poetry. The "bride" in the Hebrew poetry describes her admiration and desire for her beloved just as rapturously as her Egyptian counterpart.

What are the qualities that the speaker prizes in a good marriage?

Your love, dear man, is as lovely to me
As sweet soothing oil to the limbs of the restless,
as clean ritual robes to the flesh of gods,
As fragrance of incense to one coming home
hot from the smells of the street.

It is like nipple-berries ripe in the hand,
like the tang of grainmeal mingled with beer,
Like wine to the palate when taken with white bread.[1]

While unhurried days come and go,
Let us turn to each other in quiet affection,
walk in peace to the edge of old age.
And I shall be with you each unhurried day,
a woman given her one wish: to see
For a lifetime the face of her lord.

Translated by John L. Foster

---

[1]White bread was a delectable luxury reserved for the wealthy.

Once more you pass her house, deep in thought

To understand this humorous poem you should know that there was a widespread convention in ancient love poetry of lovers pretending to speak to the door which shut them out of their beloveds' bedrooms. In Rome men sometimes slept on the doorsill as a public demonstration of affection, hoping to charm—or shame—the woman into letting them in. The final lines make it clear that both lovers are eager to be together, and it is probably the woman's parents who have barred the door. As in Rome, each part of the door is considered a deity, with its appropriate sacrifice. By appeasing these minor gods, the lover hopes to gain entrance. But it becomes apparent as he lists the various animal sacrifices to be offered that this is all meant facetiously, for the gift of greasy suet for the hinge sockets is just lubrication to make the door open silently. The poem begins by addressing the lover, whose thoughts are then relayed in the first person until the last stanza. This poem has been compared to the Song of Solomon 5:2–8.

Why does the lover want to replace the wooden door with a new one?

Once more you pass her house, deep in thought,
darkness is fallen, hiding you:

I would gain entry there,
but for me no sort of welcome opens;
Yet the night is lovely for our soft purposes,
and doors are meant to give passage!

Doorlatch, my friend, you govern my destiny:
heaven for me needs a good turn from you;
(And once safe inside, our longhorn[1] as payment)—
oppose no spellbinding power!

Add oxen in praise to the door, as needed,
lesser beasts to the lock, slit geese
To doorjamb and lintel, suet for sockets—
and let all that moves turn quietly, quietly!

But the choicest cuts of our fine animal—
these go instead to the sawyer's apprentice
If he makes us a new door—
of rushes, and a tie-latch of brittlest straw.

O then, a man big with love could come anytime,
find her house welcoming, open,
Discover the couch decked with closewoven bedclothes,
and a lovely young lady restless among them!—

---

[1]Longhorn cow.

Egypt

(You walk back and forth in the dark)
She whispers:
"The mistress of this choice spot has been lonely.
Dear heart, who held you so long?"

Translated by John L. Foster.

If I could just be the washerman

This slightly kinky poem was undoubtedly meant to impress its object with both the young man's devotion and his passion.

Can you deduce anything about the author's attitudes toward sexuality from this poem?

If I could just be the washerman
doing her laundry for one month only,
I would be faithful to pick up the bundles,
sturdy to beat clean the heavy linens,
But gentle to touch those finespun things
lying closest the body I love.
I would rinse with pure water the perfumes
that linger still in her tunics,
And I'd dry my own flesh with the towels
she yesterday held to her face.
The touch of her clothes, their textures,
her softness in them . . .
Thank god for the body,
its youthful vigor!

Translated by John L. Foster

Dialogue of a Man With His Soul
The Two Aspects of Death (c. 2000 BCE?)

Because most of the material culture left behind by the Egyptians was preserved in their tombs, it is often assumed that they were obsessed by death. Yet a closer look at their art shows that if the upper classes made enormous efforts to attain life after death, it was because they enjoyed this life thoroughly, and dreaded to leave it. The following passages are excerpted from a poem in which a man first addresses his own soul, expressing his fear of death; then the soul replies, arguing for the blessings of the afterlife; finally, in a passage not printed here, the two are reconciled. The poem has been compared to the Hebrew book of Ecclesiastes, but the similarities between the two seem coincidental and superficial. Even out of its original context, this poem is a moving expression of the ambivalent attitudes of people everywhere toward death.

What are some of the experiences in life that the poet seems most to prize? According to this poem, how can death be a blessing?

The Curse of Death

If you think of burial, it is agony;
it is the bringing of tears through making a man miserable;
it is taking a man from his house,
being cast upon the high ground.
You shall not come up again to see suns.
They who built in granite,
who constructed in fair pyramids, in fair works,
so that the builders should become gods—
their stelae have perished, like the inert ones,[1]

those who have died on the shore for lack of a survivor,[2]
the flood having taken its toll,
and the sun likewise,
to whom only the fish of the water's edge talk.
Listen to me! Look, it is good for men to listen.
Follow the happy day! Ignore care!

---

[1]Not only did some monuments crumble, but almost all the royal tombs were robbed in ancient times. The Egyptians eventually stopped building pyramids because they failed to guard the goods and bodies of the pharaohs.
[2]Those who have not had descendents who could prepare their corpses for the life to come are compared to travelers stranded on the shore of a river, unable to cross over into the afterlife.

Egypt

The Blessings of Death

Death is to me today
like a sick man's recovery,
like going outside after confinement.

Death is to me today
like the scent of myrrh,
like sitting under a sail on a windy day.

Death is to me today
like the scent of lotuses,
like sitting on the shore of Drunkenness.

Death is to me today
like a well-trodden path,
like a man's coming home from an expedition.

Death is to me today
like the opening of the sky,
like a man's grasping what he did not know.

Death is to me today
like a man's longing to see home,
having spent many years abroad.

Yet one yonder is a living god,
punishing the wrongdoer's deed.

Yet one yonder stands in the (sun)bark,[3]
distributing choice offerings thence to the temples.

Yet one yonder is a sage,
who cannot be prevented from appealing
to Re when he speaks.

Translated by R. B. Parkinson

––––––––––––––––––––––––––
[3]The boat which daily carries the sun across the sky.

In Praise of Learned Scribes (c. 1300 BCE)

Literacy is a hallmark of most civilizations, used to keep records, maintain uniform laws, and record religious and philosophical beliefs for posterity. Yet throughout most of history, reading and writing was as narrow and specialized a skill as shipbuilding or medicine, confined to a small class of scribes who prided themselves on possessing a vital, almost magical skill. Here is one of the earliest expressions of the notion expressed in the Latin saying, Ars longa, vita brevis *("art is long, life is brief"). The belief that the writing will outlast the writer has been a powerful motive for creation throughout the centuries, being a central subject, for instance, in the sonnets of Shakespeare.*

What are the main advantages of being a scribe?

Now then, if thou dost these things, thou art skilled in the writings. As for those learned scribes from the time of those who lived after the gods, they who could foretell what was to come, their names have become everlasting, even though they are gone, they completed their lives, and all their relatives are forgotten.

They did not make for themselves pyramids of metal, with the tombstones thereof of iron. They were not able to leave heirs in children, ... pronouncing their names,[1] but they made heirs for themselves in the writings and in the books of wisdom which they composed. They gave themselves the papyrus-roll as a lector priest, the writing board as a son-he-loves,[2] books of wisdom as their pyramids, the reed-pen as their child, and the back of a stone for a wife. From great to small were made into his children.[3] As for the scribe, he is the foremost of them. If there were made for them doors and buildings, they are crumbled. Their mortuary service is gone; their tombstones are covered with dirt; and their graves are forgotten. But their names are still pronounced because of their books which they made, since they were good and the memory of him who made them lasts to the limits of eternity.

Translated by John A. Wilson

---

[1] Scribes were evidently not expected to marry. Thus they would not have left behind descendents to carry out the rituals aimed at ensuring their immortality which were performed for other nobles.

[2] The lector priest and the "son-he-loves" performed the funerary rites which beatified and maintained the deceased.

[3] Because they were made dependent upon the scribe's writings.

Hymn to the Aton of Akhnaton (c. 1372-1354 BCE)

Akhnaton is famous principally because he developed the world's first recorded monotheism. He tried to eliminate the worship of all other gods except Aton-Re (or Ra), the sun god, whose son he claimed to be. His reign also initiated the Amarna period in Egyptian art, which broke with the stereotypically rigid sculptural style of the past to create an eccentric and more natural- istic style. After his death, polytheism was quickly reasserted, and an attempt was made to obliterate Akhnaton's memory. Because his ideas had no apparent influence on later monotheis- tic religions such as Judaism, his place in the history of ideas is an ambiguous one. Yet the hymns that he wrote (or had written) to the sun movingly express adoration for a benevolent creator. In the final selection from the longest of these hymns, Aton is depicted not only as the creator of the universe, but as the begetter of individual human lives. Akhnaton is also known because of the famous portrait bust of his beautiful wife, Nefertiti, and the fabulous tomb of his otherwise obscure son-in-law, Tutankhamen.

What are some of the curses of darkness listed in this poem? Some of the blessings of sunlight? How do they function as two aspects of a single process? What are the most important powers that this hymn attributes to Aton?

Thou appearest beautifully on the horizon of heaven,
Thou living Aton, the beginning of life!
When thou art risen on the eastern horizon,
Thou hast filled every land with thy beauty.
Thou art gracious, great, glistening, and high over every land;
Thy rays encompass the lands to the limit of all that thou hast made:
As thou art Re, thou reachest to the end of them;
Thou subduest them for thy beloved son.
Though thou art far away, thy rays are on earth;
Though thou art in their faces, no one knows thy going.

When thou settest in the western horizon,
The land is in darkness, in the manner of death.
They sleep in a room, with heads wrapped up,
Nor sees one eye the other.
All their goods which are under their heads might be stolen,
But they would not perceive it.
Every lion is come forth from his den;
All creeping things, they sting.
Darkness is a shroud, and the earth is in stillness,
For he who made them rests in his horizon.

At daybreak, when thou arisest on the horizon,
When thou shinest as the Aton by day,
Thou drivest away the darkness and givest thy rays.
The Two Lands[1] are in festivity every day,
Awake and standing upon their feet,

---

[1]Upper and Lower Egypt.

30

For thou hast raised them up.
Washing their bodies, taking their clothing,
Their arms are raised in praise at thy appearance.
All the world, they do their work.

All beasts are content with their pasturage;
Trees and plants are flourishing.
The birds which fly from their nests,
Their wings are stretched out in praise to thy *ka*.[2]
All beasts spring upon their feet.
Whatever flies and alights,
They live when thou hast risen for them.
The ships are sailing north and south as well,
For every way is open at thy appearance.
The fish in the river dart before thy face;
Thy rays are in the midst of the great green sea.

Creator of seed in women,
Thou who makest fluid into man,
Who maintainest the son in the womb of his mother,
Who soothest him with that which stills his weeping,
Thou nurse even in the womb,
Who givest breath to sustain all that he has made!
When he descends from the womb to breathe
On the day when he is born,
Thou openest his mouth completely,
Thou suppliest his necessities.
When the chick in the egg speaks within the shell,
Thou givest him breath within it to maintain him.
When thou hast made him his fulfillment within the egg, to break it,
He comes forth from the egg to speak at his completed time;
He walks upon his legs when he comes forth from it.

How manifold it is, what thou hast made!
They are hidden from the face of man.
O sole god, like whom there is no other!
Thou didst create the world according to thy desire,
Whilst thou wert alone:
All men, cattle, and wild beasts,
Whatever is on earth, going upon its feet,
And what is on high, flying with its wings.

The countries of Syria and Nubia, the land of Egypt,
Thou settest every man in his place,
Thou suppliest their necessities:
Everyone has his food, and his time of life is reckoned.

---

[2]Spirit.

31

Egypt

Their tongues are separate in speech,
And their natures as well;
Their skins are distinguished,
As thou distinguishest the foreign peoples.
Thou makest a Nile in the underworld,
Thou bringest it forth as thou desirest
To maintain the people of Egypt
According as thou madest them for thyself,
The lord of all of them, wearying himself with them,
The lord of every land, rising for them,
The Aton of the day, great of majesty.

Translated by Theophile J. Meek

Judaism

The Hebrew Bible

Jewish civilization has made its impact felt not through monumental building, political supremacy, or the visual arts, but through its religious thought as expressed in the Bible. The Bible is not so much a book as a library, a collection of writings which evolved over many centuries and did not become completely fixed in its classic form until the first century CE. The core of the Hebrew Bible is the Torah, the five books which define who the Jews are through story and law. One group, the Samaritans, accepted only these five books as their Bible. The classic collection of works written in Hebrew (the ancient language of the Jews) was accepted as divine scripture not only by Jews but by early Christians, though few Christians could read Hebrew and preferred to read and quote Greek translations which contained some passages and several whole books lacking in the Hebrew text. Thus, from a very early date, the meaning of the word "Bible" differed between the two groups. The early church eventually gathered an additional number of Christian Greek-language writings and added them to the Hebrew Bible to create what is known as the "New Testament." The Hebrew Bible (with its older Greek additions) became known to Christians as "The Old Testament," and the latter was argued to have been completed, perfected, and to some extent superseded by the new writings. Faithful Jews refused to accept this view of their scriptures, of course. The process of redefinition was repeated when Islam pronounced the Bible incomplete and its existing texts flawed, and presented the Qur'an as the definitive religious scripture. Finally, during the Protestant reformation, many churches rejected the Greek additions to the Old Testament. Thus the word "Bible" has meant many things to many people. In order to avoid expressing a bias, in this reader the neutral terms "Hebrew Bible" and "Christian Scriptures" will be used to label the orthodox Jewish Bible and the New Testament, respectively.

The words "Hebrew" and "Jew" may seem to be used interchangeably in the following notes, but in fact the people known as the Hebrews do not properly become known as Jews until the dominant tribe known as Judah is reestablished in 539 BCE in the land of Judah (later called Judaea by the Romans) after the Babylonian Exile. The other half of the old Hebrew kingdom, called Israel, had been conquered and destroyed by the Assyrians long before. The Hebrew language fell out of common use in later times, being replaced by Aramaic; but the Biblical texts continued to be studied by pious men in Judaea in their original language. It was Jews living abroad in the Hellenistic world who first translated the text into Greek, incidentally providing access to these writings for the early Christians.

Christians, Muslims, and others have used these texts for many different purposes, but our aim here is to concentrate on their meaning for the people who first created them and whose sacred texts they continue to be: the Jews.

The translation used here is the New Revised Standard Version of the Bible, *a translation made primarily for Christians but which tries to give an unbiased presentation of the Hebrew text.*

The Hebrew Creation Narrative (Genesis 1–3)

The mythologies of all the world's peoples are designed to answer such questions as "Who are we as a people?" "How did we originate?" and "Why do we die?" Created by Jews, adopted by Christians, the following creation stories have had an exceptionally long and complex history which can hardly be explored in this volume's necessarily brief notes. It was about a century and a half ago that scholars first noted that Genesis seemed to contain two distinct creation stories, using different names for the creator (translated here as "God" and "the Lord"), with different emphases (physical vs. moral issues), and even a different order of creation (plants before humans, plants after humans). Scholars whose religious faith does not require them to believe otherwise have since generally agreed that the grand but starkly simple poetic opening of Genesis was the product of a much later period than the story of what traditionally is called "the Fall." The first narrative states themes typical of mature Judaism: the creator is the sole ruler of the universe, and even in the process of creation he has provided the foundation for the Jewish sabbath. Although it rejects the typical polytheism of Mesopotomian creation stories like the Enuma Elish, it shares certain features with them: land emerging out of an original watery chaos and waters above and beneath the earth. Although the universe is not created by God's dividing up a goddess like Tiamat, other passages in the Hebrew Bible suggest that the metaphor of the slaying of a primordial sea-serpent named Leviathan lurked in Hebrew thought about creation, to be linked in some passages with the miraculous division of waters which enabled the captives to leave Egypt. Note how deeply language is involved in this account: speech calls the world into being, and speech blesses it. The concept of the divine word of God was to be a central concept of Judaism, later adopted by both Christianity and Islam.

Why do you suppose plants were so important that they are depicted as being created even before the sun? What kind of plants does the narrative particularly focus on?

The Creation

In the beginning when God created the heavens and the earth, the earth was a formless void and darkness covered the face of the deep, while a wind from God swept over the face of the waters.[1] Then God said, "Let there be light;" and there was light. And God saw that the light was good; and God separated the light from the darkness. God called the light Day, and the darkness he called Night. And there was evening and there was morning, the first day.

And God said, "Let there be a dome in the midst of the waters, and let it separate the waters from the waters." So God made the dome and separated the waters that were under the dome from the waters that were above the dome. And it was so. God called the dome Sky. And there was evening and there was morning, the second day.[2]

And God said, "Let the waters under the sky be gathered together into one place, and let the dry land appear." And it was so. God called the dry land Earth, and the waters that were gathered together he called Seas. And God saw that it was good. Then God said, "Let

---

[1]Many modern interpreters see these waters as the same primordial watery chaos of other Middle Eastern creation myths; but traditionalists have usually asserted that the water is created out of the "void and darkness," a belief known by its Latin name of creation *ex nihilo* (out of nothing).

[2]Rain seemed to provide to many ancient peoples evidence that a body of water existed above the sky.

the earth put forth vegetation: plants yielding seed, and fruit trees of every kind on earth that bear fruit with the seed in it." And it was so. The earth brought forth vegetation: plants yielding seed of every kind, and trees of every kind bearing fruit with the seed in it. And God saw that it was good. And there was evening and there was morning, the third day.

And God said, "Let there be lights in the dome of the sky to separate the day from the night; and let them be for signs and for seasons and for days and years,[3] and let them be lights in the dome of the sky to give light upon the earth." And it was so. God made the two great lights—the greater light to rule the day and the lesser light to rule the night—and the stars. God set them in the dome of the sky to give light upon the earth, to rule over the day and over the night, and to separate the light from the darkness. And God saw that it was good. And there was evening and there was morning, the fourth day.

And God said, "Let the waters bring forth swarms of living creatures and let birds fly above the earth across the dome of the sky." So God created the great sea monsters and every living creature that moves, of every kind, with which the waters swarm, and every winged bird of every kind. And God saw that it was good. God blessed them, saying, "Be fruitful and multiply and fill the waters in the seas, and let birds multiply on the earth." And there was evening and there was morning, the fifth day.

And God said, "Let the earth bring forth living creatures of every kind: cattle and creeping things and wild animals of the earth of every kind." And it was so. God made the wild animals of the earth of every kind, and the cattle of every kind, and everything that creeps upon the ground of every kind. And God saw that it was good. Then God said, "Let us make humankind in our image,[4] according to our likeness; and let them have dominion over the fish of the sea, and over the birds of the air and over the cattle, and over all the wild animals of the earth, and over every creeping thing that creeps upon the earth."

So God created humankind in his image,
in the image of God he created them;
male and female he created them.[5]

God blessed them, and God said to them, "Be fruitful and multiply, and fill the earth and subdue it; and have dominion over the fish of the sea and over the birds of the air and over every living thing that moves upon the earth." God said, "See, I have given you every plant yielding seed that is upon the face of all the earth, and every tree with seed in its fruit; you shall have them for food. And to every beast of the earth, and to every bird of the air, and to everything that creeps on the earth, everything that has the breath of life, I have

---

[3]Even the heavenly bodies are seen as serving human needs, by providing the basis for a calendar.

[4]A wide variety of scholarly opinion has been expressed about this use of the plural in God's speech, unique to Genesis. Some think it reflects an earlier polytheism (an argument rejected by most scholars because of the otherwise insistent monotheism of the narrative), an exalted "royal" use of the pronoun (but no other examples are known from this culture), as addressing the angels (previously unmentioned in the story), or even—in the Middle Ages—denotes the members of the Trinity speaking among themselves (a fanciful interpretation flatly rejected by Jews as incorporating a uniquely Christian belief). No general agreement exists on this question.

[5]Some scholars maintain that God must be thought of here as having a human form; others argue that the resemblance is purely spiritual in nature. Contemporary feminists have pointed out that both sexes are created in God's image.

given every green plant for food."[6] And it was so. God saw everything that he had made, and indeed, it was very good. And there was evening and there was morning, the sixth day.

Thus the heavens and the earth were finished, and all their multitude. And on the seventh day God finished the work that he had done, and he rested on the seventh day from all the work that he had done. So God blessed the seventh day and hallowed it, because on it God rested from all the work that he had done in creation. These are the generations of the heavens and the earth when they were created.

Creation and Fall

If the first creation story answers the question "Where did we come from?" the second focuses on other questions, such as "Why do we have to die?" "Why must we work?" and "Why are women subordinate to men?"

What evidence can you find to support the theory that women's subordination to men is the result of an inherited curse? The tree of the knowledge of good and evil is often confused with the tree of life; can you distinguish between their apparent functions? In what way is the end of this story similar to the theme of the Epic of Gilgamesh?

In the day that the LORD God[7] made the earth and the heavens, when no plant of the field was yet in the earth and no herb of the field had yet sprung up—for the LORD God had not caused it to rain upon the earth, and there was no one to till the ground; but a stream would rise from the earth, and water the whole face of the ground—then the LORD God formed man from the dust of the ground, and breathed into his nostrils the breath of life, and the man became a living being. And the LORD God planted a garden in Eden, in the east; and there he put the man whom he had formed. Out of the ground the LORD God made to grow every tree that is pleasant to the sight and good for food, the tree of life also in the midst of the garden, and the tree of the knowledge of good and evil.

A river flows out of Eden to water the garden, and from there it divides and becomes four branches. The name of the first is Pishon; it is the one that flows around the whole land of Havilah, where there is gold; and the gold of that land is good; bdellium and onyx stone are there. The name of the second river is Gihon; it is the one that flows around the whole land of Cush. The name of the third river is Tigris, which flows east of Assyria. And the fourth river is the Euphrates.[8]

---

[6]The idea of absolute dominion over an abundantly productive earth must have been highly appealing to people struggling to scratch a living from the soil of ancient Israel, prey to attacks by wild animals. The image of the earth as a rich garden would have indeed seemed a paradise lost. Some interpret this passage as idealizing vegetarianism.

[7]Up to this point the original Hebrew text has called God *Elohim;* but in the subsequent passages, he is given the title now usually translated as *Yahweh.* Because this latter name was considered too sacred to utter in later Jewish tradition, various substitutes were devised. Here "LORD" in small caps indicates occurrences of the sacred name.

[8]The naming of the Tigris and Euphrates as rivers flowing from Eden locates the original Paradise somewhere in Mesopotamia, which is also the region to which the Hebrews traced their ancestry.

The LORD God took the man and put him in the garden of Eden to till it and keep it. And the LORD God commanded the man, —"You may freely eat of every tree of the garden; but of the tree of the knowledge of good and evil you shall not eat, for in the day that you eat of it you shall die." [9]

Then the LORD God said, "It is not good that the man should be alone; I will make him a helper as his partner." So out of the ground the LORD God formed every animal of the field and every bird of the air, and brought them to the man to see what he would call them; and whatever the man called every living creature, that was its name. The man gave names to all cattle, and to the birds of the air, and to every animal of the field; but for the man there was not found a helper as his partner. So the LORD God caused a deep sleep to fall upon the man, and he slept; then he took one of his ribs and closed up its place. And the rib that the LORD God had taken from the man he made into a woman and brought her to the man. Then the man said,

"This at last is bone of my bones
 and flesh of my flesh;
this one shall be called Woman,
 for out of Man this one was taken."

Therefore a man leaves his father and his mother and clings to his wife, and they become one flesh.[10] And the man and his wife were both naked, and were not ashamed.[11]

Now the serpent was more crafty than any other wild animal that the LORD God had made.[12] He said to the woman, "Did God say, 'You shall not eat from any tree in the garden'?" The woman said to the serpent, "We may eat of the fruit of the trees in the garden; but God said, 'You shall not eat of the fruit of the tree that is in the middle of the garden, nor shall you touch it, or you shall die.'" But the serpent said to the woman, "You will not die; for God knows that when you eat of it your eyes will be opened, and you will be like God, knowing good and evil."[13] So when the woman saw that the tree was good for food, and that it was a delight to the eyes, and that the tree was to be desired to make one wise, she took of its fruit and ate; and she also gave some to her husband, who was with her,

---

[9]The paradox that this prophecy is not fulfilled literally has led to many ingenious explanations, including the one dominant for centuries in Christianity: that by eating the fruit Adam and Eve fall from the state of divine grace into the death-like state of sin.

[10]Patriarchal interpretations of this story stress that the woman is a secondary creation, brought into being to serve the man; but some feminists have argued that the texts stress the unity of the two.

[11]Jews shunned nudity far more than most of their neighbors, but seemed to view the sense of shame as a curse.

[12]Later interpretations, both Jewish and Christian, identify the serpent with Satan, but the latter is a figure whom many scholars believe to have been introduced into Judaism at a comparatively late date.

[13]Again, the fact that the serpent's prophecy comes true while God's does not has led to much speculation. Whatever interpretation is followed, guilt and shame are the result of the Fall. Traditional Christianity gave the incident a sexual interpretation, often arguing that eroticism itself was a shameful by-product, whereas Jews seldom accepted this view. The doctrine of an inherited curse called "original sin" is also alien to mainstream Judaism, but is the main focus of Christian commentary on this passage.

and he ate.[14] Then the eyes of both were opened, and they knew that they were naked; and they sewed fig leaves together and made loincloths for themselves.

They heard the sound of the LORD God walking in the garden at the time of the evening breeze, and the man and his wife hid themselves from the presence of the LORD God among the trees of the garden. But the LORD God called to the man, and said to him, "Where are you?" He said, "I heard the sound of you in the garden, and I was afraid, because I was naked; and I hid myself." He said, "Who told you that you were naked? Have you eaten from the tree of which I commanded you not to eat?" The man said, "The woman whom you gave to be with me, she gave me fruit from the tree, and I ate." Then the LORD God said to the woman, "What is this that you have done?" The woman said, "The serpent tricked me, and I ate." The LORD God said to the serpent,

"Because you have done this,
   cursed are you among all animals
   and among all wild creatures;
upon your belly you shall go,
   and dust you shall eat
   all the days of your life.[15]
I will put enmity between you and the woman,
   and between your offspring and hers;
he will strike your head,
   and you will strike his heel." [16]
To the woman he said,
   "I will greatly increase your pangs in childbearing;
   in pain you shall bring forth children,
   yet your desire shall be for your husband,
   and he shall rule over you."
And to the man he said,
   "Because you have listened to the voice of your wife,
      and have eaten of the tree
   about which I commanded you,
   'You shall not eat of it,'
   cursed is the ground because of you;
      in toil you shall eat of it all the days of your life;
thorns and thistles it shall bring forth for you;
   and you shall eat the plants of the field.
By the sweat of your face you shall eat bread
until you return to the ground,
for out of it you were taken;
you are dust,
   and to dust you shall return."

---

[14]The kind of fruit is not specified. It was often identified as a fig in the early Middle Ages; but an irresistible pun eventually settled the matter for Christians: *malum* in Latin meant both "apple" and "evil."

[15]Presumably snakes originally had legs like other animals, but lost them because of this curse.

[16]Christian artists made much use of this passage to create images of the Virgin Mary crushing a serpent beneath her heel.

The Story of Abraham, from the Hebrew Bible (Genesis 16:1–3, 15–16, 17, 21:1–2)

When the Jews tried to explain that the land of Israel was theirs by divine right though they acknowledged that their ancestors had not originated there, they pointed to the promise made to Abraham (originally from the Neobabylonian city of Ur). Although the modern Zionist movement was largely non-religious, the idea of the "promised land" has had a powerful influence in creating and maintaining the modern state of Israel. Ironically, this same story also tells of the origin of another people, the offspring of Ishmael, whom Muslims identify as the Arabs. Both religions therefore trace their origins back to Abraham, and both hold the land of Israel sacred, though neither accepts the other's claims. Like Isaac, several major figures in Jewish tradition are younger brothers or outsiders who eventually triumph through virtue, wit, or skill—Jacob, Joseph, and David, for instance. This pattern reflects the self-image of a people who view themselves as survivors who needed the special intervention of God to triumph. Note the emphasis on a high reproduction rate, desirable in most ancient cultures, for only a minority of children survived infancy.

What effect on the story does the extreme age of Sarai and Abram have?

Now Sarai, Abram's wife, bore him no children. She had an Egyptian slave-girl whose name was Hagar, and Sarai said to Abram, "You see that the LORD has prevented me from bearing children; go in to my slave-girl; it may be that I shall obtain children by her." And Abram listened to the voice of Sarai. So, after Abram had lived ten years in the land of Canaan, Sarai, Abram's wife, took Hagar the Egyptian, her slave-girl, and gave her to her husband Abram as a wife. . . .

Hagar bore Abram a son; and Abram named his son, whom Hagar bore, Ishmael. Abram was eighty-six years old when Hagar bore him Ishmael.

When Abram was ninety-nine years old, the LORD appeared to Abram, and said to him, "I am God Almighty; walk before me, and be blameless. And I will make my covenant between me and you, and will make you exceedingly numerous." Then Abram fell on his face; and God said to him, "As for me, this is my covenant with you: You shall be the ancestor of a multitude of nations. No longer shall your name be Abram, but your name shall be Abraham; for I have made you the ancestor of a multitude of nations. I will make you exceedingly fruitful; and I will make nations of you, and kings shall come from you. I will establish my covenant between me and you, and your offspring after you throughout their generations, for an everlasting covenant, to be God to you and to your offspring after you. And I will give to you, and to your offspring after you, the land where you are now an alien, all the land of Canaan, for a perpetual holding; and I will be their God."

God said to Abraham, "As for you, you shall keep my covenant, you and your offspring after you throughout their generations. This is my covenant, which you shall keep, between me and you and your offspring after you: Every male among you shall be circumcised. You shall circumcise the flesh of your foreskins, and it shall be a sign of the covenant between me and you. Throughout your generations every male among you shall be circumcised when he is eight days old, including the slave born in your house and the one bought with your money from any foreigner who is not of your offspring. Both the slave born in your house and the one bought with your money must be circumcised. So shall my covenant be in your flesh an everlasting covenant. Any uncircumcised male who is not circumcised in the flesh of his foreskin shall be cut off from his people; he has broken my covenant."[1]

God said to Abraham, "As for Sarah your wife, you shall not call her Sarai, but Sarah shall be her name. I will bless her, and moreover I will give you a son by her. I will bless her, and she shall give rise to nations; kings of peoples shall come from her." Then Abraham fell on his face and laughed, and said to himself, "Can a child be born to a man who is a hundred years old? Can Sarah, who is ninety years old, bear a child?" And Abraham said to God, "O that Ishmael might live in your sight!" God said, "No, but your wife Sarah shall bear you a son, and you shall name him Isaac. I will establish my covenant with him as an everlasting covenant for his offspring after him. As for Ishmael, I have heard you; I will bless him and make him fruitful and exceedingly numerous; he shall be the father of twelve princes, and I will make him a great nation. But my covenant I will establish with Isaac, whom Sarah shall bear to you at this season next year." And when he had finished talking with him, God went up from Abraham.

Then Abraham took his son Ishmael and all the slaves born in his house or bought with his money, every male among the men of Abraham's house, and he circumcised the flesh of their foreskins that very day, as God had said to him. Abraham was ninety-nine years old when he was circumcised in the flesh of his foreskin. And his son Ishmael was thirteen years old when he was circumcised in the flesh of his foreskin. That very day Abraham and his son Ishmael were circumcised; and all the men of his house, slaves born in the house and those bought with money from a foreigner, were circumcised with him. . . .

The LORD dealt with Sarah as he had said, and the LORD did for Sarah as he had promised. Sarah conceived and bore Abraham a son in his old age, at the time of which God had spoken to him. Abraham gave the name Isaac to his son whom Sarah bore him. And Abraham circumcised his son Isaac when he was eight days old, as God had commanded him. Abraham was a hundred years old when his son Isaac was born to him. Now Sarah said, "God has brought laughter for me; everyone who hears will laugh with me." And she said, "Who would ever have said to Abraham that Sarah would nurse children? Yet I have borne him a son in his old age."

The child grew, and was weaned; and Abraham made a great feast on the day that Isaac was weaned. But Sarah saw the son of Hagar the Egyptian, whom she had borne to Abraham, playing with her son Isaac. So she said to Abraham, "Cast out this slave woman with her son; for the son of this slave woman shall not inherit along with my son Isaac." The matter was very distressing to Abraham on account of his son. But God said to Abraham, "Do not be distressed because of the boy and because of your slave woman; whatever Sarah says to you, do as she tells you, for it is through Isaac that offspring shall be named for you. As for the son of the slave woman, I will make a nation of him also, because he is your offspring." So Abraham rose early in the morning, and took bread and a skin of water, and gave it to Hagar, putting it on her shoulder, along with the child, and sent her away. And she departed, and wandered about in the wilderness of Beer-sheba.

When the water in the skin was gone, she cast the child under one of the bushes. Then she went and sat down opposite him a good way off, about the distance of a bowshot; for

---

[1]Circumcision was widely practiced in the ancient Middle East and in Egypt, but contact with people who did not follow the custom in later times made the Jews highly self-conscious of their distinctiveness. Note that in Jewish tradition the covenant (agreement) is "everlasting," not superseded by a "new covenant" as in Christianity. The whole body of the Jewish law comes to be incorporated into this covenant.

she said, "Do not let me look on the death of the child." And as she sat opposite him, she lifted up her voice and wept. And God heard the voice of the boy; and the angel of God called to Hagar from heaven, and said to her, "What troubles you, Hagar? Do not be afraid; for God has heard the voice of the boy where he is. Come, lift up the boy and hold him fast with your hand for I will make a great nation of him." Then God opened her eyes and she saw a well of water. She went, and filled the skin with water, and gave the boy a drink.

God was with the boy, and he grew up; he lived in the wilderness, and became an expert with the bow. He lived in the wilderness of Paran; and his mother got a wife for him from the land of Egypt. . . .

The Law: Exodus 20-21:27, 22:16-23:9

The Jewish Bible is divided into three parts: the Law (Torah), the Prophets, and a miscellaneous group of works known as the Writings. Of these three, the Law is in some ways the most important, for it is the Law that defines for Jews what God expects of them and provides a means to ensure his favor and protection. The Law is viewed by pious Jews as a special blessing granted God's chosen people to show them the path to virtue while other peoples languish in ignorant sin. Many people assume that the ethics of Judaism and Christianity are based primarily on the Ten Commandments; in fact, Jews are called to observe some six hundred commandments and Christians usually do not observe two of the ten, having rejected the Jewish Sabbath for the "Lord's Day" early in their history and freely violating the commandment against graven images by sculpting innumerable images of Christ as the divine savior. The first ten are set apart, are repeated later, and are obviously considered important; but in some ways the subsequent laws are more revealing. Almost all peoples have outlawed murder, theft, and adultery, however they defined them; the other Jewish laws reflect the attitudes and customs of the people who followed them. An orthodox Jew is expected to observe strictly all of the laws (except those relating to ritual sacrifice which were suspended after the destruction of the temple in Jerusalem in 70 CE). Unlike in Christianity, belief is not the central issue—obedience is. The delivery of the law is here depicted as the aftermath of generations of slavery in Egypt followed by forty years of wandering in the wilderness of the Sinai Peninsula.

What provision in the law might discourage many Hebrew slaves from seeking their freedom? What laws enforce respect for parents? In what ways are the laws on slaves different from those of Hammurabi's Code? What does the law have to say about the proper treatment of enemies and aliens?

Then God spoke all these words: I am the LORD your God, who brought you out of the land of Egypt, out of the house of slavery; you shall have no other gods before me.[1]

---

[1]Although later Judaism insists that only one god exists, some scholars have argued that this wording reflects a time when Jews acknowledged the existence of other gods but forbade their worship.

You shall not make for yourself an idol, whether in the form of anything that is in heaven above, or that is on the earth beneath, or that is in the water under the earth.[2] You shall not bow down to them or worship them; for I the LORD your God am a jealous God, punishing children for the iniquity of parents, to the third and the fourth generation of those who reject me, but showing steadfast love to the thousandth generation of those who love me and keep my commandments.

You shall not make wrongful use of the name of the LORD your God, for the LORD will not acquit anyone who misuses his name.[3]

Remember the sabbath day, and keep it holy. Six days you shall labor and do all your work. But the seventh day is a sabbath to the LORD your God; you shall not do any work—you, your son or your daughter, your male or female slave, your livestock, or the alien resident in your towns. For in six days the LORD made heaven and earth, the sea, and all that is in them, but rested the seventh day; therefore the LORD blessed the sabbath day and consecrated it.[4]

Honor your father and your mother, so that your days may be long in the land that the LORD your God is giving you.

You shall not murder.

You shall not commit adultery.

You shall not steal.

You shall not bear false witness against your neighbor.

You shall not covet[5] your neighbor's house; you shall not covet your neighbor's wife, or male or female slave, or ox, or donkey, or anything that belongs to your neighbor.

When all the people witnessed the thunder and lightning, the sound of the trumpet, and the mountain smoking, they were afraid and trembled and stood at a distance and said to Moses, "You speak to us, and we will listen; but do not let God speak to us, or we will die. "Moses said to the people, "Do not be afraid; for God has come only to test you and to put the fear of him upon you so that you do not sin." Then the people stood at a distance, while Moses drew near to the thick darkness where God was.

The LORD said to Moses: Thus you shall say to the Israelites: "You have seen for your-selves that I spoke with you from heaven. You shall not make gods of silver alongside me, nor shall you make for yourselves gods of gold. You need make for me only an altar of earth and sacrifice on it your burnt offerings and your offerings of well-being, your sheep and

---

[2]This has usually been broadly interpreted by orthodox Jews as a prohibition against all figurative art, establishing a pattern also followed by orthodox Muslims. Although at some periods Jews have decorated buildings and manuscripts with images from the Bible, their general avoidance of divine sculpture led to a historic misunderstanding when the Romans invaded the sanctuary of the Temple in Jerusalem and, finding it empty, announced to the world that the Jews were atheists. More strongly than circumcision, the rejection of idols set the Jews apart from the people who surrounded them.

[3]The desire to avoid misusing God's name led eventually to the custom of not pronouncing it or spelling it out fully. Some English-speaking Jews even today follow this pattern by writing the deity's name as "G*d."

[4]The Sabbath was a unique Jewish invention, which attracted criticism from outsiders as an excuse for laziness, but most modern people are probably grateful to it as the ultimate origin of the custom of the weekend.

[5]Sometimes interpreted as prohibiting mere envy, this may have been more narrowly aimed at those who would plot to seize what was not theirs.

your oxen; in every place where I cause my name to be remembered I will come to you and bless you. But if you make for me an altar of stone, do not build it of hewn stones; if you use a chisel upon it you profane it. You shall not go up by steps to my altar, so that your nakedness may not be exposed on it."[6]

These are the ordinances that you shall set before them: When you buy a male Hebrew slave, he shall serve six years, but in the seventh he shall go out a free person, without debt.[7] If he comes in single, he shall go out single; if he comes in married, then his wife shall go out with him. If his master gives him a wife and she bears him sons or daughters, the wife and her children shall be her master's and he shall go out alone. But if the slave declares, "I love my master, my wife, and my children; I will not go out a free person, then his master shall bring him before God. He shall be brought to the door or the doorpost; and his master shall pierce his ear with an awl;[8] and he shall serve him for life."

When a man sells his daughter as a slave, she shall not go out[9] as the male slaves do. If she does not please her master, who designated her for himself, then he shall let her be redeemed;[10] he shall have no right to sell her to a foreign people since he has dealt unfairly with her. If he designates her for his son, he shall deal with her as with a daughter. If he takes another wife to himself, he shall not diminish the food, clothing, or marital rights of the first wife.[11] And if he does not do these three things for her, she shall go out without debt, without payment of money.

Whoever strikes a person mortally shall be put to death. If it was not premeditated, but came about by an act of God, then I will appoint for you a place to which the killer may flee.[12] But if someone willfully attacks and kills another by treachery, you shall take the killer from my altar for execution.

Whoever strikes father or mother shall be put to death.

Whoever kidnaps a person, whether that person has been sold or is still held in possession, shall be put to death.

Whoever curses father or mother shall be put to death.

When individuals quarrel and one strikes the other with a stone or fist so that the injured party, though not dead, is confined to bed, but recovers and walks around outside with the help of a staff, then the assailant shall be free of liability, except to pay for the loss of time, and to arrange for full recovery.

When a slaveowner strikes a male or female slave with a rod and the slave dies immediately, the owner shall be punished. But if the slave survives a day or two, there is no punishment; for the slave is the owner's property.

When people who are fighting injure a pregnant woman so that there is a miscarriage, and yet no further harm follows, the one responsible shall be fined what the woman's

---

[6]Steps might cause the skirt which men wore to part indecently.

[7]Following the pattern of six days of labor followed by a day of rest.

[8]A mark of enslavement, comparable to branding.

[9]Be freed.

[10]Bought back by her parents. It is assumed that she has been bought as a wife or concubine.

[11]Compare the prohibition in the Qur'an against treating multiple wives unequally.

[12]The concept of "places of refuge" or "sanctuary" was also held in ancient Greece, and to some extent in Medieval Europe. A fleeing criminal could take refuge at an altar or other sacred spot and demand protection from justice. Here the law provides an exception for what is now called "involuntary manslaughter."

husband demands, paying as much as the judges determine. If any harm follows, then you shall give life for life, eye for eye, tooth for tooth, hand for hand, foot for foot, burn for burn, wound for wound, stripe for stripe.[13]

When a slaveowner strikes the eye of a male or female slave, destroying it, the owner shall let the slave go, a free person, to compensate for the eye. If the owner knocks out a tooth of a male or female slave, the slave shall be let go, a free person, to compensate for the tooth. . . .

When a man seduces a virgin who is not engaged to be married, and lies with her, he shall give the bride-price for her and make her his wife. But if her father refuses to give her to him, he shall pay an amount equal to the bride-price for virgins.

You shall not permit a female sorcerer to live.[14]

Whoever lies with[15] an animal shall be put to death.

Whoever sacrifices to any god, other than the Lord alone, shall be devoted to destruction.

You shall not wrong or oppress a resident alien, for you were aliens in the land of Egypt. You shall not abuse any widow or orphan. If you do abuse them, when they cry out to me, I will surely heed their cry; my wrath will burn, and I will kill you with the sword, and your wives shall become widows and your children orphans.[16]

If you lend money to my people, to the poor among you, you shall not deal with them as a creditor; you shall not exact interest from them.[17] If you take your neighbor's cloak in pawn, you shall restore it before the sun goes down; for it may be your neighbor's only clothing to use as cover; in what else shall that person sleep? And if your neighbor cries out to me, I will listen, for I am compassionate.

You shall not revile God, or curse a leader of your people.

You shall not delay to make offerings from the fullness of your harvest and from the outflow of your presses. The firstborn of your sons you shall give to me.[18] You shall do the same with your oxen and with your sheep: seven days it shall remain with its mother; on the eighth day you shall give it to me.

---

[13]Note that the death of a fetus is treated as much less serious than lasting injury to the mother. The "eye for an eye" pattern used here and elsewhere was moderated later in Jewish practice by allowing money fines to substitute for mutilation; but in various periods both Christians and Muslims have also used the severing of members as punishment.

[14]Used as the classic justification for witch-burning by Christians.

[15]I. e., has intercourse with. Many of the laws prohibit various sexual activities.

[16]This unequivocal demand for mercy and hospitality to foreigners is repeated elsewhere in the Jewish Bible, and becomes a hallmark of the prophetic era.

[17]This prohibition against charging interest to coreligionists was also maintained by the Medieval Catholic Church; but the capital necessary for trade was provided by allowing Jews, who could not charge each other interest, to be lenders to Christians. Christians then bitterly reproached them for their greed. One of the crucial foundation stones for modern capitalism was laid when Protestants accepted the legitimacy of interest.

[18]To the Hebrews, this dedication of first-born sons to God (as priests) reflected the biblical story that their first-born had been spared when God killed those of the Egyptians. Christian theologians later saw in it an anticipation of the sacrificial offering of Jesus as God's son in the crucifixion.

You shall be people consecrated to me; therefore you shall not eat any meat that is mangled by beasts in the field; you shall throw it to the dogs.[19]

You shall not spread a false report. You shall not join hands with the wicked to act as a malicious witness. You shall not follow a majority in wrongdoing; when you bear witness in a lawsuit, you shall not side with the majority so as to pervert justice; nor shall you be partial to the poor in a lawsuit.[20]

When you come upon your enemy's ox or donkey going astray, you shall bring it back.

When you see the donkey of one who hates you lying under its burden and you would hold back from setting it free, you must help to set it free.

You shall not pervert the justice due to your poor in their lawsuits. Keep far from a false charge, and do not kill the innocent and those in the right, for I will not acquit the guilty. You shall take no bribe, for a bribe blinds the officials, and subverts the cause of those who are in the right.

You shall not oppress a resident alien; you know the heart of an alien, for you were aliens in the land of Egypt.

---

[19]Muslims are also prohibited from eating carrion.

[20]This passage spells out in more detail what is meant by the commandment against bearing false witness.

Passover (Deuteronomy 6:20-24)

This is the central statement of faith for one of the holiest of holy days in Judaism, Passover. The Biblical account of the miraculous escape of the Hebrews from Egypt is contained in Exodus 1–15. The Lord wreaks havoc in Egypt, including killing all the Egyptians' firstborn children; but the angel of death spares (passes over) the Hebrew children. This epic of liberation has appealed to many oppressed groups who have identified themselves with the Hebrews, notably African Americans.

What does the passage say is the function of the statutes (laws) which God has given the Jews?

When your children ask you in time to come, "What is the meaning of the decrees and the statutes and the ordinances that the Lord our God has commanded you?" then you shall say to your children, "We were Pharaoh's slaves in Egypt, but the Lord brought us out of Egypt with a mighty hand. The LORD displayed before our eyes great and awesome signs and wonders against Egypt, against Pharaoh and all his household. He brought us out from there in order to bring us in, to give us the land that he promised on oath to our ancestors. Then the Lord commanded us to observe all these statutes, to fear the Lord our God, for our lasting good, so as to keep us alive, as is now the case."

The Shema (Deuteronomy 6:4-9)

The Shema expresses the essence of Judaism, that God must be loved and obeyed at all times. The following words are inscribed on small scrolls contained in a box called a mezzuzah *fastened to the doorpost of Jewish homes. The wearing of a small mezzuzah (usually a cylinder) around the neck on a chain is a modern adaptation of the ancient custom.*

Why might the attitudes expressed in the Shema have led to the Jews having an unusually high literacy rate among the world's people?

Hear, O Israel: The Lord is our God, the Lord alone. You shall love the Lord your God with all your heart, and with all your soul, and with all your might. Keep these words that I am commanding you today in your heart. Recite them to your children and talk about them when you are at home and when you are away, when you lie down and when you rise. Bind them as a sign on your hand, fix them as an emblem on your forehead, and write them on the doorposts of your house and on your gates.

Proverbs (28:27, 27:5, 25:21-22, 27:14)

Like other ancient cultures in the region, the Jews delighted in creating and reciting sayings encapsulating their concepts of wisdom. Though some Hebrew proverbs are distinctively Jewish, others strongly resemble the sayings of their neighbors. Indeed, it has been argued that one collection in the Book of Proverbs in the Hebrew Bible (22:17–24:22) is a fairly straightforward adaptation of an Egyptian collection called The Wisdom of Amenemophis. *Some proverbs are pious, others express a more worldly wisdom. They are among the most vivid and pointed of the works contained in the Writings.*

What attitudes toward charity are expressed in these proverbs?

Whoever gives to the poor will lack nothing,
but one who turns a blind eye will get many a curse.

Better is open rebuke
than hidden love.[1]

If your enemies are hungry, give them bread to eat;
and if they are thirsty, give them water to drink;
for you will heap coals of fire on their heads,
and the Lord will reward you.[2]

---

[1]This lovely but seldom-quoted proverb seems to express a typically modern demand for the open expression of positive emotions. Rebuking someone is bad; but it is worse to love someone and not tell him or her.

[2]It has been suggested that carrying a pan of hot coals on the head was a form of penance for sin. The meaning of the proverb would then be that when you forgive those who have wronged you, you will make them feel painfully guilty. The best revenge is no revenge. Compare this proverb with the attitude expressed toward enemies above (Exodus 23:4–5).

Whoever blesses a neighbor with a loud voice,
rising early in the morning,
will be counted as cursing.[3]

---

[3] Clearly the speaker likes to sleep in!

Psalm 19

It is highly appropriate that the psalms should have frequently been set to music in modern times, for they were originally songs which would have been sung by soloists or choruses, often to instrumental accompaniment. Very probably some were also accompanied by dancing. Though some seem like private meditations, many psalms seem to call for public performance. The collection which exists in the Hebrew Bible is a varied one, probably gathering together established favorites written over several centuries by different authors, some of whom are mentioned by name in the introductions. The most famous of these is the great musician-king David, who is not only said to be the author of many of the psalms, but to whom Jewish and Christian tradition alike attributes all of them, including those clearly labeled as being by others. Modern scholars have questioned whether in fact any of the psalms can be traced to David. Whatever their origin, they reflect a common poetic heritage which made skillful use of parallelism: one line expresses an idea and the following line parallels it by expressing the same or a related idea in different wording. The effect is often majestic. Psalm 19 is typical of a number of psalms which share the Genesis creation story's vision of a natural world providing witness of a powerful and loving creator. The first stanza explores the paradox that although nature cannot speak literally, it nevertheless testifies to God's greatness. The second stanza focuses on one aspect of nature: the glorious sun, whose warmth penetrates everywhere, like God's knowledge. The third stanza shifts from the natural world to one of Judaism's favorite themes: the greatness of the law. Far from being seen as a burden or a curse, it is compared to honey in the mouth. The next stanza refers to the main function of the law: to make clear to the believer what should be done to please God; but the author is concerned that he may inadvertently violate laws of which he is unaware, and asks to be protected from such errors. The closing stanza makes a fitting conclusion, and is frequently used in worship services.

Although Jews praise God through nature, he is not nature itself, as in many other religions. How does the first stanza make this clear?

The heavens are telling the glory of God;
and the firmament proclaims his handiwork.
Day to day pours forth speech,
and night to night declares knowledge.
There is no speech, nor are there words;
their voice is not heard;
yet their voice goes out through all the earth,
and their words to the end of the world.[1]

---

[1] I. e., to the farthest reaches of the world (in space) not "the end of the world" in time.

In the heavens he has set a tent for the sun,
which comes out like a bridegroom from his wedding canopy,[2]
and like a strong man runs its course with joy.
Its rising is from the end of the heavens
and its circuit to the end of them;
and nothing is hid from its heat.

The law of the Lord is perfect,
reviving the soul;
the decrees of the Lord are sure,
making wise the simple;
the precepts of the Lord are right,
rejoicing the heart;
the commandment of the Lord is clear,
enlightening the eyes;
the fear of the Lord is pure,[3]
enduring forever;
the ordinances of the Lord are true
and righteous altogether.
More to be desired are they than gold,
even much fine gold;
sweeter also than honey,
and drippings of the honeycomb.

Moreover by them is your servant[4] warned;
in keeping them there is great reward.
But who can detect their errors?
Clear me from hidden faults.
Keep back your servant also from the insolent;
do not let them have dominion over me.
Then I shall be blameless,
and innocent of great transgression.

Let the words of my mouth
and the meditation of my heart[5]
be acceptable to you,
O Lord, my rock and my redeemer.

---

[2] Jewish weddings take place under a canopy, here compared to the nightly refuge of the sun, from which it rises triumphantly and joyously like a man who has just been married.
[3] "The fear of the Lord" is a kind of respectful awe before his majesty and justice which is often praised in the Writings as the essence of wisdom.
[4] The speaker, representing any worshipper.
[5] The opening stanza portrays speech not literally uttered; later the poet turns to sins which are unconscious and involuntary, and here the subject is thoughts which remain unspoken. Despite its varied themes, there is a strong unity running throughout the poem.

Psalm 137

The history of the great royal period of the kingdoms of Judah and Israel is framed by two periods of exile and captivity: in Egypt and in Babylon. The conquest of Samaria, the capital of Israel, by Assyria in 721 BCE and of Jerusalem, the capital of Judah, by the Neobabylonians in 587 BCE were only the most striking events in a centuries-long process of repeated attacks and shifting alliances. Because the Covenant with God had been seen as promising an everlasting kingdom for his chosen people, Jewish prophets argued that the Covenant had been broken and vitiated by the failure of the Jews to remain faithful to its terms. The prophetic writings are filled with attacks on the Hebrew people, principally because continued worship of other Gods was commonplace. This psalm, either written in exile, or on the way home, takes a much more sympathetic tone as it portrays the Jews longing for their homeland and seething for revenge against their former neighbors, the Edomites, who had allied themselves with the Babylonians.

How do the Jews react when the Babylonians ask to be entertained with some of their exotic folk songs?

By the rivers of Babylon—[1]
there we sat down and there we wept
when we remembered Zion[2]
On the willows there
we hung up our harps.
For there our captors
asked us for songs,
and our tormentors asked for mirth, saying,
"Sing us one of the songs of Zion!"

How could we sing the Lord's song
in a foreign land?
If I forget you, O Jerusalem,
let my right hand wither!
Let my tongue cling to the roof of my mouth,
if I do not remember you,
if I do not set Jerusalem
above my highest joy.[3]

---

[1]Babylon was situated on the banks of the Euphrates.

[2]"Zion" is a poetic religious name for the mountain on which Jerusalem was built and where the great temple was erected by Solomon. It is often used to refer to the future re-establishment of the temple (torn down by the Babylonians) and later, to a kind of paradise on earth to be established during the Messianic age. In modern times "Zionism" has described the drive to reestablish a Jewish political state in Israel, ending the third great Jewish exile known as "The Diaspora" (the scattering).

[3]This stanza is self-consciously paradoxical: singing about the fact that one refuses to sing about Jerusalem.

Remember, O Lord, against the Edomites
the day of Jerusalem's fall,
how they said, "Tear it down!
Tear it down!
Down to its foundations!"
O daughter of Babylon, you devastator!
Happy shall they be who pay you back what you have done to us!
Happy shall they be who take your little ones
and dash them against the rock![4]

---

[4]This vindictive final stanza is often omitted in public recitations, but it has had its influence. During the First Crusade, Christian knights are said to have slain Jewish and Muslim children while chanting these verses.

Song of the Suffering Servant, Isaiah 42:1-9

Of the Books of the Prophets, Isaiah is by far the most famous and influential outside of Judaism, not only because much of it is brilliantly written, but because it contains a series of poems about a mysterious figure known as the Suffering Servant. To Jews, this figure remains mysterious. The context has suggested to some readers that at least one of these poems may be about Cyrus, the leader of the Persians who conquered the Neobabylonian Empire and allowed those Jews who desired it to return to Jerusalem in 538 BCE. Jews have sometimes seen the Servant as a symbol of themselves. However, orthodox Jews do not identify the Servant with the Messiah, the promised future king who will restore and transform the ancient Kingdom of Israel and reign over the whole earth forever. Although Isaiah may have anticipated the coming of the Messiah with the end of the Babylonian captivity, Jewish belief came to view this figure as having yet to arrive. The Servant could not be the Messiah precisely because he is depicted as suffering. The Jewish Messiah is a triumphant military and political figure whose coming marks the end of the era of mortality: neither he nor his followers will ever die. Christian theology radically reworked this material to combine the two figures into one: a suffering Messiah who dies and is resurrected. Hence these lines are frequently applied to Jesus, as in George Frederick Handel's famous oratorio Messiah.

Here is my servant, whom I uphold,
my chosen, in whom my soul delights;
I have put my spirit upon him;
he will bring forth justice to the nations.
He will not cry or lift up his voice,
or make it heard in the street;
a bruised reed he will not break,
and a dimly burning wick he will not quench;[1]
he will faithfully bring forth justice.

---

[1]It is in this passage that the Servant's "suffering" is alluded to. Although he brings justice, he is meek and submissive. This attitude is described much more clearly in the third Song of the Suffering Servant (see Isaiah 50: 5–6) where he is struck and spat upon.

He will not grow faint or be crushed
until he has established justice in the earth;
and the coastlands wait for his teaching.

Thus says God, the Lord,
who created the heavens and stretched them out,
who spread out the earth and what comes from it,
who gives breath to the people upon it
and spirit to those who walk in it:
I am the Lord, I have called you in righteousness,
I have taken you by the hand and kept you;
I have given you as a covenant to the people,
a light to the nations,
to open the eyes that are blind,
to bring out the prisoners from the dungeon,
from the prison those who sit in darkness.
I am the Lord, that is my name;
my glory I give to no other,
nor my praise to idols.
See the former things have come to pass,
and new things I now declare;
before they spring forth,
I tell you of them.[2]

---

[2]This insistence on the ability to foretell the future raises a highly controversial point. Conservative Christians insist that various passages in Isaiah, including this one, accurately predict various events, including the coming of Christ. Other scholars maintain that the book of Isaiah was compiled from the writings of various authors at different times, and that this passage was probably written while the liberation was underway, while overstating its consequences.

Greece

Homer: *The Odyssey:* Odysseus & the Cyclops, from Book VII (before 700 BCE)

At the end of the great dark age which followed the collapse of the Minoan and Mycenean civilizations, tales circulated of the heroic deeds of that far-off era. Recited to musical accompaniment by oral poets, they were given their definitive form by the genius named Homer. Exactly how they came to be written down is still disputed, but no one disputes the brilliance of the telling. So successful were his two epics, the Iliad *and the* Odyssey, *that eventually rival works were all but forgotten. By classical times, Homer was accorded almost godlike status. Lacking an accepted sacred scripture, the Greeks sometimes used his works as a sort of substitute. Even during the Middle Ages, when Western Europeans forgot how to read Greek, they never forgot that Homer was supposed to have been a great poet. From the Renaissance onward, generations of readers have delighted in his vivid retellings of the great war at Troy and the adventure-filled ten-year voyage of Odysseus, trying to return home from that war to his home in Ithaca. In the following passage he is telling a rapt audience at the court which has rescued him from the sea about his encounter with the vicious one-eyed giant (cyclops) Polyphemos. The Greeks were proud of their intelligence and their civilization; and to them the cyclopes represented the essence of crude and stupid barbarism. The cyclops is vulnerable to the wine served him by Odysseus because he is a barbaric milk-drinker, unlike the civilized Greeks.*

What aspects of Odysseus' plan to escape demonstrate his cleverness? What other character traits can you deduce from Odysseus' actions and words?

"Lightly we made our way to the cave, but we did not find him
there, he was off herding on the range with his fat flocks.
We went inside the cave and admired everything inside it.
Baskets were there, heavy with cheeses, and the pens crowded
with lambs and kids. They had all been divided into separate
groups, the firstlings in one place, and then the middle ones,
the babies again by themselves. And all his vessels, milk pails
and pans, that he used for milking into, were running over
with whey. From the start my companions spoke to me and begged me
to take some of the cheeses, come back again, and the next time
to drive the lambs and kids from their pens, and get back quickly
to the ship again, and go sailing off across the salt water;
but I would not listen to them, it would have been better their way,
not until I could see him, see if he would give me presents.[1]
My friends were to find the sight of him in no way lovely.

"There we built a fire and made sacrifice, and helping
ourselves to the cheeses we ate and sat waiting for him
inside, until he came home from his herding. He carried a heavy

---

[1] Odysseus is usually more cautious than his men, but there are some instances like this in which his curiosity (or greed) gets the better of him. It was considered obligatory to give guests of a certain social status presents; hence his hopes of the cyclops are not irrational.

load of dried-out wood, to make a fire for his dinner,
and threw it down inside the cave, making a terrible
crash, so in fear we scuttled away into the cave's corners.
Next he drove into the wide cavern all from the fat flocks
that he would milk, but he left all the male animals, billygoats
and rams, outside in his yard with the deep fences. Next thing,
he heaved up and set into position the huge door stop,
a massive thing; no twenty-two of the best four-wheeled
wagons could have taken that weight off the ground and carried it,
such a piece of sky-towering cliff that was he set over
his gateway. Next he sat down and milked his sheep and his bleating
goats, each of them in order, and put lamb or kid under each one
to suck, and then drew off half of the white milk and put it
by in baskets made of wickerwork, stored for cheeses,
but let the other half stand in the milk pails so as to have it
to help himself to and drink from, and it would serve for his supper.
But after he had briskly done all his chores and finished,
at last he lit the fire, and saw us, and asked us a question:
'Strangers, who are you? From where do you come sailing over the watery
ways? Is it on some business, or are you recklessly roving
as pirates do, when they sail on the salt sea and venture
their lives as they wander, bringing evil to alien people?'[2]
So he spoke, and the inward heart in us was broken
in terror of the deep voice and for seeing him so monstrous;
but even so I had words for an answer, and I said to him:
'We are Achaians coming from Troy, beaten off our true course
by winds from every direction across the great gulf of the open
sea, making for home, by the wrong way, on the wrong courses.
So we have come. So it has pleased Zeus to arrange it.
We claim we are of the following of the son of Atreus,
Agamemnon,[3] whose fame now is the greatest thing under heaven,
such a city was that he sacked and destroyed so many
people; but now in turn we come to you and are suppliants
at your knees, if you might give us a guest present or otherwise
some gift of grace, for such is the right of strangers. Therefore
respect the gods, O best of men. We are your suppliants,
and Zeus the guest god, who stands behind all strangers with honors
due them, avenges any wrong toward strangers and suppliants.'
So I spoke, but he answered me in pitiless spirit:
'Stranger, you are a simple fool, or come from far off,
when you tell me to avoid the wrath of the gods or fear them.

---

[2]Odysseus, though he claims not to be a pirate, often behaves like one; and, when he reaches Ithaca, he tells a series of stories which associates himself with piracy. There seems to have been little difference between legitimate travellers and pirates.

[3]The general who assembled and led the army to conquer Troy. His brother's wife had been seized by the Trojan prince Paris, starting the conflict.

The Cyclopes do not concern themselves over Zeus of the aegis,
nor any of the rest of the blessed gods, since we are far better
than they, and for fear of the hate of Zeus I would not spare
you or your companions either, if the fancy took me
otherwise. But tell me, so I may know: where did you
put your well-made ship when you came? Nearby or far off?'
So he spoke, trying me out, but I knew too much and was not
deceived, but answered him in turn, and my words were crafty:
'Poseidon, Shaker of the Earth,[4] has shattered my vessel.
He drove it against the rocks on the outer coast of your country,
cracked on a cliff, it is gone, the wind on the sea took it;
but I, with these you see, got away from sudden destruction.'
So I spoke, but he in pitiless spirit answered
nothing, but sprang up and reached for my companions,
caught up two together and slapped them, like killing puppies,
against the ground, and the brains ran all over the floor, soaking
the ground. Then he cut them up limb by limb and got supper ready,
and like a lion reared in the hills, without leaving anything,
ate them, entrails, flesh and the marrowy bones alike.
We cried out aloud and held our hands up to Zeus, seeing
the cruelty of what he did, but our hearts were helpless.
But when the Cyclops had filled his enormous stomach, feeding
on human flesh and drinking down milk unmixed with water,
he lay down to sleep in the cave sprawled out through his sheep.
Then I took counsel with myself in my great-hearted spirit
to go up close, drawing from beside my thigh the sharp sword,
and stab him in the chest, where the midriff joins on the liver,
feeling for the place with my hand; but the second thought stayed me;
for there we too would have perished away in sheer destruction,
seeing that our hands could never have pushed from the lofty
gate of the cave the ponderous boulder he had propped there.
So mourning we waited, just as we were, for the divine Dawn.
But when the young Dawn showed again with her rosy fingers,
he lit his fire, and then set about milking his glorious
flocks, each of them in order, and put lamb or kid under each one.
But after he had briskly done all his chores and finished,
again he snatched up two men, and prepared them for dinner,
and when he had dined, drove his fat flocks out of the cavern,
easily lifting off the great doorstone, but then he put it
back again, like a man closing the lid on a quiver.
And so the Cyclops, whistling loudly, guided his fat flocks
to the hills, leaving me there in the cave mumbling my black thoughts
of how I might punish him, how Athene[5] might give me that glory.

---

[4] Poseidon was god of both the sea and of earthquakes. Unfortunately for Odysseus, he also happens to be Polyphemus' father.

[5] Athene (more commonly spelled "Athena") is the goddess of wisdom and Odysseus' special protector.

And as I thought, this was the plan that seemed best to me.
The Cyclops had lying there beside the pen a great bludgeon
of olive wood, still green. He had cut it so that when it dried out
he could carry it about, and we looking at it considered
it to be about the size for the mast of a cargo-carrying
broad black ship of twenty oars which crosses the open
sea; such was the length of it, such the thickness, to judge by
looking. I went up and chopped a length of about a fathom,
and handed it over to my companions and told them to shave it
down, and they made it smooth, while I standing by them sharpened
the point, then put it over the blaze of the fire to harden.
Then I put it well away and hid it under the ordure
which was all over the floor of the cave, much stuff lying
about. Next I told the rest of the men to cast lots, to find out
which of them must endure with me to take up the great beam
and spin it in Cyclops' eye when sweet sleep had come over him.
The ones drew it whom I myself would have wanted chosen,
four men, and I myself was the fifth, and allotted with them.
With the evening he came back again, herding his fleecy
flocks, but drove all his fat flocks inside the wide cave
at once, and did not leave any outside in the yard with the deep fence,
whether he had some idea, or whether a god so urged him.
When he had heaved up and set in position the huge door stop,
next he sat down and started milking his sheep and his bleating
goats, each of them in order, and put lamb or kid under each one.
But after he had briskly done all his chores and finished,
again he snatched up two men and prepared them for dinner.
Then at last I, holding in my hands an ivy bowl
full of the black wine, stood close up to the Cyclops and spoke out:
'Here, Cyclops, have a drink of wine, now you have fed on
human flesh, and see what kind of drink our ship carried
inside her. I brought it for you, and it would have been your libation
had you taken pity and sent me home, but I cannot suffer
your rages. Cruel, how can any man come and visit
you ever again, now you have done what has no sanction?'
So I spoke, and he took it and drank it off, and was terribly
pleased with the wine he drank and questioned me again, saying:
'Give me still more, freely, and tell me your name straightway
now, so I can give you a guest present to make you happy.
For the grain-giving land of the Cyclopes also yields them
wine of strength, and it is Zeus' rain that waters it for them;
but this comes from where ambrosia and nectar flow in abundance.'[6]
So he spoke, and I gave him the gleaming wine again. Three times
I brought it to him and gave it to him, three times he recklessly
drained it, but when the wine had got into the brains of the Cyclops,

---

[6]Ambrosia and nectar were the food and drink of the gods, and were available only in their paradise, Elysium.

then I spoke to him, and my words were full of beguilement:
'Cyclops, you ask me for my famous name. I will tell you
then, but you must give me a guest gift as you have promised.
Nobody is my name. My father and mother call me
Nobody, as do all the others who are my companions.'
So I spoke, and he answered me in pitiless spirit:
'Then I will eat Nobody after his friends, and the others
I will eat first, and that shall be my guest present to you.'
He spoke and slumped away and fell on his back, and lay there
with his thick neck crooked over on one side, and sleep who subdues all
came on and captured him, and the wine gurgled up from his gullet
with gobs of human meat. This was his drunken vomiting.
Then I shoved the beam underneath a deep bed of cinders,
waiting for it to heat, and I spoke to all my companions
in words of courage, so none should be in a panic, and back out;
but when the beam of olive, green as it was, was nearly
at the point of catching fire and glowed, terribly incandescent,
then I brought it close up from the fire and my friends about me
stood fast. Some great divinity breathed courage into us.
They seized the beam of olive, sharp at the end, and leaned on it
into the eye, while I from above leaning my weight on it
twirled it, like a man with a brace-and-bit who bores into
a ship timber, and his men from underneath, grasping
the strap on either side whirl it, and it bites resolutely deeper.
So seizing the fire-point-hardened timber we twirled it
in his eye, and the blood boiled around the hot point, so that
the blast and scorch of the burning ball singed all his eyebrows
and eyelids, and the fire made the roots of his eye crackle.
As when a man who works as a blacksmith plunges a screaming
great ax blade or plane into cold water, treating it
for temper, since this is the way steel is made strong, even
so Cyclops' eye sizzled about the beam of the olive.
He gave a giant horrible cry and the rocks rattled
to the sound, and we scuttled away in fear. He pulled the timber
out of his eye, and it blubbered with plenty of blood, then
when he had frantically taken it in his hands and thrown it
away, he cried aloud to the other Cyclopes, who live
around him in their own caves along the windy pinnacles.
They hearing him came swarming up from their various places,
and stood around the cave and asked him what was his trouble:
'Why, Polyphemos, what do you want with all this outcry
through the immortal night and have made us all thus sleepless?
Surely no mortal against your will can be driving your sheep off?
Surely none can be killing you by force or treachery?'
Then from inside the cave strong Polyphemos answered:
'Good friends, Nobody is killing me by force or treachery.'
So then the others speaking in winged words gave him an answer:
'If alone as you are none uses violence on you,

why, there is no avoiding the sickness sent by great Zeus;
so you had better pray to your father, the lord Poseidon.'
So they spoke as they went away, and the heart within me
laughed over how my name and my perfect planning had fooled him.
But the Cyclops, groaning aloud and in the pain of his agony,
felt with his hands, and took the boulder out of the doorway,
and sat down in the entrance himself, spreading his arms wide,
to catch anyone who tried to get out with the sheep, hoping
that I would be so guileless in my heart as to try this;
but I was planning so that things would come out the best way,
and trying to find some release from death, for my companions
and myself too, combining all my resource and treacheries,
as with life at stake, for the great evil was very close to us.
And as I thought, this was the plan that seemed best to me.
There were some male sheep, rams, well nourished, thick and fleecy,
handsome and large, with a dark depth of wool. Silently
I caught these and lashed them together with pliant willow
withes, where the monstrous Cyclops lawless of mind had used to
sleep. I had them in threes, and the one in the middle carried
a man, while the other two went on each side, so guarding
my friends. Three rams carried each man, but as for myself,
there was one ram, far the finest of all the flock. This one
I clasped around the back, snuggled under the wool of the belly,
and stayed there still, and with a firm twist of the hands and enduring
spirit clung fast to the glory of this fleece, unrelenting.
So we grieved for the time and waited for the divine Dawn.
But when the young Dawn showed again with her rosy fingers,
then the male sheep hastened out of the cave, toward pasture,
but the ewes were bleating all through the pens unmilked, their udders
ready to burst. Meanwhile their master, suffering and in
bitter pain, felt over the backs of all his sheep, standing
up as they were, but in his guilelessness did not notice
how my men were fastened under the breasts of his fleecy
sheep. Last of all the flock the ram went out of the doorway,
loaded with his own fleece, and with me, and my close counsels.
Then, feeling him, powerful Polyphemos spoke a word to him:
'My dear old ram, why are you thus leaving the cave last of
the sheep? Never in the old days were you left behind by
the flock, but long-striding, far ahead of the rest would pasture
on the tender bloom of the grass, be first at running rivers,
and be eager always to lead the way first back to the sheepfold
at evening. Now you are last of all. Perhaps you are grieving
for your master's eye, which a bad man with his wicked companions
put out, after he had made my brain helpless with wine, this
Nobody, who I think has not yet got clear of destruction.
If only you could think like us and only be given
a voice, to tell me where he is skulking away from my anger,
then surely he would be smashed against the floor and his brains go

57

spattering all over the cave to make my heart lighter
from the burden of all the evils this niddering[7] Nobody gave me.'
So he spoke, and sent the ram along from him, outdoors. . . ."

Translated by Richmond Lattimore

_____

[7]Cowardly.

Herodotus: *The Histories:* Xerxes at the Hellespont (5th Century BCE)

Whereas many Middle-Eastern peoples welcomed the advent of the Persian Empire, the Greeks viewed their own victories over the Persians as making possible the very continuance of their civilization. The army of Darius was defeated at the Battle of Marathon in 490 BCE and that of Xerxes I at Salamis in 486 BCE. The Greeks considered their poleis—many of them democracies—as infinitely superior to the absolute monarchy of Persia. Europeans have traditionally maintained that, if these battles had not been won, history would have been utterly changed, with Europe falling under the sway of Eastern despotism. Whether or not this theory is true can never be known; but the theory itself helped to shape centuries of European hostility to and contempt for the nations of the Middle East. Part of that contempt is expressed in the following story, which expresses typical Greek prejudice against the Persians. The great Xerxes is depicted by the Greek historian Herodotus as a superstitious fool and a bloodthirsty tyrant. His massive army is preparing to cross the narrow strait (the Hellespont, now in Turkey) which separated Asia from Europe.

What incidents described below depict Xerxes as superstitious? As tyrannical? What values can you infer the Herodotus would be in favor of, based on the faults he ascribes to Xerxes?

They then began to build bridges across the Hellespont from Abydos to that headland between Sestus and Madytus, the Phoenicians building one of ropes made from flax, and the Egyptians building a second one out of papyrus. From Abydos to the opposite shore it is a distance of almost two-thirds of a mile. But no sooner had the strait been bridged than a great storm came on and cut apart and scattered all their work.

Xerxes flew into a rage at this, and he commanded that the Hellespont be struck with three hundred strokes of the whip and that a pair of foot-chains be thrown into the sea. It's even been said that he sent off a rank of branders[1] along with the rest to the Hellespont! He also commanded the scourgers to speak outlandish and arrogant words: "You hateful water, our master lays his judgement on you thus, for you have unjustly punished him even though he's done you no wrong! Xerxes the king will pass over you, whether you wish it or not! It is fitting that no man offer you sacrifices,[2] for you're a muddy and salty river!" In these ways he commanded that the sea be punished and also that the heads be severed from all those who directed the bridging of the Hellespont.

And this scourging was done by those appointed to this graceless honor, and other builders were chosen. The bridging was done in the following way: fifty-oared ships and triremes were set side by side, about three hundred and sixty to form the Euxinian bridge, and about three hundred and fourteen to form the other bridge, all of them at right angles to the Pontus and parallel to the Hellespont, thus taking off some of the tension from the ropes. Once the ships were alongside one another, they released huge anchors, both from the end near the Pontus because of the winds blowing from that sea, and on the other end towards the west and the Aegean because of the western and southern winds. A passage was left in the opening of the fifty-oared ships and triremes in order that, if he wished to go into or out of the Pontus, he could pass through in a small ship. Having done all this, they stretched ropes from the land and twisted them with wooden pulleys, and they did not

---

[1]Men with hot branding irons.

[2]Bodies of water were routinely treated as gods, and offered sacrifices.

keep each separate, but assigned two flaxen cables and four papyrus cables for each bridge. Each type of cable was thick and comely, but the report goes that the flaxen cables were heavier, a single yard weighing over 100 pounds.[3] When the sea was bridged, wooden timbers equal to the breadth of the floating ships were felled and were laid on the stretched cables, and laying them alongside one another they tied them fast. Having done this, they put down brushwood, laying it on the timbers, and they put down earth on top of the brushwood, stamping it down and building a fence on the earth on each side in order that the beasts of burden and the horses would not be frightened by the sea flowing beneath them.

When they had built the bridges, the work around Athos, and the dikes around the mouths of the canals, these built because of the sea breaking on the shore which would silt up the mouths of the canals, and these canals being reported as completely finished, the army then and there prepared to winter and, when spring came, was ready and set forth to Abydos from Sardis. When they had started to set forth, the sun eclipsed itself and was not to be seen in its place in the heavens, even though the sky was unclouded and as clear as can be, so that the day turned to night. When Xerxes perceived this he became anxious, and he asked the Magians to clarify what this omen meant. These said that the god, Pythian Apollo, was foreshowing to the Greeks the eclipse of their city, for the sun was a prophet to the Greeks, as the moon was to them. Hearing that, Xerxes' mood became exceedingly sunny and he continued the march.

As he marched out the army, Pythias the Lydian, dreading the heavenly omen and encouraged by the gifts given to him by Xerxes, came up to Xerxes and said, "Master, I wish to ask a favor of you, which would be a small favor for you to render, but would be a great favor for me to receive." Xerxes, thinking that he knew everything Pythias could ask for, answered that he would grant the favor and asked him to proclaim what it was he wished. "Master, it happens that I have five sons, and they are all bound to soldier for you against the Greeks. I pray you, king, that you have pity on one who has reached my age and that you set free one of my sons, even the oldest, from your army, so that he may provide for me and my possessions. Take the other four with you, and may you return having accomplished all you intended."

Xerxes flew into a horrible rage and replied, "You villainous man, you have the effrontery, seeing me marching with my army against the Greeks, with my sons and brothers and relatives and friends, to remind me of your son, you, my slave, who should rather come with me with your entire household, including your wife! You may now be certain of this, that since the spirit lives in a man's ears, hearing good words it fills the body with delight, when it hears the opposite it swells up. When you at one time performed well and promised more, you had no reason to boast that you outperformed your king in benefits; and now that you have turned most shameless, you shall receive less than what you deserve. You and four of your sons are saved because of your hospitality; but one of your sons, the one you most desire to hold your arms around, will lose his life!" Having answered thus, he commanded those charged to accomplish this to find the eldest of Pythias's sons and cut him in half, and having cut him in two to set one half of his corpse on the right side of the road and the other on the left side, and between these the army moved forth.

Translated by Richard Hooker

---

[3]Literally: "18 1/2 inches weighing about 57 3/4 pounds."

Tyrtaios: *Spartan Soldier* (7th Century BCE)

Athens was famed for culture, Sparta for paranoid militarism. Yet Sparta produced a number of fine lyric poets early in its history, while Athens produced few. However, this poem, by the Spartan Tyrtaios, reinforces the standard image of Sparta as a land which valued courage in battle above all.

What does Tyrtaios say is the responsibility of the young towards the old?

It is beautiful when a brave man of the front ranks
    falls and dies, battling for his homeland,
and ghastly when a man flees planted fields and city
    and wanders begging with his dear mother,
aging father, little children and true wife.
    He will be scorned in every new village,
reduced to want and loathsome poverty; and shame
    will brand his family line, his noble
figure. Derision and disaster will hound him.
    A turncoat gets no respect or pity;
so let us battle for our country and freely give
    our lives to save our darling children.
Young men, fight shield to shield and never succumb
    to panic or miserable flight,
but steel the heart in your chests with magnificence
    and courage. Forget your own life
when you grapple with the enemy. Never run
    and let an old soldier collapse
whose legs have lost their power. It is shocking
    when an old man lies on the front line
before a youth: an old warrior whose head is white
    and beard gray, exhaling his strong soul
into the dust, clutching his bloody genitals
    in his hands: an abominable vision,
foul to see: his flesh naked. But in a young man
    all is beautiful when he still
possesses the shining flower of lovely youth.
    Alive he is adored by men,
desired by women, and finest to look upon
    when he falls dead in the forward clash.
Let each man spread his legs, rooting them in the ground,
    bite his teeth into his lips, and hold.

Translated by Willis Barnstone

Sappho: *To Anaktoria* (7th Century BCE)

The term "lesbian" as we use it today is derived from the works of this famed poet from Lesbos, which in fact reflect bisexual tendencies, for she wrote passionately about both men and women. Some reviled her frank sensuality and openly-expressed desire for other women. The Catholic Church made a systematic and largely successful attempt to destroy her works; and all that survives of the works of perhaps the greatest lyric poet of antiquity are short fragments and a few complete poems.

How do the ideas in this poem contrast with those in Tyrtaios' "Spartan Soldier?"

Some say cavalry and others claim
infantry or a fleet of long oars
is the supreme sight on the black earth.
I say it is

the one you love. And easily proved.
Did not Helen—who far surpassed all
mortals in beauty—desert the best
of men, her king,
and sail off to Troy and forget
her daughter and dear kinsmen?[1] Merely
the Kyprian's gaze[2] made her bend and led
her from her path;

these things remind me now
of Anaktoria who is far,
and I
for one

would rather see her warm supple step
and the sparkle of her face—than watch
all the dazzling chariots and armored
hoplites[3] of Lydia.

Translated by Willis Barnstone

---

[1]Queen Helen abandoned King Menelaus for Prince Paris of Troy, starting the Trojan War.
[2]Aphrodite, whose birthplace was the island of Kypris, was considered capable of inspiring overpowering feelings of desire.
[3]Foot soldiers.

Seizure

This poem describes Sappho's envy as she watches her beloved conversing with a man. The other woman listens absorbed, as if she were worshipping a god. She wishes she could speak as freely with the woman as the woman is speaking with the man; but her passion and her jealousy overwhelm her. Although seldom as eloquently expressed, the description of such painful emotions as being caused by desire led to the widespread belief in Western Civilization in the concept of lovesickness. Love was for centuries interpreted literally as a disease.

What are some of the physical sensations described in this poem?

To me he seems like a god
as he sits facing you and
hears you near as you speak
softly and laugh

in a sweet echo that jolts
the heart in my ribs.
For now as I look at you my voice
is empty and

can say nothing as my tongue
cracks and slender fire is quick
under my skin. My eyes are dead
to light, my ears

pound, and sweat pours over me.
I convulse, paler than grass,[1]
and feel my mind slip as I
go close to death.

Translated by Willis Barnstone

---

[1]For most of the year the grass is a pale straw color.

Greece

Sophocles: *Antigone*

The Athenian Greeks invented drama in the Western World by creating tragedies and farcical satyr plays out of the annual celebration of the festival of the god of wine, Dionysus, beginning with a chorus, and then adding individual actors to portray individual characters, with the chorus being retained as commentators on the action. From an early period, these plays focused on conflicts within Greek culture for which there were no simple resolutions. Playwrights like Sophocles do not preach, but instead invite their audience to contemplate the fact that in real life sometimes there is no happy ending. Contemplating how people face their fates can be as important as helping people solve their less intractable problems. The following scene from Sophocles' Antigone explores the tension between two important values: individual responsibility and public order. Antigone's twin brothers, Eteocles and Polyneices, have killed each other in a civil war in which it could be said that each side had some justification for its actions. However, Antigone's uncle, Creon, who has taken over the power, identifies with Polyneices, the brother who had held the throne of Thebes before him, stressing the importance of respect for state authority. He condemns Eteocles' body to lie unburied in the open as an example to other potential rebels. In so doing, he is violating one of the most fundamental laws of Greek society, for it is the solemn duty of the living to bury the dead. Antigone is able to accomplish only a token funeral, sprinkling dirt on the body and pouring out libations to his memory; but this is enough to satisfy the demands of religion. The guard who brings her in has been threatened with death for having failed to catch her earlier.

What are Antigone's main arguments against Creon's position? What are the main arguments that Creon uses against her? How does the fact that she is a woman affect his reactions? What attitude toward this dispute is expressed in the final speech by the chorus?

(The guard enters with Antigone.)

CREON
My mind is split at this awful sight.
I know her. I cannot deny
Antigone is here.
Alas, the unhappy girl,
her unhappy father's[1] child.
Oh what is the meaning of this?
It cannot be you that they bring
for breaking the royal law,
caught in open shame.

GUARD
This is the woman who has done the deed.
We caught her at the burying. Where's the king?

CHORUS
Back from the house again just when he's needed.

CREON
What must I measure up to? What has happened?

(Creon enters.)

---

[1]Antigone's father was Oedipus, the incestuous and father-killing protagonist of another Sophocles tragedy.

GUARD
    Lord, one should never swear off anything.
    Afterthought makes the first resolve a liar.
    I could have vowed I wouldn't come back here
    after your threats, after the storm I faced.
    But joy that comes beyond the wildest hope
    is bigger than all other pleasure known.
    I'm here, though I swore not to be, and bring
    this girl. We caught her burying the dead.
    This time we didn't need to shake the lots;
    mine was the luck, all mine.
    So now, lord, take her, you, and question her
    and prove her as you will. But I am free.
    And I deserve full clearance on this charge.
CREON
    Explain the circumstance of the arrest.
GUARD
    She was burying the man. You have it all.
CREON
    Is this the truth? And do you grasp its meaning?
GUARD
    I saw her burying the very corpse
    you had forbidden. Is this adequate?
CREON
    How was she caught and taken in the act?
GUARD
    It was like this: when we got back again
    struck with those dreadful threatenings of yours,
    we swept away the dust that hid the corpse.
    We stripped it back to slimy nakedness.
    And then we sat to windward on the hill
    so as to dodge the smell.
    We poked each other up with growling threats
    if anyone was careless of his work.
    For some time this went on, till it was noon.
    The sun was high and hot. Then from the earth
    up rose a dusty whirlwind to the sky,
    filling the plain, smearing the forest-leaves,
    clogging the upper air. We shut our eyes,
    sat and endured the plague the gods had sent.
    So the storm left us after a long time.
    We saw the girl. She cried the sharp and shrill
    cry of a bitter bird which sees the nest
    bare where the young birds lay.
    So this same girl, seeing the body stripped,
    cried with great groanings, cried a dreadful curse
    upon the people who had done the deed.
    Soon in her hands she brought the thirsty dust,

and holding high a pitcher of wrought bronze
she poured the three libations for the dead.
We saw this and surged down. We trapped her fast;
and she was calm. We taxed her with the deeds
both past and present. Nothing was denied.
And I was glad, and yet I took it hard.
One's own escape from trouble makes one glad;
but bringing friends to trouble is hard grief.
Still, I care less for all these second thoughts
than for the fact that I myself am safe.

CREON

You there, whose head is drooping to the ground,
do you admit this, or deny you did it?

ANTIGONE

I say I did it and I don't deny it.

CREON *(to the* GUARD*)*

Take yourself off wherever you wish to go
free of a heavy charge.

CREON *(to Antigone)*

You—tell me not at length but in a word.
You knew the order not to do this thing?

ANTIGONE

I knew, of course I knew. The word was plain.

CREON

And still you dared to overstep these laws?

ANTIGONE

For me it was not Zeus who made that order.
Nor did that Justice who lives with the gods below
mark out such laws to hold among mankind.
Nor did I think your orders were so strong
that you, a mortal man, could over-run
the gods' unwritten and unfailing laws.
Not now, nor yesterday's, they always live,
and no one knows their origin in time.
So not through fear of any man's proud spirit
would I be likely to neglect these laws,
draw on myself the gods' sure punishment.
I knew that I must die; how could I not?
even without your warning. If I die
before my time, I say it is a gain.
Who lives in sorrows many as are mine
how shall he not be glad to gain his death?
And so, for me to meet this fate, no grief.
But if I left that corpse, my mother's son,
dead and unburied I'd have cause to grieve
as now I grieve not.
And if you think my acts are foolishness
the foolishness may be in a fool's eye.

CHORUS
 The girl is bitter. She's her father's child.
 She cannot yield to trouble; nor could he.
CREON
 These rigid spirits are the first to fall.
 The strongest iron, hardened in the fire,
 most often ends in scraps and shatterings.
 Small curbs bring raging horses back to terms.
 Slave to his neighbor, who can think of pride?
 This girl was expert in her insolence
 when she broke bounds beyond established law.
 Once she had done it, insolence the second,
 to boast her doing, and to laugh in it.
 I am no man and she the man instead
 if she can have this conquest without pain.
 She is my sister's child, but were she child
 of closer kin than any at my hearth,
 she and her sister should not so escape
 their death and doom. I charge Ismene too.
 She shared the planning of this burial.
 Call her outside. I saw her in the house,
 maddened, no longer mistress of herself.
 The sly intent betrays itself sometimes
 before the secret plotters work their wrong.
 I hate it too when someone caught in crime
 then wants to make it seem a lovely thing.
ANTIGONE
 Do you want more than my arrest and death?
CREON
 No more than that. For that is all I need.
ANTIGONE
 Why are you waiting? Nothing that you say
 fits with my thought. I pray it never will.
 Nor will you ever like to hear my words.
 And yet what greater glory could I find
 than giving my own brother funeral?
 All these would say that they approved my act
 did fear not mute them.
 (A king is fortunate in many ways,
 and most, that he can act and speak at will.)
CREON
 None of these others see the case this way.
ANTIGONE
 They see, and do not say. You have them cowed.
CREON
 And you are not ashamed to think alone?

ANTIGONE

    No, I am not ashamed. When was it shame
    to serve the children of my mother's womb?

CREON

    It was not your brother who died against him, then?

ANTIGONE

    Full brother, on both sides, my parents' child.

CREON

    Your act of grace, in his regard, is crime.

ANTIGONE

    The corpse below[2] would never say it was.

CREON

    When you honor him and the criminal just alike?

ANTIGONE

    It was a brother, not a slave, who died.

CREON

    Died to destroy this land the other guarded.

ANTIGONE

    Death yearns for equal law for all the dead.

CREON

    Not that the good and bad draw equal shares.

ANTIGONE

    Who knows that this is holiness below?

CREON

    Never the enemy, even in death, a friend.

ANTIGONE

    I cannot share in hatred, but in love.

CREON

    Then go down there, if you must love, and love
    the dead. No woman rules me while I live.

                           (Ismene is brought from the palace under guard.)

CHORUS

    Look there! Ismene is coming out.
    She loves her sister and mourns,
    with clouded brow and bloodied cheeks,
    tears on her lovely face.

CREON

    You, lurking like a viper in the house,
    who sucked me dry. I looked the other way
    while twin destruction planned against the throne.
    Now tell me, do you say you shared this deed?
    Or will you swear you didn't even know?

ISMENE

    I did the deed, if she agrees I did.
    I am accessory and share the blame.

---

[2]In Hades, the dwelling place of the dead.

68

ANTIGONE
Justice will not allow this. You did not
wish for a part, nor did I give you one.
ISMENE
You are in trouble, and I'm not ashamed
to sail beside you into suffering.
ANTIGONE
Death and the dead, they know whose act it was.
I cannot love a friend whose love is words.
ISMENE
Sister, I pray, don't fence me out from honor,
from death with you, and honor done the dead.
ANTIGONE
Don't die along with me, nor make your own
that which you did not do. My death's enough.
ISMENE
When you are gone what life can be my friend?
ANTIGONE
Love Creon. He's your kinsman and your care.
ISMENE
Why hurt me, when it does yourself no good?
ANTIGONE
I also suffer, when I laugh at you.
ISMENE
What further service can I do you now?
ANTIGONE
To save yourself. I shall not envy you.
ISMENE
Alas for me. Am I outside your fate?
ANTIGONE
Yes. For you chose to live when I chose death.
ISMENE
At least I was not silent. You were warned.
CREON
Some will have thought you wiser. Some will not.
ISMENE
And yet the blame is equal for us both.
ANTIGONE
Take heart. You live. My life died long ago.
And that has made me fit to help the dead.
CREON
One of these girls has shown her lack of sense
just now. The other had it from her birth.
ISMENE
Yes, lord. When people fall in deep distress
their native sense departs, and will not stay.

CREON
    You chose your mind's distraction when you chose
    to work out wickedness with this wicked girl.
ISMENE
    What life is there for me to live without her?
CREON
    Don't speak of her. For she is here no more.
ISMENE
    But will you kill your own son's promised bride?
CREON
    Oh, there are other furrows for his plow.
ISMENE
    But where the closeness that has bound these two?
CREON
    Not for my sons will I choose wicked wives.
ISMENE
    Dear Haemon, your father robs you of your rights.
CREON
    You and your marriage trouble me too much.
ISMENE
    You will take away his bride from your own son?
CREON
    Yes. Death will help me break this marriage off.
CHORUS
    It seems determined that the girl must die.
CREON
    You helped determine it. Now, no delay!
    Slaves, take them in. They must be women now.
    No more free running.
    Even the bold will fly when they see Death
    drawing in close enough to end their life.
CHORUS
    Fortunate they whose lives have no taste of pain.
    For those whose house is shaken by the gods
    escape no kind of doom. It extends to all the kin
    like the wave that comes when the winds of Thrace
    run over the dark of the sea.
    The black sand of the bottom is brought from the depth;
    the beaten capes sound back with a hollow cry.
    Ancient the sorrow of Labdacus'[3] house, I know.
    Dead men's grief comes back, and falls on grief.
    No generation can free the next.
    One of the gods will strike. There is no escape.
    So now the light goes out
    for the house of Oedipus, while the bloody knife
    cuts the remaining root. Folly and Fury have done this.

---

[3]The grandfather of Oedipus.

What madness of man, O Zeus, can bind your power?
Not sleep can destroy it who ages all,
nor the weariless months the gods have set. Unaged in time
monarch you rule of Olympus' gleaming light.
Near time, far future, and the past,
one law controls them all:
any greatness in human life brings doom.
Wandering hope brings help to many men.
But others she tricks from their giddy loves,
and her quarry knows nothing until he has walked into flame.
Word of wisdom it was when someone said,
"The bad becomes the good
to him a god would doom."
Only briefly is that one from under doom.

Translated by Elizabeth Wykoff

Greek Philosophy

Early Greek Philosophy

What we know of the origins of philosophy (including science) among the Greeks comes from later quotations from lost texts or reports of doctrines which were passed down orally. Philosophical thinking began with a group of Ionians who were asking about what is ultimately real: isn't there some simpler, underlying reality behind the varied appearances which our senses give us of the world? And isn't that elementary stuff eternal, such that it doesn't itself have to be created (come into being) and cannot be destroyed (cease to exist)? Thales thought that the elemental stuff must be water; others thought it to be air or fire. Anaximander made an enormous leap by proposing that the underlying, elemental stuff must be unlike any of the things which we see or touch in the world, hence something indefinable (or "infinite," apeiron in Greek). (Think of modern science, which tells us that this page is made up of extremely small particles—or of configurations of energy—which are in no way like the page that you are aware of holding. The page may be burned to ashes or decay into dust, but the atoms which make it up go on existing unchanged. Then Greek speculation doesn't seem so far-fetched.) Translations on pp. 72–75 are by G. S. Kirk and J. E. Raven.

Thales (c. 636–c. 546 BCE):

What reason does Thales seem to have given for taking water to be the basic stuff?

Others say that the earth rests on water. For this is the ancient account we have received, which they say was given by Thales the Milesian, that it stays in place through floating like a log or some other such thing (for none of these rests by nature on air, but on water). . . .

Most of the first philosophers thought that principles[1] in the form of matter were the only principles of all things: for the original source of all existing things, that from which a thing first comes-into-being and into which it is finally destroyed, the substance persisting but changing in its qualities, this they declare is the element and first principle of existing things, and for this reason they consider that there is no absolute coming-to-be or passing away, on the ground that such a nature is always preserved . . . for there must be some natural substance, either one or more than one, from which the other things come into being, while it is preserved. Over the number, however, and the form of this kind of principle they do not all agree; but Thales, the founder of this type of philosophy, says that it is water (and therefore declared that the earth is on water), perhaps taking this supposition from seeing the nature of all things to be moist, and the warm itself coming-to-be from this and living by this (that from which they come-to-be being the principle of all things)—taking the supposition both from this and from the seeds of all things having a moist nature, water being the natural principle of moist things.

For moist natural substance, since it is easily formed into each different thing, is accustomed to undergo very various changes: that part of it which is exhaled is made into air,

---

[1]Underlying essences, the "stuff."

72

and the finest part is kindled from air into aither,[2] while when water is compacted and changes into slime it becomes earth. Therefore Thales declared that water, of the four elements,[3] was the most active, as it were, as a cause.

---

[2]A very refined kind of "air" which the Greeks supposed to be the least solid of all substances. More often spelled "ether."
[3]In the Greek system of the elements, later adopted for centuries by Europeans, all substances can be classified into four categories: earth, air, fire, and water. Traces of this system still persist in superstitions such as astrology.

Anaximander (c. 611–c. 547 BCE)

Where does Anaximander think that the "infinite" (the apeiron*) came from? Or didn't it "come from" anywhere?*

... of the infinite[1] there is no beginning ... but this seems to be the beginning of the other things, and to surround all things and steer all, as all those say who do not postulate other causes, above and beyond the infinite. And this is the divine; for it is immortal and indestructible, as Anaximander says and most of the physical speculators.[2]

---

[1]"Infinite" *(apeiron)* means not just unlimited in size or in number but having no qualities at all which would serve to delimit it from other things. Thus hot and cold, wet and dry, single and double, etc., while positive features of a thing, are also "limitations" of it; they *wouldn't*, on Anaximander's account, be features of the ultimate reality.
[2]Thinkers who speculate or theorize about the nature of the world.

The Atomists: Leucippus (5th century BCE), Democritus (c. 460-c. 370 BCE), Epicurus (341-270 BCE)

The Atomists held that everything consists of matter (little tiny earthy particles, like grains of sand, but too small to be seen) and void (the empty space within which the atoms move and cluster together to make visible things like this page). With this theory they could give particularly persuasive explanations of various phenomena: for example, why some things are heavy and hard (lots of atoms closely packed) while other things are light and soft (few atoms with more space between them); or why frequently used stairsteps eventually wear down and become concave (the gradual sloughing off of a few atoms at a time). The Atomists also were introducing the radical notion that space was real in itself, an empty container in which things can move around. (That's the notion which Isaac Newton later held, and which most of us grow up believing in.) In the third selection below we are given Leucippus' theory that the earth is round(!) and his account of how it came to be from a conglomeration of atoms in the midst of an infinite space, an account strikingly similar to that given by modern cosmologists.

How, according to Leucippus and Democritus, can the shapes of the atoms, their arrangements (comparable to bonding in modern atomic physics), and their positions (locations) cause differences in the objects large enough for us to see and touch?

Leucippus and his associate Democritus hold that the elements are the full[1] and the void; they call them being and not-being respectively. Being is full and solid, not-being is void and rare. Since the void exists no less than body, it follows that not-being exists no less than being. The two together are the material causes of existing things. And just as those who make the underlying substance one generate other things by its modifications, and postulate rarefaction and condensation[2] as the origin of such modifications, in the same way these men too say that the differences in atoms are the causes of other things. They hold that these differences are three—shape, arrangement and position; being, they say, differs only in "rhythm, touching and turning," of which "rhythm" is shape, "touching" is arrangement and "turning" is position; for A differs from N in shape, AN from NA in arrangement, and Z from N in position.

They suppose their primary bodies to be impassable (some of them, e.g. Epicurus' School, regarding them as unbreakable[3] because of their hardness, others, e.g. the school of Leucippus, as indivisible because of their smallness) . . .

Leucippus holds that the whole is infinite . . . part of it is full and part void. Hence arise innumerable worlds, and are resolved again into these elements. The worlds come into being as follows: many bodies of all sorts of shapes move "by abscission[4] from the infinite" into a great void; they come together there and produce a single whirl, in which, colliding with one another and revolving in all manner of ways, they begin to separate apart, like to like. But when their multitude prevents them from rotating any longer in equilibrium, those that are fine go out towards the surrounding void as if sifted,[5] while the rest "abide together" and, becoming entangled, unite their motions and make a first spherical structure.[6] This structure stands apart like a "membrane" which contains in itself all kinds of bodies; and as they whirl around owing to the resistance of the middle, the surrounding membrane becomes thin, while contiguous atoms keep flowing together owing to contact with the whirl. So the earth came into being, the atoms that had been borne to the middle abiding together there. Again, the containing membrane is itself increased, owing to the attraction of bodies outside; as it moves around in the whirl it takes in anything it touches. Some of these bodies that get entangled form a structure that is at first moist and muddy, but as they revolve with the whirl of the whole they dry out and then ignite to form the substance of the heavenly bodies.

---

[1] I.e., that which is solid, matter.

[2] Making less or more dense.

[3] In Greek the word "atom" means "uncuttable." The idea is that if you divide a substance into smaller and smaller pieces, eventually you will reach a point when what is left can no longer be cut. These would be its "atoms." In our day the word "atom" has, of course, lost that sense of indivisibility, but the shapes of atoms in the Greek theory can be compared to the configurations of electrons and protons in modern atoms, or to the configurations of atoms in molecules.

[4] Being cut off, separated from.

[5] These would make up the air surrounding the earth.

[6] Leucippus, lacking a theory of gravity, has to depend on friction to get his atoms to stick together.

Xenophanes:

Xenophanes was perhaps the first philosopher to be critical of contemporary Greek religion, his basic point being that people believed in gods who were supposed to be too much like humans—what we now call "anthropomorphism" (something in the form, morph-, of humans, anthropo-). His second remark criticizes the idea that the gods could be immoral. He may have had a notion of a unified, monotheistic deity—or more likely a pantheistic deity, living throughout nature—as indicated by his last two remarks. Despite their lively pantheon of gods, Greek philosophers developed remarkably sophisticated ideas about the divine which were to fuse later with Jewish ones as Christian theology went through its early evolution.

What does Xenophanes seem to be saying is the basic process humans go through in creating their ideas of gods?

Homer and Hesiod have attributed to the gods everything that is a shame and reproach among men, stealing and committing adultery and deceiving each other.

But mortals consider that the gods are born, and that they have clothes and speech and bodies like their own.

The Ethiopians say that their gods are snub-nosed and black, the Thracians that theirs have light blue eyes and red hair.

But if cattle and horses or lions had hands, or were able to draw with their hands and do the works that men can do, horses would draw the forms of the gods like horses, and cattle like cattle, and they would make their bodies such as they each had themselves.

One god, greatest among gods and men, in no way similar to mortals either in body or in thought.

Always he remains in the same place, moving not at all; nor is it fitting for him to go to different places at different times, but without toil he shakes all things by the thought of his mind.

Protagoras

Protagoras was one of the famous "sophists," who traveled among the Greek cities teaching rhetoric (persuasive speaking) and grammar. In general, the Sophists argued that laws of states and societies are just conventional rules, varying from one place to another, with none of them being really right or wrong. Thus they were the earliest thinkers to espouse relativism, the view that what is right and good for my group isn't necessarily right and good for your group, hence that there can be no universally valid moral standards. In the first paragraph Protagoras seems to mean that each of us sees the world with our own eyes, thus each of us sees things differently, but each of us is right — hence, that no one can know what is "really the case." In the second paragraph he suggests a skepticism much more common in the classical world than in any other ancient society, and which foreshadows modern secularism. It goes beyond the refusal of Confucius to speculate about the spiritual world. He preferred to focus on ethical concerns, not theology. But Protagoras suggests that we can never truly know the gods.

What reasons does Protagoras give for thinking that we cannot have any religious knowledge?

Protagoras also holds that "Man is the measure of all things, of existing things that they exist, and of non-existing things that they exist not": and by "measure" he means the criterion and by "things" the objects, so that he is virtually asserting that "Man is the criterion of all objects, of those which exist that they exist, and of those which exist not that they exist not." And consequently he posits only what appears to each individual, and thus he introduces relativity.

"As to the gods, I have no means of knowing either that they exist or that they do not exist. For many are the obstacles that impede knowledge, both the obscurity of the question and the shortness of human life."

Translated by Milton C. Nahm

Socrates

Socrates opposed the Sophists, arguing that there are absolute, transcultural standards of right and wrong, good and bad. He argued (as in the first passage below) that once we recognize what is truly good, we will act in accord with that knowledge—hence his claim that "the virtues are a kind of knowledge." He also firmly believed (as shown in the second passage) that the cosmos is grounded in goodness, hence that a good person cannot suffer unduly and that death is not something to be feared.

Socrates, then, the elder, thought the knowledge of virtue to be the end, and used to inquire what is justice, what bravery, and each of the parts of virtue; and his conduct was reasonable, for he thought all the virtues to be kinds of knowledge, so that to know justice and to be just came simultaneously; for the moment we have learned geometry or architecture we are architects and geometers. Therefore he inquired what virtue is, not how or from what it arises . . . .

Translated by Milton C. Nahm from Aristotle

Socrates' Defense, from Plato's *Apology*

In this passage Plato relates the end of Socrates' defense in his speech before the Athenian court. Then, in the passage from the Phaedo, *he recounts the last hours of Socrates' life. That the condemned should drink a cup of hemlock was a standard method of execution. All selections from Plato are from translations by Benjamin Jowett.*

What reasons does Socrates give for not fearing death? Why is Socrates so little concerned with how his body is to be buried?

Now as you see there has come upon me that which may be thought, and is generally believed to be, the last and worst evil. But the oracle made no sign of opposition . . . I regard this as a proof that what has happened to me is a good, and that those of us who think that death is an evil are in error . . . . Let us reflect in another way, and we shall see that there is great reason to hope that death is a good, for one of two things:—either death is a state of nothingness and utter unconsciousness, or, as men say, there is a change and migration of the soul from this world to another. Now if you suppose that there is no consciousness, but a sleep like the sleep of him who is undisturbed even by the sight of dreams, death will be an unspeakable gain. . . . Now if death is like this, I say that to die is gain; for eternity is then only a single night. But if death is a journey to another place, and there, as men say, all the dead are, what good, O my friends and judges, can be greater than this? . . . What would not a man give if he might converse with Orpheus and Musaeus and Hesiod and Homer? Nay, if this be true, let me die again and again. . . . Above all, I shall be able to continue my search into true and false knowledge; as in this world, so also in that; I shall find out who is wise, and who pretends to be wise, and is not. . . . The hour of departure has arrived, and we go our ways—I to die, and you to live. Which is better, God only knows.

The Death of Socrates, from Plato's *Phaedo*

Then he turned to us, and added with a smile: "I cannot make Crito believe that I am the same Socrates who has been talking and conducting the argument; he fancies that I am the other Socrates whom he will soon see, a dead body—and he asks, How shall he bury me? And though I have spoken many words in the endeavor to show that when I have drunk the poison I shall leave you and go to the joys of the blessed—these words of mine, with which I was comforting you and myself, have had, as I perceive, no effect upon Crito. And therefore I want you to be surety for me to him now, as at the trial he was surety to the judges for me: but let the promise be of another sort; for he was surety for me to the judges that I would remain, and you must be my surety to him that I shall not remain, but go away and depart; and then he will suffer less at my death, and not be grieved when he sees my body being burned or buried. . . .

Socrates said: "You, my good friend, who are experienced in these matters, shall give me directions how I am to proceed."

The man answered: "You have only to walk about until your legs are heavy, and then to lie down, and the poison will act."

At the same time he handed the cup to Socrates, who in the easiest and gentlest manner, without the least fear or change of color or feature, looking at the man with all his eyes, . . . as his manner was, took the cup and said: "What do you say about making a libation out of this cup to any god? May I, or not?"

The man answered: "We only prepare, Socrates, just so much as we deem enough."

"I understand," he said; "but I may and must ask the gods to prosper my journey from this to the other world—even so—and so be it according to my prayer."

Then raising the cup to his lips, quite readily and cheerfully he drank off the poison. And hitherto most of us had been able to control our sorrow; but now when we saw him drinking, and saw too that he had finished the draft, we could not longer forbear, and in spite of myself my own tears were flowing fast; so that I covered my face and wept, not for him, but at the thought of my own calamity in having to part from such a friend. Nor was I the first; for Crito, when he found himself unable to restrain his tears, had got up, and I followed; and at that moment, Apollodorus, who had been weeping all the time, broke out in a loud and passionate cry which made cowards of us all.

Socrates alone retained his calmness: "What is this strange outcry?" he said. "I sent away the women mainly in order that they might not misbehave in this way, for I have been told that a man should die in peace. Be quiet then, and have patience."

When we heard his words we were ashamed, and refrained our tears; and he walked about until, as he said, his legs began to fail, and then he lay on his back, according to the directions, and the man who gave him the poison now and then looked at his feet and legs; and after a while he pressed his foot hard, and asked him if he could feel; and he said, "No;" and then his leg, and so upwards and upwards, and showed us that he was cold and stiff. And he felt them himself, and said: "When the poison reaches the heart, that will be the end."

He was beginning to grow cold about the groin, when he uncovered his face, for he had covered himself up, and said—they were his last words—he said: "Crito, I owe a cock to Asclepius;[1] will you remember to pay the debt?

"The debt shall be paid," said Crito; "is there anything else?"

There was no answer to this question; but in a minute or two a movement was heard, and the attendants uncovered him; his eyes were set, and Crito closed his eyes and mouth.

Such was the end . . . of our friend; concerning whom I may truly say, that of all the men of his time whom I have known, he was the wisest and justest and best.

---

[1]The god of health and medicine.

Plato: The Allegory of the Cave, from *The Republic*

Plato, the most creative and influential of Socrates' disciples, wrote dialogues in which he frequently used the figure of Socrates to espouse his own (Plato's) full-fledged philosophy. In The Republic, *Plato sums up his views in an image of ignorant humanity, trapped in the depths and not even aware of its own limited perspective. The rare individual escapes the limitations of that cave and, through a long, tortuous intellectual journey, discovers a higher realm, a true reality, with a final, almost mystical awareness of Goodness as the origin of everything that exists. Such a person is then the best equipped to govern in society, having a knowledge of what is ultimately most worthwhile in life and not just a knowledge of techniques; but that person will frequently be misunderstood by those ordinary folks back in the cave who haven't shared in his intellectual insight. If he were living today, Plato might replace his rather awkward cave metaphor with a movie theater, with the projector replacing the fire, the film replacing the objects which cast shadows, the shadows on the cave wall with the projected movie on the screen, and the echo with the loudspeakers behind the screen. The essential point is that the prisoners in the cave are not seeing reality, but only a shadowy representation of it. The importance of the allegory lies in Plato's belief that there are invisible truths lying under the apparent surface of things which only the most enlightened can grasp. Used to the world of illusion in the cave, the prisoners at first resist enlightenment, as students resist education. But those who can achieve enlightenment deserve to be the leaders and rulers of all the rest. At the end of the passage, Plato expresses another of his favorite ideas: that education is not a process of putting knowledge into empty minds, but of making people realize that which they already know. This notion that truth is somehow embedded in our minds was also powerfully influential for many centuries.*

Judging by this passage, why do you think many people in the democracy of Athens might have been antagonistic to Plato's ideas? Is a resident of the cave (a prisoner, as it were) likely to want to make the ascent to the outer world? Why or why not? What does the sun symbolize in the allegory?

And now, I said, let me show in a figure how far our nature is enlightened or unenlightened:—Behold! human beings living in an underground den, which has a mouth open towards the light and reaching all along the den; here they have been from their childhood, and have their legs and necks chained so that they cannot move, and can only see before them, being prevented by the chains from turning round their heads. Above and behind them a fire is blazing at a distance, and between the fire and the prisoners there is a raised way; and you will see, if you look, a low wall built along the way, like the screen which marionette players have in front of them, over which they show the puppets.

I see.

And do you see, I said, men passing along the wall carrying all sorts of vessels, and statues and figures of animals made of wood and stone and various materials, which appear over the wall? Some of them are talking, others silent.

You have shown me a strange image, and they are strange prisoners.

Like ourselves, I replied; and they see only their own shadows, or the shadows of one another, which the fire throws on the opposite wall of the cave?

True, he said; how could they see anything but the shadows if they were never allowed to move their heads?

And of the objects which are being carried in like manner they would only see the shadows?

Yes, he said.

And if they were able to converse with one another, would they not suppose that they were naming what was actually before them?

Very true.

And suppose further that the prison had an *echo* which came from the other side, would they not be sure to fancy when one of the passers-by spoke that the voice which they heard came from the passing shadow?

No question, he replied.

To them, I said, the truth would be literally nothing but the shadows of the images.

That is certain.

And now look again, and see what will naturally follow if the prisoners are released and disabused of their error. At first, when any of them is liberated and compelled suddenly to stand up and turn his neck round and walk and look towards the light, he will suffer sharp pains; the glare will distress him, and he will be unable to see the realities of which in his former state he had seen the shadows; and then conceive some one saying to him, that what he saw before was an illusion, but that now, when he is approaching nearer to being and his eye is turned towards more real existence, he has a clearer vision,—what will be his reply? And you may further imagine that his instructor is pointing to the objects as they pass and requiring him to name them,—will he not be perplexed? Will he not fancy that the shadows which he formerly saw are truer than the objects which are now shown to him?

Far truer.

And if he is compelled to look straight at the light, will he not have a pain in his eyes which will make him turn away to take refuge in the objects of vision which he can see, and which he will conceive to be in reality clearer than the things which are now being shown to him?

True, he said.

And suppose once more, that he is reluctantly dragged up a steep and rugged ascent, and held fast until he is forced into the presence of the sun himself, is he not likely to be pained and irritated? When he approaches the light his eyes will be dazzled, and he will not be able to see anything at all of what are now called realities.

Not all in a moment, he said.

He will require to grow accustomed to the sight of the upper world. And first he will see the shadows best, next the reflections of men and other objects in the water, and then the objects themselves; then he will gaze upon the light of the moon and the stars and the spangled heaven; and he will see the sky and the stars by night better than the sun or the light of the sun by day?

Certainly.

Last of all he will be able to see the sun, and not mere reflections of him in the water, but he will see him in his own proper place, and not in another; and he will contemplate him as he is.

Certainly.

He will then proceed to argue that this is he who gives the season and the years, and is the guardian of all that is in the visible world, and in a certain way the cause of all things which he and his fellows have been accustomed to behold?

Clearly, he said, he would first see the sun and then reason about him.

And when he remembered his old habitation, and the wisdom of the den and his fellow-prisoners, do you not suppose that he would felicitate himself on the change, and pity them?

Certainly, he would.

And if they were in the habit of conferring honors among themselves on those who were quickest to observe the passing shadows and to remark which of them went before, and which followed after, and which were together; and who were therefore best able to draw conclusions as to the future, do you think that he would care for such honors and glories, or envy the possessors of them? Would he not say with Homer, "Better to be the poor servant of a poor master, and to endure anything, rather than think as they do and live after their manner?"[1]

Yes, he said, I think that he would rather suffer anything than entertain these false notions and live in this miserable manner.

Imagine once more, I said, such a one coming suddenly out of the sun to be replaced in his old situation; would he not be certain to have his eyes full of darkness?

To be sure, he said.

And if there were a contest, and he had to compete in measuring the shadows with the prisoners who had never moved out of the den, while his sight was still weak, and before his eyes had become steady (and the time which would be needed to acquire this new habit of sight might be very considerable), would he not be ridiculous? Men would say of him that up he went and down he came without his eyes;[2] and that it was better not even to think of ascending; and if any one tried to loose another and lead him up to the light, let them only catch the offender, and they would put him to death.[3]

No question, he said.

This entire allegory, I said, you may now append, dear Glaucon, to the previous argu-

---

[1] This refers to a famous passage in Homer's *Odyssey* in which the ghost of the great hero Achilles, when asked if he is not proud of the fame his deeds have spread throughout the world, answers that he would rather be a slave on a worn-out farm than king over all of the famous dead. Interestingly, Plato quotes the same passage elsewhere disapprovingly as depicting life after death in such a negative manner that it may undermine the willingness of soldiers to die in war.

[2] The comic playwright Aristophanes had mocked Socrates by portraying Plato's master as a foolish intellectual with his head in the clouds.

[3] Plato undoubtedly has in mind the fact that the Athenians had condemned to death Socrates, whom Plato considered supremely enlightened.

ment; the prison-house is the world of sight, the light of the fire is the sun, and you will not misapprehend me if you interpret the journey upwards to be the ascent of the soul into the intellectual world according to my poor belief, which, at your desire, I have expressed— whether rightly or wrongly God knows. But whether true or false, my opinion is that in the world of knowledge the idea of good appears last of all, and is seen only with an effort; and, when seen, is also inferred to be the universal author of all things beautiful and right, parent of light and of the lord of light in this visible world,[4] and the immediate source of reason and truth in the intellectual; and that this is the power upon which he who would act rationally either in public or private life must have his eye fixed.

I agree, he said, as far as I am able to understand you.

Moreover, I said, you must not wonder that those who attain to this beatific vision are unwilling to descend to human affairs; for their souls are ever hastening into the upper world where they desire to dwell; which desire of theirs is very natural, if our allegory may be trusted.

Yes, very natural.

And is there anything surprising in one who passes from divine contemplations to the evil state of man, misbehaving himself in a ridiculous manner; if, while his eyes are blinking and before he has become accustomed to the surrounding darkness, he is compelled to fight in courts of law, or in other places, about the images or the shadows of images of justice, and is endeavoring to meet the conception of those who have never yet seen absolute justice?

Anything but surprising, he replied.

Anyone who has common sense will remember that the bewilderments of the eyes are of two kinds, and arise from two causes, either from coming out of the light or from going into the light, which is true of the mind's eye; and he who remembers this when he sees any one whose vision is perplexed and weak, will not be too ready to laugh; he will first ask whether that soul of man has come out of the brighter life, and is unable to see because unaccustomed to the dark, or having turned from darkness to the day is dazzled by excess of light. And he will count the one happy in his condition and state of being, and he will pity the other; or, if he have a mind to laugh at the soul which comes from below into the light, there will be more reason in this than in the laugh which greets him who returns from above out of the light into the den.

That, he said, is a very just distinction.

But then, if I am right, certain professors of education must be wrong when they say that they can put a knowledge into the soul which was not there before, like sight into blind eyes.

They undoubtedly say this, he replied.

Whereas our argument shows that the power and capacity of learning exists in the soul already; and that just as the eye was unable to turn from darkness to light without the whole body, so too the instrument of knowledge can only by the movement of the whole soul be turned from the world of becoming into that of being, and learn by degrees to endure the sight of being and of the brightest and best of being, or in other words, of the good.

---

[4]Here Plato describes his notion of God in a way that was to influence profoundly Christian theologians.

Aristotle: On Happiness, from *The Nicomachean Ethics*

Aristotle worked on all sorts of philosophical issues and, in particular, was influential in laying the foundations of Western ethics. In our selection he argues that the highest and finest life that we can aspire to is one in which our basic needs are taken care of, we have attained moral virtue (character traits such as honesty and friendship), and we are cultivating the life of the mind, striving for intellectual virtue (above all, the practice of philosophy itself, which includes knowledge of science and history, as well as appreciation of beauty). Happiness, as Aristotle characterizes it, is an active life, good in itself and not just as a means to some other end. Thus happiness is not merely a feeling — though it will, of course, be pleasurable.

According to Aristotle, can a slave enjoy bodily pleasures? Can a slave be happy? So what does this show about happiness and pleasure?

Now that we have spoken of the virtues, the forms of friendship, and the varieties of pleasure, what remains is to discuss in outline the nature of happiness, since this is what we state the end [goal] of human affairs to be. . . . We said, then, that it is not a state; for if it were it might belong to someone who was asleep throughout his life, living the life of a plant, or, again, to someone who was suffering the greatest misfortunes. If these implications are unacceptable, and we must rather class happiness as an activity, as we have said before, and if some activities are necessary, and desirable for the sake of something else, while others are so in themselves, evidently happiness must be placed among those desirable in themselves, not among those desirable for the sake of something else; for happiness does not lack anything, but is self-sufficient. Now those activities are desirable in themselves from which nothing is sought beyond the activity. And of this nature virtuous actions are thought to be; for to do noble and good deeds is a thing desirable for its own sake. . . .

The happy life is thought to be virtuous; now a virtuous life requires exertion and does not consist in amusement. And we say that serious things are better than laughable things and those connected with amusement, and that the activity of the better of any two things— whether it be two elements of our being or two men—is the more serious; but the activity of the better is *ipso facto* superior and more of the nature of happiness. And any chance person—even a slave—can enjoy the bodily pleasures no less than the best man; but no one assigns to a slave a share in happiness—unless he assigns to him also a share in human life. For happiness does not lie in such occupations, but, as we have said before, in virtuous activities.

If happiness is activity in accordance with virtue, it is reasonable that it should be in accordance with the highest virtue; and this will be that of the best thing in us. . . . That this activity is contemplative we have already said. For, firstly, this activity is the best (since not only is reason the best thing in us, but the objects of reason are the best of knowable objects); and, secondly, it is the most continuous since we can contemplate truth more continuously than we can *do* anything. And we think happiness ought to have pleasure mingled with it, but the activity of philosophic wisdom is admittedly the pleasantest of virtuous activities; at all events the pursuit of it is thought to offer pleasures marvelous for their purity and their enduringness, and it is to be expected that those who know will pass their time more pleasantly than those who inquire. And the self-sufficiency that is spoken of must belong most to the contemplative activity. For while a philosopher, as well as a just man or one possessing any other virtue, needs the necessaries of life, when they are sufficiently equipped with things of that sort the just man needs people towards whom and with whom he shall act justly, and the temperate man, the brave man, and each of the others is in the same case, but the philosopher, even when by himself, can contemplate truth, and the better the wiser he is. He can perhaps do so better if he has fellow workers, but still he is the most self-sufficient. And this activity alone would seem to be loved for its own sake; for nothing arises from it apart from the contemplating, while from practical activities we gain more or less apart from the action. And happiness is thought to depend on leisure; for we are busy that we may have leisure, and make war that we may live in peace. Now the activity of the practical virtues is exhibited in political or military affairs, but the actions concerned with these seem to be unleisurely. Warlike actions are completely so (for no one chooses to be at war, or provokes war, for the sake of being at war; anyone would seem absolutely murderous if he were to make enemies of his friends in order to bring about battle and slaughter); but the action of the statesman also is unleisurely, and aims— beyond the political action itself—at despotic power and honors, or at all events happiness, for him and his fellow citizens—a happiness different from political action, and evidently sought as being different. So if among virtuous actions political and military actions are distinguished by nobility and greatness, and these are unleisurely and aim at an end and are not desirable for their own sake, but the activity of reason, which is contemplative, seems both to be superior in serious worth and to aim at no end beyond itself, and to have its pleasure proper to itself (and this augments the activity), and the self-sufficiency, leisureliness, unweariedness (so far as this is possible for man), and all the other attributes ascribed to the supremely happy man are evidently those connected with his activity, it follows that this will be the complete happiness of man, if it be allowed a complete term of life (for none of the attributes of happiness is *in*complete).

But such a life would be too high for man; for it is not in so far as he is man that he will live so, but in so far as something divine is present in him; and by so much as this is superior to our composite nature is its activity superior to that which is the exercise of the other kind of virtue. If reason is divine, then, in comparison with man, the life according to it is divine in comparison with human life. But we must not follow those who advise us, being men, to think of human things, and, being mortal, of mortal things, but must, so far as we can, make ourselves immortal, and strain every nerve to live in accordance with the best thing in us; for even if it be small in bulk, much more does it in power and worth surpass everything. And this would seem actually to *be* each man, since it is the authoritative and better part of him. It would be strange, then, if he were to choose not the life of himself but that of something else. And what we said before will apply now: that which is proper to each thing is by nature best and most pleasant for each thing; for man, therefore, the life according to reason is best and pleasantest, since reason more than anything else is man. This life therefore is also the happiest. . . .

Now he who exercises his reason and cultivates it seems to be both in the best state of mind and most dear to the gods. For if the gods have any care for human affairs, as they are thought to have it would be reasonable both that they should delight in that which was best and most akin to them (i.e. reason) and that they should reward those who love and honor this most, as caring for the things that are dear to them and acting both rightly and nobly. And that all these attributes belong most of all to the philosopher is manifest. He, therefore, is the dearest to the gods. And he who is that will presumably be also the happiest; so that in this way too the philosopher will more than any other be happy.

Translated by David Ross, revised by J. L. Ackerill & J. O. Urmson

Pericles' Funeral Oration (431 BCE)
from Thucydides: *The Peloponnesian War*

When Pericles was asked to give the official funeral oration for the Athenian soldiers who had died at one of the opening battles of the Peloponnesian War, he took the occasion not only to praise the dead, but Athens itself, in a speech which has been praised as enshrining the highest ideals of democracy and condemned as blatant propaganda on behalf of a warlike, imperialistic state, which—despite what Pericles says—was heartily detested by its allies. Note that he praises not only his city's freedom, but its empire. It was its oppressive and aggressive rule over this empire that was eventually to lead to Athens' downfall in the Peloponnesian War. It is unlikely that Pericles uttered precisely these words, since it was customary for ancient historians to invent the speeches of the figures they wrote about, based on what they knew about them; but it certainly reflects the attitudes of many Athenians.

What are the main virtues that Pericles praises as characteristic of the Athenians? How does he contrast Athens with Sparta? What consolations does he offer for those whose sons have died? What does he say is the proper role of women?

Most of those who have spoken here before me have commended the lawgiver who added this oration to our other funeral customs. It seemed to them a worthy thing that such an honor should be given at their burial to the dead who have fallen on the field of battle. But I should have preferred that, when men's deeds have been brave, they should be honored in deed only, and with such an honor as this public funeral, which you are now witnessing. Then the reputation of many would not have been imperiled on the eloquence or want of eloquence of one, and their virtues believed or not as he spoke well or ill. For it is difficult to say neither too little nor too much; and even moderation is apt not to give the impression of truthfulness. The friend of the dead who knows the facts is likely to think that the words of the speaker fall short of his knowledge and of his wishes; another who is not so well informed, when he hears of anything which surpasses his own powers, will be envious and will suspect exaggeration. Mankind is tolerant of the praises of others so long as each hearer thinks that he can do as well or nearly as well himself, but, when the speaker rises above him, jealousy is aroused and he begins to be incredulous. However, since our ancestors have set the seal of their approval upon the practice, I must obey, and to the utmost of my power shall endeavor to satisfy the wishes and beliefs of all who hear me.

I will speak first of our ancestors, for it is right and seemly that now, when we are lamenting the dead, a tribute should be paid to their memory. There has never been a time when they did not inhabit this land, which by their valor they will have handed down from generation to generation, and we have received from them a free state. But if they were worthy of praise, still more were our fathers, who added to their inheritance, and after many a struggle transmitted to us their sons this great empire. And we ourselves assembled here today, who are still most of us in the vigor of life, have carried the work of improvement further, and have richly endowed our city with all things, so that she is sufficient for herself both in peace and war. Of the military exploits by which our various possessions were acquired, or of the energy with which we or our fathers drove back the tide of war, Hellenic or Barbarian, I will not speak; for the tale would be long and is familiar to you. But before I praise the dead, I should like to point out by what principles of action we rose to power, and under what institutions and through what manner of life our empire became

84

great. For I conceive that such thoughts are not unsuited to the occasion, and that this numerous assembly of citizens and strangers may profitably listen to them.

Our form of government does not enter into rivalry with the institutions of others. Our government does not copy our neighbors', but is an example to them. It is true that we are called a democracy, for the administration is in the hands of the many[1] and not of the few. But while there exists equal justice to all and alike in their private disputes, the claim of excellence is also recognized; and when a citizen is in any way distinguished, he is preferred to the public service, not as a matter of privilege, but as the reward of merit. Neither is poverty an obstacle, but a man may benefit his country whatever the obscurity of his condition. There is no exclusiveness in our public life, and in our private business we are not suspicious of one another, nor angry with our neighbor if he does what he likes; we do not put on sour looks at him which, though harmless, are not pleasant. While we are thus unconstrained in our private business, a spirit of reverence pervades our public acts; we are prevented from doing wrong by respect for the authorities and for the laws, having a particular regard to those which are ordained for the protection of the injured as well as those unwritten laws which bring upon the transgressor of them the reprobation of the general sentiment.

And we have not forgotten to provide for our weary spirits many relaxations from toil; we have regular games and sacrifices throughout the year; our homes are beautiful and elegant; and the delight which we daily feel in all these things helps to banish sorrow. Because of the greatness of our city the fruits of the whole earth flow in upon us; so that we enjoy the goods of other countries as freely as our own.

Then, again, our military training is in many respects superior to that of our adversaries. Our city is thrown open to the world, though and we never expel a foreigner and prevent him from seeing or learning anything of which the secret if revealed to an enemy might profit him. We rely not upon management or trickery, but upon our own hearts and hands. And in the matter of education, whereas they from early youth are always undergoing laborious exercises which are to make them brave, we live at ease, and yet are equally ready to face the perils which they face. And here is the proof: The Lacedaemonians come into Athenian territory not by themselves, but with their whole confederacy following; we go alone into a neighbor's country; and although our opponents are fighting for their homes and we on a foreign soil, we have seldom any difficulty in overcoming them. Our enemies have never yet felt our united strength, the care of a navy divides our attention, and on land we are obliged to send our own citizens everywhere. But they, if they meet and defeat a part of our army, are as proud as if they had routed us all, and when defeated they pretend to have been vanquished by us all.

If then we prefer to meet danger with a light heart but without laborious training, and with a courage which is gained by habit and not enforced by law, are we not greatly the better for it? Since we do not anticipate the pain, although, when the hour comes, we can be as brave as those who never allow themselves to rest; thus our city is equally admirable in peace and in war. For we are lovers of the beautiful in our tastes and our strength lies, in our opinion, not in deliberation and discussion, but that knowledge which is gained by discussion preparatory to action. For we have a peculiar power of thinking before we act, and of acting, too, whereas other men are courageous from ignorance but hesitate upon

---

[1]Defined as the free adult males of pure Athenian descent, and therefore still excluding the majority of the population. But even this degree of democracy was highly unusual in the ancient world.

reflection. And they are surely to be esteemed the bravest spirits who, having the clearest sense both of the pains and pleasures of life, do not on that account shrink from danger. In doing good, again, we are unlike others; we make our friends by conferring, not by receiving, favors. Now he who confers a favor is the firmer friend, because he would rather by kindness keep alive the memory of an obligation; but the recipient is colder in his feelings, because he knows that in requiting another's generosity he will not be winning gratitude but only paying a debt. We alone do good to our neighbors not upon a calculation of interest, but in the confidence of freedom and in a frank and fearless spirit. To sum up: I say that Athens is the school of Hellas, and that the individual Athenian in his own person seems to have the power of adapting himself to the most varied forms of action with the utmost versatility and grace. This is no passing and idle word, but truth and fact; and the assertion is verified by the position to which these qualities have raised the state. For in the hour of trial Athens alone among her contemporaries is superior to the report of her. No enemy who comes against her is indignant at the reverses which he sustains at the hands of such a city; no subject complains that his masters are unworthy of him. And we shall assuredly not be without witnesses; there are mighty monuments of our power which will make us the wonder of this and of succeeding ages; we shall not need the praises of Homer or of any other panegyrist whose poetry may please for the moment, although his representation of the facts will not bear the light of day. For we have compelled every land and every sea to open a path for our valor, and have everywhere planted eternal memorials of our friendship and of our enmity. Such is the city for whose sake these men nobly fought and died; they could not bear the thought that she might be taken from them; and every one of us who survive should gladly toil on her behalf.

I have dwelt upon the greatness of Athens because I want to show you that we are contending for a higher prize than those who enjoy none of these privileges, and to establish by manifest proof the merit of these men whom I am now commemorating. Their loftiest praise has been already spoken. For in magnifying the city I have magnified them, and men like them whose virtues made her glorious. And of how few Hellenes[2] can it be said as of them, that their deeds when weighed in the balance have been found equal to their fame! Methinks that a death such as theirs has been the true measure of a man's worth; it may be the first revelation of his virtues, but is at any rate their final seal. For even those who come short in other ways may justly plead the valor with which they have fought for their country; they have blotted out the evil with the good, and have benefited the state more by their public services than they have injured her by their private actions. None of these men were enervated by wealth or hesitated to resign the pleasures of life; none of them put off the evil day in the hope, natural to poverty, that a man, though poor, may one day become rich. But, deeming that the punishment of their enemies was sweeter than any of these things, and that they could fall in no nobler cause, they determined at the hazard of their lives to be honorably avenged, and to leave the rest. They resigned to hope their unknown chance of happiness; but in the face of death they resolved to rely upon themselves alone. And when the moment came they were minded to resist and suffer, rather than to fly and save their lives; they ran away from the word of dishonor, but on the battlefield their feet stood fast, and in an instant, at the height of their fortune, they passed away from the scene, not of their fear, but of their glory.

Such was the end of these men; they were worthy of Athens, and the living need not desire to have a more heroic spirit, although they may pray for a less fatal issue. The value

---

[2] "Hellenes" is another word for "Greeks."

of such a spirit is not to be expressed in words. Any one can discourse to you for ever about the advantages of a brave defense, which you know already. But instead of listening to him I would have you day by day fix your eyes upon the greatness of Athens, until you become filled with the love of her; and when you are impressed by the spectacle of her glory, reflect that this empire has been acquired by men who knew their duty and had the courage to do it, who in the hour of conflict had the fear of dishonor always present to them, and who, if ever they failed in an enterprise, would not allow their virtues to be lost to their country, but freely gave their lives to her as the fairest offering which they could present at her feast. The sacrifice which they collectively made was individually repaid to them; for they received again each one for himself a praise which grows not old, and the noblest of all tombs—I speak not of that in which their remains are laid, but of that in which their glory survives, and is proclaimed always and on every fitting occasion both in word and deed. For the whole earth is the tomb of famous men; not only are they commemorated by columns and inscriptions in their own country, but in foreign lands there dwells also an unwritten memorial of them, graven not on stone but in the hearts of men. Make them your examples, and, esteeming courage to be freedom and freedom to be happiness, do not weigh too nicely the perils of war. The unfortunate who has no hope of a change for the better has less reason to throw away his life than the prosperous who, if he survives, is always liable to a change for the worse, and to whom any accidental fall makes the most serious difference. To a man of spirit, cowardice and disaster coming together are far more bitter than death striking him unperceived at a time when he is full of courage and animated by the general hope.

Wherefore I do not now pity the parents of the dead who stand here; I would rather comfort them. You know that your dead have passed away amid manifold vicissitudes; and that they may be deemed fortunate who have gained their utmost honor, whether an honorable death like theirs, or an honorable sorrow like yours, and whose share of happiness has been so ordered that the term of their happiness is likewise the term of their life. I know how hard it is to make you feel this, when the good fortune of others will too often remind you of the gladness which once lightened your hearts. And sorrow is felt at the want of those blessings, not which a man never knew, but which were a part of his life before they were taken from him. Some of you are of an age at which they may hope to have other children, and they ought to bear their sorrow better; not only will the children who may hereafter be born make them forget their own lost ones, but the city will be doubly a gainer. She will not be left desolate, and she will be safer. For a man's counsel cannot have equal weight or worth, when he alone has no children to risk in the general danger. To those of you who have passed their prime, I say: "Congratulate yourselves that you have been happy during the greater part of your days; remember that your life of sorrow will not last long, and be comforted by the glory of those who are gone. For the love of honor alone is ever young, and not riches, as some say, but honor is the delight of men when they are old and useless.

To you who are the sons and brothers of the departed, I see that the struggle to emulate them will be an arduous one. For all men praise the dead, and, however preeminent your virtue may be, I do not say even to approach them, and avoid living their rivals and detractors, but when a man is out of the way, the honor and goodwill which he receives is unalloyed. And, if I am to speak of womanly virtues to those of you who will henceforth be widows, let me sum them up in one short admonition: To a woman not to show more weakness than is natural to her sex is a great glory, and not to be talked about for good or for evil among men.

87

I have paid the required tribute, in obedience to the law, making use of such fitting words as I had. The tribute of deeds has been paid in part; for the dead have them in deeds, and it remains only that their children should be maintained at the public charge until they are grown up: this is the solid prize with which, as with a garland, Athens crowns her sons living and dead, after a struggle like theirs. For where the rewards of virtue are greatest, there the noblest citizens are enlisted in the service of the state. And now, when you have duly lamented every one his own dead, you may depart.

Translated by Benjamin Jowett

The First Delphic Hymn (138 BCE)

This hymn to Apollo, god both of the Delphic Oracle and of music, was found inscribed on a stone at Delphi. The text is marked with a form of music notation which makes it one of the earliest pieces of music to have survived in the western world. We have no way of determining exactly how the piece would have been performed, but recordings have been made which may convey something of the sound of the work. One version is available on the album "Music of Ancient Greece," Orata ORANGM 2013 (track 3), and another on "Musique de la Grèce Antique" Harmonia Mundi (France) HMA 1901015 (track 3).

Oh, come now, Muses,[1]
to the rocky sacred precinct
upon the far-seen, twin-peaked Parnassus,[2]
and begin the dear hymn, Pierian maidens.[3]
Lie down on the snow-clad mountain top;
sing of the Pythian Lord[4]
with the golden sword, Phoebus,
whom Latona gave birth to[5]
on the Delian rock[6] while holding with her handss
the silvery olive branch,
the luxuriant plant which the Goddess Pallas
brought forth at an earlier time..

Translated by Richard Hooker

---

[1]The muses were the goddesses of the arts, the word "music" comes from their name.

[2]Mount Parnassus was the site of the temple of the Oracle of Apollo at Delphi, the most sacred spot in Greece.

[3]The muses were also associated with a place called Pieria near Mount Olympus; but another explanation of the reference is that they were said to be the nine daughters of one Pierus.

[4]Apollo. His priestess was called the Pythia, after a legendary snake that Apollo had killed in laying claim to the shrine.

[5]There are many different accounts of how Apollo's mother wandered the earth looking for a safe place in which to bear her child.

[6]The island of Delos.

[7]Athena. Note how the Athenian poet, even while praising the chief god of Delphi manages to bring in by a loose association the chief goddess of Athens.

Rome

Lucretius (c. 99-55 BCE): *The Nature of Things*

Titus Lucretius Carus is known for one long philosophical poem, from which this passage is excerpted. It tries to explain the nature of the universe according to the doctrines of the Greek philosophers Democritus and Epicurus, who argued against the common view that all of nature is pervaded by divine beings who have created it and shaped its destiny. Their "atomic" theory differed substantially from modern atomic theory, but its most important contribution was to create a purely secular view of a universe explainable by purely natural causes. During the 18th-Century intellectual movement known as the Enlightenment, thinkers in France and England pointed back to Lucretius' argument to explain how human beings came to believe in the existence of gods. Even more powerful was the conception that existence is not a series of inexplicable mysteries, but the result of the operation of regular and knowable laws. Without this perspective, science as we know it would be impossible.

What does Lucretius say causes people to believe in gods?

This fright, this night of the mind, must be dispelled
not by the rays of the sun, nor day's bright spears,
but by the face of nature and her laws.
And this is her first, from which we take our start:
nothing was ever by miracle made from nothing.[1]
You see, all mortal men are gripped by fear
because they see so many things on earth
and in the sky, yet can't discern their causes
and hence believe that they are acts of god.
But in all this, when we have learned that nothing
can come from nothing, then we shall see straight through
to what we seek: whence each thing is created
and in what manner made, without god's help.
If things were made from nothing, then all kinds
could spring from any source: they'd need no seed.
Man could have burst from ocean, from dry land
the bearers of scales, and from thin air the birds;
cows, horses, sheep, and the rest, and all wild beasts
would breed untrue, infesting farm and forest.
Nor would one tree produce one kind of fruit;

---

[1]The denial of creation *ex nihilo* (out of nothing) was natural for the Greeks, since their creation myths more often than not envisioned "creation" as consisting of the organization of the world out of an eternally existing chaos. One of the great debates of the 18th and 19th Century was the argument between the Christian traditionalists who argued that life could arise from nonliving matter and the scientists who argued that life could only be produced from life. Ironically, the emergence of the theory of evolution eventually reversed the terms of this debate.

90

no, they would change, and all could bear all kinds.
For if there were no factors governing birth,
how could we tell who anyone's mother was?
But things are formed, now, from specific seeds,
hence each at birth comes to the coasts of light
from a thing possessed of its essential atoms.
Thus everything cannot spring from anything,
for things are unique: their traits are theirs alone.
And why in spring do we see roses, grain
in summer, vines produce at autumn's call,
if not because right atoms in right season
have streamed together to build each thing we see,
while weather favors and life-giving earth
brings delicate seedlings safe to land and light?
But if they came from nothing, they'd spring up
all helter-skelter in seasons not their own;
for there would be no atoms to be kept
from fertile union at untimely hours.
Nor would things when they grow have need of time
for seeds to combine, if they could grow from nothing.
Why! Babes in arms would turn into men forthwith,
and forests would leap from sprouts new-sprung of earth.
Yet clearly such things never occur: all growth
is gradual, regular, from specific seed,
and with identity kept. Hence learn that things
can grow only when proper substance feeds them.
To this we add: without her seasonal rains
Earth could not send up offspring rich in joy,
nor, further, could living creatures without food
beget their kind or keep their hold on life.
Better conceive of many atoms shared
by many things, as letters are by words,
than of a single thing not made of atoms.
To continue: why could nature not produce
men of such size that they could cross the seas
on foot, and with bare hands pull hills apart,
and live the lifetime of ten thousand men,
if not because each thing has but one substance
marked and designed to bring it into being?

Translated by Frank O. Copley

Horace: We All Must Die (1st C. BCE)

People in many cultures have found it proper to meditate on the inevitability of death. For Medieval Christians reminders of death were spurs to repentance, so that the believer should escape Hell and spend eternity in Heaven. Buddhists stress that focussing on the temporary nature of life helps one to become detached from it in a way that promotes an enlightened entry into Nirvana. But the ancient Romans, especially the Stoics among them, seemed to meditate on death almost for its own sake, as a sobering and steadying influence. It is not surprising that Christian writers found such poems highly edifying. This loose translation of a poem by Quintus Horatius Flaccus (65 BCE–8 BCE) was written by the great English poet Samuel Johnson in 1760. Although it is not a precise rendering of Horace's words, it captures well his use of the traditional theme of tempus fugit ("time flies"), and nothing a person can do can prevent death or other fated dooms.

What sorts of dangers does Horace say it is useless to avoid? How does he say the dead person's heir will behave?

Alas, dear friend, the fleeting years
   In everlasting circles run,
In vain you spend your vows and prayers,
   They roll, and ever will roll on.

Should hecatombs[1] each rising morn
   On cruel Pluto's[2] altar die,
Should costly loads of incense burn,
   Their fumes ascending to the sky:

You could not gain a moment's breath
   Or move the haughty king below
Nor would inexorable death
   Defer an hour the fatal blow.

In vain we shun the din of war,
   And terrors of the stormy main,[3]
In vain with anxious breasts we fear
   Unwholesome Sirius'[4] sultry reign;

---

[1]Extravagant sacrifices, consisting of a hundred oxen.
[2]The Lord of the Dead.
[3]Ocean.
[4]When the "Dog Star" Sirius was in the ascendancy in August it was thought to exert a harmful influence on human health.

We all must view the Stygian flood[5]
   That silent cuts the dreary plains,
And Cruel Danaus' bloody brood[6]
   Condemned to everduring pains.

Your shady groves, your pleasing wife,
   And fruitful fields, my dearest friend,
You'll leave together with your life:
   Alone the cypress[7] shall attend.

After your death, the lavish heir
   Will quickly drive away his woe;
The wine you kept with so much care
   Along the marble floor shall flow.

Translated by Samuel Johnson

---

[5]The Styx, the river which the dead crossed into on their way to Hades.

[6]Danaus persuaded his fifty daughters to kill their husbands because he was feuding with their new father-in-law. The women were punished in Hades by having continually to carry water in leaking vessels so that their task would never be finished.

[7]The cypress, common in Italy, is traditionally associated with mourning.

Epitaph from the tomb of a Roman wife (2nd Century BCE)

This moving testimony reflects not only affection but esteem for a woman who fulfilled her culture's ideal as a wife. Romans were far from granting women equality, but they placed great emphasis on the value of the family.

Judging by this epitaph, what seem to have been the qualities Romans prized in women?

Short is my say, O stranger. Stay and read.
Not fair this tomb, but fair was she it holds.
By her name her parents called her Claudia.
Her wedded lord she loved with all her heart.
She bore two sons, and one of them she left
On earth, the other in the earth she laid.
Her speech was pleasing and her bearing gracious.
She kept house: span her wool. I have said. Farewell.

Translated by L. R. Lind

Ovid (43 BCE–18 CE): Daedalus and Icarus from *The Metamorphoses*

The Metamorphoses *of Publius Ovidus Naso is a highly entertaining poetic retelling of most of the famous classical myths from ancient Greece and Rome. Or perhaps it would be better to say that the myths we now consider famous became so because Ovid retold them: his book was the standard collection of myths which Europeans read from the Middle Ages through recent times, the source of countless plays, paintings, sculptures, operas, ballets, and other poems. This passage from the legend of Daedalus was not only depicted in various works of art, but became a metaphor for the consequences of excessive daring or ambition—or for excessive dependence on technology. The instructions to fly neither too high nor too low were meant originally to counsel moderation, a classic Greek ideal. The great inventor Daedalus was brought to the island of Crete by King Minos to build the labyrinth in which he confined the half man, half bull known as the Minotaur; but when he had completed his task, the king would not let him go, for fear he would reveal the secret of the maze.*

Ovid's greatness lies in the way he brings the myths to life through little humanizing touches. What are some of the moments in this story that show people in the story feeling or showing emotions? What kinds of actions do you think our own society considers "flying too high"?

But Daedalus was weary; by this time,
he'd been exiled in Crete too long; he pined
for his own land; but he was blocked—the sea
stood in his way. "Though Minos bars escape
by land or waves," he said, "I still can take
the sky—there lies my path. Though he owns all,
he does not own the air!" At once he starts
to work on unknown arts, to alter nature.
He lays out feathers—all in order, first
the shorter, then the longer (you'd have said
they'd grown along a slope); just like the kind
of pipes that country people used to fashion,
where from unequal reed to reed the rise
is gradual. And these he held together
with twine around the center; at the base
he fastened them with wax; and thus arranged—
he'd bent them slightly—they could imitate
the wings of true birds.

            As he worked at this,
his young son, Icarus, inquisitive,
stood by and—unaware that what he did
involved a thing that would imperil him—
delighted, grabbed the feathers that the wind
tossed, fluttering, about; or he would ply
the blond wax with his thumb; and as he played,
the boy disturbed his father's wonder-work.

When Daedalus had given the last touch,
the craftsman thought he'd try two wings himself;
so balanced, as he beat the wings, he hung
poised in the air. And then to his dear son,
he gave another pair. "O Icarus,"
he said, "I warn you: fly a middle course.
If you're too low, sea spray may damp your wings;
and if you fly too high, the heat is scorching.
Keep to the middle then. And keep your eyes
on me and not on Helice, Boötes,[1]
or on Orion's unsheathed sword.[2] Where I
shall lead—that's where you fly: I'll be your guide."
And as he taught his son the rules of flight,
he fitted to the shoulders of the boy
those wings that none had ever seen before.
The old man worked and warned; his cheeks grew damp
with tears; and with a father's fears, his hands
began to tremble. Then he kissed his son
(he never would embrace the boy again);
and poised upon his wings, he flew ahead,
still anxious for the follower he led
(much like the bird who, from her roost on high,
leads out her tender fledglings to the sky).
He urges on his son, saying he must
keep up, not fall behind; so he instructs
the boy in flight, an art most dangerous;
and while the father beats his wings, he turns
to watch his son, to see what he has done.

A fisherman, who with his pliant rod
was angling there below, caught sight of them;
and then a shepherd leaning on his staff
and, too, a peasant leaning on his plow
saw them and were dismayed: they thought that these
must surely be some gods, sky-voyaging.

Now on their left they had already passed
the isle of Samos—Juno's[3] favorite—
Delos, and Paros, and Calymne, rich
in honey, and Labinthos, on the right.
The boy had now begun to take delight
in his audacity; he left his guide
and, fascinated by the open sky,
flew higher; and the scorching sun was close;

---

[1]Stars.
[2]Part of a constellation of stars.
[3]Wife of Jupiter, King of the Gods.

the fragrant wax that bound his wings grew soft,
then melted. As he beats upon the air,
his arms can get no grip; they're wingless—bare.

The father—though that word is hollow now—
cried: "Icarus! Where are you?" And that cry
echoed again, again till he caught sight
of feathers on the surface of the sea.
And Daedalus cursed his own artistry,
then built a tomb to house his dear son's body.
There, where the boy was buried, now his name
remains: that island is Icaria.

Translated by Allen Mandelbaum

Propertius (c. 50 BCE-16 CE): *Like Ariadne lying on the shore*

One of the unique contributions of Roman literature is informal, personal verse which conveys a vivid sense of the humanity of the poet. Its great masters are Ovid, Catullus, and Propertius. Each wrote a series of poems about a tempestuous love affair, cajoling, rejoicing, and complaining, often with a sense of humor that is lacking in classical period Greek poetry. Here Propertius portrays himself coming home to his mistress after a party, thoroughly drunk, but not so drunk as not to be struck by her beauty. Her evening has been spent very differently, however, as she lets him know.

Is Cynthia being fair to the poet? What evidence is there that Propertius means us to be sympathetic or unsympathetic with Cynthia? Try imagining this story being told about people today. What would be different? What would stay the same?

Like Ariadne lying on the shore
from which the ship of Theseus sailed away,[1]
or like Andromeda, freed from the rock,[2]
who at long last in softer slumber lay,
or like a Maenad,[3] dizzy with the dance,
flinging herself beside the river-bed,
so did my Cynthia seem the soul of rest,
her slender hands beneath her sleeping head.
So did she seem when I came reeling home,
drunk and disheveled, and the dying light
of the slaves' torches lit the dying night.

Stumbling, I came and stood beside her couch,
drunk, yet not too drunk to be unaware
that love and wine conspired within me now
to drive me to a double madness there.
And so I tried to hold her, rosy-warm
and sleeping, and my toll of kisses take—
quietly, for I know her sudden temper;
I knew how it would rage if she should wake.
Feasting my eyes, I gazed like Argus[4] gazing
on Io's horned head, and smoothed her hair,
and the wreath I had worn laid lightly there.[5]

---

[1] The Athenian lover Theseus abandoned several lovers, including Ariadne, who had helped him defeat the Minotaur.
[2] Freed by Perseus from the rock where she was menaced by a sea serpent.
[3] A bacchante, worshipper of Dionysus. They threw themselves into wild intoxicated revels.
[4] A monstrous guardian with a hundred eyes, set to guard Io when she was turned into a cow. He means simply that he gazes at her utterly absorbed.
[5] Vine-leaves were worn in the hair at banquets.

Apples for your delight:[6] each gift I had
I lavished upon Cynthia whom I love—
placing them stealthily, with hollowed hands,
holding my breath to watch, leaning above,
startled each time you stirred or sighed (although
these were vain terrors) lest your dreaming's course
bring you dark fright, or lest you picture someone—
someone not me—who took your love by force.
But now the moonlight (O officious moon,
trying the window with its lengthening beams!)
wakens her, and with wakening rage she screams,

"Tell me the truth: whose anger, or whose boredom,
has sent you forth from her bed now to mine?
where have you spent the night? whose arms have held you
and left you pale as a ghost and rank with wine?
O may you know the tortures you have taught me;
may you for me that same vain vigil keep—
see my embroidery, see my useless lyre,
how I beguiled the hours I could not sleep.
And while you lay with her, I wept, I wept,
till slumber's kind wings touched me and I slept."

Translated by J. P. Maudsley

---

[6]Fresh fruits were a luxury. He has brought some home from the banquet and places them
on her body.

Juvenal: *On the City of Rome* (late 1st, early 2nd Century CE)

Like most ancient satire, the writings of Decimus Junius Juvenalis are essentially conservative. In order to avoid censorship, or worse, he chose as his targets people who had lived a century before; but he clearly meant to describe what he saw as the faults of his own time. In his Third Satire he gives us a wonderfully intimate and lively portrait of daily life in the streets of imperial Rome. In the poem, a friend of Juvenal's is moving to a place in the countryside, and it is he who details what he can't stand about the city.

What are the main characteristics of life in the city that the speaker objects to? About what customs in ancient Rome can you learn from reading this poem?

The sick die here because they can't sleep,
Though most people complain about the food
Rotting undigested in their burning guts.
For when does sleep come in rented rooms?
It costs a lot merely to sleep in this city!
That's why everyone's sick: carts clattering
Through the winding streets,[1] curses hurled
At some herd standing still in the middle of the road,
Could rob Claudius[2] or a seal of their sleep!
When duty demands it, crowds fall back to allow
The wealthy to pass, who sail past the coast
In a mighty Liburnian ship,[3] while on the way
They read or write or even take a nap,
For the litter and its shut windows bring on sleep.
Yet he still arrives first; while we are blocked
In our hurry by a wave before us, while the great crowd
Crushes our backs from behind us; an elbow or a stick
Hits you, a beam or a wine-jar smacks you on the head;
My leg is covered in crud, from every side
I'm trampled by shoes, and some soldier spears
My foot with his spiked shoes. Look over there:
See the baskets belching out smoke? A picnic!
There must be a hundred guests and each
Dragging behind his own portable kitchen!
Corbulo[4] could scarcely carry such huge dishes—

---

[1]The emperor Trajan tried to cut down on the noise made by heavy traffic by cutting down on public building; the bulk of city wagon traffic (see below) involved building materials. As a result of Trajan's laws, most of the loading, transportation, and offloading of building materials occurred at night.
[2]The emperor Claudius was popularly considered both an idiot and perpetually drowsy; while he certainly wasn't an idiot, the latter actually seems to be a fair characterization.
[3]That is, they pass through the crowds in a closed litter. Juvenal is likening the litter carried by servants to a war-vessel; the "coast" is the crowded streets.
[4]Domitius Corbulo was a famous Roman general known for his mighty strength.

And so many—as are placed on the heads of the servants,
Poor schmucks, walking bolt upright
And madly fanning the flames while they run.
Mended tunics are torn, the massive trunk
Of a fir passes by in a cart, a pine over here
In a wagon, both sway and menace the crowd.
If the axle supporting a load of Ligurian marble[5]
Gave way, and spilled its mountain on the heads of the crowd,
What would be left over? Bodies? Hardly.
Who'd be able to find any limbs or bones?
The body of the ordinary man would utterly perish
Just like his soul. Meanwhile, his family, unawares,
Is washing dishes, blowing the fire with their mouths,
Making a racket with oily scrapers and washing
Spots from the linens. The house-boys are busy
With their chores, but the poor bastard's sitting
On the infernal shore, newly arrived,
Frightened of the horrible ferryman,[6] despairing and unhappy
For stuck in the mud he has no coin in his mouth
To offer to buy his passage across the waters.[7]

Think now about all those other perils
Of the night: how high it is to the roof up there
From which a tile falls and smashes your brains;
How many times broken, leaky jars
Fall from windows; how hard they strike and break
The pavement. You could be thought lazy and careless
If you go to dinner without writing a will.
There are as many deaths waiting for you
As there are open windows above your head.
Therefore you should hope and fervently pray
That they only dump their sewage on you.

Don't forget the drunkard who likes to fight:
If he hasn't killed anyone yet, he suffers,

---

[5]This is marble from Luna, near Carrara, in Etruria. Juvenal is describing the typical heavy traffic of Rome; the only wagons that were allowed on the streets were wagons carrying building materials.

[6]Charon. The man is dead and in the underworld. In Roman and Greek thought, the dead arrive at the shore of the river Acheron and are ferried across by Charon to the Underworld itself, where they are judged and sent either to Tartarus for punishment or Elysium for reward.

[7]In Greek and Roman funerary practices, a small coin was placed in the mouth of the deceased. Charon would not ferry across those who died before their time; they'd have to wait until their appointed hour.

And he mourns all night like Achilles for Patroclus,[8]
Lying first on his face and then on his back, tossing
And turning all night. He can't get to sleep otherwise:
Only a brawl puts some people to sleep!
But even though he's young and flushed with wine,
He carefully avoids the man with the crimson cloak
And the long procession of servants and burning lamps.
As for me, led home only by the moon
Or a small candle, whose wick I tend with care,
Me he despises. Thus begins a wretched fight—
If you can call it a fight when he punches
And I take a beating: he stands in front of me
And orders me to halt. What can I do?
Especially in the face of a frenzied maniac
Who, by the way, is stronger than I am?
"Where are you coming from? Whose beans and vinegar
Are you farting out your ass? What low-life
Shoemaker have you been eating leeks with
And stuffing your face with boiled sheep's head?
Why don't you answer me? Speak!
You want I should kick some sense in you!
Where do you beg? What synagogue
Do you pray at?"[9] You can try to say something,
Or you can try to slip quietly away,
It really doesn't matter one way or another:
You're going to get pounded, and taken to court
The next day because you bothered him.
You see, this alone is the poor man's freedom:
After being beaten and punched you have the right
To ask that a few teeth be left in your mouth.

This doesn't exhaust all the dangers in the city.
For there is always someone to rob you,
No matter how tightly you lock your house
Or seal all the shutters of your shop with fastened chains.
Sometimes thugs do their job quickly with a knife.
Whenever the Pomptine Marshes or the pine forests
Of Gallinaria[10] are protected by armed gaurds,

---

[8]The reference is to the *Iliad*, Book 24. Achilles is the great hero of the *Iliad*; when his friend, Patroclus, is killed in battle, he avenges himself on the Trojan hero responsible for his death. The irony is that Achilles refuses to fight in the *Iliad*, whereas the person described here can't wait. The emperor Nero was infamous for behavior like that Juvenal describes here.
[9]Judaism was becoming increasingly popular in Rome as one of a number of exotic Eastern religions, but conservatives like Juvenal viewed it with contempt.
[10]The Pomptine Marshes (on the Appian Way) and Gallinarian forest (near Cumae) were famous for their roving bands of armed robbers.

They all rush to Rome as if it were
A game preserve!

           On what forge or anvil
Is there anything else except heavy chains?
Iron is mainly used to fashion fetters,
So much so we risk a shortage of ploughshares
And the complete disappearance of hoes and mattocks.
Happy were our grandfathers' ancestors,
Happy those ages of the kings and tribunes of old
When Rome was content with only a single jail.

I could add many more reasons,
But the mules call and the daylight is passing away.
It's time.
The mule driver there has been signalling
For some time now with his driving stick.
Farewell, and remember me whenever Rome
Allows you to return to your native Aquinum,
For however brief a time, and tear me away
From Cumae to the altars built for Ceres by Helvius
And the ones built for Diana by your own people,
And I'll lace up my thick boots[11] and come through the fields
To your chilly country and help you write your satires.

But only if they aren't ashamed to have me in them.

                                      Translated by Richard Hooker

---

[11]Juvenal uses foot-wear to indicate character several times in this satire. Here, "thick boots" are the attire of farmers; Umbricius is saying that his move to the country is permanent.

Marcus Aurelius: *The Meditations* (167 CE)

The emperor Marcus Aelius Aurelius Antoninus, who reigned from 161 to 180 CE was the only Roman emperor besides Julius Caesar whose writings were to become part of the canon of Western classics. His Meditations *are a loosely-organized set of thoughts relating to the stoic philosophy which had been popular among the better-educated citizens of Rome for some centuries. It stressed self-discipline, virtue, and inner tranquillity. Aurelius was also a social reformer who worked for the improvement of the lot of the poor, slaves, and convicted criminals. Non-Christians in the Western World have often looked to him as a role model. He was also a fierce persecutor of Christianity, doubtless because he felt that the religion threatened the values that had made Rome great. Aurelius was not an original or brilliant thinker, but his* Meditations *reflect well the stoic strain in Greco-Roman civilization. The emphasis on morality combined with emotional detachment is also strongly reminiscent of Buddhist thought, with which Stoicism has often been compared.*

What arguments does Aurelius offer to help people accept death? How persuasive do you find them? How does this philosophy emphasize the independence of the individual? Does this emphasis on the individual result in selfishness? What theme does Aurelius share with the poem by Horace in this volume?

From Book Four:

Men seek retreats for themselves, houses in the country, at the seashore, and in the mountains; and you tend to desire such things very much. But this is a characteristic of the most common sort of men, for it is in your power whenever you will to choose to retreat into yourself. For nowhere either with more quiet or more freedom from trouble does a man retreat than into his own soul, particularly when he has within him such thoughts that by looking into them he is immediately perfectly tranquil; and I affirm that tranquillity is nothing other than the proper ordering of the mind.

Do not act as if you were going to live ten thousand years. Death hangs over you. While you live, while it is in your power, be good.

How much trouble he avoids who does not look to see what his neighbor says or does or thinks, but only to what he does himself, that it may be just and pure; or as Agathon says, do not consider the depraved morals of others, but cling to the straight and narrow path without deviating from it.

He who has a powerful desire for posthumous fame does not consider that every one of those who remember him will himself also die very soon; then again also they who have succeeded them, until the whole remembrance shall have been extinguished as it is transmitted through men who foolishly admire and then perish. But suppose that those who will remember are even immortal, and that the remembrance will be immortal, what good will this do you?

What is evil in you does not subsist in the ruling principle of another; nor in any part or transformation of your physical body. Where is it then? It is in that part of you in which has the power of forming opinions about evils.[1] Let this power then not form such opin-

---

[1]Like Buddhists and Hindus, Stoics believe that true evil exists only within the mind. It cannot be imposed from without.

ions, and all is well. And if that which is nearest to it—the poor body—is burnt, filled with excrescences and decay, nevertheless let the part which forms opinions about these things be quiet; that is, let it judge that nothing is either bad or good which can happen equally to the bad man and the good. For that which happens equally to him who lives contrary to nature and to him who lives according to nature, is neither according to nature nor contrary to nature.[2]

Constantly regard the universe as one living being, having one substance and one soul; and observe how all things have reference to one perception, the perception of this one living being; and how all things act with one movement; and how all things are the cooperating causes of all things which exist; observe too the continuous spinning of the thread and the structure of the web.

You are a little soul carrying about a corpse, as Epictetus used to say.

It is no evil for things to undergo change, and no good for things to come into being as a consequence of change.

Time is like a river made up of the events which happen, and a violent stream; for as soon as a thing has been seen, it is carried away, and another comes in its place, and this will be carried away too.

If any god told you that you shall die tomorrow, or certainly on the day after tomorrow, you would not care much whether it was on the third day or on the next, unless you had a very degraded spirit—for how small is the difference? So think it no great thing to die after as many years as you can count rather than tomorrow.[3]

Think continually how many physicians are dead after often fretting over the sick; and how many astrologers after predicting with great pretensions the deaths of others; and how many philosophers after endless discourses on death or immortality; how many heroes after killing thousands; and how many tyrants who have used their power over men's lives with terrible insolence as if they were immortal; and how many cities are entirely dead, so to speak, Helice and Pompeii and Herculaneum, and innumerable others. Add to the total all whom you have known, one after another. One man after burying another has been laid out dead, and another buries him: and all this in a short time. To conclude, always observe how ephemeral and worthless human things are, and what was yesterday a little mucus tomorrow will be a mummy or ashes. Pass then through this little space of time in the way of nature, and end your journey in contentment, just as an olive falls off when it is ripe, blessing nature who produced it, and thanking the tree on which it grew.

Be like the cliff against which the waves continually break, but which stands firm and tames the fury of the water around it.

From Book Five:

Live with the gods. And he does live with the gods who constantly shows them that his own soul is satisfied with that which is assigned to him, and that it does all that the daemon[4] wishes, which Zeus has given to every person as his guardian and guide, as a portion of himself. And this daemon is everyone's knowledge and reason.

---

[2]Like Daoists, Stoics argue that conformity to the ways of nature is best.

[3]The point is that death's inevitability must be accepted sometime; and it is well to be prepared for it at any time.

[4]A personal guardian spirit, here equated to the mind.

The best way of avenging yourself is not to become like the wrongdoer.

When we have meat before us and such food, we receive the impression that this is the dead body of a fish, and this is the dead body of a bird or of a pig; and again, that this Falernian wine is only a little grape juice, and this purple robe some sheep's wool dyed with the blood of a shell-fish: such then are these impressions, and they reach the things themselves and penetrate them, and so we see what kind of things they are. Just in the same way ought we to act all through life, and where there are things which appear most worthy of our approval, we ought to lay them bare and look at their worthlessness and strip them of all the words by which they are exalted. For outward show is a wonderful perverter of the reason, and when you are most sure that you are engaged in matters worth your while, it is then that it cheats you most. . . .

Most of the things which ordinary people admire have to do with objects of the most general kind, those which are held together by cohesion or natural organization, such as stones, wood, fig trees, vines, olives. But those which are admired by men who are a little more reasonable have to do with the things which are held together by a living principle, such as flocks and herds. Those which are admired by men who are still more enlightened are the things which are held together by a rational soul, not however a universal soul, but rational so far as it is a soul skilled in some art, or expert in some other way, or simply rational so far as it possesses a number of slaves. But he who values a rational soul, a universal soul which is fitted for political life, values nothing else except this; and above all things he keeps his soul in a condition and in activities suitable to reason and social life, and he cooperates in this with those who are of the same kind as himself.

So keep yourself simple, good, pure, serious, free from pretense, a friend of justice, a worshipper of the gods, kind, affectionate, strenuous in performing all proper acts. Strive to be the sort of person which philosophy wishes to make of you. Revere the gods and help others. Life is short. There is only one fruit of this earthly life: a pious disposition and social acts. Asia, Europe are corners of the universe; all the sea a drop in the universe; Athos[5] a little clod of the universe: all the present time is a point in eternity. All things are little, changeable, perishable. All things come from thence, from that universal ruling power either directly proceeding or by way of sequence. And accordingly the lion's gaping jaws, and that which is poisonous, and every harmful thing, like thorns, like mud, are after-products of the grand and beautiful. Do not then imagine that they are of another kind from that which you venerate, but form a just opinion of the source of all.

He who has seen present things has seen all, both everything which has taken place from all eternity and everything which will be for time without end; for all things are of one kin and of one form.

Translated by George Long, revised by Paul Brians

---

[5]A tall mountain in northeastern Greece.

Early Christianity

The Christian Scriptures (c. 70–120? CE)

These passages come from those writings which Christians call "The New Testament," to distinguish them from the Hebrew Bible, which they call "The Old Testament." Here we use the more neutral term "Christian Scriptures" to designate the four gospels which recount the life, death and resurrection of Jesus, the letters of Paul and others, and the apocalyptic book of Revelation. Centuries of controversy has surrounded almost every line of these texts, and we can hope to do little more than point to some of the significant points of debate. Traditionally Christians believed that every word of these texts was infallible and written by men who knew Jesus personally. Today many scholars have abandoned that position, arguing that the texts display an intricate history of the development of ideas in the First Century Christian community, and that most likely none of them were written by the disciples to whom they were earlier attributed. It is on the large body of scholarship supporting this belief that many of the following annotations are based; but it would be wrong to suppose that this scholarship is irreligious. Many of the finest modern Bible scholars are Catholics, for instance. The translation used in the following selections is the New Revised Standard Version of the Bible.

Background from the Jewish Bible (Isaiah 40:1-5)

The authors of the Gospels evidently knew little or no Hebrew, for they consistently quote from Greek versions of the Hebrew Bible which sometimes differ from it in significant ways. However, they lay great stress on the idea that the major events in Jesus' life can be seen as predicted by the Jewish prophets, especially Isaiah. In the following passage, Isaiah announces the coming of the Messianic age, in which the earth will be radically transformed. Probably the original context was the impending return from the Babylonian Captivity, which the poetic vision of the writer imagines as involving the creation of a highway through the wilderness back to Jerusalem. These words were memorably set to music in George Frederick Handel's Messiah.

Comfort, O comfort my people,
says your God.
Speak tenderly to Jerusalem,[1]
and cry to her
that she has served her term,
that her penalty is paid,
that she has received from the Lord's hand
double for all her sins.[2]

A voice cries out:
"In the wilderness prepare the way of the Lord,

---

[1]That is, the people of Jerusalem, the Jews.
[2]Various prophets had earlier seen the Jewish defeat by Babylon as punishment for various sins, especially insufficient faithfulness to monotheism.

Make straight in the desert a highway for our God.
Every valley shall be lifted up,
and every mountain and hill be made low;
the uneven ground shall become level,
and the rough places a plain.
Then the glory of the Lord shall be revealed,
and all people shall see it together,
for the mouth of the Lord has spoken."

The Baptism of Jesus (Matthew 3)

The following passage illustrates the early church's use of the Hebrew Bible. Lacking anything like modern quotation marks, they felt free to read the text from Isaiah above as if a voice were crying in the wilderness rather than prophesying a highway that was to be built in the wilderness. Such differences go a long way toward explaining why most Jews did not accept Jesus as the fulfillment of Jewish prophecy. Matthew's reading is not wilfully distorted; it merely comes from a tradition which views the texts in a quite different way than did the orthodox Jews of his time. The scene is the very beginning of Jesus' career, where he is baptized by the fiery preacher John in a ritual which involves pouring water over him. In Christian thought this was comparable to the Jewish tradition of anointing the head of a king, which gave rise to the term "Messiah" and its Greek translation, "Christ," both of which mean "he whose head has been anointed with oil." The scene has been frequently depicted in art.

What is John's attitude toward the Jewish Sadducees and Pharisees who have come to be baptized? What is the meaning of the imagery of the grain and the chaff?

In those days John the Baptist appeared in the wilderness of Judea, proclaiming, "Repent, for the kingdom of heaven has come near." This is the one of whom the prophet Isaiah spoke when he said, "The voice of one crying out in the wilderness: 'Prepare the way of the Lord, make his paths straight.'"

Now John wore clothing of camel's hair with a leather belt around his waist, and his food was locusts and wild honey.[1] Then the people of Jerusalem and all Judea were going out to him, and all the region along the Jordan, and they were baptized by him in the river Jordan, confessing their sins.

But when he saw many Pharisees and Sadducees[2] coming for baptism, he said to them, "You brood of vipers! Who warned you to flee from the wrath to come? Bear fruit worthy of repentance. Do not presume to say to yourselves, 'We have Abraham as our ancestor,' for I tell you, God is able from these stones to raise up children to Abraham. Even now the

---

[1] The Baptist is usually recognizable in his traditional portraits by this clothing, even when he is depicted as a small child.

[2] Although Matthew groups them together, the Pharisees were innovative scholars (rabbis) whose beliefs came closer to those Jesus is depicted as preaching than did those of the traditionalist Sadducees, who rejected the belief in the coming Messiah, the notion of a last judgment and the existence of a heaven and hell.

ax is lying at the root of the trees; every tree therefore that does not bear good fruit is cut down and thrown into the fire.[3]

"I baptize you with water for repentance, but one who is more powerful than I is coming after me; I am not worthy to carry his sandals. He will baptize you with the Holy Spirit and fire. His winnowing fork is in his hand, and he will clear his threshing floor and will gather his wheat into the granary; but the chaff he will burn with unquenchable fire."

Then Jesus came from Galilee to John at the Jordan, to be baptized by him. John would have prevented him, saying "I need to be baptized by you, and do you come to me?" But Jesus answered him, "Let it be so now; for it is proper for us in this way to fulfill all righteousness." Then he consented. And when Jesus had been baptized, just as he came up from the water, suddenly the heavens were opened to him and he saw the Spirit of God descending like a dove and alighting on him.[4] And a voice from heaven said, "This is my Son, the Beloved, with whom I am well pleased."[5]

---

[3]The early church considered that all converts, Jewish or not, could be considered a sort of adopted "chosen people," covered by many of the statements about them in the Hebrew Bible. The fire referred to is traditionally interpreted as being the eternal fire of Hell in which all unbelievers are to burn.

[4]In art the Holy Spirit is usually literally depicted as a dove. After much debate the majority of the early Church decided to consider the term "Holy Spirit" not simply as a manifestation of God but as a distinct "person." The formula "three persons in one God: Father, Son and Holy Spirit," led to endless arguments about the relationships of these persons (collectively called "the Trinity") to each other and to the view by many Muslims and Jews that Christianity is not a strictly monotheistic religion.

[5]The relationship of Jesus to God the Father has been the most hotly debated issue concerning the Trinity. Traditional Christians have taken the phrase literally and maintained that Jesus was divinely begotten. Some argue for "adoptionalism," that Jesus was singled out in maturity by God as his instrument, pointing out that the idea of a God's producing a child through a human mate was a commonplace in Greco-Roman mythology, and alien to the beliefs of Judaism. At any rate, all interpretations agree that this story is meant to portray Jesus as a divinely chosen figure destined to accomplish great things.

A Miracle Based on Faith (Mark 5:25-34)

The Gospel of Mark, generally believed to have been the first written, portrays Jesus above all as a miracle-worker. Miraculous healings were a familiar concept to Romans and Jews alike; and they did not so much set Jesus apart as validate him as having divinely derived powers. However, in this miracle, the stress is laid not on Jesus' role, which is depicted as almost involuntary, but on the woman's. The lesson being taught is not so much about healing as it is about faith, one of Mark's main themes. Mark divides those who encounter Jesus into two types: those who do not believe, and those who do.

What is it that Jesus says has caused the woman to be healed?

Now there was a woman who had been suffering from hemorrhages for twelve years. She had endured much under many physicians, and had spent all that she had; and she was no better, but rather grew worse. She had heard about Jesus, and came up behind him in the crowd and touched his cloak, for she said, "If I but touch his clothes, I will be made well."

Immediately her hemorrhage stopped; and she felt in her body that she was healed of her disease. Immediately aware that power had gone forth from him, Jesus turned about in the crowd and said, "Who touched my clothes?" And his disciples said to him, "you see the crowd pressing in on you; how can you say, 'Who touched me?'" He looked all around to see who had done it. But the woman, knowing what had happened to her, came in fear and trembling, fell down before him, and told him the whole truth. He said to her, "Daughter, your faith has made you well; go in peace, and be healed of your disease."

On Forgiveness, Sermon on the Mount (Matthew 5:38-48)

In contrast to Mark, Matthew contains far fewer miracles and a great deal of teaching, including the famous collection of sayings called "The Sermon on the Mount," some of them quite extreme. As we saw earlier, Jewish law required the fair treatment of enemies and by no means called upon all crimes to be punished by "an eye for an eye;" but it did not require forgiveness to extend as far as this.

In your opinion, which of these is the most extreme commandment? Why?

You have heard that it was said, "An eye for an eye and a tooth for a tooth."[1] But I say to you, Do not resist an evildoer.[2] But if anyone strikes you on the right cheek, turn the other also; and if anyone wants to sue you and take your coat, give your cloak as well; and if anyone forces you to go one mile, go also the second mile.[3] Give to everyone who begs from you, and do not refuse anyone who wants to borrow from you.

You have heard that it was said, "You shall love your neighbor and hate your enemy."[4] But I say to you, Love your enemies and pray for those who persecute you, so that you may be children of your Father in heaven; for he makes his sun rise on the evil and on the good, and sends rain on the righteous and on the unrighteous. For if you love those who love you, what reward to you have? Do not even the tax collectors do the same?[5] And if you

---

[1] See Genesis 21:23–25.

[2] This statement is so strong, seeming to leave no room for police, judges, or even self-defense, that some scholars have argued that it must envision a very near end of the world. In that case, civil society need not be maintained because all will shortly be judged by God. A more traditional view applies Paul's theory that salvation by works (good deeds) is literally impossible. These commandments would then be uttered *because* they are impossible to obey, in order to force the hearer to accept that only faith can save.

[3] This commandment has been explained by some as an extension of the much-resented Roman law which required subjects to carry the spear and shield of a soldier for one mile whenever requested. The early church was anxious to avoid any appearance of being hostile to Rome, unlike the Jews who rebelled against the imperial government. "Going the second mile" has come to be a popular expression for making an extra effort.

[4] This saying occurs nowhere in the Hebrew Bible. It may be simply an expression of popular attitudes.

[5] Tax collectors were hated representatives of Rome, all the more so because their income depended on charging taxpayers more than was actually due the central government.

greet only your brothers and sisters, what more are you doing than others? Do not even the Gentiles[6] do the same? Be perfect, therefore, as your heavenly Father is perfect."[7]

[6]Non-Jews.

[7]With the exception of some saints, few Christians have taken this commandment literally, seeing in it an inconsistency with Paul's doctrine of original sin. Jewish law, of course, expected perfection in that the worshipper was supposed to be able to observe all of God's law without superhuman efforts.

The Beatitudes (Luke 6:20-26)

These famous sayings must have exercised a powerful attraction for the downtrodden people who made up much of the early Christian community. Quite specific rewards are offered in compensation for present suffering. The emphasis on the wickedness of the rich is very much in the tradition of Jewish prophets like Amos. Political liberals have generally preferred this version of the Beatitudes, conservatives, the more spiritual version in Matthew 5.

What rewards are promised to those that suffer in this life?

"Blessed are you who are poor,
  for yours is the kingdom of God.
"Blessed are you who are hungry now,
  for you will be filled.
"Blessed are you who weep now,
  for you will laugh.
"Blessed are you when people hate you, and when they exclude you, revile you, and
  defame you on account of the Son of Man.[1]
"Rejoice in that Day and leap for joy, for surely your reward is great in heaven; for that is
  what their ancestors did to the prophets.[2]
"But woe to you who are rich,
  for you have received your consolation.
"Woe to you who are full now,
  for you will be hungry.
"Woe to you who are laughing now,
  for you will mourn and weep.
"Woe to you when all speak well of you, for that is what their ancestors did to the false
  prophets."

[1]Jesus himself, a Messianic title of disputed meaning.
[2]Many passages in the Christian Scriptures seem aimed at strengthening the faith of those under persecution for their beliefs. It had become a tradition to believe that all the ancient Jewish prophets had been persecuted.

The Golden Rule (Matthew 7:12)

Sometimes claimed to be a uniquely Christian contribution to ethics, the "Golden Rule" has also been argued to be an eloquent expression of the universal principal underlying the concept of law. Compare the similar saying by Confucius.

In everything do to others as you would have them do to you; for this is the law and the prophets.[1]

---

[1]The Law and the Prophets are the first two parts of the Hebrew Bible. The third, the Writings, had not been fully consolidated at this time. This commandment would then be the essence of all Jewish teaching.

Salvation and Damnation Linked to Deeds (Matthew 7:13-23)

The Christian Scriptures abound with references to the Last Judgment, to Heaven, and to Hell. This saying seems to promise salvation only to a sub-grouping within the early church, placing considerable emphasis on the performance of good deeds. In this it resembles the teachings of Jewish prophets like Isaiah (1:10–20). Such a path to salvation is far more rigorous than, for instance, the Buddhist tradition of the eventual salvation of all beings.

What metaphor in this passage seems to promise Hellfire to those who are not true followers?

Enter through the narrow gate, for the gate is wide and the road is easy that leads to destruction,[1] and there are many who take it. For the gate is narrow and the road is hard that leads to life, and there are few who find it.

Beware of false prophets, who come to you in sheep's clothing but inwardly are ravenous wolves.[2] You will know them by their fruits. Are grapes gathered from thorns, or figs from thistles? In the same way, every good tree bears good fruit, but the bad tree bears bad fruit. A good tree cannot bear bad fruit, nor can a bad tree bear good fruit. Every tree that does not bear good fruit is cut down and thrown into the fire. Thus you will know them by their fruits.

Not everyone who says to me, "Lord, Lord," will enter the kingdom of heaven, but only the one who does the will of my Father in heaven. On that day many will say to me, "Lord, Lord, did we not prophesy in your name, and cast out demons in your name, and do many deeds of power in your name?"[3] Then I will declare to them, "I never knew you; go away from me, you evil-doers."

---

[1]Traditionally interpreted as eternal torment in Hell.
[2]Aimed at teachers who disagreed with the dominant group in the early church.
[3]Note that not even the successful performance of miracles is enough to prove worthiness.

The Ascetic Ideal (Matthew 6:24-33)

The ascetic goal of holy poverty has not been nearly as central to Christianity as it has to Hinduism or Buddhism, being practiced mainly by early hermits and the stricter sort of monks and nuns. Yet this passage has often been quoted as a poetic description of that ideal. Others prefer to emphasize the theme of trust in God as bringing prosperity, though that emphasis downplays the importance of the introductory sentences.

What images from nature can you find in this passage that symbolize the gifts of God?

"No one can serve two masters; for a slave will either hate the one and love the other, or be devoted to the one and despise the other. You cannot serve God and wealth.

"Therefore I tell you, do not worry about your life, what you will eat or what you will drink, or about your body, what you will wear. Is not life more than food, and the body more than clothing? Look at the birds of the air; they neither sow nor reap nor gather into barns, and yet your heavenly Father feeds them. Are you not of more value than they? And can any of you by worrying add a single hour to your span of life? And why do you worry about clothing? Consider the lilies of the field, how they grow; they neither toil nor spin, yet I tell you, even Solomon[1] in all his glory was not clothed like one of these. But if God so clothes the grass of the field, which is alive today and tomorrow is thrown into the oven, will he not much more clothe you—you of little faith? Therefore do not worry, saying, 'What will we eat?' or 'What will we drink?' or 'What will we wear?' For it is the Gentiles who strive for all these things; and indeed your heavenly Father knows that you need all these things. But strive first for the kingdom of God and his righteousness, and all these things will be given to you as well."

---

[1]The wealthiest of the ancient Jewish kings.

The Trial and Crucifixion of Jesus (Matthew 27:15-54)

The most original contribution of Christianity to the concept of the Messiah is the concept of the suffering and dying savior. Whereas orthodox Jews would have considered a dying Messiah a contradiction in terms, in Christianity Jesus' death was portrayed as a necessary and inevitable part of his mission, and his resurrection from death was to provide the example for his followers. In its most fully-developed form, the doctrine holds that his death actually functions as a sacrifice which wipes out the sin of those who believe in him. Unlike other dying and resurrected Mediterranean and Mesopotamian gods, Christ's death is not linked to annual cycles of planting and harvest, but is seen as a unique event which begins a new era in history. It is not surprising then, that though two of the gospels do not even mention his birth, they all devote a great deal of space to his trial and death. Every aspect of this story has been illustrated in every artistic medium throughout Christendom. Unfortunately, the desire of the early church to emphasize the role of the Jews and deemphasize that of the Romans led historically to violent persecutions of Jews by Christians throughout later history.

What aspects of this account seem to lessen the responsibility of the Romans for Jesus' death? How does Jesus react to the various sufferings he goes through?

Now at the festival[1] the governor was accustomed to release a prisoner for the crowd, anyone whom they wanted. At that time they had a notorious prisoner, called Jesus Barabbas.[2] So after they had gathered, Pilate[3] said to them, "Whom do you want me to release for you, Jesus Barabbas or Jesus who is called the Messiah?" For he realized that it was out of jealousy that they had handed him over. While he was sitting on the judgment seat, his wife sent word to him, "Have nothing to do with that innocent man, for today I have suffered a great deal because of a dream about him." Now the chief priests and the elders persuaded the crowds to ask for Barabbas and to have Jesus killed. The governor again said to them, "Which of the two do you want me to release for you?" And they said, "Barabbas." Pilate said to them, "Then what should I do with Jesus who is called the Messiah?" Then he asked, "Why, what evil has he done?" But they shouted all the more, "Let him be crucified!"

So when Pilate saw that he could do nothing, but rather that a riot was beginning, he took some water and washed his hands before the crowd, saying, "I am innocent of this man's blood; see to it yourselves." Then the people as a whole answered, "His blood be on us and on your children!"[4] So he released Barabbas for them; and after flogging Jesus, he handed him over to be crucified.[5]

Then the soldiers of the governor took Jesus into the governor's headquarters, and they gathered the whole cohort around him. They stripped him and put a scarlet robe on him, and after twisting some thorns into a crown, they put it on his head. They put a reed in his right hand and knelt before him and mocked him, saying "Hail, King of the Jews!" They spat on him, and took the reed and struck him on the head. After mocking him, they stripped him of the robe and put his own clothes on him. Then they led him away to crucify him. . . .

From noon on, darkness came over the whole land until three in the afternoon. And about three o'clock Jesus cried with a loud voice, "Eli, Eli, lema sabachthani?" that is, "My God, my God, why have you forsaken me?"[6] When some of the bystanders heard it, they said, "This man is calling for Elijah."[7] At once one of them ran and got a sponge, filled it with sour wine, put it on a stick, and gave it to him to drink. But the others said, "Wait, let us see whether Elijah will come to save him." Then Jesus cried again with a loud voice and breathed his last. At that moment the curtain of the temple was torn in two, from top to bottom. The earth shook, and the rocks were split. The tombs also were opened, and many

---

[1] Passover.

[2] Perhaps a popular anti-Roman agitator.

[3] Pontius Pilate, the Roman governor of Judaea.

[4] A line unfortunately quoted frequently in history to excuse persecution of Jews.

[5] Nailing to a cross was one of the most common forms of execution used by the Romans, designed to cause a protracted, agonizing death. There were instances of people having survived quite lengthy periods of crucifixion. According to Mark 15: 44, Pilate was astonished that Jesus had not survived into the evening.

[6] Although the four gospels give strikingly similar accounts of the trial and crucifixion, they each report different "last words." Some see these words as stressing the humanity of Jesus. Others argue that since these are the opening words of Psalm 22, which ends by expressing confidence in God, that confidence is implied in the quotation.

[7] An ancient prophet who Jews believe will return in the time of the Messiah.

bodies of the saints who had fallen asleep were raised.[8] After his resurrection they came out of the tombs and entered the holy city and appeared to many. Now when the centurion[9] and those with him, who were keeping watch over Jesus, saw the earthquake and what took place, they were terrified and said, "Truly this man was God's Son!"

---

[8]"Saints" here refers to Christian converts who had died earlier ("fallen asleep"). Jesus' sacrifice is portrayed as producing life after death immediately. This incident is not mentioned elsewhere.

[9]Roman officer.

The Last Supper (John 6: 51-57)

The final meal of Jesus before his death is given a mystical significance in this account. Avoiding any appearance of Jesus being a passive victim, John portrays him as willingly offering himself as a sacrifice. The idea is related to the lamb that was sacrificed in place of the first-born children of the Hebrews in Egypt and ritually eaten on Passover. He offers his life as a substitute—not literally for the lives of others—but for their salvation after death in the life to come. However, the imagery used here would have been offensive to most Jews, since one of the earliest Jewish laws forbade the eating of blood, and dead bodies were considered ritually unclean. The concept of eating the body of the god was familiar to non-Jews from pagan rites, however; and would have been more acceptable to them. Protestants generally see this account as metaphorical, and consider the rite of the Last Supper to be a symbolic memorial. For Catholics, the bread and wine are actually and miraculously transformed into the body and blood of Christ, without, however, changing their apparent form.

"I am the living bread that came down from heaven. Whoever eats of this bread will live forever; and the bread that I will give for the life of the world is my flesh."

The Jews then disputed among themselves, saying, "How can this man give us his flesh to eat?" So Jesus said to them, "Very truly, I tell you, unless you eat the flesh of the Son of Man and drink his blood, you have no life in you. Those who eat my flesh and drink my blood have eternal life, and I will raise them up on the last day;[1] for my flesh is true food and my blood is true drink. Those who eat my flesh and drink my blood abide in me, and I in them. Just as the living Father sent me, and I live because of the Father, so whoever eats me will live because of me."

---

[1]Some passages in the Christian Scriptures imply that resurrection occurs immediately after death, others that it will be postponed until the Day of Judgment. Theologians differ among themselves on this point.

Salvation by Faith (Romans 3:21-28)

Paul, Christianity's great missionary, who founded churches all over the eastern Roman world, was also its first theologian. Born a Jew, trained as a rabbi, and at first a dedicated enemy of Christianity, he claimed to have encountered Jesus as a blinding light and a voice on the road to Damascus. Although he never met Jesus during his lifetime, he claimed to be one of the disciples and his influence far outshone that of all of the original twelve disciples put together, partly because he dedicated himself principally to converting non-Jews. He linked the new Christian ideas with older Jewish ones, but also frequently made radical breaks with tradition when he thought it necessary. No break was more radical than his rejection of the Jewish belief that obedience to the Law was the path to salvation. In the following passage Paul maintains that complete obedience is impossible because we are born damnably flawed (according to a doctrine known as "original sin"), and that only belief in Christ can bring salvation (a doctrine known as "salvation by faith"). In modern times, liberal churches tend to dwell on the Sermon on the Mount, conservative churches on writings like this.

What makes all Christians equal, in Paul's opinion?

But now, apart from law, the righteousness of God has been disclosed, and is attested by the law and the prophets, the righteousness of God through faith in Jesus Christ for all who believe. For there is no distinction, since all have sinned and fall short of the glory of God; they are now justified by his grace as a gift, through the redemption that is in Christ Jesus, whom God put forward as a sacrifice of atonement by his blood, effective through faith. He did this to show his righteousness, because in his divine forbearance he had passed over the sins previously committed; it was to prove at the present time that he himself is righteous and that he justifies the one who has faith in Jesus.

Then what becomes of boasting? It is excluded. By what law? By that of works? No, but by the law of faith. For we hold that a person is justified by faith apart from works prescribed by the law.

Paul on marriage vs.celibacy (1 Corinthians 7:25-31, 36-40)

The meaning of Paul's teachings on women and marriage has been the subject of endless controversy, particularly in modern times. Some have argued that Paul believed that the world was about to come to an end and that there was therefore no need to continue marrying and begetting children. Yet elsewhere Paul seems to be anxious to avoid the extreme asceticism of some contemporary religious thinkers. He has been called an antifeminist and a protofeminist. The Catholic Church has embraced both the concept of celibacy (for priests and nuns) and encouraged reproduction (among lay people).

What arguments does Paul use against marriage? What does he say are reasons one should get married?

Now concerning virgins, I have no command of the Lord, but I give my opinion as one who by the Lord's mercy is trustworthy. I think that, in view of the impending crisis, it is well for you to remain as you are. Are you bound to a wife? Do not seek to be free. Are you free from a wife? Do not seek a wife. But if you marry, you do not sin, and if a virgin marries, she does not sin. Yet those who marry will experience distress in this life, and I would spare you that. I mean, brothers and sisters, the appointed time has grown short; from now on, let even those who have wives be as though they had none, and those who mourn as though they were not mourning, and those who rejoice as though they were not rejoicing, and those who buy as though they had no possessions, and those who deal with the world as though they had no dealings with it. For the present form of this world is passing away. . . .

If anyone thinks that he is not behaving properly toward his fiancée, if his passions are strong, and so it has to be, let him marry as he wishes; it is no sin. Let them marry. But if someone stands firm in his resolve, being under no necessity but having his own desire under control, and has determined in his own mind to keep her as his fiancée, he will do well. So then, he who marries his fiancée does well; and he who refrains from marriage will do better.

A wife is bound as long as her husband lives. But if the husband dies, she is free to marry anyone she wishes, only in the Lord. But in my judgment she is more blessed if she remains as she is.

The Last Judgment (Revelation 20: 11-21:4)

The last book to be added to the Christian Scriptures, Revelation is an apocalypse: a vision of the end of the world. It developed further the tradition of Jewish apocalypse, which was very popular in the first century CE. Very little in the imagery quoted below would have been unfamiliar to a 1st Century pharisee. It has been read in all ages as an urgent announcement of an imminent end to the world. Its urgency is meant as a warning to convert, but was probably also intended as a source of comfort to those suffering under Roman persecution. This excerpt contains the grand climax of the book when the dead are resurrected to face judgment and be sent to Heaven or Hell. This scene was what most Medieval Christians saw depicted in stone or paint as they entered their churches.

Revelation is generally thought of as a terrifying book, but which aspects of this passage seem designed to give comfort to the reader?

Then I saw a great white throne and the one who sat on it;[1] the earth and the heaven fled from his presence, and no place was found for them.[2] And I saw the dead, great and small, standing before the throne, and books were opened. Also another book was opened, the book of life. And the dead were judged according to their works, as recorded in the books. And the sea gave up the dead that were in it. Death and Hades[3] gave up the dead that were in them, and all were judged according to what they had done. Then Death and Hades were thrown into the lake of fire. This is the second death, the lake of fire; and anyone whose name was not found written in the book of life was thrown into the lake of fire.

Then I saw a new heaven and a new earth; for the first heaven and the first earth had

---

[1]Jesus as judge. This appearance is what Christians refer to as the "Second Coming."
[2]The writer's imagery frequently reduces the cosmos to an insignificant scale before God's greatness.
[3]The Greek name for the land of the dead, used as a name for Hell.

passed away, and the sea was no more. And I saw the holy city, the new Jerusalem,[4] coming down out of heaven from God, prepared as a bride adorned for her husband. And I heard a loud voice from the throne saying,
"See, the home of God is among mortals.
He will dwell with them as their God;
They will be his peoples,
and God himself will be with them;
he will wipe every tear from their eyes.
Death will be no more;
mourning and crying and pain will be no more,
for the first things have passed away."

---

[4] The radical transformation of the earth was also a standard feature of Jewish apocalypse, as was the establishment of Jerusalem as the capitol of the Earth.

Tacitus (c. 55 –117 CE): Nero's persecution of the Christians

Tacitus was a fierce critic of Nero, and modern scholars have questioned the reliability of his account of this notorious Roman Emperor; but the following passage from his Annals *is famous because it is one of the first mentions in a non-Christian source of Christianity. In 64 CE Rome underwent a catastrophic fire, which some believed had been set at the orders of the emperor himself. Tacitus claims that Nero tried to shift the blame to the unpopular Christians, though other sources indicate that their persecution may have been unconnected to the fire. It is not clear exactly why many Romans so detested the new believers, though Christians were often confused with Jews, who were accused of being rebellious (with some reason, since the Jews of Judaea more than once created insurrections against the Roman provincial government) and lazy (since they rested on the Sabbath). Scandalous rumors about obscene Christian rituals circulated at an early date, and we know that they were accused of disloyalty because of their refusal to perform the token ritual acknowledging the divine status of the Emperor, viewed by most citizens as little different from a modern flag salute. If Tacitus shows sympathy for them, it is because he detests Nero more. Whatever their exact cause this early persecution and later ones made a profound impact on the Christian Church, and bequeathed a legacy of colorful tales of martyred saints who were celebrated in story, song, and art for the next two millennia, long after the Church had triumphed over its opponents.*

What were the main accusations brought against the Christians?

Yet no human effort, no princely largess nor offerings to the gods could make that infamous rumor disappear that Nero had somehow ordered the fire. Therefore, in order to abolish that rumor, Nero falsely accused and executed with the most exquisite punishments those people called Christians, who were infamous for their abominations. The originator of the name, Christ, was executed as a criminal by the procurator Pontius Pilate during the reign of Tiberius; and though repressed, this destructive superstition erupted again, not only through Judea, which was the origin of this evil, but also through the city of Rome, to which all that is horrible and shameful floods together and is celebrated. Therefore, first those were seized who admitted their faith, and then, using the information they provided, a vast multitude were convicted, not so much for the crime of burning the city, but for hatred of the human race. And perishing they were additionally made into sports: they were killed by dogs by having the hides of beasts attached to them, or they were nailed to crosses or set aflame, and, when the daylight passed away, they were used as nighttime lamps. Nero gave his own gardens for this spectacle and performed a Circus game, in the habit of a charioteer mixing with the plebs or driving about the race-course. Even though they were clearly guilty and merited being made the most recent example of the consequences of crime, people began to pity these sufferers, because they were consumed not for the public good but on account of the fierceness of one man.

Translated by Richard Hooker

Christian Creeds

The English word "creed" translates the Latin word credo, *which means literally "I believe." Originally credos evolved as answers to questions asked of new converts to the Christian religion, but they also functioned to defined what were considered official Christian beliefs (orthodoxy) as opposed to views the Church rejected (heresies). The rich variety of views about Jesus presented in early Christian writings, including the Scriptures, led to many debates over what precisely it was that Christians were called upon to believe, and the decision to choose a particular creed to express those beliefs was for many people a matter of life and death.*

The Apostles' Creed

The following creed summarizes what came to be viewed as the essentials in the early centuries of the history of the Christian religion. The exact phraseology translated below dates from the late 6th or early 7th century and became the official statement of faith of the Roman Catholic Church by the early 13th century. It is also used by many protestant congregations though it is not recognized by Eastern Orthodox churches.

I believe in God the Father Almighty; Maker of heaven and earth. And in Jesus Christ his only Son our Lord; who was conceived by the Holy Ghost, born of the Virgin Mary; suffered under Pontius Pilate, was crucified, dead, and buried; he descended into hell;[1] the third day he rose from the dead; he ascended into heaven; and sitteth at the right hand of God the Father Almighty; from thence he shall come to judge the quick[2] and the dead. I believe in the Holy Ghost;[3] the holy Catholic Church;[4] the communion of saints;[5] the forgiveness of sins; the resurrection of the body,[6] and the life everlasting. Amen.

Translated by Philip Schaff

---

[1]This refers to the belief that upon his death by crucifixion, Jesus descended to the underworld to free the good Jews who had been languishing there and take them to heaven. In the Middle Ages, this was a very popular scene in religious dramas, but it has been largely forgotten today, partly because it has no Biblical basis.

[2]Living: people still alive at the Last Judgment.

[3]Archaic language for the Holy Spirit.

[4]"Catholic" originally meant simply "universal," and eventually came to mean "orthodox."

[5]Refers to the community of early Christian martyrs and leaders in Heaven.

[6]Aimed at certain early groups who argued that only the soul was resurrected and the body left behind. Paul argues that a special, perfected heavenly body is resurrected in place of the old, imperfect flesh.

The Nicene Creed

In AD 325, the Emperor Constantine, the first Roman emperor to convert to Christianity, called a universal council of the church at the town of Nicaea in Asia Minor (an event later called the First Ecumenical Council). The council was called to decide how Christians should understand the nature of Jesus, who was held by the church to be both the Savior and the Son of God. The community of believers had already been divided on many issues, perhaps most seriously by a movement or series of movements called Gnosticism (the claiming of special or secret knowledge of the will of God), and wracked by schisms such as Donatism in North Africa and Meletism in Egypt. The threat to unity at Nicaea was Arianism, a view articulated by a monk, Arius of Alexandria, that if Jesus was the son of God, he was not strictly equivalent with the Creator. This view emphasized the human over the divine nature of the Christ. Arius acknowledged that the Son could represent perfect man and serve as a perfect instrument for the salvation of the world, but that he was not of "one substance" with the Father. The Council, at Constantine's urging, adopted language that directly rejected Arius' views: the committee-constructed language that became known as the Nicene creed asserts unequivocally that the Son was indeed of one substance [homoousios] or being with God. This view, called "consubstantiality," prevailed as doctrine. The three-clause structure of the creed also gives early expression to the distinctly Christian idea of the Trinity—"one God in Three Persons." In Greek philosophical language, "substance" meant the deeper reality of a thing, that out of which it is constituted, in contrast to its appearance or changable qualities. The idea of a "person," from the Greek word for mask, refers to aspects of a being, as in the Trinitarian formulation of "God in Three Persons." "Eternal" (in the phrase "eternally begotten") would mean timelessly, prior to or apart from there being any time. Thus, it is being argued that in some sense Jesus existed before his birth, and it not uncommon in later times for him to be referred to as the creator of the universe. A longer variation on this creed, probably developed in the Eastern churches, is the familiar text set to music in the "Credo" sections of many masses during the Renaissance and later. Modern Catholics and some protestants recite this creed as well as the Apostles' Creed. The Church's insistence that God was both three and one led to vast amounts of theological debate, and to the Qur'an's rejection of that view as not truly monotheistic.

What are the main differences in emphasis between the two creeds? What questions do they seem designed to answer?

We believe in one God, the Father, the Almighty, maker of heaven and earth, of all that is seen and unseen. We believe in one Lord, Jesus Christ, the only Son of God, eternally begotten of the Father, God from God, Light from Light, true God from true God, begotten, not made, one in Being with the Father. Through him all things were made. For us men and for our salvation he came down from heaven: by the power of the Holy Spirit he was born of the Virgin Mary, and became man. our sake he was crucified under Pontius Pilate; he suffered, died, and was buried. On the third day he rose again in fulfillment of the Scriptures; he ascended into heaven and is seated on the right hand of the Father. He will come again in glory to judge the living and the dead, and his kingdom will have no end. We believe in the Holy Spirit, the Lord, the giver of life, who proceeds from the Father and the Son. With the Father and the Son he is worshipped and glorified. He has spoken through the Prophets. We believe in one holy catholic and apostolic Church. We acknowledge one baptism for the forgiveness of sins. We look for the resurrection of the dead, and the life of the world to come. Amen.

St. Augustine: *The Changeable and the Permanent* from the *Letter to Coelestinus* (390 CE)

St. Augustine, the first major Christian philosopher, was deeply influenced by Platonic thought as he developed his theology and his philosophy. In wrestling with the problem of evil (i.e., why is there evil in the world if an all-powerful and all-good God is in charge?) he reaffirms that everything that God made is good, including, both the body and the soul. (Thus he cannot blame the evil we do on our bodily desires, as some thinkers had done.) But not all things are of the same status; there is a hierarchy, with God at the top, then angels and humans in the middle, brutes, plants and the inorganic realm at the bottom. The higher something is on this scale, the greater potential it has for good but also for evil — except for God, who is unchangeably good.

Augustine admits that both our body (physical nature) and our soul (spiritual nature) are subject to change, since both are part of the created realm. But which of those two does he think is more important and can make the most significant changes (i.e., toward wretchedness or toward blessedness)? Why?

As I know you well, I ask you to accept and ponder the following brief sentences on a great theme. There is a nature which is susceptible of change with respect to both place and time, namely, the corporeal.[1] There is another nature which is in no way susceptible of change with respect to place, but only with respect to time, namely, the spiritual. And there is a third Nature which can be changed neither in respect to place nor in respect to time: that is, God. Those natures of which I have said that they are mutable[2] in some respect are called creatures; the Nature which is immutable is called Creator. Seeing however, that we affirm the existence of anything only in so far as it continues and is one (in consequence of which, unity is the condition essential to beauty in every form), you cannot fail to distinguish, in this classification of natures, which exists in the highest possible manner, and which occupies the lowest place, yet is within the range of existence, and which occupies the middle place, greater than the lowest, but coming short of the highest. That highest is essential blessedness; the lowest, that which cannot be either blessed or wretched, and the intermediate nature lives in wretchedness when it stoops towards that which is lowest, and in blessedness when it turns towards that which is highest. He who believes in Christ does not sink his affections in that which is lowest, is not proudly self-sufficient in that which is intermediate, and thus he is qualified for union and fellowship with that which is highest; and this is the sum of the active life to which we are commanded, admonished, and by holy zeal impelled to aspire.

Translated by J. G. Cunningham

---

[1] Physical, bodily.
[2] Changeable.

The Nature of Good and Evil, from *Enchiridion* (421)

In his further struggles with the problem of evil, Augustine argues first that the fact that there are things of varying goodness makes for a greater goodness of things as a whole than if there weren't such variety. And he further argues that evil is not something fully real but only something dependent on that which is more real, as disease (which is an evil) can exist only in a body (which is a good). Thus God, as the source of all that is, is not in contest with a positive being or an ultimate reality which is evil and would be His counterpart. Though Augustine's ideas were bold and daring, they troubled many later Christians who felt they were unable to reconcile them with the existence of sn, Satan, and damnation. Yet variations on this theme continue to be popular: what we perceive to be evil is, in some ultimate sense, good. (It should be noted that the classic "problem of evil" exists only in those religions like Christianity, Judaism, and Islam in which there is believed to be a single, good, almighty god; and is absent in other world religions.)

According to Augustine, what happens to vices when they are not residing in a human soul? Can you find any flaws in his analogy of evil with disease? (Remember: Augustine could not have known about germs and viruses!)

By the Trinity,[1] thus supremely and equally and unchangeably good, all things were created; and these are not supremely equally and unchangeably good, but yet they are good, even taken separately. Taken as a whole, however, they are very good, because their ensemble constitutes the universe in all its wonderful order and beauty.

And in the universe, even that which is called evil, when it is regulated and put in its own place, only enhances our admiration of the good; for we enjoy and value the good more when we compare it with the evil. For the almighty God, who, as even the heathen acknowledge, has supreme power over all things, being Himself supremely good, would never permit the existence of anything evil among His works, if He were not so omnipotent and good that He can bring good even out of evil. For what is that which we call evil but the absence of good? In the bodies of animals, disease and wounds mean nothing but the absence of health; for when a cure is effected, that does not mean that the evils which were present—namely, the diseases and wounds—go away from the body and dwell elsewhere: they altogether cease to exist; for the wound or disease is not a substance,[2] but a defect in the fleshly substance—the flesh itself being a substance, and therefore something good, of which those evils—that is, privations of the good which we call health—are accidents.[3] Just in the same way, what are called vices in the soul are nothing but privations of natural good. And when they are not transferred elsewhere: when they cease to exist in the healthy soul, they cannot exist anywhere else.

Translated by J. F. Shaw

---

[1] The Father, Son, and Holy Spirit.

[2] "Substance" is a technical term, meaning that which endures through time even though it may undergo certain changes of quality or of state. The substance is thus more real than are its changeable features;.

[3] "Accident," too, is a technical term, meaning not "happening by chance" but rather "those qualities or states of a thing which might have been different than they are." Thus accidents can only exist if there is something more real of which they can be the features.

The City of God (426 CE)

St. Augustine is remembered for bringing into philosophy from the Judeo-Christian tradition a sense of history and novelty which the Greeks and their philosophers had never had. This comes out particularly as he reflects on the fall of Rome all around him. His philosophical/theological doctrine is couched in terms of the "two cities": Rome (or the new Babylon), which symbolizes all that is worldly, and Jerusalem (the city of heaven), which symbolizes the Christian community. Our world was created in the beginning, fell away from God, and then was redeemed by Christ; thus Augustine sees the world in which he lives as a mixture of the two cities. But the temporal city of this world will eventually perish, giving way to the eternal city. As he introduces this idea, he draws on Paul's notion of "original sin" derived from the rebellion of Adam and Eve to explain how the lesser, flawed "city" came into being.

What does he say God's purpose was in creating all of humanity out of one single original being? Greed (and perhaps pride), envy, and power characterize the "second city" (or the second way of life). What are their positive counterparts in the "first city"?

The Nature of the Two Cities, The Earthly and the Heavenly

Accordingly, two cities have been formed by two loves: the earthly by the love of self, even to the contempt of God; the heavenly by the love of God, even to the contempt of self. The former, in a word, glories in itself, the latter in the Lord. For the one seeks glory from men; but the greatest glory of the other is God, the witness of conscience. The one lifts up its head in its own glory; the other says to its God, "Thou art my glory, and the lifter up of mine head."[1] In the one, the princes and the nations it subdues are ruled by the love of ruling; in the other, the princes and the subjects serve one another in love, the latter obeying, while the former take thought for all. The one delights in its own strength, represented in the persons of its rulers; the other says to its God, "I will love Thee, O Lord, my strength."[2] And therefore the wise men of the one city, living according to man, have sought for profit to their own bodies or souls, or both, and those who have known God "glorified Him not as God, neither were thankful, but became vain in their imaginations, and their foolish heart was darkened; professing themselves to be wise,"—that is, glorying in their own wisdom, and being possessed by pride,—"they became fools, and changed the glory of the incorruptible man, and to birds, and four-footed beasts, and creeping things." For they were either leaders or followers of the people in adoring images, "and worshipped and served the creature more than the Creator, who is blessed for ever."[3] But in the other city there is no human wisdom, but only godliness, which offers due worship to the true God, and looks for its reward in the society of the saints, of holy angels as well as holy men, "that God may be all in all."[4]

---

[1]Psalms 3:3
[2]Psalms 18:1
[3]Romans 1:21–25
[4]1 Corinthians 15:28

How the Two Cities Differ

We have already stated in the preceding books that God, desiring not only that the human race might be able by their similarity of nature to associate with one another, but also that they might be bound together in harmony and peace by the ties of relationship, was pleased to derive all men from one individual, and created man with such a nature that the members of the race should not have died, had not the two first (of whom the one was created out of nothing, and the other out of him) merited this by their disobedience; for by them so great a sin was committed that by it human nature was altered for the worse, and was transmitted also to their posterity, liable to sin and subject to death. And the kingdom of death so reigned over men, that the deserved penalty of sin would have hurled all head-long even into the second death, of which there is no end, had not the undeserved grace of God saved some therefrom. And thus it has come to pass that, though there are very many and great nations all over the earth, whose rites and customs, speech, arms, and dress, are distinguished by marked differences, yet there are no more than two kinds of human society, which we may justly call two cities, according to the language of our Scriptures. The one consists of those who wish to live after the flesh, the other of those who wish to live after the spirit; and when they severally achieve what they wish, they live in peace, each after its kind.

Translated by Marcus Dods

India

Hymns from the *Rig Veda*

Of the several Vedic texts, the Rig Veda *is most fundamental to Indian thought, the others dealing with more particular matters such as the sacrificial formulas, melodies, and magic. Composed over a long period of time and coming into their present form between 1500 and 1000 BCE, the Vedic hymns were eventually attributed to the divine breath or to a vision of the seers. All of the selections from the Vedas are translated by Michael Myers.*

Creation Hymn

A time is envisioned when the world was not, only a watery chaos (the dark, "indistinguishable sea") and a warm cosmic breath, which could give an impetus of life. Notice how thought gives rise to desire (when something is thought of it can then be desired) and desire links non-being to being (we desire what is not but then try to bring it into being). Yet the whole process is shrouded in mystery.

Where do the gods fit in this creation scheme? What about this hymn is similar to the Hebrew creation story? What is different?

The nonexistent was not; the existent was not at that time. The atmosphere was not nor the heavens which are beyond. What was concealed? Where? In whose protection? Was it water? An unfathomable abyss?

There was neither death nor immortality then. There was not distinction of day or night. That alone breathed windless by its own power. Other than that there was not anything else.

Darkness was hidden by darkness in the beginning. All this was an indistinguishable sea. That which becomes, that which was enveloped by the void, that alone was born through the power of heat.

Upon that, desire arose in the beginning. This was the first discharge of thought. Sages discovered this link of the existent to the nonexistent, having searched in the heart with wisdom.

Their line [of vision] was extended across; what was below, what was above? There were impregnators, there were powers: inherent power below, impulses above.

Who knows truly? Who here will declare whence it arose, whence this creation? The gods are subsequent to the creation of this. Who, then, knows whence it has come into being?

Whence this creation has come into being; whether it was made or not; he in the highest heaven is its surveyor. Surely he knows, or perhaps he knows not.

To Agni (Fire)

Agni, the god of fire, whose name is the common word for fire, is a terrestrial deity, only loosely anthropomorphic. He is most often compared to animals, with wood for his food and clarified butter for his drink. He is the mouth by which the gods consume those items during the sacrifice. He is born from wood (as two sticks are rubbed together), but then devours his parents. As "Lord of the House," he is a guest in human dwellings in the form of the domestic fire.

How is Agni supposed to "bring the gods here"?

I call upon Agni, the one placed in front, the divine priest of the sacrifice, the invoker, the best bestower of gifts.

Agni is worthy of being called upon by seers past and present: may he bring the gods here!

Through Agni may one obtain wealth and prosperity day by day, splendid and abounding in heroic sons.

O Agni, the sacrifice and work of the sacrifice, which you encompass on all sides—that alone goes to the gods.

May Agni, the invoker who has the powers of a sage, true and most brilliant in glory, come here, a god with the gods!

Whatsoever favor you wish to do for a worshipper, Agni, that favor of yours surely comes true, O Angiras [member of a priestly family].

O Agni, you who gleam in the darkness, to you we come day by day, with devotion and bearing homage;

To you, ruler of the sacrifices, keeper of the Rta [cosmic law], brightly shining, growing in your abode.

So, be of easy access to us, Agni, as a father to his son. Abide with us for our well-being.

To Indra

Indra is a sky god and a war god who holds the earth and the heavens apart, on occasion making the earth tremble. As the counterpart of Zeus for the Greeks or Jupiter for the Romans, he is the god of the thunderstorm, who vanquishes drought and darkness. He is the most frequently mentioned god in the Vedas, the most nationalistic, and the most anthropomorphic. The serpent which he slew was a demon of drought, who had bottled up the streams; but Indra shattered the mountain, releasing the streams like pent up cows. "The lowly Dasa color" whom he has "put in hiding" presumably refers to the indigenous peoples of northern India who had been overcome by the Aryan invaders and either moved into the forests or migrated southward.

What is Indra supposed to do for the weary, the weak, the needy priest (a Brahman, of course) and the singer?

The one who is first and possessed of wisdom when born; the god who strove to protect the gods with strength; the one before whose force the two worlds were afraid because of the greatness of his virility: he, O people, is Indra.

The one who made firm the quaking earth; the one who made fast the shaken mountains; the one who measured out wide the atmosphere; the one who propped up heaven: he, O people, is Indra.

127

The one who, having killed the serpent, released the seven rivers; the one who drove out
the cows by undoing Vala,[1] the one who generates fire between two rocks, victor in
battles: he, O people, is Indra.

The one by whom all things here were made moving; the one who put in hiding the
lowly Dasa color; the one who, like a gambler who has won the stake, has taken the
enemy's possessions: he, O people, is Indra.

The one who is the terrible one, about whom they ask "Where is he?" and they say of
him, "He is not!" He diminished the enemy's possessions like stakes [at a game]. Put
your faith in him: he, O people, is Indra.

The one who is the impeller of the weary, of the weak, of the Brahman seeking aid, the
singer; the one with goodly mustaches who is the helper of him who works the stones,
who has pressed the Soma[2]: he, O people, is Indra.

The one in whose control are horses, cows, villages, all chariots; the one who has caused
to be born the sun, the dawn; the one who is the waters' leader: he, O people, is
Indra.

The one whom the two lines of battle, coming together, call upon separately, the nearer
and the farther, both foes; even the two who have mounted the same chariot call upon
him individually: he, O people, is Indra.

The one without whom people do not conquer; the one to whom, when fighting, they
call for help; the one who is a match for everyone; the one who shakes the unshakable:
he, O people, is Indra.

---

[1]The cave in which the cattle were imprisoned.

[2]A beverage made from the juice of a plant (probably a hallucinogenic mushroom) and
used in religious ceremonies; also a god.

Purusa, the Cosmic Person

This is one of the latest compositions in the Rig Veda, as it suggests a sort of pantheistic philosophy. Purusa is a cosmic giant, of whom the gods and the cosmos itself are composed; yet he is also the object of the sacrifice to the gods. From him then are derived the gods in the heaven and, from the remainder, all the rest of what is, both the living and the nonliving.

The top four castes are supposed to have been derived from Purusa: the Brahmans, the Rajanya (or Kshatriya), the Vaisya, and the Sudra. Which body parts are associated with each group, and what seems to be the significance of those parts?

Thousand-headed is Purusa, thousand-eyed, thousand-footed. Having covered the earth on all sides, he stood above it the width of ten fingers.

Only Purusa is all this, that which has been and that which is to be. He is the lord of the immortals, who grow by means of [ritual] food.

Such is his greatness, yet more than this is Purusa. One-quarter of him is all beings; three-quarters of him is the immortal in heaven.

Three-quarters of Purusa went upward, one-quarter of him remained here. From this [one-quarter] he spread in all directions into what eats and what does not eat.

From him the shining one was born, from the shining one was born Purusa. When born he extended beyond the earth, behind as well as in front.

When the gods performed a sacrifice with the offering Purusa, spring was its clarified butter, summer the kindling, autumn the oblation.

It was Purusa, born in the beginning, which they sprinkled on the sacred grass as a sacrifice. With him the gods sacrificed, the demi-gods, and the seers.

From that sacrifice completely offered, the clotted butter was brought together. It made the beasts of the air, the forest and the village.

From that sacrifice completely offered, the mantras [Rig Veda] and the songs [Samaveda] were born. The meters were born from it. The sacrificial formulae [Yajurveda] were born from it.

From it the horses were born and all that have cutting teeth in both jaws. The cows were born from it, also. From it were born goats and sheep.

When they divided Purusa, how many ways did they apportion him? What was his mouth? What were his arms? What were his thighs, his feet declared to be?

His mouth was the Brahman [caste], his arms were the Rajanaya [Kshatriya caste], his thighs the Vaisya [caste]; from his feet the Sudra [caste] was born.

The moon was born from his mind; from his eye the sun was born; from his mouth both Indra and Agni [fire]; from his breath Vayu [wind] was born.

From his navel arose the air; from his head the heaven evolved; from his feet the earth; the [four] directions from his ear. Thus, they fashioned the worlds.

Seven were his altar sticks, three times seven were the kindling bundles, when the gods, performing the sacrifice, bound the beast Purusa.

The gods sacrificed with the sacrifice to the sacrifice. These were the first rites. These powers reached the firmament, where the ancient demi-gods and the gods are.

The *Chandogya Upanishad* on Brahman and Atman

The Upanishads developed as part of a reform movement within Indian religion, when devout individuals sought to escape the dry formalism of ceremonial religion and the power of the Brahmans. The texts are more philosophical in their scope, and they avoid talking anthropomorphically of the transcendent. Brahman is at one and the same time the whole universe and our individual souls.

What images or comparisons are used to try to describe both the largeness and all-encompassing nature of Brahman on the one hand, and the particularity and closeness of Brahman to us on the other?

Great is the Gayatri, the most sacred verse of the Vedas; but how much greater is the Infinity of Brahman! A quarter of his being is this whole vast universe: the other three quarters are his heaven of Immortality.

There is a light that shines beyond all things on earth, beyond us all, beyond the heavens, beyond the highest, the very highest heavens. This is the Light that shines in our heart.

All this universe is in the truth Brahman. He is the beginning and end and life of all. As such, in silence, give unto him adoration.

Man in truth is made of faith. As his faith is in this life, so he becomes in the beyond: with faith and vision let him work.

There is a Spirit that is mind and life, light and truth and vast spaces. He contains all works and desires and all perfumes and all tastes. He enfolds the whole universe, and in silence is loving to all.

This is the Spirit that is mind and life, light and truth, and vast spaces. He contains all works and desires and all perfumes and all tastes. He enfolds the whole universe, and in silence is loving to all.

This is the Spirit that is in my heart, smaller than a grain of rice, or a grain of barley, or a grain of mustard-seed, or a grain of canary-seed, or the kernel of a grain of canary seed. This is the Spirit that is in my heart, greater than the earth, greater than the sky, greater than heaven itself, greater than all these worlds.

He contains all works and all perfumes and all tastes. He enfolds the whole universe and in silence is loving to all. This is the Spirit that is in my heart, this is Brahman.

To him I shall come when I go beyond this life. And to him will come he who has faith and doubts not. Thus said Sandilya, thus said Sandilya.

Translated by Juan Mascaro

The *Upanishads* on Karma and Reincarnation

The Upanishads also teach the doctrines of karma and reincarnation, namely, that our character is developed in this life by the actions which we perform. But we will be reborn in another life, moving up or down the scale of sentient beings according to how well or poorly we lived this time around. Thus moral behavior is encouraged by a belief in reincarnation.

What hope is held out for an individual to escape from a constant repetition of the birth/death/birth cycle?

According as a man acts and walks in the path of life, so he becomes. He that does good becomes good; he that does evil becomes evil. By pure actions he becomes pure; by evil actions he becomes evil.

And they say in truth that a man is made of desire. As his desire is, so is his faith. As his faith is, so are his works. As his works are, so he becomes. It was said in this verse:

A man comes with his actions to the end of his determination.

Reaching the end of the journey begun by his works on earth, from that world a man returns to this world of human action. Thus far for the man who lives under desire.

Now as to the man who is free from desire.

He who is free from desire, whose desire finds fulfillment, since the Spirit is his desire, the powers of life leave him not. He becomes one with Brahman, the Spirit, and enters into the Spirit. There is a verse that says:

When all desires that cling to the heart disappear, then a mortal becomes immortal, and even in this life attains liberation.

As the slough of a snake lies dead upon an ant-hill, even so the mortal body; but the incorporeal immortal spirit is life and light and eternity. . . .

While we are here in this life we may reach the light of wisdom; and if we reach it not, how deep is the darkness. Those who see the light enter life eternal: those who live in darkness enter into sorrow.

When a man sees the Atman, the Self in him, God himself, the Lord of what was and of what shall be, he fears no more.

Before whom the years roll and all the days of the years, him the gods adore as the Light of all lights, as Life immortal;

In whom the five hosts of beings rest and the vastness of space, him I know as Atman immortal, him I know as eternal Brahman.

Those who know him who is the eye of the eye, the ear of the ear, the mind of the mind and the life of life, they know Brahman from the beginning of time.

Even by the mind this truth must be seen: there are not many but only One. Who sees variety and not the Unity wanders on from death to death.

Behold then as One the infinite and eternal One who is in radiance beyond space, the everlasting Soul never born.

Knowing this, let the lover of Brahman follow wisdom. Let him not ponder on many words, for many words are weariness.

Translated by Juan Mascaro

The *Bhagavad Gita* (2nd Century CE)

The title means "song of the Lord," and the text was a late addition to the great epic, The
Mahabharata, *which tells the story of two branches of a noble family fighting for power as each
claims the right to the throne. At one point in the struggle Arjuna, a warrior, is hesitating about
pursuing the fight. He enters into dialogue with his charioteer, who is actually the god Krishna
(Krishna himself being one manifestation of Vishnu, the savior god of Indian religion).*

*Krishna offers Arjuna not just one but a series of justifications. He appeals first to the doctrine
of reincarnation, arguing that death is not ultimate, since one will be born again. Secondly, he
ties this to the claim that the real Self is to be distinguished from the person who can be seen and
heard at the moment—in effect, an appeal to the distinction between appearance and reality.
Thirdly, he points to the inevitability of death, and fourthly, to the particular duty [dharma]
which belongs to a warrior. Finally, he broadens out the discussion by a consideration of the
principles of yoga. Two types are particularly cited: action of a disinterested and non-profiteering
sort, and meditation or contemplation which quells the senses and the desires. But a third type of
yoga can also be discerned,* bhakti *or devotional yoga, as Krishna extols the lives of those who
"keep their minds ever absorbed in me" (i.e., devoted to Krishna himself).*

*How is Krishna's claim that "the impermanent has no reality" supposed to help Arjuna? What
is* jnana yoga, *and what is* karma yoga?

The War Within

SANJAYA
And Arjuna, standing between the two armies, saw fathers and grandfathers, teachers,
uncles, and brothers, sons and grandsons, in-laws and friends. Seeing his kinsmen established in opposition, Arjuna was overcome by sorrow. Despairing, he spoke these words:

ARJUNA
O Krishna, I see my own relations here anxious to fight, and my limbs grow weak; my
mouth is dry, my body shakes, and my hair is standing on end. My skin burns, and the
bow Gandiva has slipped from my hand. I am unable to stand; my mind seems to be
whirling. These signs bode evil for us. I do not see that any good can come from killing our
relations in battle. . . . Surely it would be better to spend my life begging than to kill these
great and worthy souls! If I killed them, every pleasure I found would be tainted. I don't
even know which would be better, for us to conquer them or for them to conquer us. . . .
My will is paralyzed, and I am utterly confused. Tell me which is the better path for me,
Let me be your disciple. I have fallen at your feet; give me instruction. What can overcome
a sorrow that saps all my vitality? Even power over men and gods or the wealth of an
empire seems empty.

SANJAYA
With the words, "O Krishna, I will not fight," he fell silent.
As they stood between the two armies, Sri Krishna smiled and replied to Arjuna, who
had sunk into despair.

SRI KRISHNA

You speak sincerely, but your sorrow has no cause. The wise grieve neither for the living nor for the dead. There has never been a time when you and I and the kings gathered here have not existed, nor will there be a time when we will cease to exist. As the same person inhabits the body through childhood, youth, and old age, so too at the time of death he attains another body. The wise are not deluded by these changes.

When the senses contact sense objects, a person experiences cold or heat, pleasure or pain. These experiences are fleeting; they come and go. Bear them patiently, Arjuna. Those who are not affected by these changes, who are the same in pleasure and pain, are truly wise and fit for immortality. Assert your strength and realize this!

The impermanent has no reality; reality lies in the eternal. Those who have seen the boundary between these two have attained the end of all knowledge. Realize that which pervades the universe and is indestructible; no power can affect this unchanging, imperishable reality. The body is mortal, but he who dwells in the body is immortal and immeasurable. Therefore, Arjuna, fight in this battle.

One man believes he is the slayer, another believes he is the slain. Both are ignorant; there is neither slayer nor slain. You were never born; you will never die. You have never changed; you can never change. Unborn, eternal, immutable, immemorial, you do not die when the body dies. Realizing that which is indestructible, eternal, unborn, and unchanging, how can you slay or cause another to slay?

As a man abandons worn-out clothes and acquires new ones, so when the body is worn out a new one is acquired by the Self, who lives within.

The Self cannot be pierced by weapons or burned by fire; water cannot wet it, nor can the wind dry it. The Self cannot be pierced or burned, made wet or dry. It is everlasting and infinite, standing on the motionless foundations of eternity. The Self is unmanifested, beyond all thought, beyond all change. Knowing this, you should not grieve.

O mighty Arjuna, even if you believe the Self to be subject to birth and death, you should not grieve. Death is inevitable for the living; birth is inevitable for the dead. Since these are unavoidable, you should not sorrow. Every creature is unmanifested at first and then attains manifestation. When its end has come, it once again becomes unmanifested. What is there to lament in this? . . .

Considering your dharma, you should not vacillate. For a warrior, nothing is higher than a war against evil. The warrior confronted with such a war should be pleased, Arjuna, for it comes as an open gate to heaven. But if you do not participate in this battle against evil you will incur sin, violating your dharma and your honor. . . .

Therefore rise up, Arjuna, resolved to fight! Having made yourself alike in pain and pleasure, profit and loss, victory and defeat, engage in this great battle and you will be freed from sin.

You have heard the intellectual explanation of Sankhya, Arjuna; now listen to the principles of yoga. By practicing these you can break through the bonds of karma. On this path effort never goes to waste, and there is no failure. Even a little effort toward spiritual awareness will protect you from the greatest fear. . . .

You have the right to work, but never to the fruit of work. You should never engage in action for the sake of reward, nor should you long for inaction. Perform work in this world, Arjuna, as a man established within himself—without selfish attachments, and alike in success and defeat. For yoga is perfect evenness of mind.

Seek refuge in the attitude of detachment and you will amass the wealth of spiritual awareness. Those who are motivated only by desire for the fruits of action are miserable, for they are constantly anxious about the results of what they do. When consciousness is unified, however, all vain anxiety is left behind. There is no cause for worry, whether things go well or ill. Therefore, devote yourself to the disciplines of yoga, for yoga is skill in action.

The wise unify their consciousness and abandon attachment to the fruits of action, which binds a person to continual rebirth. Thus they attain a state beyond all evil.

When your mind has overcome the confusion of duality, you will attain the state of holy indifference to things you hear and things you have heard. When you are unmoved by the confusion of ideas and your mind is completely united in deep samadhi, you will attain the state of perfect yoga. . . . [The wise] see themselves in all and all in them, who have renounced every selfish desire and sense craving tormenting the heart.

Neither agitated by grief nor hankering after pleasure, they live free from lust and fear and anger. Established in meditation, they are truly wise. Fettered no more by selfish attachments, they are neither elated by good fortune nor depressed by bad. Such are the seers. Even as a tortoise draws in its limbs, the wise can draw in their senses at will. Aspirants abstain from sense pleasures, but they still crave for them. These cravings all disappear when they see the highest goal. Even of those who tread the path, the stormy senses can sweep off the mind. They live in wisdom who subdue their senses and keep their minds ever absorbed in me. . . .

Selfless Service

ARJUNA
O Krishna, you have said that knowledge is greater than action; why then do you ask me to wage this terrible war? Your advice seems inconsistent. Give me one path to follow to the supreme good.

SRI KRISHNA
At the beginning of time I declared two paths for the pure heart: Jnana yoga, the contemplative path of spiritual wisdom, and karma yoga, the active path of selfless service. He who shirks action does not attain freedom; no one can gain perfection by abstaining from work. Indeed, there is no one who rests for even an instant; every creature is driven to action by his own nature.

Those who abstain from action while allowing the mind to dwell on sensual pleasure cannot be called sincere spiritual aspirants. But they excel who control their senses through the mind, using them for selfless service.

Fulfill all your duties; action is better than inaction. Even to maintain your body, Arjuna, you are obliged to act. Selfish action imprisons the world. Act selflessly, without any thought of personal profit.

At the beginning, mankind and the obligation of selfless service were created together. "Through selfless service, you will always be fruitful and find the fulfillment of your desires"; this is the promise of the creator. . . .

ARJUNA
What is the force that binds us to selfish deeds, O Krishna? What power moves us, even against our will, as if forcing us?

SRI KRISHNA

It is selfish desire and anger, arising from the guna of rajas; these are the appetites and evils which threaten a person in this life.

Just as a fire is covered by smoke and a mirror is obscured by dust, just as the embryo rests deep within the womb, knowledge is hidden by selfish desire—ridden, Arjuna, by this unquenchable fire for self-satisfaction, the inveterate enemy of the wise.

Selfish desire is found in the senses, mind, and intellect, misleading them and burying the understanding in delusion. Fight with all your strength, Arjuna! Controlling your senses, conquer your enemy, the destroyer of knowledge and realization.

The senses are higher than the body, the mind higher than the senses; above the mind is the intellect, and above the intellect is the Atman. Thus, knowing that which is supreme, let the Atman rule the ego. Use your mighty arms to slay the fierce enemy that is selfish desire.

Translated by Eknath Easwaran.

Sanskrit Poetry

Selections from the *Treasury* of Vidyakara (11th Century CE)

Vidyakara's Treasury is an anthology of brief poems of all kinds, written in many periods in Sanskrit, and organized by general theme. They give a widely varied impression of life and faith in ancient India. Little is known about the poets whose names are attached to each verse. Except where otherwise noted, the translations are by Daniel H. H. Ingalls.

Kesata: *Somewhere in Space*

This poem contrasts interestingly with the human-centered vision of the universe in Genesis, teeming with life. The Hindu emphasis on the ultimate unreality of the physical world makes the void surrounding it more significant than the earth itself. Coincidentally, it results in a vision of the universe not unlike that held by modern astronomers.

Compare this vision of the universe with that in the first chapter of Genesis.

Somewhere in Space is set the universe
with here the earth, there clouds,
here oceans garlanded by continents
and there the mountain ranges.
How marvelous it is that Space should be so great
that far from being filled by all these substances
its very name allows it to be void.

Ratnakirti: Hymn to the Buddha

Like Christ, the Buddha is here depicted both as ruler of the world and as compassionate savior.

What images make the Buddha seem appealing?

All conquering is the Savior of the World.
His lotus hand, stretched down in charity,
is dripping streams of nectar to assuage
the thirsty spirits of the dead.
His glorious face is bright with gathered moonlight
and his glance is soft
with that deep pity that he bears within.

Utpalaraja: *I pray that I may have before me songsters*

This poem seems to present a rather cynical view of Hindu ideals: the poet is willing to accept release from the cycle of rebirth and enter Brahma if more earthly pleasures are not available.

What are the pleasures the poet wants to experience?

I pray that I may have before me songsters,
beside the tasteful poets from the South
and behind me girls whose graceful bracelets
jingle as they wave the fly whisk.
If this should be, be greedy, heart,
to taste the world.
If it, however, should not be,
then enter highest Brahma.

Vatoka: *Fireflies weave the garment of the night*

Vatoka's lyrics belong to a long tradition of ancient Sanskrit love-poetry concerned with nature on the one hand, and with the ardent and forceful passions of a lover, on the other. The following lyric exemplifies such concerns, where images are drawn from nature to suggest a lover's intense desire for a physical union which, however, remains unfulfilled due to separation of the lovers.

Which nature images suggest a lover's sexual desire for union?

Fireflies weave the garment of the night
and lightning flirts with the sky,
while elephants of clouds rut and roar
and jasmine fragrance benumbs the wind.
But, O dear, do they make any difference
to a lover who only sighs in separation?

Translated by Azfar Hussain

Anonymous: *Summer Poem*

In traditional European poetry, spring and summer are treated as much the same thing; but in the tropics distinctive images are associated with summer as poets seek relief from the oppressive heat. It was customary to smear the body with cooling, sweet-smelling potions. Coolness is the opposite of passion in Western poetry; but in India they could be synonymous. The poet claims that the essence of this delightful sensation is now found only in making love with his sweetheart..

Coolness, which stayed a while beneath the waters,
made brief acquaintance with unguent of sandalwood,
set foot on lily stems and moonlight,
and rested later in the shade of tasty plantains,
now is found alone
within my sweetheart's arms.

137

Utpalaraja: *The clouds, torpid from the much water they have drunk*

The imagery of this poem, dwelling on the sounds of raindrops and croaking frogs in the night, describes a natural phenomenon somewhat like a Japanese haiku. *Early in the night, the pouring rain drowns out all other sounds, but when it clears, the frogs can sing unrivalled.*

The clouds, torpid from the much water they have drunk,
let fall the rain in steady streams
till sleep comes to our eyes from the sound of downpour.
When men then sleeping in every house are silent,
the sound of frogs, swelling without rival,
turns night to uproar.

Subhanga(?): *Rich is he who drinks his bride's red-lotus lip*

Romance in Western literature often culminates in marriage, but there are few love poems set after marriage. In a society where arranged marriages are the norm, it is the blossoming of love within marriage which is often the focus of poetry. The rainy season in India was seen as a time for lovemaking; then the torrential downpours made it impossible to work out of doors, and people turned to indoor pleasures, welcoming the cooling rain.

Rich is he who drinks his bride's red-lotus lip
in a roof pavilion screened by mats against the rain,
their amorous murmurs mingling with the sound of moorhens
wakened in their baskets by the driving downpour.[1]

---

[1] The captive moorhens hear the rain on their basket as the lovers hear the rain on their thatched roof.

Yogesvara: Early Winter Poem

India is not all tropical heat. In the north, winter can be distinctly chilly; and in the mountains, there is snow. Winter is always a hard time for peasants as food supplies for both humans and their animals shrink; but this poem is written from the point of view of a wealthy traveler, upset at the seasonal rise in the price of straw.

Compare this with one of the other poems in this volume about the life of poor people.

The peasants now grow haughty,
being flattered by a hundred travelers for their straw;
at night the cows in calf, chewing the cud,
keep warm the herdsmen with their breath;
at dawn the first rays of the sun play on the great bull's back
as he lies covered with mustard flower
and eyelids thick with frost upon the village common.

Anonymous: *The religious student carries a small and torn umbrella*

Although Hinduism idealizes asceticism as a spiritual path to liberation, Hindus still feel compassion for the poor and suffering, as is expressed in these three poems. India is famous for its beggars. It should be equally famous for its charity. The Brahman of the last line of the first poem is probably his spiritual teacher.

The religious student carries a small and torn umbrella;
his various possessions are tied about his waist;
he has tucked *bilva* leaves in his topknot;
his neck is drawn, his belly frightening from its sunkenness.
Weary with much walking, he somehow stills
the pain of aching feet and goes at evening
to the brahman's house to chop his wood.

Anonymous: *The children starving*

Among the worst sufferings of poverty is the sense of shame it brings.

The children starving, looking like so many corpses,
the relative who spurns me, the water pot
patched up with lac[1]—these do not hurt so much
as seeing the woman from next door, annoyed
and smiling scornfully when every day my wife
must beg a needle to mend her tattered dress.

---

[1]A substance derived from insects, commonly used in dyes.

Sabdarnava: *Those who feel pity for the poor*

In this poem charity is compared to another high virtue: control of the passions.

Those who feel pity for the poor:
who hold not the slightest pride in wealth;
who even when they are tired, if asked,
are glad to help their neighbor;
who keep their reason
even when that mortal fever, youth, is at its height:
such good men, although they are but few,
are the true spots of beauty that ornament the earth.

Vidyapati (1352?-1448): Love Songs to Krishna

Vidyapati was born in the village of Bisapi in Madhubani, on the eastern side of north Bihar. Courtier, scholar, and prose-writer, Vidyapati, though a Bengali poet, is primarily known for his love-lyrics composed in Maithili, a language spoken in the towns and villages of Mithila. In the well-known tradition of the Kama Sutra *and the influential early Indian poem called* Gita Govinda *by Jayadeva, Vidyapati's love-songs re-create and reveal the world of Radha and Krishna, the major erotic figures of Indian mythology and literature. Such poems convey the devotion of Krishna's worshippers through the metaphor of human erotic love. While Jayadeva's poem celebrates Krishna's love and pays comparatively little attention to Radha the woman, Vidyapati is primarily concerned with the intense passion of Radha's love. At once sensuous and sensual, descriptive and dramatic, Vidyapati's songs range beyond the mythological only to find their place in the heart of a human lover whose dreams and desires never die, whose sighs and cries never end.*

In this poem, Krishna expresses his devotion to Radha, his principal consort. Bites and finger-nail marks are considered signs of passion in Indian tradition (the Kama Sutra *devotes an entire chapter to the different patterns that may be made by fingernails on the lover's skin; the associations are not sadistic, but more like "hickeys" in American tradition). The language is violent, to express the power of the union between worshipper and god; but note how the god plays the submissive role in this poem, almost as if he were worshipping the human woman.*

For heaven's sake, listen, listen, O my darling

Considering what is said in the introduction above, how could you interpret some of these lines in religious terms?

For heaven's sake, listen, listen, O my darling;
Do not dart your cruel, angry glances at me,
For I swear by the lovely pitchers of your breasts,
And by your golden, glittering, snake-like necklace:
If ever on earth I dare touch anyone except you,
Let your necklace turn into a real snake, and bite me;
And if ever my promise and words prove false,
Chastise me, O darling, in the way you want to.
But, now, don't hesitate to take me in your arms,
Bind, bind my thirsty body with yours; bruise me
With your thighs, and bite, bite me with your teeth.
Let your fingernails dig deep, deep into my skin!
Strangle me, for heaven's sake, with your breasts,
And lock me in the prison of your body forever!

All my inhibition left me in a flash

Krishna is a playful god, associated with tricks and games. In one of the most famous incidents in the Krishna legend, he steals the clothing of a group of bathing cowherds' wives (gopis) and exhorts them to come forth from the water to reveal themselves. The religious significance of this incident is that the believer must not hold back from uniting fully with the divine, must be utterly devoted to the god. Similar attitudes are expressed in the following poem in relation to Radha.

What different emotions are expressed in this poem?

All my inhibition left me in a flash,
When he robbed me of my clothes,
But his body became my new dress.
Like a bee hovering on a lotus leaf
He was there in my night, on me!

True, the god of love never hesitates!
He is free and determined like a bird
Winging toward the clouds it loves.
Yet I remember the mad tricks he played,
My heart restlessly burning with desire
Was yet filled with fear!

He promised he'd return tomorrow

In the final poem, Radha has to deal with her jealousy. Krishna is the lover of all women (representing all humanity), and she cannot hope to keep him to herself.

What functions do you think such a poem as this might play in a polygamous society? Does it express women's feelings, or teach how they should feel?

He promised he'd return tomorrow.
 And I wrote everywhere on my floor:
"Tomorrow."

The morning broke, when they all asked:
Now tell us, when will your "Tomorrow" come?
Tomorrow, Tomorrow, where are you?
I cried and cried, but my Tomorrow never returned!

Vidyapati says: O listen, dear!
Your Tomorrow became a today
with other women.

Translated by Azfar Hussain

141

Kautilya: *The Arthashastra* (4th Century BCE)

This treatise on government is said to have been written by the prime minister of India's first great emperor, Chandragupta Maurya. Although often compared to Machiavelli's Prince *because of its sometimes ruthless approach to practical politics, Kautilya's work is far more varied—and entertaining—than usual accounts of it indicate. He mixes the harsh pragmatism for which he is famed with compassion for the poor, for slaves, and for women. He reveals the imagination of a romancer in imagining all manner of scenarios which can hardly have been commonplace in real life.*

The Institution of Spies

One of the most notorious features of the Arthashastra *is its obsession with spying on the king's subjects. Kautilya sometimes goes to amusingly absurd lengths to imagine various sorts of spies. He even cynically proposes using fake holy men for this purpose. Why do you think the emperor felt the need for such an elaborate spy network?*

A man with shaved head or braided hair and desirous to earn livelihood is a spy under the guise of an ascetic practicing austerities. Such a spy surrounded by a host of disciples with shaved head or braided hair may take his abode in the suburbs of a city, and pretend as a person barely living on a handful of vegetables or meadow grass taken once in the interval of a month or two, but he may take in secret his favorite foodstuffs.

Merchant spies pretending to be his disciples may worship him as one possessed of preternatural powers. His other disciples may widely proclaim that "This ascetic is an accomplished expert of preternatural powers."

Regarding those persons who, desirous of knowing their future, throng to him, he may, through palmistry, foretell such future events as he can ascertain by the nods and signs of his disciples concerning the works of high-born people of the country—*viz.* small profits, destruction by fire, fear from robbers, the execution of the seditious, rewards for the good, forecast of foreign affairs, saying, "This will happen to-day, that to-morrow, and that this king will do." Such assertions of the ascetic his disciples shall corroborate (by adducing facts and figures).[1]

He shall also foretell not only the rewards which persons possessed of foresight, eloquence, and bravery are likely to receive at the hands of the king, but also probable changes in the appointments of ministers.

The king's minister shall direct his affairs in conformity to the forecast made by the ascetic. He shall appease with offer of wealth and honor those who have had some well-known cause to be disaffected, and impose punishments in secret on those who are for no reason disaffected or who are plotting against the king.

---

[1] Of course these prophets, being in the employ of the King, have reason to know what he intends to do.

Formation of Villages

Far from being single-mindedly aimed at preserving the monarch's power for its own sake, like Machiavelli's The Prince, *the* Arthashastra *requires the ruler to benefit and protect his citizens, including the peasants, whom Kautilya correctly believes to be the ultimate source of the prosperity of the kingdom. He therefore advocates what is now called "land reform."*

What practical argument does Kautilya offer the king for supporting poor farmers?

Lands may be confiscated from those who do not cultivate them and given to others; or they may be cultivated by village laborers and traders, lest those owners who do not properly cultivate them might pay less (to the government). If cultivators pay their taxes easily, they may be favorably supplied with grains, cattle, and money.

The king shall bestow on cultivators only such favor and remission as will tend to swell the treasury, and shall avoid such as deplete it. . . .

The king shall provide the orphans, the aged, the infirm, the afflicted, and the helpless with maintenance. He shall also provide subsistence to helpless women when they are carrying and also to the children they give birth to.

Elders among the villagers shall improve the property of bereaved minors till the latter attain their age; so also the property of gods.

When a capable person other than an apostate or mother neglects to maintain his or her child, wife, mother, father, minor brothers, sisters, or widowed girls, he or she shall be punished with a fine of twelve panas.

When, without making provision for the maintenance of his wife and sons, any person embraces asceticism, he shall be punished with the first amercement;[1] likewise any person who converts a woman to asceticism.

Whoever has passed the age of copulation may become an ascetic after distributing the properties of his own acquisition (among his sons), otherwise he will be punished.

---

[1]A small fine, between 12 and 96 panas.

Rules Regarding Slaves and Laborers

Slaves were not as common in ancient India as in other civilizations, partly because the lower castes were forced to take on voluntarily many unsavory tasks that would have been performed by slaves elsewhere. However, they did exist, and Kautilya's regulations governing them are among the most liberal in history. Note how upper-caste slaves are protected from demeaning labor that was reserved for the lowest castes, and how the chastity of female slaves is protected (even ancient Judaism and Islam explicitly allowed a master to have sex with his slave women). It is unknown how widely observed these idealistic regulations were.

Compare these laws on slavery with those in Hammurabi's Code and the Hebrew Bible. In what ways did caste affect the way slaves were to be treated?

Deceiving a slave of his money or depriving him of the privileges he can exercise as an Arya,[1] shall be punished with half the fine (levied for enslaving the life of an Arya).

A man who takes in mortgage a person who runs away, or who dies or who is incapacitated by disease, shall be entitled to receive back [from the mortgagor] the value he paid for the slave.

Employing a slave to carry the dead or to sweep ordure, urine, or the leavings of food;[2] or a female slave to attend on her master while he is bathing naked; or hurting or abusing him or her, or violating (the chastity of) a female slave shall cause the forfeiture of the value paid for him or her. Violation [of the chastity] of nurses, female cooks, or female servants of the class of joint cultivators or of any other description shall at once earn their liberty for them. Violence towards an attendant of high birth shall entitle him to run away. When a master has connection with a nurse or pledged female slave under his power against her will, he shall be punished with the first amercement; for doing the same when she is under the power of another, he shall be punished with the middlemost amercement.[3] When a man commits or helps another to commit rape with a girl or a female slave pledged to him, he shall not only forfeit the purchase-value, but also pay a certain amount of money [sulka] to her and a fine of twice the amount [of sulka to the government].

---

[1]Aryan, an upper-caste person, a Brahman.
[2]These are defiling tasks reserved for the so-called "untouchable" castes, who are considered beneath even slaves.
[3]Between 200 and 500 panas.

Capture of the Enemy by Means of Secret Contrivances

Unlike most political treatises, the Arthashastra *makes highly entertaining reading, partly because of the mini-narratives in which Kautilya describes how a king may retain his power or preserve his life after he has been overthrown.*

Contrivances to kill the enemy may be formed in those places of worship and visit, which the enemy, under the influence of faith, frequents on occasions of worshipping gods and of pilgrimage.

A wall or stone, kept by mechanical contrivance, may, by loosening the fastenings, be let to fall on the head of the enemy when he has entered into a temple; stones and weapons may be showered over his head from the topmost story; or a door-panel may be let to fall; or a huge rod kept over a wall or partly attached to a wall may be made to fall over him; or weapons kept inside the body of an idol may be thrown over his head; or the floor of those places where he usually stands, sits, or walks may be besprinkled with poison mixed with cow dung[1] or with pure water; or, under the plea of giving him flowers, scented powders, or of causing scented smoke, he may be poisoned; or by removing the fastenings made under a cot or a seat, he may be made to fall into a pit containing pointed spears. . . .

Or having challenged the conqueror at night, he may successfully confront the attack; if he cannot do this, he may run away by a side path; or, disguised as a heretic, he may escape with a small retinue; or he may be carried off by spies as a corpse; or disguised as a woman, he may follow a corpse [as it were, of her husband to the cremation ground]; or on the occasion of feeding the people in honor of gods or of ancestors or in some festival, he may make use of poisoned rice and water, and having conspired with his enemy's traitors, he may strike the enemy with his concealed army; or, when he is surrounded in his fort, he may lie concealed in a hole bored into the body of an idol after eating sacramental food and setting up an altar; or he may lie in a secret hole in a wall, or in a hole made in the body of an idol in an underground chamber; and when he is forgotten, he may get out of his concealment through a tunnel, and, entering into the palace, slay his enemy while sleeping, or loosening the fastening of a machine he may let it fall on his enemy; or when his enemy is lying in a chamber which is besmeared with poisonous and explosive substances, or which is made of lac, he may set fire to it. Fiery spies, hidden in an underground chamber, or in a tunnel, or inside a secret wall, may slay the enemy when the latter is carelessly amusing himself in a pleasure park or any other place of recreation; or spies under concealment may poison him; or women under concealment may throw a snake, or poison, or fire or poisonous smoke over his person when he is asleep in a confined place; or spies, having access to the enemy's harem, may, when opportunities occur, do to the enemy whatever is found possible on the occasion, and then get out unknown.

Translated by R. Shamasastry

---

[1]Cow dung, like pure water, is considered ritually purifying by Hindus, and is here used to deceive the victim into thinking the poisoned substance is safe.

The Buddha: The First Sermon (Sutra of Turning the Wheel of the Doctrine)

Buddhism arose from the experiences of Gautama Siddhartha, Prince of the Sakya clan of northern India. The Middle Way which he extols lies between the extremes of pursuing pleasure on the one hand and asceticism (or "self-torture") on the other. The Eightfold Path is an outline of how to live successfully on that Middle Way. The Four Noble Truths are the insights into life's pain which one must have if one is to be convinced of the rightness of the Middle Way; but they can also be approached by starting on that path. Thus he says that the Middle Way gives successively "sight . . . calm . . . insight, enlightenment, Nirvana."

How does the Buddha think that pain can be avoided? What is the relation between enlightenment and rebirth? Compare the Eightfold Path with Christian ideas about salvation.

These two extremes, O monks, are not to be practiced by one who has gone forth from the world. What are the two? That conjoined with the passions, low, vulgar, common, ignoble, and useless, and that conjoined with self-torture, painful, ignoble, and useless. Avoiding these two extremes the Tathagata[1] has gained the knowledge of the Middle Way, which gives sight and knowledge, and tends to calm, to insight, enlightenment, Nirvana.

What, O monks, is the Middle Way, which gives sight. . . . It is the noble Eightfold Path, namely, right views, right intention, right speech, right action, right livelihood, right effort, right mindfulness, right concentration. This, O monks, is the Middle Way. . . .

(1) Now this, O monks, is the noble truth of pain: birth is painful, old age is painful, sickness is painful, death is painful, sorrow, lamentation, dejection, and despair are painful. Contact with unpleasant things is painful, not getting what one wishes is painful. In short the five khandhas of grasping are painful.

(2) Now this, O monks, is the noble truth of the cause of pain: that craving, which leads to rebirth, combined with pleasure and lust, finding pleasure here and there, namely the craving for passion, the craving for existence, the craving for non-existence.

(3) Now this, O monks, is the noble truth of the cessation of pain: the cessation without a remainder of that craving, abandonment, forsaking, release, non-attachment.

(4) Now this, O monks, is the noble truth of the way that leads to the cessation of pain: this is the noble Eightfold Path, namely, right views, right intention, right speech, right action, right livelihood, right effort, right mindfulness, right concentration. "This is the noble truth of pain." Thus, O monks, among doctrines unheard before, in me sight and knowledge arose, wisdom, knowledge, light arose. "This noble truth of pain must be comprehended." Thus, O monks, among doctrines unheard before, by me was this truth comprehended. And thus, O monks, among doctrines unheard before, in me sight and knowledge arose. *[Repeated in the same words for the other truths, except that the second, the cause of pain, is to be abandoned, the third, the cessation of pain, is to be realized, and the fourth, the noble Eightfold Path, is to be practiced.]*

As long as in these noble truths my threefold knowledge and insight duly with its twelve divisions was not well purified, even so long, O monks, in the world with its gods, Mara, Brahma, with ascetics, brahmins, gods and men, I had not attained the highest complete enlightenment. Thus I knew.

---

[1]The Buddha, Gautama Siddhartha.

But when in these noble truths my threefold knowledge and insight duly with its twelve divisions was well purified, then, O monks, in the world . . . I had attained the highest complete enlightenment. Thus I knew. Knowledge arose in me, insight arose that the release of my mind is unshakable; this is my last existence; now there is no rebirth.

Translated by Edward J. Thomas

Ashoka Maurya: Inscriptions (269–232 BCE)

The numerous inscriptions carved on pillars at the command of Ashoka Maurya depict a ruler who, after using ruthless violence to conquer most of India, turned to peace. As is apparent from the conclusion of the following inscription, however, it is clear that he was not to allow potentially rebellious groups like the precivilized forest peoples to think that they could safely defy his authority.

Inscription Thirteen

Eight years after his coronation King Devanampiya Piyadasi[1] conquered the Kalingas. In that [conquest] one hundred and fifty thousand people were deported [as prisoners], one hundred thousand were killed [or maimed] and many times that number died. Thereafter, with the conquest of Kalinga, King Devanampiya Piyadasi [adopted] the practice of morality, love of morality and inculcation of morality. For there arose in King Devanampiya Piyadasi remorse for the conquest of Kalinga. For when an unsubdued country is conquered there occur such things as slaughter, death and deportation of people and these are regarded as very painful and serious by King Devanampiya Piyadasi. Brahmans and ascetics live everywhere, as well as votaries of other sects and householders who practice such virtues as support of mother and father, service of elders, proper treatment of friends, relatives, acquaintances and kinsmen and slaves and servants and steadfastness in devotion to duties. They too suffer injury (separation from loved ones), slaughter and deportation of loved ones. And for those whose love is undiminished, their friends, acquaintances, relatives and kinsmen suffer calamity. And that is injury to them. This plight of men is regarded as serious by King Devanampiya Piyadasi. Outside of the territory of the Greeks there is no land where communities such as those of Brahmans and ascetics are not to be found. Nor is there any land where men do not have faith [religion] of one sect or another.

Hence, whatever the number of men then killed [or wounded] and died and were deported at the annexation of Kalinga, a hundredth or a thousandth part [thereof] even is regarded as serious by King Devanampiya Piyadasi. Furthermore, if anyone does wrong [to him] the person should be suffered or pardoned. To the forest folk, who live in the royal dominions of King Devanampiya Piyadasi, it may be pointed out that the king, remorseful as he is, has the strength to punish the wrongdoers who do not repent. For King Devanampiya desires that all beings should be safe, self-restrained, tranquil in thought and gentle.

---

[1]"Benevolent of the gods, of Benevolent Mien," a title used by Ashoka.

Inscription Nine

Although he was claimed as a follower by Buddhists, and boasted of his piety, Ashoka believed that virtuous deeds were more important than religious rituals. The following passage was cited by Mahatma (Teacher) Mohandas K. Gandhi in modern times as a basis for his doctrine of nonviolence, although such attitudes were not otherwise traditional in India. Considering Gandhi's use of this inscription, and his influence on Martin Luther King, it is a valuable historical document.

King Devanampiya Piyadasi says thus: People perform many and diverse propitious ceremonies. In sickness, or marriage of sons and daughters, or for the gift of a son, or for (safety in) journey, in these and other matters, people perform diverse propitious ceremonies. And in this wives and mothers particularly indulge in ceremonies that are useless and empty. But ceremonies should be performed. But such ceremonies are of little value. But that indeed is a very valuable ceremony namely the ceremony (in behalf) of morality. It comprises proper treatment of slaves and servants, respect toward teachers, restraint (noninjury) toward living beings, gifts to Brahmans and ascetics, these and many such others are the ceremony of morality. Now, therefore, this should be said by a father, or son, or master, or husband, friend or acquaintance, or a neighbor. This is good; this is the kind of ceremony that should be performed for (the accomplishment of the proper) purpose.

And this too has been said: Charity is good. There is no (greater) charity or favor than the gift of morality or favor of morality. And in this an acquaintance or friend, or kinsman or companion should instruct: This should be done; this is good. By this heaven may be gained. What more is worthy of performance for the accomplishment of heaven than this?

Inscription Seven

Hindus have generally been tolerant in matters of religious belief, partly because they have lacked a centralized, organized priesthood (though recent events have provided some sobering exceptions). Ashoka's call for tolerance is fairly typical of Indian attitudes, but would have been most unusual in any other civilization.

King Devanampiya Piyadasi desires that all sects may live everywhere. All of them desire restraint and purity of the mind. But men are of diverse desires and passions. They will practice all [points of their faith] or only a part. Even for a generous man, if he not have restraint, purity of mind, gratefulness or steadfastness in faith, there is no greatness.

Translated by Balkrishna Govind Gokhale

The Pure Land Sutra

As Buddhism moved out from India and into other areas, variations developed, with diverse sects creating their own styles of art, their own modes of worship, even their own doctrines. Those which taught the universal buddhahood of all believers came to be known collectively as Mahayana Buddhism, or The Greater Vehicle. The Pure Land sect, which began to flourish in China by the sixth century of our era taught that the Buddha was divine, that those who have been enlightened and worked their way up through the cycles of rebirth have the status of Bodhisattvas, or holy ones, who may delay their entrance into Nirvana as they assist those yet here in the world to develop their faith. Even the concept of Nirvana changed radically: early on, it was simply a mode of non-being, an escape from the suffering of this world; now there was conceived a "happy land," filled with wonders and delights, which would prepare one to enter Nirvana. The very notion of squelching our desires, so important in early Buddhism, gave way to the notion of the satisfaction of desires—at least harmless satisfactions and worthwhile delights—in a sort of Buddhist heaven. Thus the Pure Land Sutra shows us something that is true of all religions which last a long time: they evolve over the course of time, so that the early proponents might even have trouble identifying the later practices and beliefs as being part of their same faith, though the later adherents, aware of the tradition, can identify the early practices and beliefs as being the sources of current ones.

In what ways does the "Pure Land" envisioned here cater to the wishes of its inhabitants? What does its geography suggest about the preferences, and perhaps the actual habitation, of the members who belong to this sect?

This world Sukhavati, Ananda,[1] which is the world system of the Lord Amitabha,[2] is rich and prosperous, comfortable, fertile, delightful and crowded with many Gods and men. And in this world system, Ananda, there are no hells, no animals, no ghosts, no Asuras[3] and none of the inauspicious places of rebirth. And in this our world no jewels make their appearance like those which exist in the world system Sukhavati.

And that world system Sukhavati, Ananda, emits many fragrant odors, it is rich in a great variety of flowers and fruits, adorned with jewel trees, which are frequented by flocks of various birds with sweet voices, which the Tathagata's[4] miraculous power has conjured up. And these jewel trees, Ananda, have various colors, many colors, many hundreds of thousands of colors. They are variously composed of the seven precious things, in varying combinations, i.e. of gold, silver, beryl, crystal, coral, red pearls or emerald. Such jewel trees, and clusters of banana trees and rows of palm trees, all made of precious things, grow everywhere in this Buddha-field. On all sides it is surrounded with golden nets, and all round covered with lotus flowers made of all the precious things. Some of the lotus flowers

---

[1]Ananda was one of the Buddha's favorite disciples.

[2]Amitabha was an Indian ascetic who, when seeking enlightenment, made a series of vows that helped him attain Buddhahood. Among those was the vow that if anyone approaching death would call on him by name, he would personally lead that one to rebirth in his own Buddha-world, Sukhavati. There it would be much easier for the believer to gain release from his human limitations.

[3]Titanic beings who war constantly with the Gods.

[4]A title of the Buddha.

are half a mile in circumference, others up to ten miles. And from each jewel lotus issue thirty-six hundred thousand kotis[5] of rays. And at the end of each ray there issue thirty-six hundred thousand kotis of Buddhas, with golden-colored bodies, who bear the thirty-two marks of the superman, and who, in all the ten directions, go into countless world systems, and there demonstrate Dharma.

And further, Ananda, in this Buddha-field there are nowhere any mountains,—black mountains, jewel mountains, Sumerus, kings of mountains, circular mountains and great circular mountains. But the Buddha-field is everywhere even, delightful like the palm of the hand, and in all its parts the ground contains a great variety of jewels and gems.

And many kinds of rivers flow along in this world system Sukhavati. There are great rivers there, one mile broad, and up to fifty miles broad and twelve miles deep. And all these rivers flow along calmly, their water is fragrant with manifold agreeable odors, in them there are bunches of flowers to which various jewels adhere, and they resound with various sweet sounds. And the sound which issues from these great rivers is as pleasant as that of a musical instrument, which consists of hundreds of thousands of kotis of parts, and which, skillfully played, emits a heavenly music. It is deep, commanding, distinct, clear, pleasant to the ear, touching the heart, delightful, sweet, pleasant, and one never tires of hearing it, it always agrees with one and one likes to hear it, like the words "Impermanent, peaceful, calm, and not-self." Such is the sound that reaches the ears of those beings.

And, Ananda, both the banks of those great rivers are lined with variously scented jewel trees, and from them bunches of flowers, leaves and branches of all kinds hang down. And if those beings wish to indulge in sports full of heavenly delights on those river-banks, then, after they have stepped into the water, the water in each case rises as high as they wish it to,—up to the ankles, or the knees, or the hips, or their sides, or their ears. And heavenly delights arise. Again, if beings wish the water to be cold, for them it becomes cold; if they wish it to be hot, for them it becomes hot; if they wish it to be hot and cold, for them it becomes hot and cold, to suit their pleasure. And those rivers flow along, full of water scented with the finest odors, and covered with beautiful flowers, resounding with the sounds of many birds, easy to ford, free from mud, and with golden sand at the bottom. And all the wishes those beings may think of, they all will be fulfilled, as long as they are rightful.

And as to the pleasant sound which issues from the water (of these rivers), that reaches all the parts of this Buddha-field. . . . And, hearing this, one gains the exalted zest and joyfulness, which is associated with detachment, dispassion, calm, cessation, Dharma, and brings about the state of mind which leads to the accomplishment of enlightenment. And nowhere in this world-system Sukhavati does one hear of anything unwholesome, nowhere of the hindrances, nowhere of the states of punishment, the states of woe and the bad destinies, nowhere of suffering. Even of feelings which are neither pleasant nor unpleasant one does not hear here, how much less of suffering! And that, Ananda, is the reason why this world-system is called the "Happy Land" (Sukhavati). But all this describes it only in brief, not in detail. One aeon might well reach its end while one proclaims the reasons for happiness in the world system Sukhavati, and still one could not come to the end of (the enumeration of) the reasons for happiness.

Moreover, Ananda, all the beings who have been reborn in this world-system Sukhavati, who are reborn in it, or who will be reborn in it, they will be exactly like the Paranirmitavasavartin Gods: of the same color, strength, vigor, height and breadth, do-

---

[5]A huge number.

minion, store of merit and keenness of super-knowledges; they enjoy the same dresses, ornaments, parks, palaces and pointed towers, the same kind of forms, sounds, smells, tastes and touchables, just the same kinds of enjoyments. And the beings in the world-system Sukhavati do not eat gross food, like soup or raw sugar; but whatever food they may wish for, that they perceive as eaten, and they become gratified in body and mind, without there being any further need to throw the food into the body. And if, after their bodies are gratified, they wish for certain perfumes, then the whole of that Buddha-field becomes scented with just that kind of heavenly perfumes. But if someone does not wish to smell that perfume, then the perception of it does not reach him. In the same way, whatever they may wish for, comes to them, be it musical instruments, banners, flags, etc.; or cloaks of different colors, or ornaments of various kinds. If they wish for a palace of a certain color, distinguishing marks, construction, height and width, made of various precious things, adorned with hundreds of thousands of pinnacles, while inside it various heavenly woven materials are spread out, and it is full of couches strewn with beautiful cushions,—then just such a palace appears before them. In those delightful palaces, surrounded and honored by seven times seven thousand Apsaras,[6] they dwell, play, enjoy and disport themselves.

And the beings who are touched by the winds, which are pervaded with various perfumes, are filled with a happiness as great as that of a monk who has achieved the cessation of suffering.

And in this Buddha-field one has no conception at all of fire, sun, moon, planets, constellations, stars or blinding darkness, and no conception even of day and night, except (where they are mentioned) in the sayings of the Tathagata. There is nowhere a notion of monks possessing private parks for retreats.

And all the beings who have been born, who are born, who will be born in this Buddha-field, they all are fixed on the right method of salvation, until they have won Nirvana. And why? Because there is here no place for and no conception of the two other groups, i.e., of those who are not fixed at all, and those who are fixed on wrong ways. For this reason also that world-system is called "Happy Land". . . .

And further again, Ananda, in the ten directions, in each single direction, in Buddha-fields countless like the sands of the river Ganges, Buddhas and Lords countless like the sands of the river Ganges, glorify the name of the Lord Amitabha, of the Tathagata, praise him, proclaim his fame, extol his virtue. And why? Because all beings are irreversible from the supreme enlightenment if they hear the name of the Lord Amitabha, and, on hearing it, with one single thought only raise their hearts to him with a resolve connected with serene faith.

And if any beings, Ananda, again and again reverently attend to this Tathagata, if they will plant a large and immeasurable root of good, having raised their hearts to enlightenment, and if they vow to be reborn in that world system, then, when the hour of their death approaches, that Tathagata Amitabha, the Arhat, the fully Enlightened One, will stand before them, surrounded by hosts of monks. Then, having seen that Lord, and having died with hearts serene, they will be reborn in just that world-system Sukhavati. And if there are sons or daughters of good family, who may desire to see that Tathagata Amitabha in this very life, they should raise their hearts to the supreme enlightenment, they should direct their thought with extreme resoluteness and perseverance unto this Buddha-field and they should dedicate their store of merit to being reborn therein.

Translated by Edward Conze

---

[6]Beautiful divine nymphs.

Kalidasa: *The Recognition of Sakuntala* (4th-5th Century CE?)

The greatest of all ancient Indian playwrights is Kalidasa. His Abhijnanasakuntalam (The Recognition of Sakuntala) *begins with the encounter between a great king and the miraculously beautiful Sakuntala when he is hunting in the woods occupied by her stepfather's hermitage. They fall passionately in love, almost instantly. Keep in mind that women were expected to be shy and reticent with men. The audience would recognize from the way she is described that she has developed almost instantly an overwhelming passion for the king, despite the fact that she seems to reject him. In this scene he happens upon Sakuntala and her friends as they water plants near the hermitage, and observes them from hiding.*

In what ways are Sakuntala and the King compared to objects or phenomena in nature? For instance, what does the bee buzzing around Sakuntala's lips symbolize? What examples can you find of symbols for Sakuntala's "ripeness" for marriage?

KING *(walks about and looks)*
So, here is the gate to the asrama![1] Let me enter.
(enters and indicates an omen)
> How serene and profoundly peaceful is this hermitage!
> Yet my arm trembles! Oh, what does it augur for me?
> Who knows fate may open its door anywhere, any time!

A VOICE OFF-STAGE
O dear friends, let us go then . . .

KING *(listening)*
Ah, I hear voices to the right of the grove. I'll go and see *(walks about and looks)*. I see! They are the hermit-maidens coming this way, carrying pitchers proportionate to their strength and size; perhaps they will water the shrubs here.
> When such beauty, rare even in the palace,
> Dwells in the heart of a grove, then who would
> Deny that wild woodland vines far outshine
> The cultivated ones in our orchards?
> Let me conceal myself behind these trees,
> And watch a beauty to my heart's content.

Enter Sakuntala, accompanied by her two friends—Anasuya and Priyamvada.

ANASUYA
O dear Sakuntala, it is evident that Father Kanva loves these trees far more than he loves you. Indeed, it pains me to have to see that he has engaged a girl like you, as soft and delicate as a newly bloomed jasmine, in watering these plants. Such a hard task simply does not suit you, Sakuntala.

SAKUNTALA
But, dear Anasuya, I don't consider it merely as a task imposed by Father Kanva, for I love these trees like my own sister *(she begins to water the trees)*.

PRIYAMVADA
Dear Sakuntala, now that we have watered all summer-blooming trees, let us turn to new-grown ones, and earn merit for our selfless devotion.

---

[1]Hermit's dwelling place, often called "ashram" in English.

KING *(whispering to himself)*

What! Is she Sakuntala, the daughter of Sage Kanva? *(surprised)* How utterly deficient in judgement is the Sage to lock up such a lovely, delicate beauty in this asrama! Oh, how terribly she is imprisoned in her bark-garment!

> It's a pity! It's a pity!
> While trying to train her
> In ascetic austerity,
> The Sage only attempts
> To cut an acacia wood
> With the soft edge
> Of a blue lotus-leaf.

Well, let me remain hidden in the trees, and watch her without raising anyone's suspicions.

SAKUNTALA

Dear Anasuya, Priyamvada has drawn my garment too tightly. Would you please loosen it a little? *(Anusuya loosens it)*

PRIYAMVADA *(spreading a smile over her face)*

Oh, is it Priyamvada who has tied your dress too tightly? Or is it the budding youth of your body?

KING *(again whispering to himself)*

> She has observed justly!
> Her bark-dress conceals the splendid orbs
> Of her breasts, and reveals not their beauty
> And brilliance; it seems that a sallow leaf
> Has barely imprisoned a bud in the morning.
> Yet her bark-garment, howsoever restrictive,
> Radiates with its own brightness, as an ornament does.
> Even hidden in the duckweed, the lotus glows,
> And dusky scars in the face of the moon
> Only heighten its radiance; thus, Sakuntala's
> Beauty is only revealed by what her bark
> Conceals: her dress makes her far more attractive,
> For, indeed, beauty lies in concealing beauty.

SAKUNTALA *(curiously glancing at one of the trees)*

O dear, look there! It seems that the Kesara tree is fluttering his fingers of young shoots, calling me to converse with him. And how can I ignore his call? *(she walks over to the tree)*

PRIYAMVADA: O dear Sakuntala, pause there for a moment.

SAKUNTALA

But why?

PRIYAMVADA

As you are standing beside the tree, it seems that the tree has found a lover in a flowering creeper.

SAKUNTALA

O Priyamvada, you really are what your name means—a "flatterer!"

KING *(once again whispering to himself)*

> Yes, what Priyamvada says is sweet and flattering, But also true.
> Her lips are like red, red shoots of a vine,

154

Her arms are as delicate as its winding stems,
Her limbs are lovely noonday flowers
Glittering with the glory of charming youth.

ANASUYA:

Mark, Sakuntala, the fresh jasmine-flower whom you call by the name of Vana-jyostna—the "Moonlight-of-the-Grove"—seems to have chosen the mango as her bridegroom.

Sakuntala approaches the vine and gazes at it with intense delight.

SAKUNTALA

And indeed it is a splendid wedding in a delightful season. Look, the jasmine has produced fresh blossoms, while the mango tree is vibrant with its youthfulness, with its joy of bearing new fruits (she stands gazing at the flower).

PRIYAMVADA

Anasuya, do you know why Sakuntala gazes so intently at the Moonlight-of-the-Grove?

ANASUYA:

No, I don't. But why don't you tell me?

PRIYAMVADA

Well, gazing at the flower, what our dear Sakuntala thinks is simply this: "As the jasmine has found its husband in the tree, so, may I also find one worthy of me."

SAKUNTALA

Oh, thus you only speak of your own heart's desire, Priyamvada *(Sakuntala waters the flower)*.

ANASUYA:

Dear Sakuntala, why don't you take a look at the bush here—the Madhabi bush that Father Kanva has perhaps nursed more lovingly than he has nursed you. Have you forgotten her?

SAKUNTALA

I might as well forget myself *(approaches the bush and shouts in joy)*. Oh, here is a great surprise, Priyamvada! Now I'll tell you something that you'll love to hear.

PRIYAMVADA

O dear Sakuntala, please tell me what it is.

SAKUNTALA

See, what a wonderful thing has happened to our Madhavi! It's covered with buds, down to its root, though this is not the season for its blooming.

BOTH *(in great excitement)*

Is it true, Sakuntala?

SAKUNTALA

Of course, it is. Why don't you come here and see it with your own eyes?

PRIYAMVADA

I see! Well, now it is my turn to tell you something that you'll love to hear, Sakuntala. You'll get married soon.

SAKUNTALA *(crossly)*

Once again you're expressing your own heart's desire, Priyamvada.

PRIYAMVADA

Oh, this is no joke, dear. I've heard Father Kanva himself say that this would be an omen for your marriage.

ANASUYA

So, this is the reason why Sakuntala so lovingly nurses Madhavi.

SAKUNTALA

Why shouldn't I? I love her like a sister *(she begins to pour water from the pitcher)*.
KING
Ah, I wish she were the daughter of a Brahman by a wife of the Kshatriya caste. But let me do away with doubts:

> She is destined to become a warrior's bride,
> For my heart and my being sincerely desire her.
> In the face of doubt or confusion, nothing can be
> A safer guide than the inner voice of the virtuous soul.
> Yet I should try to find out more about her.

SAKUNTALA
O God, this bee is buzzing round my face...*(she tries to drive it away)*
KING *(longingly)*

> O, those dark, lovely eyes keep following
> The movement of the bee buzzing near her face,
> As a lover's eyes follow the movement of her beloved
> Though not in fear, but in love.

(annoyed)

> Hey, you rascal thief! How fearlessly you rove
> To steal the lustre from her sparkling eyes
> As she darts a glance at you. And how closely
> You hover by her ear, as if to whisper a secret!
> As she waves her delicate hand to ward you off,
> You only rush to drink the dense, sweet nectar
> Of her ripe, lower lip—oh, how blessed you are, my rival!
> While you drink ambrosia, I must stand here thirsting!

SAKUNTALA
O dear friends! Save me from this wicked bee.

BOTH FRIENDS *(with a grin)*
Who are we to save you, Sakuntala? But why don't you seek help from King Dushyanta who is responsible for protecting our asrama?

KING
I think this is the most opportune moment for me to reveal myself *(the King, however, pauses for a moment)*. No, I should not appear in such a way that they would recognize me as the King. I should rather act like an ordinary visitor.

SHAKUNTALA
I think this rascal bee would not leave off. Scat! Shoo! No, he won't listen. I must leave the place. Oh, no! Help! Help!

KING *(emerging from behind the trees)*

> Who dares disturb the peace
> Of the hermit-maidens,
> When the King of Puru's line
> Still reigns supreme in the world?

As the King appears suddenly, the asrama girls stand confused.
ANASUYA
Honorable Sir, nothing serious has happened. *(Pointing to Sakuntala)*
Our dear friend Sakuntala was being pursued by a large bee, and she was frightened.
KING
I am glad to know that you are not in a serious trouble. I trust all is well with the holy

rites.

Sakuntala stands confused, silent.

ANASUYA

Indeed, all is well, Sir. And the noble presence of a distinguished guest like you further ensures our safety.

PRIYAMVADA

We welcome you to our asrama, Sir.

ANASUYA

Dear Sakuntala, go, and bring for our distinguished guest flowers, rice and fruits from the asrama. Meanwhile, let me wash his feet with the water that we have here.

KING

O ladies! Your gracious words have already sufficed to welcome and entertain me, and nothing more is needed.

PRIYAMVADA

But, Sir, you must sit under the cool shade of the Saptaparna tree
and rest awhile.

KING

I think all of you must be tired after performing your holy duties. So, why don't we all sit down for a while?

ANASUYA *(aside)*

Dear Sakuntala, propriety demands that we provide a hospitable company to our noble guest. Come, let's sit down.

They all sit down.

SAKUNTALA *(whispering to herself)*

Oh, why do I feel so lost and shaken? Why does the sight of this man fill my heart with emotions clashing with my ascetic life?

KING *(looking at them)*

I feel honored, ladies, by the charming company and warm hospitality of three beautiful girls of the same age.

PRIYAMVADA *(aside to Anasuya)*

I wonder who this stranger could be! His manner is so dignified and majestic, yet he speaks so fluently and politely!

ANASUYA *(aside)*

O Priyamvada, I, too, am curious to know who he is. Well, let me simply ask him. *(aloud)* Noble Sir, we feel encouraged by your gracious words to ask you a few questions which we hope will not offend you. Sir, what royal family do you descend from? Which country laments your absence? And what is it that brings a delicately nurtured young man like you to this grove of penance?

SAKUNTALA *(whispering to herself)*

O heart, keep quiet! Anasuya is asking the same questions I've wanted to ask.

KING *(aside)*

What should I do now? To reveal, or to conceal—that is the question. *(thinking for a moment)* Well, then, let me do it this way. *(aloud)* I am a person well-versed in the Vedas, and the Paurava King has entrusted me with the charge of the Ministry of Religious Affairs. I am, therefore, visiting this grove of penance only to see if the holy rites are being performed without impediments.

ANASUYA

Indeed, Sir, we are happy to have a guardian like you.
Sakuntala's trembling lips, uneasy silence, and coyness look like signs of falling in love.
ANASUYA *(noticing the behavior of both the King and Sakuntala, aside)*
Sakuntala, if only your father returns today. . .
SAKUNTALA *(frowning, aside)*
So?
BOTH
He would then reward this guest in the most befitting manner by offering him the greatest treasure of his life.
SAKUNTALA *(petulantly)*
Oh, you two with all your silly notions! Would you please stop prattling?
KING
Now if you permit, let me ask you something about your friend.
BOTH
We will feel honored to answer your question, Sir.
KING
So far as I know the holy Sage Kanva has hitherto observed celibacy. How, then, can your friend be his daughter?
ANASUYA
That's easy to answer, Sir. Have you heard of a royal sage called Kausika?
KING
Yes, I have.
ANASUYA:
Yes, it is Kausika who is Sakuntala's real father. Father Kanva only adpoted and reared her after she was found abandoned.
KING
Abandoned? The word arouses my curiosity. Would you please relate the story from the beginning?
ANASUYA
Once, a long time ago, Sage Kausika was deeply immersed in meditation for many years. His unflinching devoutness made the gods jealous and nervous. So, they sent Menaka to tempt him.
KING
Yes, the gods are well-known for showing resentment of human accomplishments. But what happened then?
ANASUYA
It was spring then, and Menka's irresistible beauty. . .*(she stops short, in embarrassment)*
KING
I can guess what the rest was. So, your friend is Menaka's daughter?
ANASUYA:
Yes, Sir.
KING

> So, there is no incongruity. . .
> Indeed, how could such a rare beauty be mortal?
> Can the radiance of the tremulous lightening
> Ever spring upward from the womb of the earth?

Sakuntala remains seated with her eyes downcast.
KING *(whispering to himself)*

Now my heart's longings have true scope for their indulgence.

PRIYAMVADA (*looking with a smile at Sakuntala, and then turning to the King*):

Noble Sir, it seems that you want to say something.

Sakuntala makes a reproving gesture with her forefinger.

KING

Yes, yes, you have made a right guess. May I ask you yet another question?

PRIYAMVADA

Please feel free to ask, Sir. Asrama girls may be asked questions freely.

KING

> What I wish to ask is this—
> Should she observe, until betrothal,
> Her ascetic vow that resists love and marriage,
> Or is she condemned to living forever the life
> Of a hermit in this Grove of Righteousness,
> With those small antelopes so dear to her,
> Whose lovely eyes only parallel the beauty
> Of her own eyes.

PRIYAMVADA

True, Sir, she follows her father's instructions in religious duties. But I'm sure her father will love to see her happily married to a husband worthy of her.

KING (*whispering to himself in delight*)

> O my heart, now harbor what is devoutly
> To be wished, for all doubts are now dissolved.
> What you feared might be a flame
> Is now turned into a lovely gem,
> Worthwhile to possess.

SAKUNTALA (*pretending to be annoyed*)

Anasuya, I'm leaving now.

ANASUYA

But, dear Sakuntala, it is improper to desert a distinguished guest, neglecting the duties of hospitality.

KING (*whispering to himself*)

Oh, is she leaving? No! (*makes a move to restrain her, but instantly checks himself, aside*) Ah, a lover's act reflects his feelings. . .

> As I was about to stop her on the way
> Decorum restrained my desire, all at once.
> I did not leave my place at all,
> Yet I seemed to rise and return.

PRIYAMVADA (*holding Sakuntala back*)

> Are you out of your senses, Sakuntala?
> You must not leave now.

SAKUNTALA

Why not?

PRIYAMVADA

Simply because you owe me your turn to water a couple of plants here. First, pay the debt, and then, leave. (*forces her back*)

KING

> Well, I can see that she is tired now.
> Her shoulders droop, her palms glow red,
> As she lifted up the heavy watering jar;
> Her bosom heaves rapidly, while she breathes.
> Rounded blobs of sweat glinting on her cheek
> Only tend to catch the flower of her ear.
> With her one hand, she restrains her lock
> Dishevelled, almost falling.

Let me free her of the debt she owes to you, if you please permit me *(offers his ring)*.
The two friends take the ring, and reading the royal seal on it, stare at each other.

KING

O ladies, do not get confused by the royal seal on the ring. I received it as a gift from the King.

PRIYAMVADA

In that case, Sir, you should not part with such a precious gift. Your gracious words suffice to set her free.

ANASUYA

O dear Sakuntala, now that you are free by the grace of this noble man or of the King, shouldn't you leave?

SAKUNTALA *(whispering to herself)*

Oh, what is this strange, anonymous power that has robbed me of all my movement?

PRIYAMVADA

Hey, Sakuntala, why don't you leave now?

SAKUNTALA

Am I still bound to answer your question, Priyamvada? I will leave whenever I feel like doing so.

KING *(looking closely at Sakuntala, aside)*

Is it likely that she feels in the same way I feel towards her? Oh, if it is so, my desire will be fulfilled. Yet I believe I have reasons to hope.

> Even though she keeps her words hidden
> Beneath her silences, she lends her ears
> To whatever I say. And even though
> She keeps her eyes downcast, she watches me
> Only when I watch her not!

(A VOICE OFF-STAGE)

Watch, all people of the hermitage! Get ready to save the creatures of the grove, for King Dushyanta who revels in hunting has entered our grove.

> Swirls of thick dust, stirred up by the hoof-beats
> Of wildly prancing horses, are falling on the branches
> Of our trees like swarms of locusts, thus clouding
> The afternoon sunglow and the immense azure
> Of the grove. . .

KING *(to himself)*

O, what a bad luck! I think my armed guards are rummaging through the grove in search of me.

(AGAIN A VOICE OFF-STAGE)

Be careful, everybody! Here comes a wild elephant, chasing children, women, and men.

> Frightened by the royal chariot

An elephant invades the grove,
Smashing tree-trunks, and chasing
And scattering antelope-herds.
With its sound and fury, the elephant
Also drags along the fetter of uprooted
Vines at its feet. All these, to our penance,
Are nothing but impediments incarnate.

All the girls now rise in alarm.

KING (*quickly*)

Oh, what a mess! I have indeed greatly harmed the sages here. I must leave the place now.

FRIENDS

Noble Sir! The warning about the elephant makes us feel very nervous. If your good self permits us, we may return to our asrama.

ANASUYA *(looking at Sakuntala)*

Dear Sakuntala, Mother Gautami must be worrying about us. Come, let us return as soon as we can.

SAKUNTALA *(showing difficulty in walking)*

Oh, God, I cannot walk, for a strange numbness pains my thighs.

KING

Take care, gracious ladies. I will try to protect the grove from any possible damage.

FRIENDS

Forgive this inadvertent interruption, my Lord! May we request you to visit us again so that we can compensate for the lack of our hospitality to you.

KING

O dear ladies, don't worry; what can be better hospitality than the lively company of three charming girls like you?

SAKUNTALA

Wait, Anasuya. My foot has been pricked by the pointed blade of the Kusa grass. . .and my dress is caught in an amaranth twig. Wait a little, and let me free myself.

Sakuntala follows her friends, but keeps looking back at the King.

KING *(with a deep sigh)*

Oh, gone! Gone are all of them! Sakuntala has robbed me of all my desire to return to the capital. Well, I will set up a camp with my companions in the vicinity of this grove. Oh, how impossible it is to punctuate, even for a moment, the stream of my thoughts that flows towards only one destination it has known—Sakuntala. Oh, Sakuntala! Sakuntala!

My body has an apparent movement,
But my heart? Oh, it only turns back
Like a silken pennon, borne against
The gale.

Translated by Azfar Hussain

China

Confucius: *Analects* (5th Century BCE?)

The sayings of Confucius were remembered by his followers and were later compiled in a book of Analects *(sayings), perhaps having been expanded on in the meantime. Through them we discover Confucius' notions of the virtues, i.e., the positive character traits, to which we should aspire. Foremost among these is filial piety, the respect which children owe to parents—and by extension, wives owe to husbands, sisters to brothers, and everyone to ancestors. When such virtue is cultivated in the home, it is supposed to carry over into one's relations in affairs of state as well.*

How does Confucius formulate the equivalent of the Golden Rule ("do unto others as you would have them do unto you")? Is his a stronger injunction or a less demanding one?

On Filial Piety

Mang I asked what filial piety is. The Master said, "It is being obedient." Soon after, as Fan Chi was driving him, the Master told him "Mang asked me what filial piety is, and I answered him 'being obedient.'" Fan Chi asked, "What exactly did you mean?" The Master replied, "That parents, when alive, should be served according to ritual; that, when dead, they should be buried according to ritual; and that they should be sacrificed to according to ritual."

Ziyou asked what filial piety is. The Master said, "The filial piety of now-a-days means providing nourishment for one's parents. But dogs and horses likewise are able to do something along that line for their own kind. Without reverence, what is there to distinguish the one support given from the other?"

On Goodness

The Master said, "A youth, when at home, should behave well toward his parents, and when abroad, respectfully to his elders. He should be earnest and truthful. He should overflow in love to all, and cultivate the friendship of the good. When he has time and opportunity, after doing those things, he should study the polite arts."

The Master said, "With coarse rice to eat, with water to drink, and my bended arm for a pillow, I still have joy in the midst of these things. Riches and honors acquired by unrighteousness are to me as a floating cloud."

Zhonggong asked about perfect virtue. The Master said, "When abroad, behave to everyone as if you were receiving an important guest; treat people as if you were assisting at a great sacrifice; do not do to others as you would not wish done to yourself. Thereby you will let no murmuring rise against you in the country, and none in the family. . . ."

Confucius took the notion of the gentleman, as one who owned land and had some political power, and reworked it into a moral notion which captures the essence of the good life. The graciousness and self-discipline which characterize such a gentleman are fostered by, and expressed in, ritual and music. But this also leads to many detailed guidelines about how to dress and how to perform the rituals. (The counterpart would be rules of etiquette in our society.)

162

Why is ritual supposed to be important? What happens to otherwise virtuous traits without such ritual?

On the Gentleman

The Master said, "Riches and honors are what men desire; but if they cannot be obtained in the proper way, they should be let go. Poverty and meanness are what men dislike; but if they cannot be avoided in the proper way, they should not be avoided. If a gentleman abandons virtue, how can he fulfill the requirements of his title? A gentleman will not, even for the space of a single meal, act contrary to virtue. Even in moments of haste, and in times of danger, he clings to virtue."

The Master said, "A gentleman, well studied in literature, and abiding by the rules of ritual, will not go very wrong."

"When gentlemen perform well all their duties to their relations, the people are inspired to virtue. When they remain true to their old friends, the people are preserved from irresponsible behavior."

The Master said, "A gentleman points out the admirable qualities of men and does not point out their bad qualities. A petty man does just the opposite."

The Master said, "A gentleman is distressed by his lack of ability, but he is not distressed by men's not knowing him."

The Master said, "What the gentleman demands is something of himself. What the petty man demands is something of others."

A gentleman does not wear a deep purple or a puce color, nor in his at-home clothes does he wear red. In warm weather, he wears a single-layered garment, either of coarse or fine texture, but when going out he wears it over another garment. He wears lambskin with a garment of black, fawn with white, and fox with yellow. His fur dressing gown should be long, but with the right sleeve short. His night clothes must be half again as long as his body. When staying at home, he wears thick furs of the fox or the badger. So long as he is not in mourning, he wears all the trimmings of his girdle. . . . He does not wear lamb's fur or a black cap when making a visit of condolence. And on the first day of the month he must put on his court robes and present himself at court.

On Ritual and Music

The Master said, "If a man lacks the human virtues, what has he to do with ritual? If a man lacks the human virtues, what has he to do with music?"

The Master said, "Respectfulness, without the rules of ritual, becomes laborious bustle; carefulness, without the rules, becomes timidity; boldness becomes insubordination; straightforwardness becomes rudeness."

The Master said, "It is by the Odes that a man's mind is aroused, by the rules of ritual that his character is established, and by music that he is perfected [finished]. . . ."

Education is, of course, important to Confucius, as one needs to learn the traditions and profit from the wisdom of the past. Government can then be carried on by "moral force," as opposed to requiring military or legal force. As to religion, Confucius does not challenge it, but he doesn't put his hope in it either. His stress is always on living well, which means living properly, here and now and by our own actions.

Which is more important for an orderly state: food, weapons, or a government that one can trust?

On Education

The Master said, "Anyone learning without thought is lost; anyone thinking, but not learning, is in peril."

The Master said, "Yu, shall I teach you what knowledge is? When you know a thing, to realize that you know it; and when you do not know a thing, to allow that you do not know it: this is knowledge." The Master said, [I have been] "a transmitter and not a maker, believing in and loving the ancients. . ."

When the Master went to Wei, Ran Yu acted as driver of his carriage. The Master observed, "How numerous the people are!" Ran Yu asked, "When they are more numerous, what more shall be done for them?" "Enrich them," was the reply. "And when they have been enriched, what more shall be done?" The Master said, "Instruct them."

On Government

The Master said, "To rule a country of a thousand chariots requires reverent attention to business, sincerity, economy in expenditures, and love for men, as well as the employment of the people only in the right seasons."

The Master said, "If the people are governed by laws and punishment is used to maintain order, they will try to avoid the punishment but have no sense of shame. If they are governed by virtue and rules of propriety [ritual] are used to maintain order, they will have a sense of shame and will become good as well."

Ji Kang Zi asked Confucius about government, saying, "What do you say to killing those who are unprincipled [i.e., the immoral] for the good of those who are principled?" Confucius replied, "Sir, in carrying on your government, why should you use killing at all? Let your obvious desires be for what is good, and the people will be good. The relation between superiors and inferiors is like that between the wind and the grass: the grass is bound to bend when the wind blows across it."

Zigong asked about government. The Master said, "The requisites of government are that there be sufficient food, sufficient military equipment, and the confidence of the people in their ruler." Zigong said, "If one had to dispense with one of those three, which should be given up first?" "The military equipment," said the Master. Zigong again asked, "If one had to dispense with one of the two remaining, which should be given up?" The Master answered, "Give up the food. From of old, death has always been the lot of men; but if the people have no faith in their rulers, they cannot stand."

On Religion

Someone asked the meaning of the great sacrifice. The Master said, "I do not know. Anyone who knew its meaning would find it as easy to govern the kingdom as to look on this," and he pointed to the palm of his hand.

Zilu asked about serving the ghosts of the dead. The Master said, "Until you are able to serve men, how can you serve their ghosts?" When Zilu ventured to ask about death, the answer was: "While you do not know life, how can you [hope to] know about death?"

Translated by James Legge, revised by Michael Neville

Ta-Hsüeh: "The Great Learning" (3rd Century BCE)

Originally the Ta Hsüeh *was a chapter of the* Li-chi, *the "Book of Rites," one of the five Chinese classics. Literary analysis suggests that it was written in the 3rd century BCE. During the Song Dynasty (960-1280), the* Ta Hsüeh *was considered sufficiently important to be singled out as one of the canonical "Four Books." Since both the Five Classics and the Four Books had to be memorized by Chinese students aspiring for a position in the Chinese civil service, the* Ta-Hsüeh *had to be studied twice.*

How does the Ta Hsüeh *emphasize the traditional Confucian value of the importance of knowledge?*

The Ancients, wishing to illuminate with shining virtue all under heaven, would first establish order in their own states.[1]
Wishing to establish order in their own states, they would first harmonize their families.
Wishing to harmonize their families, they would first cultivate their own persons.
Wishing to cultivate their own persons, they would first rectify their minds.[2]
Wishing to rectify their minds, they would first seek to verify their opinions.
Wishing to verify their opinions, they would first expand their knowledge.

The expansion of knowledge lies in the investigation of things.[3]

Once things are investigated, knowledge will be completed.
Once knowledge is complete, opinions will be verified.
Once opinions are verified, minds will be rectified.
Once minds are rectified, persons will be cultivated.
Once persons are cultivated, families will be harmonized.
Once families are harmonized, states will be put in order.
Once states are in order, there will be peace all under heaven.

From the emperor to the common people, all must see the cultivation of their own person as the root of all else.
If roots are in disarray, there will never be healthy branches.

Translated by Lydia Gerber

---

[1]"All under heaven" (Chinese *t'ien-hsia*) was a term used for the Chinese empire rather than for the world at large. Before 221 BCE, the Chinese empire consisted of a number of very strong, independent states.

[2]"Mind" (*hsin*) can also be translated as "heart." Classical Chinese does not differentiate between the rational and emotional aspects of a person the way western languages do.

[3]The Chinese term *wu*—translated as "things"—basically means "all that is outside oneself." It is usually translated either as "things" or "affairs".

Laozi: *Dao de Jing*

The Dao de Jing (Tao te Ching) (literally, "the classic of the way and virtue") is attributed to Laozi (Lao Tzu), though scholars disagree about his actual existence. In its very poetic form it teaches that there is a dynamic, cosmic structure underlying everything that happens in the world. We humans need to discover that Way (Dao), which is immanent in all aspects of the world, not a rule imposed from without; and we need to fit into it, letting things take their course, not exerting ourselves in opposition to it by trying to bend things to our will.

Our naming (describing) of things always falls short of the way things are, since things are not limited as our language presupposes. Even the Dao which we are trying to talk about here eludes our words. The original polarity is that of being and non-being, and it will be found to inter-play throughout the world, with non-being (emptiness, what is not) having as much significance as does being (the fullness of things, what is). Thus the notion of the Dao recaptures the earlier Chinese concept of Yin and Yang, the polarities running through all things.

What price is paid when people come to know beauty and goodness (i.e., what comes along with such knowledge)? Is that bad, according to Daoism? What are the advantages and disadvantages of an ideal which cannot be fully expressed in words?

1

The Dao that can be spoken of is not the enduring and unchanging Dao. The name that can be named is not the enduring and unchanging name.

Having no name, it is the Originator of heaven and earth; having a name, it is the Mother of all things.

We should rid ourselves of desires if we wish to observe its subtlety; we should allow our desires if we wish to see something of its manifestations.

Under these two aspects, it is really the same; but as development takes place, it receives the different names. Together we call them the mystery; where the mystery is the deepest is the gate of all that is subtle and wonderful.

2

All in the world know the beauty of the beautiful, and in doing so they have the idea of ugliness; they all know the good, and in doing so they have the idea of what is the bad.

So it is that being and non-being give birth each to the other; that difficulty and ease each produce the idea of the other; that the ideas of height and lowness arise from the contrast of the one with the other; that the musical notes and tones become harmonious through the relation of one with another; and that being before and behind give the idea of one following the other.

Therefore the sage manages affairs without doing anything, and conveys his teachings without the use of speech.

[In that way] all things come forth, and there is not one which declines to show itself; they grow, and there is no ownership claim made upon them; they go through their processes, and there is no expectation placed on them. The work is accomplished, and there is no disruption of order.

Daoism eschews many of the practices and principles of Confucianism, as in the following passage, where we are urged not to single out exemplary individuals and not to store up treasures and invest in fancy clothing and such. The sage rules his people not by force from the top but by subtly encouraging those trends and inclinations which are in keeping with the Dao; thus he can "act without action."

Which kind of knowledge is it that the sage ruler protects his people from?

3

Not to value and employ men of superior ability is the way to keep the people from rivalry among themselves; not to prize articles which are precious is the way to keep them from becoming thieves; not to show them what is likely to excite their desires is the way to keep their minds from disorder.

Therefore the sage, in the exercise of his government, empties their minds,[1] fills their bellies, weakens their wills, and strengthens their bones.

He constantly (tries to) keep them without knowledge and without desire, and where there are those who have knowledge, to keep them from presuming to act (on it). When there is this abstinence from action, good order is universal.

The Dao de Jing uses a series of images to show the potency of that which is not. The vessel or bowl is essentially an empty space, but it makes containment, hence drinking and life, possible. Similarly a room gets its usefulness from being empty; and doors and windows are important because there is nothing there. The valley, as a female receptacle, is rich and productive. The hub of the wheel is the empty space to which the spokes connect. Water becomes an image for the moral character of humans (at least in its passive mode), for it "does not compete" but fills in the cracks between other things. While our task is to fit in quietly, we may still "love the earth," i.e., extreme asceticism is not called for.

A brief list of what Daoists love and appreciate can be gleaned from Section 8. What are those sorts of things?

4

The Dao is (like) the emptiness of a vessel; and in our employment of it we must be on our guard against all fullness. How deep and unfathomable it is, as if it were the Honored Ancestor of all things!

We should blunt our sharp points and unravel the complications of things; we should moderate our brightness and bring ourselves into agreement with the obscurity of others. How pure and still the Dao is, as if it would ever so continue!

I do not know whose son it is. It might appear to have been before God.

6

The spirit of the valley dies not, but remains the same;
Thus we name it the mysterious female.

---

[1]"Emptying the mind" seems here to mean "freeing from concerns which might press in upon them."

Its gate is called the root from which grew heaven and earth.
Long and unbroken does its power remain,
Used gently, it will never be exhausted.

8

The highest excellence[2] is like that of water. The excellence of water appears in its benefiting all things, and in its occupying, without striving, the low place which all men dislike. Hence it is near to the Dao.

The excellence of a residence is in the suitability of the place; that of the mind is in the stillness of the abyss; that of relationships is in their being with the virtuous; that of government is in its securing good order; that of the conduct of affairs is in its ability; and that of any movement is its timeliness. And when one with the highest excellence does not strive against his low position, no one finds fault with him.

11

The thirty spokes unite in the one center; but it is on the empty space for the axle that the use of the wheel depends. Clay is fashioned into vessels; but it is on their empty hollowness that their use depends. The door and windows are cut out from the walls to form an apartment; but it is on the empty space that its use depends. Therefore, whatever has being is profitable, but what does not have being can be put to use.

Translated by James Legge, adapted by Michael Neville

---

[2]Some translators take this to be "the good man." In any case, it is human virtue that is being talked about.

Han Fei-tzu (d. 233 BCE): Legalist Views on Good Government

The Confucian ideal of "government through virtue" and the tendency of Confucianists to seek guidance in the rule of former kings was strongly criticized by another school of thought: the Legalists or School of Law. According to the Legalists, neither the wisdom of ancient kings nor an ethical code would make a state strong. Instead "good" and "bad" were defined by whatever the self-interest of the ruler demanded. A system of harsh punishments and rewards, regulated through laws and enforced without exceptions, should guarantee good behavior within the state. The Legalists considered military service and agriculture as the only occupations beneficial to the welfare of the state and discouraged all scholarship.

The state of Qin in Western China was the first to adopt Legalist doctrines. The Qin were so successful that by 221 BCE they had conquered the other Chinese states and unified the empire after centuries of war. The following paragraph was taken from Han Fei-tzu, The "[book of] Master Han Fei," *chapter 50. Han Fei-tzu had studied under the Confucian scholar Hsun-tzu and became the major theorist of the Legalist school. Confucian scholars vigorously denounced his teachings in all subsequent generations; yet his harsh pragmatism, often compared to that of Machiavelli and Kautilya, more accurately explains the actions of many rulers than does the idealistic Confucian model.*

What attitude does Han Fei express toward the common people? What kinds of stern measures does he suggest should be enacted for their own good? How practical do you think this advice is for maintaining a successful government?

When a sage governs a state, he does not rely on the people to do good out of their own will. Instead, he sees to it that they are not allowed to do what is not good. If he relies on people to do good out of their own will, within the borders of the state not even ten persons can be counted on [to do good]. Yet, if one sees to it that they are not allowed to do what is not good, the whole state can be brought to uniform order. Whoever rules should consider the majority and set the few aside: He should not devote his attention to virtue, but to law.

If it were necessary to rely on a shaft that had grown perfectly straight, within a hundred generations there would be no arrow. If it were necessary to rely on wood that had grown perfectly round, within a thousand generations there would be no cart wheel. If a naturally straight shaft or naturally round wood cannot be found within a hundred generations, how is it that in all generations carriages are used and birds shot? Because tools are used to straighten and bend. But even if one did not rely on tools and still got a naturally straight shaft or a piece of naturally round wood, a skillful craftsman would not value this. Why? Because it is not just one person that needs to ride and not just one arrow that needs to be shot. Even if without relying on rewards and punishments there would be someone doing good out of his own will, an enlightened ruler would not value this. Why? Because a state's law must not be neglected, and not just one person needs to be governed. Therefore, the skilled ruler does not go after such unpredictable goodness, but walks the path of certain success. . . .

Praising the beauty of Ma Ch'iang or Hsi shih[1] does not improve your own face. But using oil to moisten it, and powder and paint will make it twice as attractive.

---

[1] The beauty of these women is proverbially famous.

Praising the benevolence and righteousness of former kings does not improve your own rule. But making laws and regulations clear and rewards and punishments certain, is like applying oil, powder and paint to a state.

An enlightened ruler holds up facts and discards all that is without practical value. Therefore he does not pursue righteousness and benevolence, and he does not listen to the words of scholars. These days, whoever does not understand how to govern will invariably say: "Win the hearts of the people." If winning the hearts of the people is all that one needs in order to govern, a Yi Yin or a Kuan Chung[2] would be useless. Listening to the people would be enough. But the wisdom of the people is useless: They have the minds of little infants! If an infant's head is not shaved, its sores will spread, and if its boil is not opened, it will become sicker. Yet while its head is being shaved and its boil opened, one person has to hold it tight so that the caring mother can perform the operation, and it screams and wails without end. Infants and children don't understand that the small pain they have to suffer now will bring great benefit later.

Likewise, if the people are forced to till their land and open pastures in order to increase their future supplies, they consider their ruler harsh. If the penal code is being revised and punishments are made heavier in order to wipe out evil deeds, they consider their ruler stern. If light taxes in cash and grain are levied in order to fill granaries and the treasury so that there will be food in times of starvation and sufficient funds for the army, they consider their ruler greedy. If it is required that within the borders everybody is familiar with warfare, that no one is exempted from military service, and that the state is united in strength in order to take all enemies captive, the people consider their ruler violent. These four types of measures would all serve to guarantee order and peace, yet the people do not have the sense to welcome them. Therefore one has to seek for an enlightened [ruler] to enforce them.

Translated by Lydia Gerber

---

[2]Ancient Chinese statesmen famous for their wisdom.

Ban Zhao: *Lessons for Women* (1st Century CE)

Ban Zhao was the sister of a famous Han historian, and became his assistant when her husband died. So brilliant was she that after her brother's death the emperor appointed her court historian in his place. Despite her own unconventional and distinguished career, the book she wrote teaching women how they should behave followed traditional Confucian values, urging submissiveness.

On what one subject does Ban Zhao insist on the rights of women? Does she hold a romantic view of marriage? Which of her demands on women do you object to the most? Are there any you approve of?

Humility

On the third day after the birth of a girl the ancients observed three customs: [first] to place the baby below the bed; [second] to give her a potsherd with which to play; and [third] to announce her birth to her ancestors by an offering. Now to lay the baby below the bed plainly indicated that she is lowly and weak, and should regard it as her primary duty to humble herself before others. To give her potsherds with which to play indubitably signified that she should practice labor and consider it her primary duty to be industrious. To announce her birth before her ancestors clearly meant that she ought to esteem as her primary duty the continuation of the observance of worship in the home. . . .

Let a woman modestly yield to others; let her respect others; let her put others first, herself last. Should she do something good, let her not mention it; should she do something bad, let her not deny it. Let her bear disgrace; let her even endure when others speak or do evil to her. Always let her seem to tremble and to fear. . . .

Let a woman retire late to bed, but rise early to duties; let her not dread tasks by day or by night. Let her not refuse to perform domestic duties whether easy or difficult.

Education

Yet only to teach men and not to teach women—is that not ignoring the essential relation between them? According to the "Rites," it is the rule to begin to teach children to read at the age of eight years, and by the age of fifteen years they ought then to be ready for cultural training. Only why should it not be [that girls' education as well as boys' be] according to this principle?

Respect and Caution

If husband and wife have the habit of staying together, never leaving one another, and following each other around within the limited space of their own rooms, then they will lust after and take liberties with one another. From such action improper language will arise between the two. This kind of discussion may lead to licentiousness. Out of licentiousness will be born a heart of disrespect to the husband. Such a result comes from not knowing that one should stay in one's proper place.

Be "Womanly"

A woman ought to have four qualifications: [1] womanly virtue; [2] womanly words; [3] womanly bearing; and [4] womanly work. Now what is called womanly virtue need not be brilliant ability, exceptionally different from others. Womanly words need be neither clever in debate nor keen in conversation. Womanly appearance requires neither a pretty nor a perfect face and form. Womanly work need not be work done more skillfully than that of others.

To guard carefully her chastity; to control her behavior; in every motion to exhibit modesty; and to model each act in the best usage, this is womanly virtue.

To choose her words with care; to avoid vulgar language; to speak at appropriate times; and not to weary others [with much conversation], may be called the characteristics of womanly words.

To wash and scrub filth away; to keep clothes and ornaments fresh and clean; to wash the head and bathe the body regularly, and to keep the person free from disgraceful filth, may be called the characteristics of womanly bearing.

With whole-hearted devotion to sew and to weave; to love not gossip and silly laughter; In cleanliness and order [to prepare] the wine and food for serving guests, may be called the characteristics of womanly work.

Whole-hearted Devotion

Now in the Rites is written the principle that a husband may marry again, but there is no [law] that authorizes a woman to be married the second time. Therefore it is said of husbands as of Heaven, that as certainly as people cannot run away from Heaven, so surely a wife cannot leave [a husband's home].

Implicit Obedience

Now to "win the love of one man is the crown of a woman's life; to lose the love of one man is her eternal disgrace." This saying advises a fixed will and a whole-hearted devotion for a woman. Ought she then to lose the hearts of her father- and mother-in-law? . . . Whenever the mother-in-law says, "Do not do that," and if what she says is right, unquestionably the daughter-in-law obeys. Whenever the mother-in-law says, "Do that," even if what she says is wrong, still the daughter-in-law submits unfailingly to the command.

Translated by Nancy Lee Swann

Examples of Filial Piety (14th Century CE)

According to Chinese tradition, filial piety (hsiao) was the primary duty of all Chinese. Being a filial son meant complete obedience to one's parents during their lifetime and—as they grew older—taking the best possible care of them. After their death the eldest son was required to perform ritual sacrifices at their grave site or in the ancestral temple. A son could also express his devotion to his parents by passing the Civil Service examinations, winning prestige for the whole family. Most important of all, a son had to make sure that the family line would be continued. Dying without a son therefore was one of the worst offenses against the concept of filial piety. If a marriage remained barren, it was a son's duty to take a second wife or adopt a child in order to continue the family. Since Chinese women became part of their husband's family through marriage, filial conduct for a woman meant faithfully serving her in-laws, in particular her mother-in-law, and giving birth to a son. By fulfilling these duties, she also gained prestige for her own family. If the mother and daughter-in-law did not get along, filial piety demanded that a man should get rid of his wife in order to please his mother. He could always get another wife, but he would only have one mother. While continuing the family line was probably the most important issue for the vast majority of the Chinese, Buddhist monks and nuns were required to remain celibate. Their refusal to fulfill the obligations of filial piety made them suspect in the eyes of other Chinese. Along with the eunuchs at the emperor's court and Taoist priests they were often believed to conduct themselves in an immoral or criminal manner.

Stories about exemplary filial conduct abound in Chinese history. The Twenty-Four Examples of Filial Piety (Er-shih-ssu hsiao) were chosen and compiled by Kuo Chü-ching during the Yuan Dynasty (1280–1368 CE) while he was mourning the death of his father. Other collections followed. Even today, these stories form an important part of Chinese folklore. You may be surprised at how brief these stories are and how little background is given. Two reasons may explain this: On the one hand, everyone was so familiar with the heroes of these examples that it was unnecessary to give any details about their lives. On the other hand, brevity is considered to be good style in the classic Chinese tradition.

Choose a western fairy tale which involves children's relationship to their parents and compare the attitudes in that tale with the attitudes expressed here. What strikes you as familiar? Where do you see differences?

Freezing in a Thin Coat in Obedience to His Stepmother

Min Tzu-chien had lost his mother at a young age. His father remarried and had two more sons with his second wife. She always dressed her own sons in thickly padded robes. But to her stepson she gave only a thin coat padded with cattails [instead of cotton]. One winter day, when Min Tzu-chien was told to hold the reins of his father's cart, he was shivering so badly that he dropped the reins. This way his father found out that his wife dressed his oldest son very poorly. In his rage he decided to dismiss his second wife. But Min Tzu-chien said: "If she stays, one son will be freezing. But if she leaves, all three sons will suffer from the cold." When his stepmother heard this, she changed her attitude towards Min Tzu-chien.

Allowing Mosquitoes to Feast on His Blood

During the Chin Dynasty (4th–5th Century CE), a boy named Wu Meng[1] was already serving his parents in exemplary filial piety although he was just eight years old. The family was so poor that they could not even afford a gauze net against the mosquitoes. Therefore every night in the summer swarms of mosquitoes would come and bite them. Wu Meng let them all feast on his naked stomach. Even though there were so many, he did not drive them away. He feared that the mosquitoes, having left him, would instead bite his parents. His heart was truly filled with love for his parents.

Sacrificing His Son for the Sake of His Mother

Kuo Chi, who lived during the Han Dynasty (200 BCE–200 CE) and his family were very poor. He had a three-year-old son. Even though there was little food, Kou Chi's mother would always give part of her share to her grandson so that he did not suffer hunger.

One day Kuo Chi said to his wife, "We are so poor and needy that we cannot give mother enough to eat, and on top of this our son is eating part of mother's share. It were better if we buried our son."[2] He started digging a grave. When he had dug a hole of about three *chih*[3], he discovered a pot filled with gold and the inscription: "Officials may not take it, people may not steal it."

Wearing Children's Clothes to Amuse His Parents

During the time of the Chou Dynasty (11th–3rd Century BCE), there was a man named Lao Lai-tzu[4] who was by nature extremely filial. He took care of both his parents and provided for them with the choicest delicacies. After he himself turned seventy, he never spoke about his age.[5] He often wore clothes striped in five colors and acted like an infant in front of his parents. He would carry a bowl of water to them, and then stumble on purpose. Lying on the floor he would cry like a little child in order to make his parents laugh.

---

[1]According to Chinese tradition, Wu Meng later in life studied black magic and could cross a river without a boat, waving a fan of white feathers over the water. His body did not decompose after death and finally disappeared.

[2]Chinese texts sometimes continue this conversation: "We can always get another son, but it is impossible to get another mother."

[3]One chih is approximately 11 inches long.

[4]Lao Lai-tzu lived during the Spring and Autumn Period (770-476 CE) of the Chou Dynasty and was a native of Ch'u in South-West China. According to Chinese tradition, the king of Ch'u eventually heard of his ability to make people laugh and gave him a post in his court.

[5]In China it is quite unusual even today for both men and women above seventy not to mention their age with pride. In some colloquial versions of this story it is said that he does not mention his age so that his parents would not be sad and realize that both their son and they themselves might be near death.

Crying in the Bamboo-Grove and Making the Bamboo Sprout

During the era of the Three Kingdoms (3rd Century CE) there lived a man named Meng Sung, also known as [Meng] Chien-wu[6]. He had lost his father during his childhood. When his mother was old and sick she craved fresh bamboo-shoots even though it was winter. Sung had no idea how he could get them. In desperation, he went into a bamboo grove, clasped a bamboo stem and broke into tears. His filial devotion moved heaven and earth and they forced the earth to crack open. Numerous shoots of bamboo came out. Meng Sung carried them home and made them into a soup for his mother. As soon as she had eaten she felt much better.

Cleaning his Mother's Chamberpot

Huang T'ing-chien[7] of the Sung Dynasty, also known as [Huang] Shan-gu, became a member of the Hanlin academy[8] during the Yuan-Yu reign (1086–1094 CE)[9].

He was by nature extremely filial. Even though he was such an esteemed and famous person, he served his mother with utmost devotion. Every evening he would personally clean his mother's chamber pot. Not a moment passed without his fulfilling his filial duties.

Translated by Lydia Gerber

---

[6]Meng Sung eventually became keeper of the imperial fish ponds under the first emperor of the succeeding Chin dynasty.

[7]Huang T'ing-chien (1050–1110 CE) was a well-known poet and calligrapher.

[8]The Hanlin academy was the central institution of learning in Imperial China. This appointment was very prestigious for any scholar.

[9]Upon his ascension to the throne and whenever he considered it beneficial, a Chinese emperor proclaimed a new maxim for his reign. "Yuan yu" means "great protection."

Chinese Poetry

Tu Fu (T'ang, 712-770 CE): Banquet at the Tso Family Manor

Tu Fu and Li Po are the two most famous Chinese lyric poets. Friends and companions during some of the most tumultuous years of the T'ang dynasty, they were often separated by events from each other and from other friends. Like many Chinese poems, this one begins by making observations of the natural world surrounding the poet at a particular moment, then moves on to describe his individual mood. The pale moon sends its light through the scattered clouds onto the trees, which in itself suggests decline or loss. In the darkness he is aware of the trickling stream by its sound and knows that the stars are shining overhead, though he can see neither. The poet is participating in a poetry contest, writing new songs and performing them to the accompaniment of his lute. As they sing and drink, the contestants are enjoying themselves until someone sings a song which reminds Tu Fu of his home in the south, bringing over him a wave of homesickness.

The windy forest is checkered
By the light of the setting,
Waning moon. I tune the lute,
Its strings are moist with dew.
The brook flows in the darkness
Below the flower path. The thatched
Roof is crowned with constellations.
As we write the candles burn short.
Our wits grow sharp as swords while
The wine goes round. When the poem
Contest is ended, someone
Sings a song of the South. And
I think of my little boat,
And long to be on my way.

Translated by Kenneth Rexroth

Li Po (701–762 CE): *No long rope can tie the running sun*

The poetry of Tu Fu's friend Li Po is more lighthearted than that of his friend. If he also sees that life is transient, he argues that life can still be enjoyed. His enthusiasm for the pleasures of wine is legendary. The poem begins like a Buddhist meditation on impermanence, but ends with a call to celebrate.

No long rope can tie the running sun—[1]
All ages share this great sorrow in common.
Had I the yellow metal[2] piled up to the stars,

---

[1]That is, nothing can stop the passage of time.
[2]Gold.

I should use it to buy youth and fun.
A little spark of fire from the stone—
That is life in this world.
A moment past is a dream done;
What will become of us later is known to none.
Tell me not that you are too poor to drink,
Let us get wine and call our neighbors to our feast.
I doubt if there are immortals in the world,
But we can find sure happiness in the wine at least.

Translated by John C. H. Wu

In Spring how sweet is sleep!

Such an enthusiastic party-goer as Li Po was undoubtedly not fond of waking early under any circumstances, but on this night his sleep has been disturbed by a storm. Tree-blossoms, the most typical and fragile of spring beauties, must have suffered from the weather. In this sort of very compact mood piece, beginning with a reference to the seasons, going on to a natural observation, implying rather than stating a mood, we see the sort of poem that was to so powerfully influence Japanese waka *and—later—*haiku.

In Spring how sweet is sleep! I don't know the day has dawned!
But what a riotous chorus of birds I hear all around!
Last night the sound of wind and rain stole into my ears—
I wonder how many flowers have fallen on the ground.

Translated by John C. H. Wu

The Sun has set behind the western slope

Compare this poem with the similar poem above by Tu Fu.

The Sun has set behind the western slope,
The eastern moon lies mirrored in the pool;
With streaming hair my balcony I ope,[1]
And stretch my limbs to enjoy the cool.
Loaded with lotus-scent the breeze sweeps by,
Clear dripping drops from tall bamboos I hear,
I gaze upon my idle lute and sigh:
Alas no sympathetic soul is near!
And so I doze, the while before mine eyes
Dear friends of other days in dream-clad forms arise.

Translated by John C. H. Wu

---

[1]"Open."

Po Chü-i (772–846 CE): Passing T'ien-Men Street in Ch'ang-an and Seeing a Distant View of Chung-Nan Mountain[1]

Chinese poets and artists concentrate heavily on the beauties of nature, but ordinary life went on in the T'ang Dynasty as in most places and times.

The snow has gone from Chung-nan; spring is almost come.
Lovely in the distance its blue colors, against the brown of the streets.
A thousand coaches, ten thousand horsemen pass down the Nine Roads;
Turns his head and looks at the mountains,—not one man!

Translated by Arthur Waley

---

[1]Part of the great Nan Shan range, fifteen miles south of Ch'ang-an.

The Charcoal-Seller

Po Chü-i is famous for the simplicity of his language and his sympathy with the oppressed, as in this poem depicting the sufferings of a charcoal-vendor exploited by arrogant aristocrats.

An old charcoal seller
Cutting wood and burning charcoal in the forest of the Southern Mountain.
His face, stained with dust and ashes, has turned to the color of smoke.
The hair on his temples is streaked with gray: his ten fingers are black.
The money he gets by selling charcoal, how far does it go?
It is just enough to clothe his limbs and put food in his mouth.
Although, alas, the coat on his back is a coat without lining,
He hopes for the coming of cold weather, to send up the price of coal!
Last night, outside the city,—a whole foot of snow;
At dawn he drives the charcoal wagon along the frozen ruts.
Oxen,—weary; man,—hungry: the sun, already high;
Outside the Gate, to the south of the Market, at last they stop in the mud.
Suddenly, a pair of prancing horsemen. Who can it be coming?
A public official in a yellow coat and a boy in a white shirt.
In their hands they hold a written warrant: on their tongues—the words of an order;
They turn back the wagon and curse the oxen, leading them off to the north.
A whole wagon of charcoal,
More than a thousand pieces!
If officials choose to take it away, the woodman may not complain.
Half a piece of red silk and a single yard of damask,
The Courtiers have tied to the oxen's collar, as the price of a wagon of coal!

Translated by Arthur Waley

Lao-tzü

Po Chü-i impishly taunts one of the most influential of all Chinese philosophers in this poem.

"Those who speak know nothing
Those who know are silent."
These words, as I am told,
Were spoken by Lao-tzü.
If we are to believe that Lao-tzü
Was himself one who knew,
How comes it that he wrote a book
Of five thousand words?

Translated by Arthur Waley

Fu Hsüan: Woman (3rd C. CE)

Chinese civilization has often been considered one of the least favorable toward women, yet their problems are largely common from culture to culture. At least a number of Chinese women were able to articulate their plight in poems that came to be considered classics. Here the theme of distance is used throughout the poem to emphasize the emotional isolation that is women's lot.

How sad it is to be a woman!
Nothing on earth is held so cheap.
Boys stand leaning at the door
Like Gods fallen out of Heaven.
Their hearts brave the Four Oceans,
The wind and dust of a thousand miles.
No one is glad when a girl is born:
By her the family sets no store.
Then she grows up, she hides in her room
Afraid to look a man in the face.
No one cries when she leaves her home—
Sudden as clouds when the rain stops.
She bows her head and composes her face,
Her teeth are pressed on her red lips:
She bows and kneels countless times.
She must humble herself even to the servants.
His love is distant as the stars in Heaven,
Yet the sunflower bends toward the sun.
Their hearts more sundered than water and fire—
A hundred evils are heaped upon her.
Her face will follow the years' changes:
Her lord will find new pleasures.
They that were once like substance and shadow
Are now as far as Hu from Ch'in.[1]

---

[1] Two lands.

Yet Hu and Ch'in shall sooner meet
Than they whose parting is like Ts'an and Ch'en.[2]

Translated by Arthur Waley

_____

[2]Two stars.

Mei Yao Ch'en (Sung, 1002-1060)

Despite the fact that Chinese civilization has not generally provided much freedom or status for women, clearly many men loved their wives dearly, for they said so in poems like this lament of a bereaved husband. In China it was believed that the spirits of the departed continued to surround the living; so his experience is in no way unusual.

In what role does the husband think affectionately of his late wife? How has her death affected his own attitude toward life?

In broad daylight I dream I
Am with her. At night I dream
She is still at my side. She
Carries her kit of colored
Threads. I see her image bent
Over her bag of silks. She
Mends and alters my clothes and
Worries for fear I might look
Worn and ragged. Dead, she watches
Over my life. Her constant
Memory draws me towards death.

Translated by Kenneth Rexroth

Su Tung-p'o (1036–1101 CE): On the Birth of his Son

The Confucian examination system for recruiting officials into the bureaucracy may have been far more egalitarian than anything comparable in its heyday; yet it had its limits. Wealthy men were able to hire tutors to ensure their success, and poor but intelligent men seldom rose to the top. Su Tung-p'o, usually considered the greatest poet of the Sung Dynasty, often commented cynically on the system he considered corrupt and was dismissed from various positions for his pains. His sarcasm in the following poem sounds a strikingly contemporary note in this age of cynicism about politicians. The poet's revenge lies in the fact that his poems are still read and memorized when all those who persecuted him have been forgotten.

Families, when a child is born
Want it to be intelligent.
I, through intelligence,
Having wrecked my whole life,
Only hope the baby will prove
Ignorant and stupid.
Then he will crown a tranquil life
By becoming a Cabinet Minister.

Translated by Arthur Waley

The Secret History of the Mongols (13th Century CE)

This work, probably written in Mongolian in the mid-13th century, exists only in a late 14th-century Chinese text. It served as the official account of the origins of the ruling clan of the Mongols and the life story of Chingis Khan[1] (ca. 1162–1227). Although most of us are familiar with the later exploits of the conqueror, we know little of his early life. The first section of this work presents a familiar pattern of trials and tribulations experienced by Chingis Khan during his early life. When he was only nine, upon his father's untimely death, his relatives seized all the family goods and drove him, his mother, and his younger brothers into the mountains. This bitter experience and the harsh life in the mountains seems to have been a major influence in the development of his character—indomitable, resourceful, and ruthless. As the chief provider for his mother and younger brothers, he once tracked down and killed one of his half-brothers for stealing the fish he caught. This passage below describes what happened some years later when his relatives returned and tried to kill him.

What events does Chingis Khan interpret as showing that he is protected by Heaven (and might therefore be justifieed in later claiming the "Mandate of Heaven")?

Targhutai Kiriltugh,[2] the Tayichigud chief, said to himself:
"Hogelun's brood must have molted by now.
Her droolers must have grown into little men."
He gathered some of his soldiers and rode back down the river to find them.
When the family saw the soldiers approaching they were frightened.
The mother and her children,
young ones and old ones,
built a quick fortress in the woods.
Belgutei[3] pulled down small trees to fashion a barricade
and Khasar[4] fired off a volley of arrows to hold the soldiers back.
While these two older boys fought
Hogelun took Khadigun, Temuge, and Temulun[5]
and she hid them in the opening of a nearby cliff.
Then the Tayichigud shouted to them:
"Send out your elder brother, Temujin.
We're not here to fight with you.
We're here to get him."
But the Tayichigud realized that Temujin had escaped them.
He'd slipped out and run for the woods with his horse.
They pursued him until he reached the woods at the top of Mount Tergune.
Then they stopped there
since the forest was too thick to ride into

---

[1]Traditionally known as "Genghis Khan" in the West. His original name was Temujin. In 1206, the chieftains of all the Mongol clans and tribes gave Temujin the title "Chingis Khan," meaning universal ruler, and committed themselves to his leadership.

[2]The relative who took away all of Chingis Khan's possessions after his father's death.

[3]One of Chingis Khan's younger half-brothers.

[4]Another younger brother.

[5]More younger brothers.

and the Tayichigud stood watch at the entrance
waiting for Temujin to come out.
Temujin hid in the woods for three nights
then said to himself:
"Now I'll escape."
But as he led out his horse
his saddle seemed to fall off by itself.
He went back to where the saddle had fallen and looked at it closely.
The breast strap was still buckled and the belly cinch was in place,
yet somehow it fell off the horse.
He said to himself:
"The belly cinch could stay fastened and it could still slip back,
but how could a breast strap come off without coming unbuckled?
I think Heaven[6] wants me to stay here."
So he returned to his hiding place and spent three more nights.
Then again he tried to escape
but as he neared the edge of the forest
a white boulder the size of a tent
fell down in the path and blocked the way out.
He said to himself:
"I think Heaven wants me to stay here,"
and for three more nights he stayed in the woods.
For nine nights now he'd been without food
and he said to himself:
"I don't want to die here, forgotten and nameless.
I've got to escape."
He cut a new path around the boulder
using the knife he carried to cut himself arrows.
The brush was so thick there
he couldn't push through until he'd hacked a new path.
But as he led his horse out the Tayichigud were still waiting.
They captured him there and took him away.

Targhutai Kiriltugh had Temujin taken back to his camp as a prisoner,
ordering that he be passed around from tent to tent,
spending one night in each tent.
On the sixteenth day of the summer's first moon,
the Red Circle Day of that year,

the Tayichigud held a big feast on the banks of the Onan.
By twilight the people began to disperse.
A weak little fellow had been given the job of guarding Temujin that day,
and when all the people had passed out or gone home

---

[6]Eternal Blue Heaven (*Koko Mongke Tengri*), the supreme deity in Mongolian religious
belief, appears as the protector of Chingis Khan throughout the story. Chingis Khan later
attributed all his success to Heaven's will.

Temujin yanked his cangue away from his guard.
He swung the wood collar around and hit his guard once in the head with it,
then ran for the river as fast as he could.
He thought to himself:
"If I run for the woods they'll spot me there,"
so he went to the river,
and using his cangue as a float,
he lay back in the river with only his face sticking out of the water.
When the fellow he'd beaten came to, he yelled:
"I've lost him! Temujin's escaped!"
When they heard that
all the Tayichigud who had gone back to their tents
came out to search for him.
It was the night of full moon
and the moonlight was bright as the day.
Most went to look in the forest
thinking that's where he'd run.
But as Sorkhan Shira passed by the river
he saw Temujin lying there and said to him quietly:
"It's because you're a clever young man that the Tayichigud are afraid of you.
They say that your eyes contain fire,
that your face fills with light.
Just stay where you are.
I won't tell them I've seen you,"
and he kept right on pretending to search.
When they all came back to the feasting grounds someone said:
"Let's search again."
Sorkhan Shira spoke up, saying:
"Yes, let's go back again.
Each of us go back to the place we just searched and look again."
They agreed and went back to the same places,
and as Sorkhan Shira passed by the river, he whispered to Temujin:
"They're still after you.
Don't move yet."
They came back to the feasting ground and again someone said:
"Let's go back and search for him more."
And Sorkhan Shira spoke up this time, saying:
"My Tayichigud leaders, you've lost a man in broad daylight.
How can you expect to find him at night?
Let's look in the same places once more,
then go back to our tents.
Tomorrow we'll gather again and we'll find him.
How far can he go with a cangue on his neck?"
All agreed and went back to searching one last time for the night.
As Sorkhan Shira passed Temujin's hiding place he whispered:
"They said, 'Let's search one more time.
Then we'll go back to our tents and search tomorrow again.'
Lie quiet until they've gone away.

183

And don't tell anyone about this.
If you're captured don't tell them I saw you."
Temujin lay still in the water
waiting until all the men had gone back to their tents.
He tried to figure out what to do next,
and looking into his heart he thought:
"As I was passed from family to family,
from tent to tent,
I was taken to the tent of Sorkhan Shira.
His sons Chimbai and Chilagun were kind to me.
They even took the cangue off my neck
so I could sleep one night without it.
Now it's Sorkhan Shira who found me but didn't let them know.
Maybe that family will save me."
He pulled himself out of the river
and went off to find Sorkhan Shira's tent.
Temujin knew that theirs was the tent where the kumis was made.
During the day the leather jars were filled with mare's milk,
then all night they would beat the jars till the milk had fermented to kumis.
He found their tent by listening in the dark for the sound of the beater.
As he slipped in the door,
Sorkhan Shira cried out in a hushed voice:
"What are you doing here?
Didn't I tell you, 'Go find your mother and brothers' ?"
But his sons, Chimbai and Chilagun, protested, saying:
"If a falcon chases a sparrow into a bush,
then the bush saves the sparrow.
Now that he's here you can't throw him out."
They wouldn't listen to their father,
and removing Temujin's cangue,
they burnt it up in the fireplace.
They had him hide in a cart full of wool
and ordered their sister, Khadagan, to take care of him, telling her:
"Don't let anyone know that he's here."
After searching for him three days the Tayichigud leaders said:
"Someone in camp must be hiding him.
Let's search all the tents."
They came to Sorkhan Shira's tent and began searching everything.
They went through his chests,
through his carts,
even looking under his beds.
Finally they came to the cart filled with wool,
and began throwing the wool on the floor,
approaching the back of the cart.
"How could anyone survive all the heat,
buried under so much wool?" Sorkhan Shira said to the searchers,
and they looked at him,
looked at the wool,

threw it back in the cart and left.
Once they'd gone Temujin came out from under the wool.
Sorkhan Shira looked at him and said:
"You almost got us all killed,
blown away like the ashes.
Now get out of here.
Go find your mother and brothers."
He gave Temujin a straw-yellow mare,
a barren one with a white mouth.
He boiled him a fat lamb who'd been fed by two ewes,
and gave him two leather buckets of kumis to drink.

He gave him no saddle nor flint to light fires,
and gave a bow with only two arrows.
This was to make sure that Temujin wouldn't stop to hunt on the way back.
Giving him these things and no more,
Sorkhan Shira told Temujin to leave.
Temujin rode without stopping
till he came to the place where his brothers had thrown up their fortress.
Reading their tracks in the grass,
he followed them up the banks of the Onan.
The Kimurgha River enters the Onan from the west there,
and he saw they'd gone up that way.
He found their new camp up this river near Khorchukhui Hill.
He rejoined his family and they moved camp again.
This time they went to Blue Lake
below Mount Khara Jirugen in the Sengur River valley.
There in the Gurelgu mountains,
in sight of Mount Burkhan Khaldun,
they lived on the marmots and field mice they caught.
                        Translated by Paul Kahn & Francis Woodman Cleaves

The Travels of Marco Polo (late 13th C. CE)

When the Venetian merchant-traveler Marco Polo returned to Italy after a quarter-century absence, not only did he find himself largely forgotten, few took seriously his wild tales of the lavish court of Kublai Khan, whom he had been loyally serving in China for the past twenty years. He was mocked as "Marco Millions" for what they imagined were his wild exaggerations. Yet Polo's account of his travels, dictated while he was languishing in a Venetian prison, provided Europe with its first detailed images of China and many other far-off lands, and continues to be a valuable source for historians, though recently some have questioned whether he actually reached all the places he described.

Of the Figure and Stature of the Grand Khan, of his Four Principal Wives, and of the Annual Selection of Young Women for him in the Province of Ungut

Wealthy, powerful men in all cultures have usually surrounded themselves with beautiful women. The Catholic Polo sounds distinctly envious as he describes the Khan's imperial harem. The image of Asia as an erotic fantasyland was one that was to haunt the imaginations of Europeans for centuries to come.

Kublai, who is styled the grand khan, or lord of lords, is of the middle stature, that is, neither tall nor short; his limbs are well formed, and in his whole figure there is a just proportion. His complexion is fair, and occasionally suffused with red, like the bright tint of the rose, which adds much grace to his countenance. His eyes are black and handsome, his nose is well shaped and prominent. He has four wives of the first rank, who are esteemed legitimate, and the eldest born son of any one of these succeeds to the empire, upon the decease of the grand khan. They bear equally the title of empress, and have their separate courts. None of them have fewer than three hundred young female attendants of great beauty, together with a multitude of youths as pages, and other eunuchs, as well as ladies of the bedchamber; so that the number of persons belonging to each of their respective courts amounts to ten thousand. When his majesty is desirous of the company of one of his empresses, he either sends for her, or goes himself to her palace. Besides these, he has many concubines provided for his use, from a province of Tartary named Ungut, having a city of the same name, the inhabitants of which are distinguished for beauty of features and fairness of complexion. Thither the grand khan sends his officers very second year, or oftener, as it may happen to be his pleasure, who collect for him, to the number of four or five hundred, or more, of the handsomest of the young women, according to the estimation of beauty communicated to them in their instructions.

Of the style in which the Grand Khan holds his public courts, and sits at table with all his nobles

The Venetians were amazed by the lavishness of the Yuan court, though Marco Polo saw it after its peak. Polo could not have known that by the time he had reached home, "the Great Khan" was dead and his empire crumbling.

When his Majesty holds a grand and public court, those who attend it are seated in the following order. The table of the sovereign before his elevated throne, and he takes his seat on the northern side, with his face turned towards the south; and next to him, on his left

186

hand, sits the Empress. On his right hand, upon seats somewhat lower, are placed his sons, grandsons, and other persons connected with him by blood, that is to say, who are descended from the imperial stock. The seat, however, of Chingis, his eldest son, is raised a little above those of his othr sons, whose heads ar nearly on a level with the feet of the grand khan. The other princes and the nobility have their places at still lower tables; and the same rules are observed with respect to the females, the wives of the sons, grandsons, and other relatives of the grand khan being seated on the left hand, at tables in like manner gradually lower; then follow the wives of the nobility and military officers: so that all are seated according to their respective ranks and dignities, in the places assigned to them, and to which they are entitled. The tables are arranged in such a manner that the grand khan, sitting on his elevated throne, can overlook the whole. It is not, however, to be understood that all who assemble on such occasions can be accommodated at tables. The greater part of the officers, and even of the nobles, on the contrary, eat, sitting upon carpets, in the hall; and on the outside stand a great multitude of persons who come from different countries, and bring with them many rare and curious articles. . . .

In the middle of the hall, where the Great Khan sits at table, there is a magnificent piece of furniture, made in the form of a square coffer, each side of which is three paces in length, exquisitely carved in figures of animals, and gilt. It is hollow within, for the purpose of receiving a capacious vase, shaped like a jar, and of precious materials, calculated to hold about a hogshead , one of which is filled with mare's milk, another with that of the camel,[1] and so of the others, according to the kinds of beverage in use. Within this buffet are also the cups or flagons belonging to his majesty, for serving the liquors. Some of them are of beautiful gilt plate. Their size is such that, when filled with wine or other liquor, the quantity would be sufficient for eight or ten men. Before every two persons who have seats at the tables, one of these flagons is placed, together with a kind of ladle, in the form of a cup with a handle, also of plate; to be used not only for taking the wine out of the flagon, but for lifting it to the head. This is observed as well with respect to the women as the men. The quantity and richness of the plate belonging to his Majesty is quite incredible. Officers of rank are likewise appointed, whose duty it is to see that all strangers who happen to arrive at the time of the festival, and are unacquainted with the etiquette of the court, are suitably accommodated with places; and these stewards are continually visiting every part of the hall, inquiring of the guests if there is anything with which they are unprovided, or whether any of them wish for wine, milk, meat, or other articles, in which case it is immediately brought to them by the attendants. . . .

The numerous persons who attend at the sideboard of his majesty, and who serve him with victuals and drink, are all obliged to cover their noses and mouths with handsome veils or cloths of worked silk, in order that his victuals or his wine may not be affected by their breath. When drink is called for by him, and the page in waiting has presented it, he retires three paces and kneels down, upon which the courtiers, and all who are present, in like manner make their prostration. At the same moment all the musical instruments, of which there is a numerous band, begin to play, and continue to do so until he has ceased drinking, when all the company recover their posture. This reverential salutation is made as often as his majesty drinks. It is unnecessary to say anything of the victuals, because it may well be imagined that their abundance is excessive. When the repast is finished, and the tables have been removed, persons of various descriptions enter the hall, and amongst

---

[1]The traditional drinks of the nomadic Mongols, who brought them with them to the court they founded.

these a troop of comedians and performers on different instruments, as also tumblers and jugglers, who exhibit their skill in the presence of the grand khan, to the high amusement and gratification of all the spectators. When these sports are concluded, the people separate, and each returns to his own house.

From the Han to the early Ming Dynasties (corresponding to the period from classical Rome through the Middle Ages) China developed a wide variety of technologies far in advance of their European use. Gunpowder and printing are two familiar examples, but there were many others. Polo did not observe their use of distilled petroleum, but he was astonished by coal fires and by printed money, which involved three marvels: paper, printing, and the concept of nonmetallic money itself.

What reasons does Polo give that the Chinese have had to resort to burning these strange "stones?"

Concerning the Black Stones Dug in Cathay Used for Fuel

Throughout this province there is found a sort of black stone, which they dig out of the mountains, where it runs in veins. When lighted, it burns like charcoal, and retains the fire much better than wood; insomuch that it may be preserved during the night, and in the morning be found still burning. These stones do not flame, excepting a little when first lighted, but during their ignition give out a considerable heat. It is true there is no scarcity of wood in the country, but the multitude of inhabitants is so immense, and their stoves and baths, which they are continually heating, so numerous, that the quantity could not supply the demand; for there is no person who does not frequent a warm bath at least three times in the week, and during the winter daily, if it is in their power. Every man of rank or wealth has one in his house for his own use; and the stock of wood must soon prove inadequate to such consumption; whereas these stones may be had in the greatest abundance, and at a cheap rate.

The Kind of Paper Money Issued by the Grand Khan and Made to Pass Current Throughout His Dominions

In this city of Kanbalu is the mint of the Great Khan, who may truly be said to possess the secret of the alchemists,[1] as he has the art of producing money by the following process. He causes the bark to be stripped from those mulberry trees the leaves of which are used for feeding silk-worms, and takes from it that thin inner rind which lies between the coarser bark and the wood of the tree. This being steeped, and afterwards pounded in a mortar, until reduced to a pulp, is made into paper, resembling, in substance, that which is manufactured from cotton, but quite black. When ready for use, he has it cut into pieces of money of different sizes, nearly square, but somewhat longer than they are wide. Of these, the smallest pass for a denier tournois; the next size for a Venetian silver groat; others for two, five, and ten groats, others for one, two, three, and as far as ten bezants of gold. The coinage of this paper money is authenticated with as much form and ceremony as if it were

---

[1] Who claimed to be able to transform inexpensive metals like lead into gold.

actually of pure gold or silver; for to each note a number of officers, specially appointed, not only subscribe their names, but affix their signets also; and when this has been regularly done by the whole of them, the principal officer, appointed by his majesty, having dipped into vermilion the royal seal committed to his custody, stamps with it the piece of paper, so that the form of the seal tinged with the vermilion remains impressed upon it, by which it receives full authenticity as current money, and the act of counterfeiting it is punished as a capital offense. When thus coined in large quantities, this paper currency is circulated in every part of the Great Khan's dominions; nor dares any person, at the peril of his life, refuse to accept it in payment. All his subjects receive it without hesitation, because, wherever their business may call them, they can dispose of it again in the purchase of merchandise they may have occasion for; such as pearls, jewels, gold, or silver. With it, in short, every article may be procured.

Several times in the course of the year, large caravans of merchants arrive with such articles as have just been mentioned, together with gold tissues, which they lay before the grand khan. He thereupon calls together twelve experienced and skillful persons, selected for this purpose, whom he commands to examine the articles with great care, and to fix the value at which they should be purchased. Upon the sum at which they have been thus conscientiously appraised he allows a reasonable profit, and immediately pays for them with this paper; to which the owners can have no objection, because, as has been observed, it answers the purpose of their own disbursements; and even though they should be inhabitants of a country where this kind of money is not current, they invest the amount in other articles of merchandise suited to their own markets. When any persons happen to be possessed of paper money which from long use has become damaged, they carry it to the mint, where, upon the payment of only three per cent., they receive fresh notes in exchange. Should any be desirous of procuring gold or silver for the purposes of manufacture, such as of drinking-cups, girdles, or other articles wrought of these metals, they in like manner apply to the mint, and for their paper obtain the bullion they require. All his Majesty's armies are paid with this currency, which is to them of the same value as if it were gold or silver. Upon these grounds, it may certainly be affirmed that the grand khan has a more extensive command of treasure than any other sovereign in the universe.

Translated by William Marsden

Japan

Japanese Creation Myth (712 CE)
From Genji Shibukawa: *Tales from the Kojiki*

The following is a modern retelling of the creation story from the Kojiki, *Japan's oldest chronicle, compiled in 712 CE by O No Yasumaro. The quest for Izanami in the underworld is reminiscent of the Greek demigod Orpheus' quest in Hades for his wife, Eurydice, and even more of the Sumerian myth of the descent of Innana to the underworld.*

How does this story reflect the sense of its creators that Japan is the most important place in the world? Choose another creation story in this volume and compare it with this one.

The Beginning of the World

Before the heavens and the earth came into existence, all was a chaos, unimaginably limitless and without definite shape or form. Eon followed eon: then, lo! out of this boundless, shapeless mass something light and transparent rose up and formed the heaven. This was the Plain of High Heaven, in which materialized a deity called Ame-no-Minaka-Nushi-no-Mikoto (the Deity-of-the-August-Center-of-Heaven). Next the heavens gave birth to a deity named Takami-Musubi-no-Mikoto (the High-August-Producing-Wondrous-Deity), followed by a third called Kammi-Musubi-no-Mikoto (the Divine-Producing-Wondrous-Deity). These three divine beings are called the Three Creating Deities.

In the meantime what was heavy and opaque in the void gradually precipitated and became the earth, but it had taken an immeasurably long time before it condensed sufficiently to form solid ground. In its earliest stages, for millions and millions of years, the earth may be said to have resembled oil floating, medusa-like, upon the face of the waters. Suddenly like the sprouting up of a reed, a pair of immortals were born from its bosom. . . .

Many gods were thus born in succession, and so they increased in number, but as long as the world remained in a chaotic state, there was nothing for them to do. Whereupon, all the heavenly deities summoned the two divine beings, Izanagi and Izanami, and bade them descend to the nebulous place, and by helping each other, to consolidate it into terra firma. "We bestow on you," they said, "this precious treasure, with which to rule the land, the creation of which we command you to perform." So saying they handed them a spear called Ama-no-Nuboko, embellished with costly gems. The divine couple received respectfully and ceremoniously the sacred weapon and then withdrew from the presence of the Deities, ready to perform their august commission. Proceeding forthwith to the Floating Bridge of Heaven, which lay between the heaven and the earth, they stood awhile to gaze on that which lay below. What they beheld was a world not yet condensed, but looking like a sea of filmy fog floating to and fro in the air, exhaling the while an inexpressibly fragrant odor. They were, at first, perplexed just how and where to start, but at length Izanagi suggested to his companion that they should try the effect of stirring up the brine with their spear. So saying he pushed down the jeweled shaft and found that it touched something. Then drawing it up, he examined it and observed that the great drops which

190

fell from it almost immediately coagulated into an island, which is, to this day, the Island of Onokoro. Delighted at the result, the two deities descended forthwith from the Floating Bridge to reach the miraculously created island. In this island they thenceforth dwelt and made it the basis of their subsequent task of creating a country. Then wishing to become espoused, they erected in the center of the island a pillar, the Heavenly August Pillar, and built around it a great palace called the Hall of Eight Fathoms. Thereupon the male Deity turning to the left and the female Deity to the right, each went round the pillar in opposite directions. When they again met each other on the further side of the pillar, Izanami, the female Deity, speaking first, exclaimed: "How delightful it is to meet so handsome a youth!" To which Izanagi, the male Deity, replied: "How delighted I am to have fallen in with such a lovely maiden!" After having spoken thus, the male Deity said that it was not in order that woman should anticipate man in a greeting. Nevertheless, they fell into connubial relationship, having been instructed by two wagtails which flew to the spot. Presently the Goddess bore her divine consort a son, but the baby was weak and boneless as a leech. Disgusted with it, they abandoned it on the waters, putting it in a boat made of reeds. Their second offspring was as disappointing as the first. The two Deities, now sorely disappointed at their failure and full of misgivings, ascended to Heaven to inquire of the Heavenly Deities the causes of their misfortunes. The latter performed the ceremony of divining and said to them: "It is the woman's fault. In turning round the Pillar, it was not right and proper that the female Deity should in speaking have taken precedence of the male. That is the reason." The two Deities saw the truth of this divine suggestion, and made up their minds to rectify the error. So, returning to the earth again, they went once more around the Heavenly Pillar. This time Izanagi spoke first saying: "How delightful to meet so beautiful a maiden!" "How happy I am," responded Izanami, "that I should meet such a handsome youth!" This process was more appropriate and in accordance with the law of nature. After this, all the children born to them left nothing to be desired. First, the island of Awaji was born, next, Shikoku, then, the island of Oki, followed by Kyushu; after that, the island Tsushima came into being, and lastly, Honshu, the main island of Japan. The name of Oyashi- ma-kuni (the Country of the Eight Great Islands) was given to these eight islands. After this, the two Deities became the parents of numerous smaller islands destined to surround the larger ones.

The Birth of the Deities

Having, thus, made a country from what had formerly been no more than a mere floating mass, the two Deities, Izanagi and Izanami, set about begetting those deities destined to preside over the land, sea, mountains, rivers, trees, and herbs. Their first-born proved to be the sea-god, Owatatsumi-no-Kami. Next they gave birth to the patron gods of harbors, the male deity Kamihaya-akitsu-hiko having control of the land and the goddess Haya-akitsu-hime having control of the sea. These two latter deities subsequently gave birth to eight other gods.

Next Izanagi and Izanami gave birth to the wind-deity, Kami-Shinatsuhiko-no-Mikoto. At the moment of his birth, his breath was so potent that the clouds and mists, which had hung over the earth from the beginning of time, were immediately dispersed. In consequence, every corner of the world was filled with brightness. Kukunochi-no-Kami, the deity of trees, was the next to be born, followed by Oyamatsumi-no-Kami, the deity of mountains, and Kayanuhime-no-Kami, the goddess of the plains. . . .

191

The process of procreation had, so far, gone on happily, but at the birth of Kagutsuchi-no-Kami, the deity of fire, an unseen misfortune befell the divine mother, Izanami. During the course of her confinement, the goddess was so severely burned by the flaming child that she swooned away. Her divine consort, deeply alarmed, did all in his power to resuscitate her, but although he succeeded in restoring her to consciousness, her appetite had completely gone. Izanagi, thereupon and with the utmost loving care, prepared for her delectation various tasty dishes, but all to no avail, because whatever she swallowed was almost immediately rejected. It was in this wise that occurred the greatest miracle of all. From her mouth sprang Kanayama-biko and Kanayama-hime, respectively the god and goddess of metals, whilst from other parts of her body issued forth Haniyasu-hiko and Haniyasu-hime, respectively the god and goddess of earth. Before making her "divine retirement," which marks the end of her earthly career, in a manner almost unspeakably miraculous she gave birth to her last-born, the goddess Mizuhame-no-Mikoto. Her demise marks the intrusion of death into the world. Similarly the corruption of her body and the grief occasioned by her death were each the first of their kind.

By the death of his faithful spouse Izanagi was now quite alone in the world. In conjunction with her, and in accordance with the instructions of the Heavenly Gods, he had created and consolidated the Island Empire of Japan. In the fulfillment of their divine mission, he and his heavenly spouse had lived an ideal life of mutual love and cooperation. It is only natural, therefore, that her death should have dealt him a truly mortal blow.

He threw himself upon her prostrate form, crying: "Oh, my dearest wife, why art thou gone, to leave me thus alone? How could I ever exchange thee for even one child? Come back for the sake of the world, in which there still remains so much for both us twain to do." In a fit of uncontrollable grief, he stood sobbing at the head of the bier. His hot tears fell like hailstones, and lo! out of the tear-drops was born a beauteous babe, the goddess Nakisawame-no-Mikoto. In deep astonishment he stayed his tears, and gazed in wonder at the new-born child, but soon his tears returned only to fall faster than before. It was thus that a sudden change came over his state of mind. With bitter wrath, his eyes fell upon the infant god of fire, whose birth had proved so fatal to his mother. He drew his sword, Totsuka-no-tsurugi, and crying in his wrath, "Thou hateful matricide," decapitated his fiery offspring. Up shot a crimson spout of blood. Out of the sword and blood together arose eight strong and gallant deities. "What! more children?" cried Izanagi, much astounded at their sudden appearance, but the very next moment, what should he see but eight more deities born from the lifeless body of the infant firegod! They came out from the various parts of the body—head, breast, stomach, hands, feet, and navel—and, to add to his astonishment, all of them were glaring fiercely at him. Altogether stupefied he surveyed the new arrivals one after another.

Meanwhile Izanami, for whom her divine husband pined so bitterly, had quitted this world for good and all and gone to the Land of Hades.

Izanagi's Visit to the Land of Hades

As for the Deity Izanagi, who had now become a widower, the presence of so many offspring might have, to some extent, beguiled and solaced him, and yet when he remembered how faithful his departed spouse had been to him, he would yearn for her again, his heart swollen with sorrow and his eyes filled with tears. In this mood, sitting up alone at midnight, he would call her name aloud again and again, regardless of the fact that he could hope for no response. His own piteous cries merely echoed back from the walls of his chamber.

Unable any longer to bear his grief, he resolved to go down to the Nether Regions in order to seek for Izanami and bring her back, at all costs, to the world. He started on his long and dubious journey. Many millions of miles separated the earth from the Lower Regions and there were countless steep and dangerous places to be negotiated, but Izanagi's indomitable determination to recover his wife enabled him finally to overcome all these difficulties. At length he succeeded in arriving at his destination. Far ahead of him, he espied a large castle. "That, no doubt," he mused in delight, "may be where she resides."

Summoning up all his courage, he approached the main entrance of the castle. Here he saw a number of gigantic demons, some red, some black, guarding the gates with watchful eyes. He retraced his steps in alarm, and stole round to a gate at the rear of the castle. He found, to his great joy, that it was apparently left unwatched. He crept warily through the gate and peered into the interior of the castle, when he immediately caught sight of his wife standing at the gate at an inner court. The delighted Deity loudly called her name. "Why! There is some one calling me," sighed Izanami-no-Mikoto, and raising her beautiful head, she looked around her. What was her amazement but to see her beloved husband standing by the gate and gazing at her intently! He had, in fact, been in her thoughts no less constantly than she in his. With a heart leaping with joy, she approached him. He grasped her hands tenderly and murmured in deep and earnest tones: "My darling, I have come to take thee back to the world. Come back, I pray thee, and let us complete our work of creation in accordance with the will of the Heavenly Gods—our work which was left only half accomplished by thy departure. How can I do this work without thee? Thy loss means to me the loss of all." This appeal came from the depth of his heart. The goddess sympathized with him most deeply, but answered with tender grief: "Alas! Thou hast come too late. I have already eaten of the furnace of Hades. Having once eaten the things of this land, it is impossible for me to come back to the world." So saying, she lowered her head in deep despair.

"Nay, I must entreat thee to come back. Canst not thou find some means by which this can be accomplished?" exclaimed her husband, drawing nearer to her. After some reflection, she replied: "Thou hast come a very, very long way for my sake. How much I appreciate thy devotion! I wish, with all my heart, to go back with thee, but before I can do so, I must first obtain the permission of the deities of Hades. Wait here till my return, but remember that thou must not on any account look inside the castle in the meantime." " I swear I will do as thou biddest," quoth Izanagi, "but tarry not in thy quest." With implicit confidence in her husband's pledge, the goddess disappeared into the castle.

Izanagi observed strictly her injunction. He remained where he stood, and waited impatiently for his wife's return. Probably, to his impatient mind, a single heart-beat may have seemed an age. He waited and waited, but no shadow of his wife appeared. The day gradually wore on and waned away, darkness was about to fall, and a strange unearthly wind began to strike his face. Brave as he was, he was seized with an uncanny feeling of apprehension. Forgetting the vow he had made to the goddess, he broke off one of the teeth of the comb which he was wearing in the left bunch of his hair, and having lighted it, he crept in softly and glanced around him. To his horror he found Izanagi lying dead in a room: and lo! a ghastly change had come over her. She, who had been so dazzlingly beautiful, was now become naught but a rotting corpse, in an advanced stage of decomposition. Now, an even more horrible sight met his gaze; the Fire Thunder dwelt in her head, the Black Thunder in her belly, the Rending-Thunder in her abdomen, the Young Thunder in her left hand, the Earth-Thunder in her right hand, the Rumbling-Thunder in her left foot, and the Couchant Thunder in her right foot:—altogether eight Thunder-Deities had been born and were dwelling there, attached to her remains and belching forth flames from their mouths. Izanagi-no-Mikoto was so thoroughly alarmed at the sight, that he dropped the light and took to his heels. The sound he made awakened Izanami from her death-like slumber. "Forsooth!" she cried: "he must have seen me in this revolting state. He has put me to shame and has broken his solemn vow. Unfaithful wretch! I'll make him suffer, for his perfidy."

Then turning to the Hags of Hades, who attended her, she commanded them to give chase to him. At her word, an army of female demons ran after the Deity.

Translated by Yaichiro Isobe

The Pillow Book of Sei Shonagon (967–1013 CE)

*This informal collection of jottings delightfully depicts the Heian court from a woman's per-
spective. Sei Shonagon was learned, noble, witty, and beautiful. Like many women of her era,
she was able to cultivate the art of writing in Japanese because a sexist society reserved the more
prestigious Chinese writing for men. The result is that there are more famous women writers
from this period than any other in ancient history, a fact that makes one realize how tragic has
been the loss to literature and learning of the repression of women. Many of her pieces are small,
poem-like lists of images or ideas.*

The Beauties Belonging to Each Season

Which is the only season about which she has something negative to say?

In spring it is the dawn that is most beautiful. As the light creeps over the hills, their
outlines are dyed a faint red and wisps of purplish cloud trail over them.

In summer the nights. Not only when the moon shines, but on dark nights too, as the
fireflies flit to and fro, and even when it rains, how beautiful it is!

In autumn the evenings, when the glittering sun sinks close to the edge of the hills and
the crows fly back to their nests in threes and fours and twos; more charming still is a file
of wild geese, like specks in the distant sky. When the sun has set, one's heart is moved by
the sound of the wind and the hum of the insects.

In winter the early mornings. It is beautiful indeed when snow has fallen during the
night, but splendid too when the ground is white with frost; or even when there is no snow
or frost, but it is simply very cold and the attendants hurry from room to room stirring up
the fires and bringing charcoal, how well this fits the season's mood! But as noon approaches and the cold wears off, no one bothers to keep the braziers alight, and soon
nothing remains but piles of white ashes.

The Women's Apartments along the Gallery

*The women at court lived in semi-seclusion. Even when they socialized with men it was
usually from behind screens or darkened rooms where their faces could seldom be made out
clearly. Yet they led very active social and sexual lives. Through the shutters of their windows and
the openings in their screens they observed more of the outside world than the outside world
observed of them.*

*What aspects of the following passage show that these women had very little privacy, despite
their seclusion? What seem to you to be the disadvantages of being a woman in this setting? The
advantages? Explain.*

The women's apartments along the gallery of the Imperial Palace are particularly pleasant. When one raises the upper part of the small half-shutters, the wind blows in extremely
hard; it is cool even in summer, and in winter snow and hail come along with the wind,
which I find agreeable. As the rooms are small, and as the page-boys (even though employed in such august precincts) often behave badly, we women generally stay hidden
behind our screens or curtains. It is delightfully quiet there; for one cannot hear any of the

loud talk and laughter that disturb one in other parts of the palace.

Of course we must always be on the alert when we are staying in these apartments. Even during the day we cannot be off our guard, and at night we have to be especially careful. But I rather enjoy all this. Throughout the night one hears the sound of footsteps in the corridor outside. Every now and then the sound will stop, and someone will tap on a door with just a single finger. It is pleasant to think that the woman inside can instantly recognize her visitor. Sometimes the tapping will continue for quite a while without the woman's responding in any way. The man finally gives up, thinking that she must be asleep; but this does not please the woman, who makes a few cautious movements, with a rustle of silk clothes, so that her visitor will know she is really there. Then she hears him fanning himself as he remains standing outside the door.

In the winter one sometimes catches the sound of a woman gently stirring the embers in her brazier. Though she does her best to be quiet, the man who is waiting outside hears her; he knocks louder and louder, asking her to let him in. Then the woman slips furtively towards the door where she can listen to him.

On other occasions one may hear several voices reciting Chinese or Japanese poems. One of the women opens her door, though in fact no one has knocked. Seeing this, several of the men, who had no particular intention of visiting this woman, stop on their way through the gallery. Since there is no room for them all to come in, many of them spend the rest of the night out in the garden—most charming.

Bright green bamboo blinds are a delight, especially when beneath them one can make out the many layers of a woman's clothes emerging from under brilliantly colored curtains of state. The men who glimpse this sight from the verandah, whether they be young noblemen with their over-robes informally left unsewn in the back, or Chamberlains of the Sixth Rank in their costumes of green, do not as a rule dare enter the room where the woman is seated. It is interesting to observe them as they stand there with their backs pressed to the wall and with the sleeves of their robes neatly arranged. Charming also, when one is watching from the outside, is the sight of a young man clad in laced trousers of dark purple and in a dazzling Court robe over an array of varicolored garments, as he leans forward into the woman's room, pushing aside the green blind. At this point he may take out an elegant inkstone and start writing a letter, or again, he may ask the woman for a mirror and comb his sidelocks; either is delightful.

When a three-foot curtain of state has been set up, there is hardly any gap between the top of the frame and the bottom of the head-blind; fortunately the little space that remains always seems to come precisely at the face level of the man who is standing outside the curtains and of the woman who is conversing with him from inside. What on earth would happen if the man was extremely tall and the woman very short? I really cannot imagine. But, so long as people are of normal height, it is satisfactory.

I particularly enjoy the rehearsal before the Special Festival when I am staying in the women's apartments at the Palace. As the men from the Office of Grounds walk along, they hold their long pine torches high above them; because of the cold their heads are drawn into their robes, and consequently the ends of the torches are always threatening to bump into things. Soon there is the pleasant sound of music as the players pass outside the women's apartments playing their flutes. Some of the young noblemen in the Palace, fascinated by the scene, appear in their Court costumes and stand outside our rooms chatting with us, while their attendants quietly order people to make way for their masters. All the voices mingle with the music in an unfamiliar and delightful way.

Since the night is already well advanced, one does not bother to go to bed but waits for the dawn when the musicians and dancers return from their rehearsal. Soon they arrive, and then comes the best part of all when they sing "The rice flowers from the freshly-planted fields."

Almost everyone enjoys these things; but occasionally some sober-sides will hurry by, without stopping to watch the scene. Then one of the women calls out laughingly to him, "Wait a moment, Sir! How can you abandon the charms of such a night? Stay for a while and enjoy yourself!" But evidently the man is in a bad mood, for he scurries along the corridor, almost tumbling over himself in his haste, as though in terror of being pursued and captured.

Things That Make One's Heart Beat Faster

Sparrows feeding their young. To pass a place where babies are playing. To sleep in a room where some fine incense has been burnt. To notice that one's elegant Chinese mirror has become a little cloudy.[1] To see a gentleman stop his carriage before one's gate and instruct his attendants to announce his arrival. To wash one's hair, make one's toilet,[2] and put on scented robes; even if not a soul sees one, these preparations still produce an inner pleasure.

It is night and one is expecting a visitor. Suddenly one is startled by the sound of rain-drops, which the wind blows against the shutters.

Good and Bad Lovers

The court ladies seemed to engage extensively in love affairs, though they were expected to be reasonably discreet about them. Sei Shonagon here evaluates men's behavior based on her own experiences.

What qualities does she particularly appreciate in a lover?

A lover who is leaving at dawn announces that he has to find his fan and his paper.[3] "I know I put them somewhere last night," he says. Since it is pitch dark, he gropes about the room, bumping into the furniture and muttering, "Strange! Where on earth can they be?" Finally he discovers the objects. He thrusts the paper into the breast of his robe with a great rustling sound; then he snaps open his fan and busily fans away with it. Only now is he ready to take his leave. What charmless behavior! "Hateful" is an understatement.

Equally disagreeable is the man who, when leaving in the middle of the night, takes care to fasten the cord of his headdress. This is quite unnecessary; he could perfectly well put it gently on his head without tying the cord. And why must he spend time adjusting his cloak or hunting costume? Does he really think someone may see him at this time of night and criticize him for not being impeccably dressed?

A good lover will behave as elegantly at dawn as at any other time. He drags himself out of bed with a look of dismay on his face. The lady urges him on: "Come, my friend, it's getting light. You don't want anyone to find you here." He gives a deep sigh, as if to say that

---

[1]Bronze mirrors tarnished with time.
[2]Make-up, etc.
[3]Courtiers routinely carried fancy paper with them for writing notes and poetry.

the night has not been nearly long enough and that it is agony to leave. Once up, he does not instantly pull on his trousers. Instead he comes close to the lady and whispers whatever was left unsaid during the night. Even when he is dressed, he still lingers, vaguely pretending to be fastening his sash.

Presently he raises the lattice, and the two lovers stand together by the side door while he tells her how he dreads the coming day, which will keep them apart; then he slips away. The lady watches him go, and this moment of parting will remain among her most charming memories.

Indeed, one's attachment to a man depends largely on the elegance of his leave-taking. When he jumps out of bed, scurries about the room, tightly fastens his trouser-sash, rolls up the sleeves of his Court cloak, over-robe, or hunting costume, stuffs his belongings into the breast of his robe and then briskly secures the outer sash—one really begins to hate him.

Translated by Ivan Morris

Murasaki Shikibu: *The Tale of Genji* (c. 1000 CE)
The Festival of the Cherry Blossoms

Lady Murasaki's Genji Monogatari, Japan's greatest novel (and often claimed to be the world's first), is largely concerned with the many love affairs of the handsome and charming Prince Genji. He illustrates his skills in several arts, including the crucial one: improvising brief poems. Part of the game of such improvisation is to reply to someone else's poem using the same imagery, but in a different way. All the courtiers had memorized vast quanities of such poetry, so even a slight allusion to a verse would immediately suggest the whole poem (here given in footnotes) to the listeners. In the following episode, he blunders into seducing his brother's intended wife in what would now be seen as little better than an act of rape. As in all Heian literature, the narrative is very discreet about alluding to actual sex acts; but the context makes clear that the couple spent the night making love. Genji can remain ignorant of the identity of his bed-partner because court women lived behind screens in semi-darkened rooms, with most of their social life being conducted during the hours of darkness. Women were hardly sequestered in the classic sense of the word, since love-affairs seem to have been commonplace and widely accepted, but their faces were seldom clearly seen.

What argument does Genji give to get the young woman to give in to him?

Other high courtiers danced, in no fixed order, but as it was growing dark one could not easily tell who were the better dancers. The poems were read. Genji's was so remarkable that the reader paused to comment upon each line. The professors were deeply moved. Since Genji was for the emperor a shining light, the poem could not fail to move him too. As for the empress, she wondered how Kokiden could so hate the youth—and reflected on her own misfortune in being so strangely drawn to him.

"Could I see the blossom as other blossoms,
Then would there be no dew to cloud my heart."

She recited it silently to herself. How then did it go the rounds and presently reach me? The festivities ended late in the night.

The courtiers went their ways, the empress and the crown prince departed, all was quiet. The moon came out more brightly. It wanted proper appreciation, thought Genji. The ladies in night attendance upon the emperor would be asleep. Expecting no visitors, his own lady might have left a door open a crack. He went quietly up to her apartments, but the door of the one whom he might ask to show him in was tightly closed. He sighed. Still not ready to give up, he made his way to the gallery by Kokiden's pavilion. The third door from the north was open. Kokiden herself was with the emperor, and her rooms were almost deserted. The hinged door at the far corner was open too. All was silent. It was thus, he thought, that a lady invited her downfall. He slipped across the gallery and up to the door of the main room and looked inside. Everyone seemed to be asleep.

"'What can compare with a misty moon of spring?'" It was a sweet young woman, so delicate that its owner could be no ordinary serving woman.

She came (could he believe it?) to the door. Delighted, he caught at her sleeve.

"Who are you?" She was frightened.

"There is nothing to be afraid of."

"Late in the night we enjoy a misty moon.
There is nothing misty about the bond between us."

Quickly and lightly he lifted her down to the gallery and slid the door closed. Her surprise pleased him enormously.

Trembling, she called for help.

"It will do you no good. I am always allowed my way. Just be quiet, if you will, please."

She recognized his voice and was somewhat reassured. Though of course upset, she evidently did not wish him to think her wanting in good manners. It may have been because he was still a little drunk that he could not admit the possibility of letting her go; and she, young and irresolute, did not know how to send him on his way. He was delighted with her, but also very nervous, for dawn was approaching. She was in an agony of apprehension lest they be seen.

"You must tell me who you are," he said. "How can I write to you if you do not? You surely don't think I mean to let matters stand as they are?"

"Were the lonely one to vanish quite away,
Would you go the grassy moors to ask her name?"

Her voice had a softly plaintive quality.

"I did not express myself well.

"I wish to know whose dewy lodge it is
Ere winds blow past the bamboo-tangled moor."

"Only one thing, a cold welcome, could destroy my eagerness to visit. Do you perhaps have some diversionary tactic in mind?"

They exchanged fans and he was on his way. Even as he spoke a stream of women was moving in and out of Kokiden's rooms. There were women in his own rooms too, some of them still awake. Pretending to be asleep, they poked one another and exchanged whispered remarks about the diligence with which he pursued these night adventures.

He was unable to sleep. What a beautiful girl! One of Kokiden's younger sisters, no doubt. Perhaps the fifth or sixth daughter of the family, since she had seemed to know so little about men? He had heard that both the fourth daughter, to whom To no Chujo was uncomfortably married, and Prince Hotaru's wife were great beauties,[1] and thought that the encounter might have been more interesting had the lady been one of the older sisters. He rather hoped she was not the sixth daughter, whom the minister had thoughts of marrying to the crown prince. The trouble was that he had no way of being sure. It had not seemed that she wanted the affair to end with but the one meeting. Why then had she not told him how he might write to her? These thoughts and others suggest that he was much interested. He thought too of Fujitsubo's pavilion, and how much more mysterious and inaccessible it was, indeed how uniquely so.

He had a lesser spring banquet with which to amuse himself that day. He played the thirteen-stringed koto, his performance if anything subtler and richer than that of the day before. Fujitsubo went to the emperor's apartments at dawn.

---

[1] The crown prince, Genji, and Prince Hotaru are all brothers.

Genji was on tenterhooks, wondering whether the lady he had seen in the dawn moonlight would be leaving the palace. He sent Yoshikiyo and Koremitsu, who let nothing escape them, to keep watch; and when, as he was leaving the royal presence, he had their report, his agitation increased.

"Some carriages that had been kept out of sight left just now by the north gate. Two of Kokiden's brothers and several other members of the family saw them off; so we gathered that the ladies must be part of the family too. They were ladies of some importance, in any case—that much was clear. There were three carriages in all."

How might he learn which of the sisters he had become friends with? Supposing her father were to learn of the affair and welcome him gladly into the family—he had not seen enough of the lady to be sure that the prospect delighted him. Yet he did want very much to know who she was. He sat looking out at the garden.

Murasaki[2] would be gloomy and bored, he feared, for he had not visited her in some days. He looked at the fan he had received in the dawn moonlight. It was a "three-ply cherry." The painting on the more richly colored side, a misty moon reflected on water, was not remarkable, but the fan, well used, was a memento to stir longing. He remembered with especial tenderness the poem about the grassy moors.

He jotted down a poem beside the misty moon:

"I had not known the sudden loneliness
Of having it vanish, the moon in the sky of dawn."

He had been neglecting the Sanjo mansion of his father-in-law for rather a long time, but Murasaki was more on his mind. He must go comfort her. She pleased him more, she seemed prettier and cleverer and more amiable, each time he saw her. He was congratulating himself that his hopes of shaping her into his ideal might not prove entirely unrealistic. Yet he had misgivings—very unsettling ones, it must be said—lest by training her himself he put her too much at ease with men. He told her the latest court gossip and they had a music lesson. So he was going out again—she was sorry, as always, to see him go, but she no longer clung to him as she once had.

At Sanjo it was the usual thing: his wife kept him waiting. In his boredom he thought of this and that. Pulling a koto to him, he casually plucked out a tune. "No nights of soft sleep,"[3] he sang, to his own accompaniment.

The minister came for a talk about the recent pleasurable events.

"I am very old, and I have served through four illustrious reigns, but never have I known an occasion that has added so many years to my life. Such clever, witty poems, such fine music and dancing—you are on good terms with the great performers who so abound in our day, and you arrange things with such marvelous skill. Even we aged ones felt like cutting a caper or two."

"The marvelous skill of which you speak, sir, amounts to nothing at all, only a word here and there. It is a matter of knowing where to ask. 'Garden of Willows and Flowers' was much the best thing, I thought, a performance to go down as a model for all the ages. And

[2]Murasaki has been raised by Genji to be his ideal mistress. It is her name which has been traditionally used for the author of this work.
[3]The rest of the song is, "Soft as the reed pillow,/The waves of the river Nuki./My father comes between us."

what a memorable day it would have been, what an honor for our age, if in the advancing spring of your life you had followed your impulse and danced for us."

Soon To no Chujo and his brothers, leaning casually against the veranda railings, were in fine concert on their favorite instruments.

The lady of that dawn encounter, remembering the evanescent dream, was sunk in sad thoughts. Her father's plans to give her to the crown prince in the Fourth Month were a source of great distress. As for Genji, he was not without devices for searching her out, but he did not know which of Kokiden's sisters she was, and he did not wish to become involved with that unfriendly family.

Late in the Fourth Month the princes and high courtiers gathered at the mansion of the Minister of the Right, Kokiden's father, for an archery meet.[4] It was followed immediately by a wisteria banquet. Though the cherry blossoms had for the most part fallen, two trees, perhaps having learned that mountain cherries do well to bloom late,[5] were at their belated best. The minister's mansion had been rebuilt and beautifully refurnished for the initiation ceremonies of the princesses his granddaughters. It was in the ornate style its owner preferred, everything in the latest fashion.

Seeing Genji in the palace one day, the minister had invited him to the festivities. Genji would have preferred to stay away, but the affair seemed certain to languish without him. The minister sent one of his sons, a guards officer, with a message:

"If these blossoms of mine were of the common sort,
Would I press you so to come and look upon them?"

Genji showed the poem to his father.

"He seems very pleased with his flowers," laughed the emperor. "But you must go immediately. He has, after all, sent a special invitation. It is in his house that the princesses your sisters are being reared. You are scarcely a stranger."

Genji dressed with great care. It was almost dark when he finally presented himself. He wore a robe of a thin white Chinese damask with a red lining and under it a very long train of magenta. Altogether the dashing young prince, he added something new to the assembly that so cordially received him, for the other guests were more formally clad. He quite overwhelmed the blossoms, in a sense spoiling the party, and played beautifully on several instruments. Late in the evening he got up, pretending to be drunk. The first and third princesses were living in the main hall. He went to the east veranda and leaned against a door. The shutters were raised and women were gathered at the southwest corner, where the wisteria was in bloom. Their sleeves were pushed somewhat ostentatiously out from under blinds, as at a New Year's poetry assembly. All rather overdone, he thought, and he could not help thinking too of Fujitsubo's reticence.

"I was not feeling well in the first place, and they plied me with drink. I know I shouldn't, but might I ask you to hide me?" He raised the blind at the corner door.

"Please, dear sir, this will not do. It is for us beggars to ask such favors of you fine gentlemen." Though of no overwhelming dignity, the women were most certainly not common.

[4]Note that the poems at the end of this selection have archery themes.
[5]An allusion to the following poem: "These mountain cherries with no one to look upon them:/Might they not bloom when all the others have fallen?"

202

Incense hung heavily in the air and the rustling of silk was bright and lively. Because the princesses seemed to prefer modern things, the scene may perhaps have been wanting in mysterious shadows.

The time and place were hardly appropriate for a flirtation, and yet his interest was aroused. Which would be the lady of the misty moon?

"A most awful thing has happened," he said playfully. "Someone has stolen my fan."[6] He sat leaning against a pillar.

"What curious things that Korean does do." The lady who thus deftly returned his allusion did not seem to know about the exchange of fans.

Catching a sigh from another lady, he leaned forward and took her hand.

> "I wander lost on Arrow Mount and ask:
> May I not see the moon I saw so briefly?

"Or must I continue to wander?"

It seemed that she could not remain silent:

> "Only the flighty, the less than serious ones,
> Are left in the skies when the longbow moon is gone."

It was the same voice. He was delighted. And yet—

Translated by Edward G. Seidensticker.

[6]Because the words for "fan" and "sash" are similar, this is an allusion to the following poem: "A most awful thing has happened. Someone has stolen my sash. 'Tis the Korean of Ishikawa."

Japanese Poetry

Poetry has been a major Japanese influence on the literature of many countries. In the early waka and later haiku forms, poets strove for the utmost conciseness and vividness; always linking emotions or ideas to natural objects. The gem-like brilliance of these extremely restricted forms has attracted many modern Western poets. The following poems are from two classic collections of Japanese verse, the Manyoshu and the Kokinoshu.

Anonymous: *In the autumn fields*

From the early section of the love poems of the Kokinoshu.

In the autumn fields
mingled with the pampas grass
flowers are blooming
should my love too, spring forth
or shall we never meet?

Translated by Jon LaCure

Mibu no Tadamine: *On Kasuga plain*

Having seen a young lady at the Kasuga festival, Tadamine asked where she lived and sent this poem.

On Kasuga plain
between those patches of snow
just beginning to sprout,
glimpsed, the blades of grass,
like those glimpses of you.

Translated by Jon LaCure

Ono no Komachi: *The hue of the cherry* (9th C. CE)

Ono no Komachi was a fine poet, but she was also a great court beauty whose love affairs inspired the plots of more than one Noh drama. Many of her poems used multiple puns (called "pivot words") to create complex layers of meaning.

In what way does the poet compare herself to the cherry blossoms in the spring rain?

The hue of the cherry
fades too quickly from sight
all for nothing
this body of mine grows old —
spring rain ceaselessly falling.

Translated by Jon LaCure

204

Sugawara Michizane (845–903 CE): *The autumn breeze rises*

Japanese poets often delight in exploring ambiguities. One of their favorite themes is the difficulty of discerning one white object from another: a white spider on a white flower, or here, white flowers and the foam of waves beating against the shore. Nature in the Heian period (794–1186) was never an untamed wilderness but most typically represented by the carefully tended garden or a painting on a folding screen. This poem was attached to a chrysanthemum during a courtly competition where the flower was placed in a miniature representation of the beach at Fukiage done in a tray. The author is best known as a scholar and poet of Chinese verse.

Write a poem of your own comparing two things which are close to each other in appearance.

The autumn breeze rises
on the shore at Fukiage—
and those white chrysanthemums
are they flowers? or not?
or only breakers on the beach?

Translated by Jon LaCure

Ki no Tsurayuki (c. 872–945 CE): *The night approaches*

Ki no Tsurayuki was the foremost poet of his age. He was one of the editors of the Kokinshu *and wrote one of the prefaces to the anthology. He was also the author of a travel diary, the* Tosa *diary.*

In what way is the approach of night like autumn?

The night approaches,
darkness on Mt. Ogura
where the deer cry out
and in their voices calling
is it autumn on the wane?

Translated by Jon LaCure

Japan

Prince Otsu (663-686 CE): Poem sent by Prince Otsu to Lady Ishikawa

In the classical age much of the verse was occasional poetry, and poetic exchanges were a necessary part of courtship. In this exchange the Lady Ishikawa has taken Prince Otsu's poem and cleverly rearranged it. She repeats in the fourth line what Prince Otsu has repeated in lines two and five of his poem.

How does Lady Ishakawa turn Prince Otsu's complaint at having been stood up into a compliment which reassures him of her continuing love?

Gentle foothills, and
in the dew drops of the mountains,
soaked, I waited for you—
grew wet from standing there
in the dew drops of the mountains.

Translated by Jon LaCure

Lady Ishikawa (7th C. CE): Poem by Lady Ishikawa in response

Waiting for me,
you grew wet there
in gentle foothills,
in the dew drops of the mountains—
I wish I'd been such drops of dew.

Translated by Jon LaCure

Lady Horikawa (mid-12th Century CE): *Will he always love me?*

Much classic poetry concerns love affairs often conducted in secrecy. Here the poet is anxious on the morning after an encounter with her lover which has left her hair and emotions equally tangled.

Will he always love me?
I cannot read his heart.
This morning my thoughts
Are as disordered
As my black hair.

Translated by Kenneth Rexroth

Kakinomoto Hitomaro (7th C. CE): *In the sea of ivy clothed Iwami*

Not all love poetry concerns illicit relationships. Here one of Japan's greatest poets expresses the anguish of being separated from his young bride. Usually bureaucratic service at a distant shoreline outpost was viewed with dread by the urbanized courtiers; but as the poet returns to the capital, he remembers the tangled seaweed near the shore at Iwami, and its motion reminds him fondly of their honeymoon lovemaking there.

What different ways can you find in this poem that Hitomaro has used nature imagery to convey his feelings?

In the sea of ivy clothed Iwami
Near the cape of Kara,
The deep sea miru weed
Grows on the sunken reefs:
The jewelled sea tangle
Grows on the rocky foreshore,
Swaying like the jewelled sea tangle
My girl would lie with me,
My girl whom I love with a love
Deep as the miru[1] growing ocean.
We slept together only a few
Wonderful nights and then
I had to leave her.
It was like tearing apart braided vines.
My bowels are knotted inside me
With the pain of my heart.
I long for her and look back.
A confusion of colored leaves
Falls over Mount Watari.[2]
I can no longer see
Her waving sleeves.
The moon rushes through rifted clouds
Over the honeymoon cottage
On Mount Yagami.
The setting sun has left the sky.
The light grows dim.
I thought I was a brave man,
My thin sleeves are wet with tears.

Translated by Geoffrey Bownas & Anthony Thwaite

---

[1]A type of seaweed.

[2]This mountain stands between him and his bride. It is autumn, so he sees the colored leaves instead of her as he remembers her at his departure, waving goodbye.

I loved her like the leaves

In this poem Hitomaro writes of a bereaved husband, yearning for his late wife. Her soul is described as having flown toward the heavens like the lightest of scarves. He cannot feed adequately the child she was still nursing. Japanese tradition places great emphasis on encounters with ghosts, but here the narrator is unsuccessful in his search for the spirit of his dead wife.

I loved her like the leaves,
The lush leaves of spring
That weighed the branches of the willows
Standing on the jutting bank
Where we two walked together
While she was of this world.
My life was built on her;
But man cannot flout
The laws of this world.
To the wide fields where the heat haze shimmers,
Hidden in a white cloud,
White as white mulberry scarf,
She soared like the morning bird
Hidden from our world like the setting sun.
The child she left as token
Whimpers, begs for food; but always
Finding nothing that I might give,
Like birds that gather rice-heads in their beaks,
I pick him up and clasp him in my arms.
By the pillows where we lay,
My wife and I, as one.
The daylight I pass lonely till the dusk,
The black night I lie sighing till the dawn.
I grieve, yet know no remedy:
I pine, yet have no way to meet her.
The one I love, men say,
Is in the hills of Hagai,
So I labor my way there,
Smashing rock-roots in my path,
Yet get no joy from it.
For, as I knew her in this world,
I find not the dimmest trace.

Translated by Geoffrey Bownas & Anthony Thwaite

Lady Kasa (2nd half 8th Century CE): Six Tanka written for Otomo Yakamochi

Tanka or waka is an ancient form in Japan, and is still widely used. Several of the poems above are tanka as well. In the first poem Lady Kasa says she will die of longing separated so far from her beloved.

Like the pearl of dew
On the grass in my garden
In the evening shadows,
I shall be no more.

The next two poems speak of love for one who has been posted to a remote location—a common theme. All nobles hoped to spend their lives at court.

Even the grains of sand
On a beach eight hundred days wide
Would not be more than my love,
Watchman of the island coast.

The breakers of the Ise Sea
roar like thunder on the shore,
As fierce as they, as proud as they,
Is he who pounds my heart.

Why would a woman dreaming she has a sword remind her of a man?

I dreamt of a great sword
Girded to my side.
What does it signify?
That I shall meet you?

The bell has rung, the sign
For all to go to sleep,
Yet thinking of my love
How can I ever sleep?

To love a man without return
Is to offer a prayer
To a devil's back[1]
In a huge temple.

Translated by Geoffrey Bownas & Anthony Thwaite

[1]These are guardian demons, mighty but not prone to answer prayers.

The Islamic World

The *Qur'an*

The Qur'an *(often spelled "Koran" in English), the sacred book of Islam, is believed by Muslims to be literally the word of God as dictated by an angel to the Prophet Muhammad and recited by him to his followers, who wrote it down and assembled it after his death into the book that we have now. It is divided into 114 suras (chapters), in ascending order of length. According to tradition no true translation from the original Arabic is possible, so this rendering into English is called an "interpretation" rather than a "translation;" but it attempts to capture some of the poetic beauty which characterizes the original and makes it not only the dominant religious work in Islam but also the most influential literary work in the Arabic-speaking world. Note that "Allah" is simply the Arabic word for the same god called "El" in ancient Hebrew, and is therefore here rendered simply as "God." All selections from the* Qur'an *are from the version by A. J. Arberry.*

The Opening (Sura 1)

Islam, like Christianity and later Judaism, accepts the idea of a Day of Judgment in which God will send the believers to Paradise and condemn the unbelievers to eternal torment. Yet the theme announced at the very beginning of the Qur'an *and running throughout it is God's mercy, praised in the first verse of this and every chapter of the book. Like Jews, Muslims count themselves especially blessed to have been given God's word to guide them through life.*

In the name of God, the Merciful, the Compassionate

Praise be to God, the Lord of the Universe,
the Merciful, the Compassionate,
the Authority on Judgment Day.

It is You whom we worship
and You whom we ask for help.

Show us the upright way;
the way of those whom You have favored,
not of those with whom You have been angry
and those who have gone astray.

The Forenoon (Sura 93)

Islam, like Judaism, Christianity, Hinduism, and Buddhism, places emphasis on charity to the poor. Zakat (alms) is one of the "five pillars of Islam," which every believer must perform. As in Judaism, the reader is reminded of God's mercy in calling on the believer to be merciful to others.

What three duties are specifically given the believer at the end of this passage?

In the Name of God, the Merciful, the Compassionate

By the white forenoon
and the brooding night!
Thy Lord has neither forsaken thee nor hates thee
and the Last shall be better for thee than the First.
Thy Lord shall give thee, and thou shalt be satisfied.

Did He not find thee an orphan, and shelter thee?
Did He not find thee erring, and guide thee?
Did He not find thee needy, and suffice thee?

As for the orphan, do not oppress him,
and as for the beggar, scold him not;
and as for thy Lord's blessing, declare it.

On Belief and Unbelief (Sura 2)

Islam and Judaism are the most insistently monotheistic religions in the world. Both have criticized Christianity for its doctrine of the Holy Trinity: three gods in one. However, Islam accepts as believers anyone who is basically monotheistic and shuns idol-worship.

What is said to be the fate of idol-worshippers?

God
there is no god but He, the
Living, the Everlasting.
Slumber seizes Him not, neither sleep;
to Him belongs
all that is in the heavens and the earth.
Who is there that shall intercede with Him
save by His leave?
He knows what lies before them and what is after them,
and they comprehend not anything of His knowledge save such as He wills.
His Throne comprises the heavens and earth;
the preserving of them oppresses Him not;
He is the All-high, the All-glorious.

No compulsion is there in religion.
Rectitude has become clear from error.
So whosoever disbelieves in idols
and believes in God, has laid hold of
the most firm handle, unbreaking; God is
All-hearing, All-knowing.

God is the Protector of the believers;
He brings them forth from the shadows into the light.

And the unbelievers—their protectors are
idols, that bring them forth from the light into the shadows;
those are the inhabitants of the Fire,
therein dwelling forever.

Description of Heaven and Hell (Sura 38)

*The Qur'an describes the afterlife in more detail than do the Christian Scriptures, and with
more emphasis on the blessings of Heaven. Asceticism is not as prized in Islam as in Christianity, Buddhism, and Hinduism. The pleasures of Paradise are a kind of heightened and purified
version of some of the pleasures of Earth.*

What blessings are promised the saved?

This is a Remembrance; and for the godfearing is a fair resort,
Gardens of Eden,[1] whereof the gates are open to them,
wherein they recline, and wherein
they call for fruits abundant, and sweet potions,
and with them maidens restraining their glances of equal age.
"This is what you were promised for the Day of Reckoning;
this is Our provision, unto which there is no end."
All this; but for the insolent awaits an ill resort,
Gehenna,[2] wherein they are roasted—an evil cradling!
All this; so let them taste it—boiling water and pus,
and other torments of the like kind coupled together.

---

[1]As in Christian tradition, Eden is both the place of human origins and a name for the
Paradise of the blessed.
[2]Also used as the Jewish word for Hell.

On Women (Sura 4)

*No aspect of Islam has come in for more severe criticism by Europeans than its treatment of
women; but it is worth remembering that only a few centuries ago Europeans agreed that
women were meant to be strictly subordinate to men and wife-beating was sometimes preached
from the pulpits. The Muslim law on polygamy is not meant to encourage the practice, but to
restrict it. Indeed, some modern Muslims argue that so stringent are the* Qur'an's *demands for
the equal treatment of wives that polygamy is effectively ruled out. As in ancient Sumer, a man
who divorces his wife is supposed to return her dowry, unless the wife has voluntarily surrendered it to her husband. Note that daughters inherit less than sons.*

How does the Qur'an *say disputes between husband and wife are to be settled?*

In the Name of God, the Merciful, the Compassionate

Mankind, fear your Lord, who created you
of a single soul, and from it created

its mate, and from the pair of them scattered
abroad many men and women; and fear God
by whom you demand one of another,
and the wombs; surely God ever watches over you.

Give the orphans their property, and do not
exchange the corrupt for the good; and devour
not their property with your property; surely that is a great crime.
If you fear that you will not act justly
towards the orphans, marry such women
as seem good to you, two, three, four:
but if you fear you will not be equitable,
then only one, or what your right hands own;[1]
so it is likelier you will not be partial.
And give the women their dowries as a gift
spontaneous; but if they are pleased
to offer you any of it, consume it with wholesome appetite.
But do not give to fools their property
that God has assigned to you to manage;
provide for them and clothe them out of it,
and speak to them honorable words.
Test well the orphans, until they reach
the age of marrying; then, if you perceive
in them right judgment, deliver to them
their property; consume it not wastefully and hastily
ere they are grown. If any man is rich,
let him be abstinent; if poor, let him consume in reason.
And when you deliver to them their property,
take witnesses over them; God suffices for a reckoner.

To the men a share of what parents and kinsmen
leave, and to the women a share of what
parents and kinsmen leave, whether it be
little or much, a share apportioned;
and when the division is attended by
kinsmen and orphans and the poor,
make provision for them out of it,
and speak to them honorable words.
And let those fear who, if they left
behind them weak seed, would be afraid
on their account, and let them fear
God, and speak words hitting the mark.
Those who devour the property of orphans
unjustly, devour Fire in their bellies,
and shall assuredly roast in a Blaze.

---

[1]Your female slaves. As in patriarchal Hebrew society, sex with such women is not considered adultery.

God charges you, concerning your children:
to the male the like of the portion
of two females, and if they be women
above two, then for them two-thirds of what he leaves, but if she be one
then to her a half; and to his parents
to each one of the two the sixth
of what he leaves, if he has children;
but if he has no children, and his
heirs are his parents, a third to his
mother, or, if he has brothers, to his
mother a sixth, after any bequest
he may bequeath, or any debt.
Your fathers and your sons—you know not
which out of them is nearer in profit
to you. So God apportions; surely God is All-knowing, All-wise. . . .

Men are the managers of the affairs of women
for that God has preferred in bounty
one of them over another, and for that
They have expended of their property.
Righteous women are therefore obedient,
guarding the secret for God's guarding.
And those you fear may be rebellious
admonish; banish them to their couches,
and beat them. If they then obey you,
look not for any way against them; God is
All-high, All-great.
And if you fear a breach between the two,
bring forth an arbiter from his people
and from her people an arbiter, if they
desire to set things right; God will
compose their differences; surely God is
All-knowing, All-aware.

The People of the Book (Sura 48)

Islam sees itself as a the continuation and fulfillment of the faith developed in the Jewish Torah and the Christian Scriptures, as Christianity sees itself as the continuation and fulfillment of Judaism. All are called "People of the Book" because they have sacred scriptures promoting monotheism. Jews and Christians are not counted among the faithful, but they are not to be treated as harshly as polytheists, either.

Muhammad is the Messenger of God,
and those who are with him are hard
against the unbelievers, merciful
one to another. Thou seest them
bowing, prostrating, seeking bounty
from God and good pleasure. Their

mark is on their faces, the trace of
prostration.[1] That is their likeness
in the Torah, and their likeness
in the Gospel: as a seed that puts
forth its shoot, and strengthens it,
and it grows stout and rises straight
upon its stalk, pleasing the sowers,
that through them He may enrage
the unbelievers. God has promised
those of them who believe and do deeds
of righteousness forgiveness and a mighty wage.

---

[1]A mark on the forehead left by fervent praying, involving striking of the head against the ground.

On the Jews (Sura 3)

Muslims and Jews have at times lived together in peace and prosperity, and at other times fought bitterly. The Qur'an expresses an ambivalent view of the Jews as greatly blessed, but failing to live up to their promise; ironically the Qur'an uses the prophetic denunciations of much of the Hebrew Bible to criticize the actual behavior of some Jews.

What are said to be the characteristics of good Jews?

You are the best nation ever brought forth
to men, bidding to honor, and forbidding
dishonor, and believing in God. Had the People
of the Book believed, it were better for them;
some of them are believers, but the most of them are ungodly.
They will not harm you, except a little hurt; and if
they fight with you, they will turn on you
their backs; then they will not be helped.
Abasement shall be pitched on them, whenever
they are come upon, except they be in a bond
of God, and a bond of the people; they will be laden
with the burden of God's anger, and poverty shall be
pitched on them; that, because they disbelieved in
God's signs, and slew the Prophets without right;
that, for that they acted rebelliously and were transgressors.
Yet they are not all alike; some of the People
of the Book are a nation upstanding, that
recite God's signs in the watches of the night, bowing themselves,
believing in God and in the Last Day,
bidding to honor and forbidding dishonor,
vying one with the other in good works; those are of the righteous.
And whatsoever good you do, you shall not
be denied the just reward of it; and God knows the godfearing.

As for the unbelievers, their riches shall not
avail them, neither their children, against God;
those are the inhabitants of the Fire, therein dwelling forever.
The likeness of that they expend in this present life
is as the likeness of a freezing blast that smites
the tillage of a people who wronged themselves,
and it destroyed that; God wronged them not, but themselves they wronged.

On Christianity, from Sura 4 ("Women")

As Christians had tried to amend Judaism, the Qur'an tries to amend Christianity. Its strong monotheism rejects the idea of God's having a mortal son, or taking on human flesh himself. Muhammad is the greatest of the prophets, especially blessed by God: but he is not God nor the son of God. The Judeo-Christian idea of the Messiah undergoes yet another transformation in Islam: as in Christianity, he is identified with Jesus; but as in Judaism, he is the servant of God, not God himself.

What aspects of traditional Christianity are accepted here?

O men, the Messenger[1] has now come to you
with the truth from your Lord; so believe;
better is it for you. And if you disbelieve,
to God belongs all that is in the heavens
and in the earth; and God is
All-knowing, All-wise.

People of the Book, go not beyond the bounds
in your religion, and say not as to God
but the truth. The Messiah, Jesus, son of Mary,
was only the Messenger of God, and His Word
that He committed to Mary, and a Spirit from Him.
So believe in God and His Messengers, and say not, "Three."
Refrain; better is it for you. God is only One God.
Glory be to Him—that He should have a son!
To Him belongs all that is in the heavens
and in the earth; God suffices for a guardian.
The Messiah will not disdain to be a servant
of God, neither the angels who are near stationed to Him.
Whosoever disdains to serve Him, and waxes
proud, He will assuredly muster them to Him, all of them.
As for the believers, who do deeds of righteousness,
He will pay them in full their wages,
and He will give them more, of His bounty;
and as for them who disdain, and wax proud,
them He will chastise with a painful chastisement,
and they shall not find for them, apart from God, a friend or helper.

---

[1]Muhammad.

On the unbelievers, from "The Cow" (Sura 2)

The concept of holy war exists in the traditions of Judaism, Christianity, and Islam alike. Because Muhammad and his followers engaged directly in the war for the faith called jihad, *it is often especially associated with Muslims; yet it would be difficult to show that either side has been more peace-loving or aggressive in Christian-Muslim conflicts throughout history.*

On what condition will God be merciful to those who fight against Muslims?

And fight in the way of God with those
who fight with you, but aggress not: God loves
not the aggressors.
And slay them wherever you come upon them,
and expel them from where they expelled you;
persecution is more grievous than slaying.
But fight them not by the Holy Mosque
until they should fight you there;
then, if they fight you, slay them—
such is the recompense of unbelievers—
but if they give over,[1] surely God is
All-forgiving, All-compassionate.

Fight them, till there is no persecution
and the religion is God's; then if they
give over, there shall be no enmity
save for evildoers.
The holy month for the holy month;[2]
holy things demand retaliation.
Whoso commits aggression against you,
do you commit aggression against him
like as he has committed against you;
and fear you God, and know that God is
with the godfearing.

---

[1]Surrender.
[2]Ramadan, the holy month of fasting and religious observances.

Sufi Wisdom Literature

Hafiz of Shiraz (d. 1389 CE?): *The dawn is breaking*

The ghazals [songs] of the Persian poet born Shams ad-Din Muhammad, and known as Hafiz, are among the most famous and popular works in the Muslim world. Although they are filled with celebrations of the joys of wine-drinking, which is strongly forbidden to Muslims, they are consistently read as allegories of spiritual intoxication. Mysticism is generally suspect among Muslims who are more likely to view God with respectful awe than to seek to merge with him; but the sufi tradition, which incorporates meditation, singing, and even dancing to induce a state of spiritual ecstasy, is popular among Muslims from Africa to Pakistan and beyond. The great Persian sufi poets all use the metaphor of intoxication to explain their feelings when in communion with the divine.

Which lines in this poem emphasize the shortness of life? How does the poet make clear in the last lines that this is a religious poem?

The dawn is breaking, cup-bearer; fill up with wine:
The revolving heavens will not delay, so hurry!

Let us get drunk with a cup of the rose-red wine—
Before this transient world has itself passed out.

The sun of wine has risen upon the east of the bowl:
If pleasure is what you aim at, waste no time in sleep.

Since one day we'll be clay for Fate to make pitchers of,
Let my skull be a cup kept sweet, being filled with wine.

We are not bigots nor puritans; we need no penance:
Preach to us only with a cup of the unmixed wine.

This worship of wine, Hafiz, is a virtuous business,
So be resolute in performance of righteous works.

Translated by Peter Avery & John Heath-Stubbs

Jalal al-Din Rumi (1207-1273 CE): *There's hidden sweetness*

For most Muslims, asceticism is not an ideal. Even during the month of Ramadan, when believers fast during the daylight hours, feasting is carried on after dark. But Sufis praise the power generated by abstaining from food. Similarly, music has been somewhat suspect in strict Muslim traditions, but here the Sufi poet uses a musical metaphor to explain how emptiness can be rewarding, replacing mortal food with spiritual nourishment.

What three kinds of music-making are referred to in this poem?

There's hidden sweetness in the stomach's emptiness.
We are lutes, no more, no less. If the soundbox
is stuffed full of anything, no music.
If the brain and the belly are burning clean
with fasting, every moment a new song comes out of the fire.
The fog clears, and new energy makes you
run up the steps in front of you.
Be emptier and cry like reed instruments cry.
Emptier, write secrets with the reed pen.
When you're full of food and drink, Satan sits
where your spirit should, an ugly metal statue
in place of the Kaaba.[1] When you fast,
good habits gather like friends who want to help.
Fasting is Solomon's ring.[2] Don't give it
to some illusion and lose your power,
but even if you have, if you've lost all will and control,
they come back when you fast, like soldiers appearing
out of the ground, pennants flying above them.
A table descends to your tents,
Jesus' table.
Expect to see it, when you fast, this table
spread with other food, better than the broth of cabbages.

Translated by John Moyne and Coleman Barks

---

[1] One of the Prophet Muhammad's most important deeds was removing from the Kaaba in Mecca the many idols which had been placed there.

[2] A magical wishing ring: it can produce anything desired.

Rumi: *I was, on the day when the heavens were not*

Many Westerners are drawn to sufism because it emphasizes mysticism in terms that are familiar from many religious traditions. In this poem Rumi seems to describe a kind of spirituality which transcends religion itself, although sufis would see the discovery of God within as the highest form of Islam. The poet argues that spiritual truth dwells not in houses of worship, but within the human heart. In the opening lines, Rumi expresses his belief that the human soul existed before creation.

I was, on the day when the heavens were not;
   no hint was there that anything with a name existed.
Through us named and names became apparent
   on the day when no "I" or "We" were there.
A hint came in the revelation of the tip of the Beloved's[1] Tress
   when the tip of the Beloved's Tress was not.
Cross and Christianity from end to end
   I traversed. He was not in the Cross.
To the idol-house[2] I went, the ancient cloister;[3]
   in that no tinge of it was perceptible.
I went to the mountain of Herat and Kandahar;
   I looked. He was not in the depths or the heights there.
With purpose I ascended to the summit of Mount Qaf;[4]
   in that place was nought but the 'Anqa.[5]
I turned the reins of search towards the Ka'ba;[6]
   He was not in that place to which old and young aspire.
I questioned Avicenna[7] about him;
   He was not within Avicenna's range.
I journeyed to the scene of "the two bow-lengths' distance;"[8]
   He was not in that sublime Court.
I looked into my own heart.
   There I saw him; He was nowhere else.

Translated by Reynold Alleyne Nicholson

---

[1] Muhammad's. The Prophet also existed in some sense before his birth.
[2] Refers to Hindu temples.
[3] A Zarathustrian fire-temple.
[4] A legendary mountain, about 1750 miles high, haunted by magical creatures and considered the most inaccessible place on earth.
[5] The Simurgh, a mysterious bird which sufis often use to represent the unknown God.
[6] The holiest shrine of Islam, in Mecca.
[7] Ibn Sina (980–1037), Persian philosopher and physician. His interpretation of Aristotle and his works on medicine were widely influential in both the Muslim and Christian worlds during the Middle Ages.
[8] In the Qur'an it is said (Sura 53) that Muhammad approached the throne of God at a distance of two bows' length or nearer.

Sa'di: A story about wealth vs. virtue, from the *Gulistan* (early 13th Century CE)

Sa'di's Gulistan (Rose-Garden) is one of the most popular books in the Islamic world. A collection of poems and stories, it is widely quoted as a source of wisdom. A native of Shiraz, Sa'di was also the father-in-law of another great Persian writer, Hafiz.

What is the moral of this story?

I saw the son of a rich man seated at the head of his father's sepulcher, and engaged in a dispute with the son of a poor man, and saying, "My father's sarcophagus is of stone, and the inscription colored with a pavement of alabaster and turquoise bricks. What resemblance has it to that of thy father which consists of a brick or two huddled together, with a few handfuls of dust sprinkled over it?" The son of the poor man heard him, and answered, "Peace! for before thy father can have moved himself under this heavy stone, my sire will have arrived in paradise. This is a saying of the Prophet: *'The death of the poor is repose.'*"

Translated by Nathan Haskell Dole and Belle M. Walker

Secular Literature

Nizami: *Layla and Majnun* (1188 CE)

Many passionate love poems attributed to one Qays circulated in the Arabic world; and so extravagant was the love they spoke of that they gradually gave rise to the legend of their author, who, because he went insane out of frustrated love for Layla, was nicknamed "Majnun" ("madman"). Nizami's version of their story reflects the kind of idealized romanticism that can spring up in a culture where marriages are arranged and real-life romance is rare; but it is also a warning against such romances, since Majnun's passion destroys both lovers, their families, and many others. This brief passage illustrates Nizami's ornate style, embroidered with figures of speech which strain to reflect the intense feelings of the lovers.

Choose a pair of metaphors and explain what they tell us about Layla and Majnun.

Once more the young day donned his morning coat, woven from shimmering brocade. He adorned the ear of the sky with the precious golden ornament of the sun and the quicksilver of the stars melted in its red flames.

Majnun appeared, together with his friends, near the tent of his beloved. So far he had only come by night, wrapped in the cloak of darkness, but now he could bear it no longer. His patience was at an end; he had to see her, Layla, for whom his heart was crying out. The closer he came to his goal, the less certain were his steps; drunk with longing and confused by feverish hope, his lips trembled like the verses of the poem he was chanting.

Suddenly he stopped. In front of him he saw the tent—and what else? Seldom do dreams become so real. The curtain was withdrawn and in the entrance of the tent unveiled in the light of day, clearly visible against the dark interior, Layla was sitting; Layla, his moon.

Majnun sighed deeply. Now Layla saw him, and they recognized in the mirror of each other's face their own fear, their own pain and love. Neither stirred; only their eyes met, their voices caressed each other, softly exchanging plaintive sighs, which they were used to confide to the wind and to the night.

Layla was a lute, Majnun a viola.

All the radiance of this morning was Layla, yet a candle was burning in front of her, consuming itself with desire. She was the most beautiful garden and Majnun was a torch of longing. She planted the rose-bush; he watered it with his tears.

What shall I say about Layla? She was a fairy, not a human being. How shall I describe Majnun? He was a fairy's torch, alight from head to foot.

Layla was a jasmine-bush in spring, Majnun a meadow in autumn, where no jasmine was growing. Layla could bewitch with one glance from beneath her dark hair, Majnun was her slave and a dervish dancing before her. Layla held in her hand the glass of wine scented with musk. Majnun had not touched the wine, yet he was drunk with its sweet smell. . . .

Only this encounter, brief and from afar was permitted to the lovers, then Majnun, afraid of guards and spies, ran away, lest the wheel of fate should turn even this fleeting happiness to disaster. He escaped from Layla in order to find her.

Translated by E. Martin & G. Hill

Ibn Hazm al-Andalusi (994-1064 CE): *Tawq al-Hamamah, The Dove's Necklace*

Searching for the roots of the Western idea of love, many scholars have detected the influence of Arabic and Persian poetry, especially via Moorish Spain. These writers praise women in lavish terms reminiscent of those used by the early European troubadours, making romance almost into an alternative religion. The following passage, from a long treatise on love by the Moorish writer Ibn Hazm, quotes a woman who speaks of her devotion to her beloved, arguing in the final lines that he is the stairway to Heaven.

What are some of the metaphors that the speaker uses to describe how much she loves the man?

I enjoy conversation when, in it, he is mentioned to me and exhales a scent of sweet ambergris[1] for me.

If he should speak, among those who sit in my company, I listen only to the words of that marvelous charmer.

Even if the Prince of the Faithful[2] should be with me, I would not turn aside from my love for the former.

If I am compelled to leave him, I look back at him constantly and walk like [an animal] wounded in the hoof.

My eyes remain fixed firmly upon him though my body has departed, as the drowning man looks at the shore from the fathomless sea.[3]

If I recall my distance from him, I choke as though with water, like the man who yawns in the midst of a dust storm and the sun's noonday heat.

And if you say: "It is possible to reach the sky," I reply: "Yes, and I know where the stairs may be found."

Translated by James T. Monroe

---

[1]A substance produced by diseased whales which was often used in creating perfumes.

[2]The ruler, the king.

[3]Unfathomable, bottomless. The line means that the beloved is vivid in her imagination even when he is not physically present.

Wallada (early 1000s CE): To Ibn Zaidun

Various romantic stories are told about this Arabic woman poet. Like European poets, she uses burning coals as a metaphor for passion; but unlike the writers of the wet and chilly north, she naturally uses rain as symbol of her love.

Can't we find some way
to meet again
and speak our love?

In winter with you near
no need for coals—
our passion blazed.

Now—cut off, alone
day darkens deep
the fate I feared

Nights pass. You're still away
Longing chains me and
Patience brings no release

Where morning finds you
may God stream down upon your land
refreshing, fertile rain.

Translated by James T. Monroe

Firdausi (died c. 1020-1025 CE): The struggle between Esfandiyar and Goshtasp

Author of the famous Shahnama (Book of Kings) *the national epic of Iran, Firdausi is one of the earliest and most outstanding poets in the modern Persian language. His honorific title was "Abul Qasem," while "Firdausi" is a poetic name under which he composed verses for about half a century. Firdausi belonged to the class of dehqans, or landed gentry, though his family owned very little land and lived in extreme poverty. The* Shahnama, *the composition of which took about thirty-five years, is a collection of episodes from the history of the Iranian empire from the creation of the world, followed by the reign of the first mythological shah, Kiumars, through the times of the earlier kings founding civilization, to the defeat and death of the last Sassanian emperor, Yazdegerd III, as a result of the conquest of Iran by the Muslim Arabs in the middle of the seventh century CE. Composed in metrical and rhymed couplets, the* Shahnama *purports to provide an account of fifty kings and queens. Not a formal epic like the* Aeneid *or the* Lusiad, *but orally spontaneous like the* Iliad *and structurally episodic like* chansons de geste, *the* Shahnama, *however, is not so much about kings and queens and their noble deeds as it is about individuals exhibiting their strengths and weaknesses, virtues and vices, and their inner conflicts. The following selection from the* Shahnama *constitutes part of its fourteenth episode called "Esfandiyar and Rostam."*

What is the cause of the crisis in the events narrated below? What does it mean to say that the silk of Esfandyiar's mother turned to thorns? How is a belief in fate reflected in this story?

I have heard from the nightingale a story which it repeats after an ancient legend. It is that Esfandiyar once returned home intoxicated and in savage mood from the king's palace. His mother, Katayun, daughter of the Caesar, took him to her heart in the darkness of the night. Halfway through the night he awoke from his sleep, called for a cup of wine and gave vent to speech. He said to his mother,

"The king behaves evilly towards me. He told me that the kingship and the army would one day be mine, as well as the treasury, the throne and the diadem, but only after I had boldly exacted vengeance for king Lohrasp from king Arjasp and delivered his sisters from captivity. Thus I would exalt your repute in the world, which must be cleansed of evildoers, rid of defects and be made anew with adornment. When the sky next brings up the sun and his Majesty's head awakens from slumber, I will repeat to him the words he spoke; he will not withhold the truth from me. If he surrenders the royal crown to me, I will serve him as a priest serves his idols. But if no gleam lights up his face, by the God who keeps the sky established, if I do not set that crown on my head, I will surrender the whole country to the Iranians, make you queen of the realm of Iran and violently and fearlessly act the part of the lion."

His mother was saddened by this speech and all the silk of her bosom turned to thorns, for she knew that the Shah, ever jealous for his name, would not surrender the treasury, throne and diadem. She said to him,

"My much-afflicted son, what does a noble heart demand? You have everything—treasure, command and power of decision— which concerns the army. Seek for nothing further. Your father has the crown, my son, but you have all the troops, the lands and country. What is better than a fierce male lion standing in his father's presence and girt for service? When he passes away, crown and throne will be yours; his greatness, majesty and good fortune will come to you."

Esfandiyar replied to his mother,

"The wise axiom which told one never to utter secrets before women, hit the mark truly. Once you have spoken a word to her you will find it in the street. In no matter ought you to listen to a woman's behest, for you will never find her counsel to be wise."

Esfandiyar went to Goshtasp no more, but spent his time in dalliance with musicians and the maids who handed round the wine. For two days and nights he imbibed, and delighted the hearts of the beauteous ladies. By the third day Goshtasp perceived that his son was ambitious to take his place, that the thought was growing in his mind that he must possess the crown and throne of the sovereign. He thereupon summoned Jamasp [his wise counsellor] together with Lohrasp's astrologers, who came embracing their star-tables. The king plied them with questions about the hero Esfandiyar, asking whether he would enjoy long life and dwell in happiness, peace and comfort, whether he would place on his head the sovereign's crown and firmly hold to his virtue and greatness.

When the sage of Iran [Jamasp] heard the questions he looked into his ancient star-tables and his eyelashes dripped with tears, his eyebrows wrinkling as he uncovered the truth. He said,

"Evil is my fate and evil my star; and evil will come on my head from the truth which I impart. I would that in the presence of the blessed Zarir destiny had cast me into the claws of a lion, or that my father had slain me before a baleful star had been destined for Jamasp. When Esfandiyar has rid the earth entirely of his foes, he will have no more fear or concern about war. He will have freed the world from apprehension of any who design evil and he will cut the dragon's body into two."

"My dear friend," said the king to him, "tell me all, and turn not aside from the path of true knowledge. If his fate is to be that of Zarir [who was killed in the war against Arjasp], the commander of armies, then my life henceforth will be unhappy. Tell me in haste—for out of this knowledge bitterness has invaded my countenance—at whose hand out of the whole world he will meet his death. That will be a loss over which we shall have to weep."

Jamasp replied,

"Your Majesty, may no evil fate devolve on me! His death will come in Zabolestan at the hand of Dastan's heroic son [Rostam]."

Then said the king to Jamasp,

"Do not reckon this matter as one of little moment. If I vacate the sovereign's throne and surrender it to him, with the treasury and the crown, he will not need to see the land and soil of Zabolestan and none will know him in Kabolestan. He will be secure against the turns of fortune; his good star will direct him."

To that the star-calculator answered, "Who can escape from the turning wheel? Out of it the sharpclawed dragon springs. Who can find deliverance, either by courage or wisdom? What is to be will be, without fail, and wise men do not seek to know the hour of it. His fate will come upon him at the hand of a mighty warrior, were even an angel lying before him as his shield."

Translated by Reuben Levy

Esfandiyar reminds his father of his past exploits and demands the throne which had been promised him. Goshtasp praises him for his past deeds but feels that his son has yet to accomplish one great task: defeating Rustam, the great Iranian hero and warrior. Esfandiyar suspects that his father is simply trying to get rid of him by involving him in a battle with Rustam. Nevertheless, he sets out on the campaign but is shot through the eye by Rustam and dies of his wounds. When his body is carried back to Iran, he is deeply mourned.

Usamah Ibn-Mundqidh (1095–1188 CE): The Character and Customs of the Franks

Following their devastation of Jerusalem in 1099, Western Europeans reigned over kingdoms in Palestine and other parts of the Middle East for about a century. Although some Muslims were scandalized by their occupation of Islam's third most holy city, much of the time they ignored the newcomers until they were driven out by the great warrior Saladin in 1187. For a young Muslim like Usamah growing up among them, they were exotic barbarians, by turns amusing and disgusting, but no serious threat. His lively memoirs give his reactions to these semibarbaric invaders from a distant land. The tendency of Europeans to fantasize erotically about the Middle East has been much discussed in recent years. The passage on Europeans' lack of jealousy displays the same tendency in a reverse direction. Usamah is so amazed by the trust that Western men place in women that he assumes they must be easily cuckolded.

What does Usamah think are the main virtues of the Franks? What is his opinion of Western medicine?

Their lack of sense.

Mysterious are the works of the Creator, the author of all things! When one comes to recount cases regarding the Franks,[1] he cannot but glorify Allah (exalted is he!) and sanctify him, for he sees them as animals possessing the virtues of courage and fighting, but nothing else; just as animals have only the virtues of strength and carrying loads. I shall now give some instances of their doings and their curious mentality.

In the army of King Fulk, son of Fulk, was a Frankish reverend knight who had just arrived from their land in order to make the holy pilgrimage and then return home. He was of my intimate fellowship and kept such constant company with me that he began to call me "my brother." Between us were mutual bonds of amity and friendship. When he resolved to return by sea to his homeland, he said to me:

"My brother, I am leaving for my country and I want thee to send with me thy son (my son, who was then fourteen years old, was at that time in my company) to our country, where he can see the knights and learn wisdom and chivalry. When he returns, he will be like a wise man."[2]

Thus there fell upon my ears words which would never come out of the head of a sensible man; for even if my son were to be taken captive, his captivity could not bring him a worse misfortune than carrying him into the lands of the Franks. However, I said to the man: "By thy life, this has exactly been my idea. But the only thing that prevented me from carrying it out was the fact that his grandmother, my mother, is so fond of him and did not this time let him come out with me until she exacted an oath from me to the effect that I would return him to her."

---

[1]Although not all the crusaders were from France, they were uniformly referred to as "Franks."

[2]This is not quite as bizarre a proposition as it sounds, since it was routine for Frankish nobles to send their sons to other courts to be brought up and trained in the chivalric arts.

Their curious medication.[3]

A case illustrating their curious medicine is the following:

The lord of al-Munaytirah[4] wrote to my uncle asking him to dispatch a physician to treat certain sick persons among his people. My uncle sent him a Christian physician named Thabit. Thabit was absent but ten days when he returned. So we said to him, "How quickly hast thou healed thy patients!" He said: "They brought before me a knight in whose leg an abscess had grown; and a woman afflicted with imbecility. To the knight I applied a small poultice until the abscess opened and became well; and the woman I put on diet and made her humor wet. Then a Frankish physician came to them and said, 'This man knows nothing about treating them.' He then said to the knight, 'Which wouldst thou prefer, living with one leg or dying with two?' The latter replied, 'Living with one leg.' The physician said, 'Bring me a strong knight and a sharp ax.' A knight came with the ax. And I was standing by. Then the physician laid the leg of the patient on a block of wood and bade the knight strike his leg with the ax and chop it off at one blow. Accordingly he struck it—while I was looking on—one blow, but the leg was not severed. He dealt another blow, upon which the marrow of the leg flowed out and the patient died on the spot. He then examined the woman and said, 'This is a woman in whose head there is a devil which has possessed her. Shave off her hair.' Accordingly they shaved it off and the woman began once more to eat their ordinary diet—garlic and mustard. Her imbecility took a turn for the worse. The physician then said, 'The devil has penetrated through her head.' He therefore took a razor, made a deep cruciform incision on it, peeled off the skin at the middle of the incision until the bone of the skull was exposed and rubbed it with salt. The woman also expired instantly. Thereupon I asked them whether my services were needed any longer, and when they replied in the negative I returned home, having learned of their medicine what I knew not before."

I have, however, witnessed a case of their medicine which was quite different from that.

The king of the Franks[5] had for treasurer a knight named Bernard *[barnad]*, who (may Allah's curse be upon him!) was one of the most accursed and wicked among the Franks. A horse kicked him in the leg, which was subsequently infected and which opened in fourteen different places. Every time one of these cuts would close in one place, another would open in another place. All this happened while I was praying for his perdition. Then came to him a Frankish physician and removed from the leg all the ointments which were on it and began to wash it with very strong vinegar. By this treatment all the cuts were healed and the man became well again. He was up again like a devil.

Another case illustrating their curious medicine is the following:

In Shayzar we had an artisan named abu-al-Fath, who had a boy whose neck was afflicted with scrofula. Every time a part of it would close, another part would open. This man happened to go to Antioch on business of his, accompanied by his son. A Frank noticed the boy and asked his father about him. Abu-al-Fath replied, "This is my son." The Frank said to him, "Wilt thou swear by thy religion that if I prescribe to thee a medicine which will cure thy boy, thou wilt charge nobody fees for prescribing it thyself? In that

---

[3]Historians agree that the Muslim lands were for centuries far more advanced in medicine than Western Europe; and indeed Europeans learned much of their medicine from Muslim sources.

[4]In Lebanon, near Afqah.

[5]Fulk of Anjou, king of Jerusalem.

case, I shall prescribe to thee a medicine which will cure the boy." The man took the oath and the Frank said: "Take uncrushed leaves of glasswort, burn them, then soak the ashes in olive oil and sharp vinegar. Treat the scrofula with them until the spot on which it is growing is eaten up. Then take burnt lead, soak it in ghee butter *[samn]* and treat him with it. That will cure him."

The father treated the boy accordingly, and the boy was cured. The sores closed and the boy returned to his normal condition of health.

I have myself treated with this medicine many who were afflicted with such disease, and the treatment was successful in removing the cause of the complaint.

Newly arrived Franks are especially rough: One insists that Usamah should pray eastward.

Everyone who is a fresh emigrant from the Frankish lands is ruder in character than those who have become acclimatized and have held long association with the Moslems. Here is an illustration of their rude character:

Whenever I visited Jerusalem I always entered the Aqsa Mosque, beside which stood a small mosque which the Franks had converted into a church. When I used to enter the Aqsa Mosque, which was occupied by the Templars *[al-dawiyyah]*, who were my friends, the Templars would evacuate the little adjoining mosque so that I might pray in it. One day I entered this mosque, repeated the first formula, "Allah is great," and stood up in the act of praying, upon which one of the Franks rushed on me, got hold of me and turned my face eastward saying, "This is the way thou shouldst pray!"[6] A group of Templars hastened to him, seized him and repelled him from me. I resumed my prayer. The same man, while the others were otherwise busy, rushed once more on me and turned my face eastward, saying, "This is the way thou shouldst pray!" The Templars again came in to him and expelled him. They apologized to me, saying, "This is a stranger who has only recently arrived from the land of the Franks and he has never before seen anyone praying except eastward." Thereupon I said to myself, "I have had enough prayer." So I went out and have ever been surprised at the conduct of this devil of a man, at the change in the color of his face, his trembling and his sentiment at the sight of one praying towards the *qiblah*.[7]

Another wants to show to a Moslem God as a child.

I saw one of the Franks come to al-Amir Mu'in-al-Din (may Allah's mercy rest upon his soul!) when he was in the Dome of the Rock,[8] and say to him, "Dost thou want to see God as a child?" Mu'in-al Din said, "Yes." The Frank walked ahead of us until he showed us the picture of Mary with Christ (may peace be upon him!) as an infant in her lap. He then said, "This is God as a child." But Allah is exalted far above what the infidels say about him!

---

[6]European Christians normally prayed toward the east, which was taken to be the direction of Jerusalem. Muslims were much more precise in calculating the direction of Mecca, which they faced when they prayed. In this case, the proper direction is more south than east.

[7]The *qiblah* in any mosque marks the proper direction of prayer.

[8]The shrine honoring Muhammad's miraculous ascent into heaven, built on the site of the ancient Jewish temple which was destroyed by the Romans in 70 CE.

Franks lack jealousy in sex affairs.

The Franks are void of all zeal and jealousy. One of them may be walking along with his wife. He meets another man who takes the wife by the hand and steps aside to converse with her while the husband is standing on one side waiting for his wife to conclude the conversation. If she lingers too long for him, he leaves her alone with the conversant and goes away.

Here is an illustration which I myself witnessed:

When I used to visit Nablus, I always took lodging with a man named Mu'izz, whose home was a lodging house for the Moslems. The house had windows which opened to the road, and there stood opposite to it on the other side of the road a house belonging to a Frank who sold wine for the merchants. He would take some wine in a bottle and go around announcing it by shouting, "So and so, the merchant, has just opened a cask full of this wine. He who wants to buy some of it will find it in such and such a place." The Frank's pay for the announcement made would be the wine in that bottle. One day this Frank went home and found a man with his wife in the same bed. He asked him, "What could have made thee enter into my wife's room?" The man replied, "I was tired, so I went in to rest." "But how," asked he, "didst thou get into my bed?" The other replied, "I found a bed that was spread, so I slept in it." "But," said he, "my wife was sleeping together with thee!" The other replied, "Well, the bed is hers. How could I therefore have prevented her from using her own bed." "By the truth of my religion," said the husband, "if thou shouldst do it again, thou and I would have a quarrel." Such was for the Frank the entire expression of his disapproval and the limit of his jealousy.

Translated by Philip K. Hitti

The European Middle Ages

Hildegard of Bingen (1098–1179 CE): Hymn to the Virgin

Hildegard of Bingen was the brilliant head of a community of nuns near Bingen, Germany. Besides her poetry, she wrote books on natural history and medicine. She composed a great deal of highly original and beautiful music, including a long music drama entitled Ordo Virtutum (Play of the Virtues). *She experienced intense mystical visions which she described to the nuns under her, and they rendered them in vivid paintings which now survive in modern copies. Most of her poems praise various saints, but above all the Virgin Mary. In this hymn to the Virgin, like many other Medieval and Renaissance Christian mystics, she borrows from the biblical Song of Songs to describe Mary's relationship with God in sensuous language which compares them to human lovers. It seems likely that in the second stanza Hildegard is thinking of her own experiences, in which she felt flooded with the Holy Spirit in a way that compelled her to express the experience in song. This hymn is performed on the album* A Feather on the Breath of God *(Hyperion CDA66039, track 2, "Ave, generosa").*

In which lines does Hildegard compare the begetting of Jesus to the creation of music?

In the pupil of chastity's eye
I beheld you
untouched.[1]
Generous maid![2] Know that it's God
who broods over you.

For heaven flooded you like
unbodied speech
and you gave it a tongue.

Glistening
lily: before all worlds
you lured the supernal one.[3]

---

[1] Medieval Christians believed not only that Mary was a virgin when she conceived Jesus, but remained one throughout her life. Thus she was a special role model for nuns, who took vows of perpetual virginity. The image of the untouched pupil of the eye as a symbol of virginity is striking.
[2] "Maid" as used here means "virgin."
[3] See Song of Songs 2:1 for the source of the traditional comparison of Mary to a lily. Hildegard is saying that before her birth, even before the creation of the world, Mary was chosen to be Jesus' mother by God ("the supernal one").

How he reveled
in your charms! how your beauty
warmed to his caresses
till you gave your breast to his child.

And your womb held joy when heaven's
harmonies rang from you,
a maiden with child by God,
for in God your chastity blazed.

Yes your flesh held joy like the grass
when the dew falls, when heaven
freshens its green: O mother
of gladness, verdure of spring.

Ecclesia,[4] flush with rapture! Sing
for Mary's sake, sing
for the maiden, sing
for God's mother. Sing!

Translated by Barbara Newman

---

[4]Ecclesia is the Church.

Stabat mater dolorosa
Anonymous 13th Century Franciscan Hymn to Mary

Beginning in the mid-12th Century religious poetry took a striking turn toward emotional-ism, asking the reader to identify with the sufferings of Christ and his mother, Mary. The following is one of the most famous hymns of this type, and has often been set to music. Some believers went so far as to subject themselves to prolonged whipping to share in Christ's agony. The Latin original has been printed alongside the translation to allow listeners hearing a musical version to follow the text.

Stabat mater dolorosa	There stood the Mother deeply sorrowing
Iuxta crucem lacrimosa	At the Cross-side, tears outpouring,
Dum pendebat filius;	As they hanged her Son, her Christ;
Cuius animam gementem	How her heart was gravely groaning,
Contristantem et dolentem	Wracked with pain and full of moaning,
Pertransivit gladius.	As the swords inside her sliced.
O quam tristis et afflicta	Ah, the grieving, great affliction
Fuit illa benedicta	Heaped on this maid of benediction,
Mater unigeniti	Mother of the Chosen One;
Quæ mærebat, et dolebat,	Full of suffering, filled with pining
Et tremebat cum videbat	She stood shuddering while divining[1]
Nati pœnas incliti.	The penalties for her great Son.
Quis est homo qui non fleret	Where's the man who is not weeping
Matrem Christi si videret	As he sees Christ's Mother keeping
In tanto supplicio?	Watch upon such bitterness?
Quis non posset contristari	Who's not filled with agitation
Piam matrem contemplari	In the Virgin's contemplation
Dolentem cum filio?	of her Son's most dire duress?
Pro peccatis suae gentis	She sees Jesus stretched on the yoke,[2]
Iesum vidit in tormentis	Paying for the sins of other folk,
Et flagellis subditum.	Handed over to the whips;
Vidit suum dulcem natum	There she sees her Boy-Child mild
Morientem, desolatum,	In the death-grip, alone, defiled,
Dum emisit spiritum.	As his man-soul from him slips.[3]
Eia, mater! fons amoris,	Eia,[4] Mother, fount of loving,
Me sentire vim doloris	Let me bear with you the groveling,
Fac, ut tecum lugeam;	Let me suffer woe with you;
Fac ut ardeat cor meum	Let my heart be filled with burning;

---

[1]Foreseeing.

[2]Cross.

[3]As she sees the adult Jesus dying, she thinks of him as the infant he used to be.

[4]Alas!

In amando Christum Deum,	For the Lord Christ set me yearning,
Ut sibi complaceam.	Make your child love me too.[5]
Sancta mater, istud agas,	Holy Mother, please abide me
Crucifixi fige plagas	Let the nail-blows pound inside me,
Cordi meo valide;	Let them strike within my heart;
Tui nati vulnerati,	As I spy those sundering blows
Tam dignati pro me pati,	That your loved one undergoes
Pœnas mecum divide!	Let me also share a part!
Fac me vere tecum flere,	Let me with you stand there crying,
Crucifixo condolere,	Lending comfort at the crucifying
Donec ego vixero.	For as long as I have breath;
Iuxta crucem tecum stare,	At the Cross-side let me stand
Te libenter sociare	Offering you a kindly hand
In planctu desidero.	As we keen the dirge[6] of death.
Virgo virginum praeclara	Maiden, foremost among maidens,
Mihi iam non sis amara;	Let me not be overladen,
Fac me tecum plangere,	Let me mourn along with you;
Fac, ut portem Christi mortem,	Let the Christ-death be my ration,
Passionis eius sortem	Make me consort to his Passion,[7]
Et plagas recolere.	Let me bear the beatings too!
Fac me plagis vulnerari,	Let me feel the flails aflying,
Cruce hac inebriari	Make me drunk in the crucifying
Ob amorem filii;	In the blest love of your Son;
Inflammatus et accensus	Save me from the Hell-flames' kindling:
Per te, virgo, sin defensus	Virgin! save this sinner spindling
In die iudicii.	When the Judgment Day has come!
Fac me cruce custodiri,	Let the Cross attend my breath,
Morte Christi praemuniri,	Stay with me until my death
Confoveri gratia;	And the grace of princely prize;
Quando corpus morietur	When this body knows it's dying,
Fac ut animæ donetur	Let this soul go upward flying
Paradisi gloria.	To the praise of Paradise.

Translated by James J. Wilhelm

---

[5] Mary is often portrayed as an intercessor, a more approachable figure to whom prayers can be directed and who will then relay them to Christ. The image of a compassionate mother figure also exists in Buddhism in the person of Kuan Yin or Kannon.
[6] Wail the funeral lament.
[7] Partner in his suffering and death.

The Wife's Lament (c. 780–830 CE)

This anonymous Anglo-Saxon poem expresses the anguish of a woman whose husband has gone into exile, evidently because of a blood feud such as are often described in early northern European narratives. Rejected by his family, she has herself been forced into exile, but is pining away for her absent husband. As in most Anglo-Saxon poetry, each line is marked by four strong accents and divided in two by a pause. Instead of rhyme, which was not to become popular for several more centuries, the verses are held together by alliteration: in the original at least three of the accented words begin with the same consonant (for instance, "pour," "poem," and "pathetic" in the first line). Whether it was actually written by a woman will never be known, but it expresses powerfully a woman's anguish.

What images from the description of the place where she is living reflect the speaker's depression?

I pour forth this poem   of my life pathetic,
Tracing the self's trip.   This I can say:
How I suffered miseries   once I had grown up,
Some new, some old,   but none more than now.
Fore'er I've experienced   expeditions in exile.
First fared my liegelord[1]   hence from his land
Over waves' winnows.   I suffered wan-care,
Wondering where my lord   wandered abroad.
I took then to traveling,   seeking out service,
A winsomeless[2] wanderer   out of woeful need.
The kin of my kind one   began to conspire
In soft, secret whispering   to split us apart
So that sundered completely   I would be cast forth
To a most loathsome life—   ah, indeed how I longed!
Here did my dear lord   command me take dwelling.
I had little to love   here in this land,
Very few loyal friends.   And so is my soul sad,
For I found that companion[3]   most fit for my side
Suddenly sad-spirited,   strangely ill-starred,
Mulling over murders,   hiding his mind.
Before we were both   blithe in our bearing,
Promising ever that   nothing would part us
Unless it were death.   All went helter-skelter:
And now it's as nothing. . . . . . .
Our loyal love. Whether far,   whether near
I must bide[4] the bad   cheer of my cherished one.
A man has commanded: go live in that grove!
Under an oak tree,   deep in a den.

---

[1]Husband.
[2]Lacking charm.
[3]Again, her husband.
[4]Abide, put up with.

Old is my cave-lodge;   I languish with longing;
Dark are the dales round;   high are the hills;
Sharp are the hamlet-hedges   brittle with briars,
A home full of groans.   The going of my good lord
Fills me with grief.   Other lovers are living
Lively on earth,   with leisure in the bedstead;
But I walk at daybreak   alone in the dawning
Under the oak tree   or deep in my den.
There I may sit   the whole summer day;
There I may weep   the wreck of my roaming,
Hardships so heavy,   never knowing any rest
From the dark depression   that dogs all my days
And seizes my soul now   for the length of my life.
A young man may ever[5] be   melancholy and mourning,
Heavy in his heart,   yet he should e'er show
Blitheness of bearing[6]   despite all his breast-cares,
His sufferings endless,   whether all the world's weal[7]
He holds in his hands   or even if exiled
Among some far folk—   where my friend is sitting
Under some stone heap,   stung by the storm,
Ever mournful in mind,   wet by the water
In some ruined gloom.   Ah, my lord labors
With glumness that's great: too oft he remembers
Our hilarious halls.   Woe is the winning[8]
Of one who's awaiting   a lover with longing.

Translated by James J. Wilhelm

---

[5]Always.
[6]He should always act happy.
[7]Wealth.
[8]Sorrow is what one gets.

The Will of Wulfgyth

Judging by several surviving wills of Anglo-Saxon women, many of them were quite prosperous. Unlike women in later ages, they could evidently legally hold land and other wealth in their own names and bestow it on either sons or daughters.

Here in this document it is made known how Wulfgyth grants after her death the things which Almighty God has allowed her to enjoy in life.

First to my lord. . . And I grant the estate at Stisted, with the witness of God and my friends, to Christchurch for the sustenance of the monks in the community, on condition that my sons Aelfketel and Ketel may have the use of the estate for their lifetime; and afterwards the estate is to go to Christchurch. . . for my soul and for my lord Aelfwine's and for the souls of all my children:[1] and after their lifetime half the men[2] are to be free . . .

And I grant to my sons Ulfketel and Ketel the estates at Walsingham and at Carleton and at Harling; and I grant to my two daughters, Gode and Bote, Saxlingham and Somerleyton. And to the church at Somerleyton sixteen acres of land and one acre of meadow. And to my daughter Ealdgyth I grant the estates at Chadacre and at Ashford, and the wood which I attached to the latter. . . .

And I grant to Christ's altar at Christchurch a little gold crucifix, and a seat-cover. And I grant to St. Edmund's two ornamented horns. And I grant to St. Etheldreda's a woolen gown.

Translated by Dorothy Whitelock

---

[1] Although it was not possible to buy salvation, it was believed that gifts to the church could shorten the time one's soul spent suffering in Purgatory on the way to Heaven. Such gifts were a form of penance for sin. By stipulating that her sons shall have the use of the property during their lifetimes, Wulfgyth is providing both for the welfare of their souls and for that of their mortal bodies in this world.

[2] Presumably bonded or indentured servants.

The Song of Roland (early 12th Century CE): The Death of Roland

Among the earliest Medieval epic forms is the French chanson de geste (song of deeds). *Chansons de geste recount the heroic tales of warriors associated with Charlemagne. The most famous of them is the* Chanson de Roland, *in which the martyrdom of a 8th Century hero is turned into a sort of allegory for the Crusades over three hundred years later. Besides illustrating European views of Muslims, the poem well depicts the ideal of loyalty to one's feudal lord. Count Roland, pledged to defend the rear of his uncle Charlemagne's army as it triumphantly leaves Spain, has been betrayed by his wicked uncle Ganelon, who has counseled the Saracens to attack him in the narrow pass of Ronceval. (In fact Charlemagne never fought Muslims in Spain, and the battle on which this story is based involved a skirmish with fellow Christians, but the anti-Muslim fervor surrounding the First Crusade may have influenced the writing of this imaginative poetic account.) Despite a heroic defense by the French, the Saracens have been all too successful. Roland had refused early in the battle to blow his ivory oliphant (horn made from an elephant's tusk) to summon the main body of the army back to rescue him; but he did so at last so that his death and those of his comrades should not remain unavenged. So mighty a blast has he blown on his horn that his brain has burst out through his skull. No Muslim foe could kill him, but his own strength finally proves his undoing. As a loyal soldier and pious Christian, he now prepares for death.*

Why does Roland try to destroy his sword?

Count Roland realizes death is near:
his brains begin to ooze out through his ears.
He prays to God to summon all his peers,[1]
and to the angel Gabriel, himself.
Eschewing blame, he takes the horn in hand
and in the other Durendal, his sword,
and farther than a crossbow fires a bolt,
heads out across a fallow field toward Spain
and climbs a rise. Beneath two lovely trees
stand four enormous marble monoliths.
Upon the green grass he has fallen backward
and fainted, for his death is near at hand.

The hills are high, and very high the trees;
four massive blocks are there, of gleaming marble;
upon green grass Count Roland lies unconscious.
And all the while a Saracen is watching:
he lies among the others, feigning death;
he smeared his body and his face with blood.
He rises to his feet and starts to run—
a strong, courageous, handsome man he was;
through pride he enters into mortal folly—

---

[1]The heroic companions who have died before him, and who he hopes are on their way to Heaven.

and pinning Roland's arms against his chest,
he cries out: "Charles's nephew has been vanquished;
I'll take this sword back to Arabia."
And as he pulls, the count revives somewhat.

Now Roland feels his sword is being taken
and, opening his eyes, he says to him:
"I know for certain you're not one of us!"
He takes the horn he didn't want to leave
and strikes him on his jeweled golden casque;
he smashes through the steel and skull and bones,
and bursting both his eyeballs from his head,
he tumbles him down lifeless at his feet
and says to him: "How dared you, heathen coward,
lay hands on me, by fair means or by foul?
Whoever hears of this will think you mad.
My ivory horn is split across the bell,
and the crystals and the gold are broken off."

Now Roland feels his vision leaving him,
gets to his feet, exerting all his strength;
the color has all vanished from his face.
In front of him there is a dull gray stone;
ten times he strikes it, bitter and dismayed:
the steel edge grates, but does not break or nick.
"Oh holy Mary, help me!" says the count,
"Oh Durendal, good sword, you've come to grief!
When I am dead, you won't be in my care.
I've won with you on many battlefields
and subjugated many spacious lands
now ruled by Charles, whose beard is shot with gray.
No man who flees another should possess you!
A loyal knight has held you many years;
your equal holy France will never see."

Roland strikes the great carnelian stone:
the steel edge grides, but does not break or chip.
And when he sees that he cannot destroy it,
he makes this lamentation to himself:
"Oh Durendal, how dazzling bright you are—
you blaze with light and shimmer in the sun!
King Charles was in the Vales of Moriane
when God in Heaven had His angel tell him
that he should give you to a captain-count:
the great and noble king then girded me.
With this I won Anjou and Brittany,
and then I won him both Poitou and Maine,
with this I won him Normandy the Proud,

and then I won Provence and Aquitaine,
and Lombardy, as well as all Romagna.
With this I won Bavaria, all Flanders,
and Burgundy, the Poliani lands,
Constantinople, where they did him homage—
in Saxony they do what he commands.
With this I won him Scotland, Ireland too,
and England, which he held as his demesne.[2]
With this I've won so many lands and countries
which now are held by Charles, whose beard is white.
I'm full of pain and sorrow for this sword;
I'd rather die than leave it to the pagans.
Oh God, my Father, don't let France be shamed!"

Roland hammers on a dull gray stone
and breaks off more of it than I can say:
the sword grates, but it neither snaps nor splits,
and only bounces back into the air.
The count, on seeing he will never break it,
laments it very softly to himself:
"Oh Durendal, so beautiful and sacred,
within your golden hilt are many relics—
Saint Peter's tooth, some of Saint Basil's blood,
some hair belonging to my lord, Saint Denis,
a remnant, too, of holy Mary's dress.
It isn't right that pagans should possess you;
 you ought to be attended on by Christians.
You never should be held by one who cowers!
With you I've conquered many spacious lands
now held by Charles, whose beard is streaked with white;
through them the emperor is rich and strong."

Now Roland feels death coming over him,
descending from his head down to his heart.
He goes beneath a pine tree at a run
and on the green grass stretches out, face down.
He puts his sword and ivory horn beneath him
and turns his head to face the pagan host.
He did these things in order to be sure
that Charles, as well as all his men, would say:
"This noble count has died a conqueror."
Repeatedly he goes through his confession,
and for his sins he proffers God his glove. AOI[3]

---

[2]This is a wildly exaggerated statement of the territory ruled by Charlemagne.
[3]This mysterious syllable recurs periodically throughout the poem; there is little agreement about its significance.

Now Roland is aware his time is up:
he lies upon a steep hill, facing Spain,
and with one hand he beats upon his chest:
"Oh God, against Thy power I have sinned,
because of my transgressions, great and small,
committed since the hour I was born
until this day when I have been struck down!"[4]
He lifted up his right-hand glove to God:
from Heaven angels came to him down there. AOI

Count Roland lay down underneath a pine,
his face turned so that it would point toward Spain
he was caught up in the memory of things—
of many lands he'd valiantly subdued,
of sweet France, of the members of his line,
of Charlemagne, his lord, who brought him up;
he cannot help but weep and sigh for these.
But he does not intend to slight himself;
confessing all his sins, he begs God's mercy:
"True Father, Who hath never told a lie,
Who resurrected Lazarus from the dead,
and Who protected Daniel from the lions,
protect the soul in me from every peril
brought on by wrongs I've done throughout my life!
He offered up his right-hand glove to God:[5]
Saint Gabriel removed it from his hand.
And with his head inclined upon his arm,
hands clasped together, he has met his end.
Then God sent down his angel Cherubin
and Saint Michael of the Sea and of the Peril;
together with Saint Gabriel they came
and took the count's soul into Paradise.

Translated by Robert Harrison

---

[4]As a good Catholic, Roland makes his last confession. This is almost certainly not meant to suggest that he has been a wicked man, or that his actions during the battle have been anything other than virtuous, as some readers have supposed. His death is that of a very pious Christian, even a saintly one.
[5]The glove is a symbol of his feudal obedience both to Charlemagne and to God. Having finished his assigned tasks in life, he renders the glove back to his Master.

Anna Comnena: *The Alexiad* (c. 1148 CE)

When in 1095 Emperor Alexius Comnenus appealed to Pope Urban II for help in fighting the Turks, what caught the pontiff's attention was not the plight of his fellow Christians in Byzantium, but the fact that the places where Christ had lived and died were in Muslim hands (as they had been for centuries). Although Urban was responsible for initiating the drive to "liberate" the Holy Land, it was a common monk, Peter the Hermit, who got the credit in the popular imagination. The crusaders who arrived from Northern Europe were filled with religious passion and the desire to acquire kingdoms for themselves; but they had scant understanding of the people they were supposed to be assisting. The emperor's daughter Anna, in her history of Alexius' reign, disdainfully depicts the crusaders as violent, ignorant boors.

According to Anna, what were the main faults of the crusaders?

A Celt[1] named Peter, called "Peter the Hermit," left to worship at the Holy Sepulcher.[2] After having suffered much bad treatment at the hands of the Turks and the Saracens who were ravaging all of Asia he returned to his home only with great difficulty. Since he could not bear to have failed in his aim, he decided to begin the same voyage over again. But he understood that he should not retravel the route to the Holy Sepulcher alone for fear that a worse mishap might occur to him; and he thought up a clever scheme, which was to preach throughout all the countries of the Latins[3] as follows: "A divine voice has ordered me to proclaim before all the nobles of France that they should all leave their homes to go worship at the Holy Sepulcher and try with all their ability and with all their passion to free Jerusalem from the domination of the Agarenes."[4]

In fact he succeeded. As if he had made a divine voice heard in the heart of each person, Celts from all over assembled, arriving one after the others with their arms, horses, and the rest of their military equipment. These men were so passionately enthusiastic they filled all the roads. These Celtic soldiers were accompanied by a multitude of unarmed people, more numerous than grains of sand or stars, carrying palm branches[5] and crosses over their shoulders: women and children who had left their countries. To see them one would have thought they were streams which flowed together from everywhere—from Dacia mostly, they headed toward us with their entire army.

The arrival of so many people was preceded by locusts which spared the wheat but despoiled and devoured the vines. It was truly the sign such as the prophets of that time had predicted, that this formidable Celtic army, when it arrived, would not intervene in Christian affairs, but would crush in a terrible manner the barbaric Ishmaelites[6] who are slaves of drunkenness, of wine and of Dionysus.[7] For this race, which is ruled by Dionysus

---

[1]Anna calls the crusaders "Celts," "Latins," and "Normans" interchangeably.

[2]The tomb of Christ is in Jerusalem.

[3]Countries dominated by the Roman Catholic Church, whose official language was Latin.

[4]The Turks.

[5]It was traditional for pilgrims to the Holy Land to carry palm branches over their shoulders.

[6]Muslims.

[7]The Greek god of wine. It is difficult to know what caused Anna to judge the Muslims as drunkards, for Islam strictly forbids its followers to drink wine.

and Eros, is so degenerate in regard to sexual relations of every kind that, if it is circumcised in the flesh, is not in its passions: it is enslaved—entirely enslaved—by the vices of Aphrodite. This is also the reason that the Ishmaelites adore in their worship Astarte and Ashtaroth, and that they make so much of an image of a star and the golden statue of Chobar.[8] Besides, wheat was considered as the symbol of Christianity because it is not a stimulant and is very nourishing. This is how the prophets interpreted the symbolism of the wheat and the vines.

But enough about prophets; these signs also accompanied the approach of the barbarians, and intelligent people could expect something novel. In fact the arrival of such a multitude did not take place at the same moment, nor by the same road. (In fact, how could such masses setting out from different countries have all assembled to cross from Italy?[9]) One group crossed, then another, then another after that: thus one after another they all crossed over, then continued across the continent. Each army was preceded by a cloud of locusts, as I said above; so everyone having experienced this several times, knew that this phenomenon portended the arrival of French troops.

When these groups began crossing the Straits of Lombardy, the emperor summoned some of the leaders of the Roman troops and sent them to the region around Dyrrachium and Avlona, with orders that the travelers who had crossed over should be received kindly and provided all along their route with abundant provisions from all regions; and instructions to observe them discretely, constantly observing them, so that if they were observed making raids or pillaging neighboring regions, they should be repelled by light skirmishes. These officers were aided by interpreters who knew the Latin language and could settle the conflicts which might arise.

I would like to give a clearer and more detailed account of this matter. Inspired by word of the preaching which circulated everywhere, Godefroi[10] was the first to sell his lands and set out on the road. He was a very rich man, extremely proud of his noble birth, his courage, and the glory of his ancestry, for every Celt wanted to surpass all others. There arose a movement including both men and women such as no one could remember having ever seen before: the simplest people were truly motivated by their desire to worship at the sepulcher of the Lord and to visit the holy places; but villainous men like Bohemond and his like had an ulterior motive, and the hope that perhaps they might seize the imperial city itself[11] on the way since they had stumbled on this opportunity for profit. Bohemond confused the minds of many noble warriors because he cherished an old grudge against the emperor.

Meanwhile, Peter, after having preached as I have described above, crossed the Strait of Lombardy before any of them with 80,000 infantrymen and 100,000 horsemen, and arrived at the imperial palace after having crossed through Hungary. The Celtic people, as can be guessed, are in any case very hotheaded and passionate: once they've caught fire they are unstoppable. Informed of all that Peter had had to endure previously at the hands of the Turks, the emperor advised him to wait for the arrival of the other counts; but he,

---

[8]Both Western and Eastern Medieval Christians insisted that Muslims were polytheistic idol-worshipers, although in fact they were strict monotheists and forbad images.

[9]Anna wrongly assumes that all of the crusaders crossed over from Italy, probably because the first to arrive came from that direction.

[10]Godefroi of Bouillon, Duke of Lower Lorraine.

[11]Constantinople, which was indeed invaded, pillaged and conquered by the soldiers of the Fourth Crusade in 1204.

refusing to listen to him, feeling his company strong in numbers, crossed the strait and set up camp near a small village called Helenopolis. Normans followed him: about 10,000 of them. They broke off from the rest of the army and began pillaging the region around Nicaea, conducting themselves with extreme cruelty toward all. Suckling infants, for example, were either mutilated or speared on spits and roasted over the fire. As for older people, they inflicted all manner of tortures on them. When the inhabitants of the city heard these things, they opened the gates and made a sortie against the Normans. A violent combat followed; but in the face of the belligerent ferocity of the Normans the native troops retreated into the citadel. The attackers returned to Helenopolis with all their booty. But a dispute arose between them and those who had not gone with them on the raid, as often happens in such cases; envy inflamed those who had remained behind and there followed between the two groups a quarrel which ended by the audacious Normans making a new separate sortie and taking Xerigordon in a single assault.

The sultan reacted to these events by sending Elkhanes against them with a substantial force. As soon as he arrived, he recaptured Xerigordon. As for the Normans, he put many to the sword and took the rest prisoner while planning a surprise assault on the others who had remained behind with Peter. He set up ambushes in appropriate spots where those who were traveling toward Nicaea would be fallen upon and massacred. Knowing the Celts were greedy, he summoned two courageous men and ordered them to go to Peter's camp and say that the Normans, having conquered Nicaea, were in the process of dividing up the riches of the city. This news spread among those with Peter and threw them into a terrible confusion; for as soon as they heard of dividing riches, they rushed off in disorder along the road to Nicaea, almost entirely forgetting the military experience and discipline proper to fighting men. Since they did march in ranks or troops, they fell into a Turkish ambush near Drakon and were wretchedly massacred. So many Celts and Normans were victims of the Ishmaelite sword that when the bodies of the slaughtered warriors which were scattered about were collected, they were piled—not in a huge pile, nor even a mound, or a hill—but into a high mountain of considerable dimensions, so great was the mass of bones. Later men belonging to the same race as the massacred men built walls like those of the city, filling the holes between the stones with bones instead of mortar, and thus made this city into their tomb. The fortified place exists still today, surrounded by a wall made of stones and bones mixed together.

When all these had been slain by the sword, Peter alone with a few others returned to Helenopolis and entered it. The Turks, who wanted to seize the city, raised new ambushes. But when the emperor learned all of this and had verified the facts of this appalling massacre, he realized how tragic it would have been if Peter had also been taken prisoner. So he sent for Constantine Euphorbenos Katakalon, whom I have mentioned often above, and had him assemble a large body of warships and sent them to rescue those on the other side of the strait. As soon as the Turks saw these troops arrive, they fled. Constantine, without losing a moment, gathered Peter and his few companions and led them safe and sound to the emperor. When the latter reminded him of his imprudence from the beginning and told them that he had undergone such a disaster because he had disregarded the emperor's advice, the proud Latin, far from admitting that he was responsible for this disaster, accused the others of not having obeyed him, following their own whims, and spoke of them as thieves and brigands, which is why the Lord had not allowed them to reach the Holy Sepulcher.

Those Latins who, like Bohemond and his kind, had for a long time coveted the Roman[12] Empire and wished to seize it, took advantage of the pretext of Peter's preaching which had provoked this enormous movement by deceiving the more honest among them. Selling their lands, they pretended to go off to war against the Turks to free the Holy Sepulcher.

Translated by Paul Brians

---

[12]Byzantine.

Omittamus Studia from *Carmina Burana* (12th–13th Century? CE)

Students in the Middle Ages often employed the Latin which was the medium of formal education for highly informal purposes. Many of their boldly satirical poems were collected some time in the early 13th century, some with musical settings. This poem is an impudent parody of two odes by the Latin writer Horace (IV.12 and I.11) whose moralistic works the poet had undoubtedly been forced to memorize. The theme is Carpe diem *("seize the day"): a common-place in late Roman poetry. Most students were either clergymen or clergymen in training, but that didn't stop many of them from appreciating wine, women, and song.*

What is the poet's reaction to the shortness of life? What is his attitude toward old age?

Let's put aside our studying:
Sweet it is to play the fool.
Let's seize all the sweeter things
Youth offers in its languid rule.
There'll be time for pondering
Weighty things when life grows cool.
   Time too swiftly rushes;
      Study crushes;
   Young blood strongly urges
      Love's sweet surges.

The spring of age away is slipping,
Winter soon comes rushing on
Life feels loss against it chipping
Until the flesh with care's all gone;
Heart is hardened; blood just trickles;
One by one goes all that pleases
Old Age hails us with his sickle
Coming with his family of diseases.
   Time too swiftly rushes . . .

Let's imitate the gods above![1]
That's a maxim well worth heeding.
Toward us come those nets of love
To ensnare fair men of breeding.
Let us pay heed to our prayers!
That's the code the gods maintain.
Let's go down then to the square
And watch the virgins entertain.[2]
Time too swiftly rushes . . .

---

[1]Medieval satirical poets often imitate their Roman models by speaking of "the gods," although as Christians they certainly did not believe in them.

[2]That is, let's go watch the young women.

Ah, there's plenty there for grabbing
If it's only with the eyes.
Shiny arms the air are stabbing,
Slender slink those splendid thighs.

While the girls are leaping, stalking
With the beat that never dies,
I stand gaping; in my gawking
Feel my soul outside me rise!
 Time too swiftly rushes;
  Study crushes;
 Young blood strongly urges
  Love's sweet surges.

        Translated by James J. Wilhelm

La Comtessa de Dia (1150–1200? CE): *I've suffered great distress*

The first Europeans to develop the literary approach to the subject which later came to be called "courtly love" were the troubadours of southern France. It is often said that their poetry idealizes love by depicting unfulfilled romantic yearnings; but in fact much of it is about frankly physical desire, and is often strikingly explicit. Marriage among the nobles was the product of business negotiations between families; so romance blossomed in secret affairs, usually with a married woman as the lover's object. The few women among the troubadours seem to have held attitudes similar to those of the men. A musical setting of this poem (Estat ai en greu cossirier) *is performed by Sinfonye on their album* The Sweet Look and the Loving Manner: Trobairitz Love Lyrics and Chansons de femme from Medieval France *(Hyperion CDA66625, track 15) and by the Boston Camerata on their album* Tristan and Iseult *(Erato ECD 75528, track 7).*

What qualities does the poet say her lover possesses?

I've suffered great distress
From a knight whom I once owned.[1]
Now, for all time, be it known:
I loved him—yes, to excess.
His jilting I've regretted,
Yet his love I never really returned.
Now for my sin[2] I can only burn:
Dressed, or in my bed.

O if I had that knight to caress
Naked all night in my arms,
He'd be ravished by the charm
Of using, for cushion, my breast.
His love I more deeply prize
Than Floris did Blancheflor's.[3]
Take that love, my core,
My sense, my life, my eyes!

Lovely lover, gracious, kind,
When will I overcome your fight?
O if I could lie with you one night!
Feel those loving lips on mine!
Listen, one thing sets me afire:
Here in my husband's place I want you,
If you'll just keep your promise true:
Give me everything I desire.

Translated by James J. Wilhelm

---

[1]In the sense that she possessed his love.
[2]In the language of courtly love, her "sin" was refusing his love.
[3]A famous pair of Medieval lovers.

Provençal Dawn Song:
In a garden under a hawthorn bower (12th Century CE)

This is the earliest known example of a "dawn song," a poem about illicit lovers in anguish at the approach of the dawn which will separate them. The form became extremely popular, and variations on it proliferated in France and Germany. The words in quotation marks are spoken by the lady to her lover, whom she affectionately calls "pretty boy." Her frenzied passion is aroused by pre-dawn birdsongs.

In a garden under a hawthorn bower[1]
A lover to his lady's closely drawn
Until a watchman shouts the morning hour.
O God! O God! how swift it comes—the dawn!

"Dear God, if this night would never fail[2]
And my lover never far from me was gone,
And the watchman never saw the morning pale—
But, O my God! how swift it comes—the dawn!

"Come, pretty boy, give me a little kiss
Down in the meadow where birds sing endless song.
Forget my husband! Think—just think of this—
For, O my God! how swift it comes—the dawn!

"Hurry, my boy. The new games end at morn.
Down to that garden—those birds—that song!
Play, play till the crier blows his horn,
For, O my God! how swift it comes—the dawn!

"Down in the sweet air over the meadow hovering
I drank a sweet draught—long, so long—
Out of the air of my handsome, noble lover."
O God! O God! how swift it comes—the dawn!

The lady's pretty. She has many charms.
Toward her beauty many men are drawn.
But she lies happy in one pair of arms.[3]
O God! O God! how swift it comes—the dawn!

Translated by James J. Wilhelm

---

[1]The hawthorn forms a large prickly hedge which often encloses a hollowed-out interior. With very little privacy in most Medieval homes, lovers often resorted to outdoor lovemaking.
[2]End.
[3]Although a lady might be unfaithful to her husband, according to the conventions of courtly love she was supposed to have only one lover.

Dante Alighieri: *The Inferno*, Canto 3 (early 14th Century CE)

Dante Alighieri is generally considered the greatest poet of the Middle Ages. He was forced to leave his beloved home city of Florence as the result of a bitter political dispute, and spent the rest of his life in various cities in Italy and France. His Commedia *(in English traditionally called* The Divine Comedy) *is a vast allegorical work in three parts, in which the poet is taken on a grand tour of Hell, Purgatory, and Paradise. His guide is the spirit of the ancient Roman poet Virgil, whom Medieval scholars mistakenly believed to have miraculously predicted the birth of Christ. Since he was not a Christian, Virgil lives in Limbo, the area of Hell reserved for pious pagans and unbaptized infants. Arranged below them in rings are various kinds of sinners being punished in ways appropriate to their particular sort of evil. It is important to keep in mind that neither Dante nor his readers supposed that his poem depicted the actual reality of Heaven and Hell: rather it is a symbolic story which is designed to convey Christian ideas about the nature of sin and salvation. Medieval readers delighted in such allegorical verse and were skilled in interpreting it; but the* Inferno *is the only poem of its kind still popular today. In the following scene Dante and Virgil stand before the gateway into Hell. The canto begins with the inscription written over the gate.*

I AM THE WAY INTO THE CITY OF WOE.
I AM THE WAY TO A FORSAKEN PEOPLE.
I AM THE WAY INTO ETERNAL SORROW.

SACRED JUSTICE MOVED MY ARCHITECT.
I WAS RAISED HERE BY DIVINE OMNIPOTENCE,
PRIMORDIAL LOVE[1] AND ULTIMATE INTELLECT.

ONLY THOSE ELEMENTS TIME CANNOT WEAR
WERE MADE BEFORE ME, AND BEYOND TIME I STAND.
ABANDON ALL HOPE YE WHO ENTER HERE.[2]

These mysteries I read cut into stone
above a gate. And turning I said: "Master,
what is the meaning of this harsh inscription?"

And he then as initiate to novice:[3]
"Here must you put by all division of spirit
and gather your soul against all cowardice.

This is the place I told you to expect.
Here you shall pass among the fallen people,
souls who have lost the good of intellect."[4]

[1]The threat of Hell is meant to inspire a fear of sin and lead to salvation, so its creation can be said to be an act of love; but this saying seems harsh even to Dante.
[2]In traditional Christian belief, no salvation is possible once one has entered Hell.
[3]Fully-educated monk to student.
[4]The soul was often identified with the mind in Medieval theology.

So saying, he put forth his hand to me,
and with a gentle and encouraging smile
he led me through the gate of mystery.

Here sighs and cries and wails coiled and recoiled
on the starless air, spilling my soul to tears.
A confusion of tongues and monstrous accents toiled

in pain and anger. Voices hoarse and shrill
and sounds of blows, all intermingled, raised
tumult and pandemonium that still

whirls on the air forever dirty with it
as if a whirlwind sucked at sand. And I,
holding my head in horror, cried: "Sweet Spirit,

what souls are these who run through this black haze?"
And he to me: "These are the nearly soulless
whose lives concluded neither blame nor praise.[5]

They are mixed here with that despicable corps
of angels who were neither for God nor Satan,
but only for themselves.[6] The High Creator

scourged them from Heaven for its perfect beauty,
and Hell will not receive them since the wicked
might feel some glory over them." And I:

"Master, what gnaws at them so hideously
their lamentation stuns the very air?"
"They have no hope of death," he answered me,[7]

"and in their blind and unattaining state
their miserable lives have sunk so low
that they must envy every other fate.

---

[5]According to a common interpretation of Luke 11:23 neutrality of faith is impermisible. Those who were not firmly on the side of Christ in life are sent to Hell along with those who openly opposed his teachings, but in order to symbolize the fact that they failed to align themselves decisively with either side, he places them in this antechamber, on the far side of the river Acheron which marks the border of Hell proper. Despite the fact that their sin is only passive neutrality, their damnationis just as complete as that of those who committed more overt, active sins..

[6]Tradition says that a group of angels, led by Satan, rebelled against God, and were punished by being cast down into Hell. Dante puts those angels who stood on the sidelines during this conflict in Hell for not vigorously defending the right.

[7]According to Christian belief, all souls live on after death, so physical mortality is not final for anyone.

No word of them survives their living season.
Mercy and Justice deny them even a name.
Let us not speak of them: look, and pass on."[8]

I saw a banner there upon the mist.
Circling and circling, it seemed to scorn all pause.
So it ran on, and still behind it pressed

a never-ending rout of souls in pain.
I had not thought death had undone so many[9]
as passed before me in that mournful train.

And some I knew among them; last of all
I recognized the shadow of that soul
who, in his cowardice, made the Great Denial.[10]

At once I understood for certain: these
were of that retrograde and faithless crew
hateful to God and to His enemies.

These wretches never born and never dead
ran naked in a swarm of wasps and hornets
that goaded them the more the more they fled,

and made their faces stream with bloody gouts
of pus and tears that dribbled to their feet
to be swallowed there by loathsome worms and maggots.

Then looking onward I made out a throng
assembled on the beach of a wide river,
whereupon I turned to him: "Master, I long

to know what souls these are, and what strange usage
makes them as eager to cross as they seem to be
in this infected light." At which the Sage:

"All this shall be made known to you when we stand
on the joyless beach of Acheron." And I
cast down my eyes, sensing a reprimand

---

[8]Throughout the poem Virgil urges Dante not to identify emotionally with the damned, but to learn from their fate.

[9]Dante makes these apathetic souls behave like fanatics in the afterlife, chasing in a mob after a banner. This is the first of many symbolic punishments he invents for the inhabitants of Hell. This line is memorably quoted in T. S. Eliot's poem "The Waste Land."

[10]The identity of this figure is disputed. One translator argues that it may be Pontius Pilate, who washed his hands to symbolize his refusal to either condemn or acquit Jesus during his trial.

in what he said, and so walked at his side
in silence and ashamed until we came
through the dead cavern to that sunless tide.

There, steering toward us in an ancient ferry
came an old man with a white bush of hair,[11]
bellowing: "Woe to you depraved souls! Bury

here and forever all hope of Paradise:
I come to lead you to the other shore,
into eternal dark, into fire and ice.[12]

And you who are living yet, I say begone
from these who are dead." But when he saw me stand
against his violence he began again:

"By other windings and by other steerage
shall you cross to that other shore. Not here! Not here!
A lighter craft than mine must give you passage."

And my Guide to him: "Charon, bite back your spleen:
this has been willed where what is willed must be,
and is not yours to ask what it may mean."

The steersman of that marsh of ruined souls,
who wore a wheel of flame around each eye,
stifled the rage that shook his woolly jowls.

But those unmanned and naked spirits there
turned pale with fear and their teeth began to chatter
at sound of his crude bellow. In despair

They blasphemed God, their parents, their time on earth,
the race of Adam, and the day and the hour
and the place and the seed and the womb that gave them birth.

But all together they drew to that grim shore
where all must come who lose the fear of God.
Weeping and cursing they come for evermore,

---

[11] This is Charon, the boatman of Greek mythology, who ferried the souls of the dead into Hades.

[12] It is a common misconception that the worst sinners in *The Inferno* are punished in its hottest region. In fact, some of the worst sinners are punished by being buried in ice, symbolizing their distance from the warmth of God's love.

and demon Charon with eyes like burning coals
herds them in, and with a whistling oar
flails on the stragglers to his wake of souls.

As leaves in autumn loosen and stream down
until the branch stands bare above its tatters
spread on the rustling ground, so one by one

the evil seed of Adam in its Fall[13]
cast themselves, at his signal, from the shore
and streamed away like birds who hear their call.[14]

So they are gone over that shadowy water,
and always before they reach the other shore
a new noise stirs on this, and new throngs gather.

"My son," the courteous Master said to me,
"all who die in the shadow of God's wrath
converge to this from every clime and country.

And all pass over eagerly, for here
Divine Justice transforms and spurs them so
their dread turns wish: they yearn for what they fear.[15]

No soul in Grace comes ever to this crossing;
therefore if Charon rages at your presence
you will understand the reason for his cursing."

When he had spoken, all the twilight country
shook so violently, the terror of it
bathes me with sweat even in memory:

the tear-soaked ground gave out a sigh of wind
that spewed itself in flame on a red sky,
and all my shattered senses left me. Blind,

like one whom sleep comes over in a swoon,
I stumbled into darkness and went down.

Translated by John Ciardi

---

[13]According to the doctrine of Original Sin, all humans have inherited the sin of Adam.
[14]Falcons were trained to swoop down and attack a target on command.
[15]Catholic doctrine places great emphasis on the belief that the individual is free to choose either salvation or damnation. No one goes to Hell inadvertently. Hence the damned are depicted as eager to cross into Hell even though they must dread the prospect.

St. Thomas Aquinas on Moral Principles from *The Summa of Theology* (1265 CE)

Aquinas revived Aristotle's thought in Europe at a time when it was better known among the Arabic-speaking peoples, and he used it in developing his theology and his philosophy much as St. Augustine had earlier used Platonic thought. Most moral rules, he claims, are grounded in nature (in the very being of things, in our case, "human nature") and are knowable by human reason. Aquinas thus acknowledges that rules such as most of the Ten Commandments are commonplace in human societies; but he argues that there are other moral rules which are known only by revelation ("divine instruction"). All translations from Aquinas are by Vernon J. Bourke.

If the moral rules discernible by reason pertain to our actions toward our fellow humans (e.g., honoring, not killing, not stealing), which of our actions (or which kinds of actions) are governed by the rules in which humans need divine instruction?

Moral Rules and Natural Law

Moral rules are concerned with those matters that essentially pertain to good behavior. Now, since human morals are spoken of in relation to reason (for it is the proper principle of human acts), those customs that are in conformity with reason are called good, and those that are in discord with reason are deemed bad. Just as every judgment of speculative reason proceeds from the natural knowledge of first principles, so, too, does every judgment of practical reason from certain naturally known principles, as we have explained before. . . .

And so, it becomes evident that since moral precepts belong among the matters that pertain to good behavior, and these are items that are in conformity with reason, and since every judgment of human reason is derived in some fashion from natural reason, it must be true that all moral rules belong to the law of nature, but not all in the same way.

For, there are some things that the natural reason of every man judges immediately and essentially as things to be done; for example, *Honor thy father and mother; Thou shalt not kill; Thou shalt not steal.* Precepts of this kind belong in an unqualified way to the law of nature.

Then, there are other things that are judged by a more rational consideration, on the part of the wise men, matters of obligation. Now, these belong to the law of nature in this way: they of course require instruction, by which less favored people are taught by those who are wise; for example, *Rise up before the hoary head, and honor the face of the aged man* (Leviticus 19:32), and other injunctions of this kind.

Finally, there are other matters for the judgment of which human reason needs divine instruction, whereby we are taught concerning matters of divinity; for example, *Thou shalt not make to thyself a graven thing, nor the likeness of any thing . . . . Thou shalt not take the name of thy God in vain* (Exodus 20:4, 7).

St. Thomas Aquinas on Faith and Reason:
Faith is Not Demonstrative Knowledge, from *The Summa of Theology*

Aquinas' emphasis on reason to discover divine truths led to elaborate systems of theology based on the logic of Aristotle which dominated late Medieval thought. Although Renaissance humanists were to ridicule these "scholastic" thinkers, much of the later history of Western philosophy and science was to be based on their methods of analysis. But Aquinas uses his distinction between reason and revelation more generally to distinguish those things which can be known by philosophy and those which can only be known by theology as founded on faith. An example of the latter (in the first selection below) is the doctrine of the Trinity, namely, that God has three persons: the Father, who creates the world, the Son (Christ), who redeems the world, and the Holy Spirit, who continues to work out the consequences of that redemption, yet together they constitute but one god.

Why can't we know by human reason that the world had a beginning?

That the world did not always exist is held by faith alone and it cannot be proved demonstratively, just as we said above of the mystery of the Trinity. The reason for this is that the beginning [*novitas*] of the world cannot receive a demonstration from the side of the world itself. Indeed, the starting point of a generation is that which is. But each thing in its specific intelligibility abstracts from the here and now. This is why it is said that "universals are everywhere and forever." Hence it cannot be demonstrated that man, or the heavens, or a stone did not always exist.

Likewise, it cannot be demonstrated from the side of the agent-cause that acts by means of will. For, the will of God cannot be investigated rationally, except for those items that it is absolutely necessary for God to will. Now, such items are not what He wills in regard to creatures, as we have said.

Of course, it is possible for the divine will to be manifested through revelation, on which faith rests. Hence, that the world had a beginning is a matter of belief [*credibile*] but not of demonstration or of science.

And this is a useful thing to consider, lest someone who perhaps presumes to demonstrate what is of faith brings forward arguments lacking in necessity; for, these would provide unbelievers with matter for ridicule and they would think that we believe items pertaining to the faith because of arguments of this kind.

St. Thomas Aquinas: Perfect Happiness as the Contemplation of God, from *Quodlibetal Questions*

How is Aquinas' notion of human happiness like Aristotle's notion, and how is it different?

Felicity or happiness consists in an operation[1] and not in a habitual state, as the Philosopher[2] proves in the *Ethics* (I, 8, 1098b30). So, happiness can be related to a potency[3] of the soul in two ways. One way is as the object of the potency; and in this sense, happiness is chiefly related to the will. Indeed, happiness is the name of the ultimate end[4] of man and of the highest good itself. Now, the end and the good are the object of the will. . . .

Now, the end of our desires is God; hence, the act whereby we are primarily joined to Him is basically and substantially our happiness. But we are primarily united with God by an act of understanding; and therefore, the very seeing of god, which is an act of the intellect, is substantially and basically our happiness. However, since this action is most perfect and most appropriate to its object, it is therefore followed by the greatest enjoyment, which adorns and perfects this operation as beauty does youth, to quote the *Ethics* (X, 4). As a result, this joy which belongs to the will is a formal complement of happiness. Thus, the ultimate basis of happiness lies in the vision, while its complement consists in the fruition.

---

[1]Process.

[2]The great philosopher, for Aquinas and his followers, is Aristotle.

[3]The powers of the soul, namely, will (wanting, deliberating and choosing) and intellect.

[4]Goal, purpose.

Jean de Venette: The Black Death (14th Century CE)

Plagues have wracked the world throughout history, but the bubonic plague which swept through parts of Asia and into Europe in the 14th Century is especially memorable, both because of its profound and lasting effects and because it was vividly described by witnesses. In many areas three-quarters of the inhabitants died, and whole villages were abandoned, reverting to the wild. The suffering caused by the bubonic plague was all the harder to bear because no one really understood its causes (the bites of fleas carrying it from infected rats), and prejudiced people were all too ready to believe wild stories about its being a Jewish plot. Thus human cruelty worsened the suffering caused by nature.

In what ways does the pious Jean de Venette feel that the plague years were actually better than those which followed?

In A.D. 1348, the people of France and of almost the whole world were struck by a blow other than war. For in addition to the famine which I described in the beginning and to the wars which I described in the course of this narrative, pestilence and its attendant tribulations appeared again in various parts of the world. In the month of August, 1348, after Vespers when the sun was beginning to set, a big and very bright star appeared above Paris, toward the west. It did not seem, as stars usually do, to be very high above our hemisphere, but rather very near. As the sun set and night came on, this star did not seem to me or to many other friars who were watching it to move from one place. At length, when night had come, this big star, to the amazement of all of us who were watching, broke into many different rays and, as it shed these rays over Paris toward the east, totally disappeared and was completely annihilated. Whether it was a comet or not, whether it was composed of airy exhalations and was finally resolved into vapor, I leave to the decision of astronomers. It is, however, possible that it was a presage of the amazing pestilence to come, which, in fact, followed very shortly in Paris and throughout France and elsewhere, as I shall tell. All this year and the next, the mortality of men and women, of the young even more than of the old, in Paris and in the kingdom of France, and also, it is said, in other parts of the world, was so great that it was almost impossible to bury the dead. People lay ill little more than two or three days and died suddenly, as it were in full health. He who was well one day was dead the next and being carried to his grave. Swellings appeared suddenly in the armpit or in the groin—in many cases both—and they were infallible signs of death. This sickness or pestilence was called an epidemic by the doctors. Nothing like the great numbers who died in the years 1348 and 1349 has been heard of or seen or read of in times past. This plague and disease came from *ymaginatione* or association and contagion, for, if a well man visited the sick he only rarely evaded the risk of death. Wherefore in many towns timid priests withdrew, leaving the exercise of their ministry to such of the religious as were more daring. In many places not two out of twenty remained alive. So high was the mortality at the Hotel-Dieu[1] in Paris that for a long time, more than five hundred dead were carried daily with great devotion in carts to the cemetery of the Holy Innocents in Paris for burial. A very great number of the saintly sisters of the Hôtel-Dieu who, not fearing to die, nursed the sick in all sweetness and humility, with no thought of honor, a number too often renewed by death, rest in peace with Christ, as we may piously believe.

---

[1] A hospital.

This plague, it is said, began among the unbelievers,[2] came to Italy, and then crossing the Alps reached Avignon, where it attacked several cardinals and took from them their whole household.[3] Then it spread, unforeseen, to France, through Gascony and Spain, little by little, from town to town, from village to village, from house to house, and finally from person to person. It even crossed over to Germany, though it was not so bad there as with us. During the epidemic, God of His accustomed goodness deigned to grant this grace, that however suddenly men died, almost all awaited death joyfully. Nor was there anyone who died without confessing his sins and receiving the holy viaticum.[4] To the even greater benefit of the dying, Pope Clement VI through their confessors mercifully gave and granted absolution from penalty to the dying in many cities and fortified towns. Men died the more willingly for this and left many inheritances and temporal goods to churches and monastic orders, for in many cases they had seen their close heirs and children die before them.

Some said that this pestilence was caused by infection of the air and waters, since there was at this time no famine nor lack of food supplies, but on the contrary great abundance. As a result of this theory of infected water and air as the source of the plague the Jews were suddenly and violently charged with infecting wells and water and corrupting the air. The whole world rose up against them cruelly on this account. In Germany and other parts of the world where Jews lived, they were massacred and slaughtered by Christians, and many thousands were burned everywhere, indiscriminately. The unshaken, if fatuous, constancy of the [Jewish] men and their wives was remarkable. For mothers hurled their children first into the fire that they might not be baptized and then leaped in after them to burn with their husbands and children. It is said that many bad Christians were found who in a like manner put poison into wells. But in truth, such poisonings, granted that they actually were perpetrated, could not have caused so great a plague nor have infected so many people. There were other causes; for example, the will of God and the corrupt humors and evil inherent in air and earth. Perhaps the poisonings, if they actually took place in some localities, reinforced these causes. The plague lasted in France for the greater part of the years 1348 and 1349 and then ceased. Many country villages and many houses in good towns remained empty and deserted. Many houses, including some splendid dwellings, very soon fell into ruins. Even in Paris several houses were thus ruined, though fewer here than elsewhere.

After the cessation of the epidemic, pestilence, or plague, the men and women who survived married each other. There was no sterility among the women, but on the contrary fertility beyond the ordinary. Pregnant women were seen on every side. Many twins were born and even three children at once. But the most surprising fact is that children born after the plague, when they became of an age for teeth, had only twenty or twenty-two teeth, though before that time men

---

[2]That is, among the Muslims to the East.
[3]During this period the Pope and his College of Cardinals lived at Avignon rather than Rome.
[4]The Eucharist, or elements of the mass, given to the dying.

commonly had thirty-two in their upper and lower jaws together.[5] What this diminution in the number of teeth signified I wonder greatly, unless it be a new era resulting from the destruction of one human generation by the plague and its replacement by another. But woe is me! the world was not changed for the better but for the worse by this renewal of population. For men were more avaricious and grasping than before, even though they had far greater possessions.[6] They were more covetous and disturbed each other more frequently with suits, brawls, disputes, and pleas. Nor by the mortality resulting from this terrible plague inflicted by God was peace between kings and lords established. On the contrary, the enemies of the king of France and of the Church were stronger and wickeder than before and stirred up wars on sea and on land. Greater evils than before pullulated everywhere in the world. And this fact was very remarkable. Although there was an abundance of all goods, yet everything was twice as dear,[7] whether it were utensils, victuals, or merchandise, hired helpers or peasants and serfs, except for some hereditary domains which remained abundantly stocked with everything. Charity began to cool, and iniquity with ignorance and sin to abound, for few could be found in the good towns and castles who knew how or were willing to instruct children in the rudiments of grammar.

Translated by Jean Birdsall

---

[5] Like the majority of Medieval "scientific" statements, this observation was insufficiently researched to be worth anything.

[6] The shortage of labor following upon the plague led to a substantial improvement in wages for workers, which was seen as a deplorable sign of greed by the wealthy.

[7] Expensive.

The Southern European Renaissance

Pico Della Mirandola: *Oration On the Dignity Of Man* (15th C. CE)

If there is such a thing as a "manifesto" of the Italian Renaissance, Pico della Mirandola's "Oration on the Dignity of Man" is it; no other work more forcefully, eloquently, or thoroughly remaps the human landscape to center all attention on human capacity and the human perspective. Pico himself had a massive intellect and literally studied everything there was to be studied in the university curriculum of the Renaissance; the "Oration" in part is meant to be a preface to a massive compendium of all the intellectual achievements of humanity, a compendium that never appeared because of Pico's early death. Pico was a "humanist," following a way of thinking that originated as far back as the fourteenth century. Late Medieval and Renaissance humanism was a response to the dry concerns for logic and linguistics that animated the other great late Medieval Christian philosophy, Scholasticism. The Humanists, rather than focussing on what they considered futile questions of logic and semantics, focussed on the relation of the human to the divine, seeing in human beings the summit and purpose of God's creation. Their concern was to define the human place in God's plan and the relation of the human to the divine; therefore, they centered all their thought on the "human" relation to the divine, and hence called themselves "humanists." At no point do they ignore their religion; humanism is first and foremost a religious movement, not a secular one (what we call "secular humanism" in modern political discourse is a world view that arises in part from "humanism" but is, nevertheless, essentially conceived in opposition to "humanism").

Where is humanity's place on the "chain of being?" What choices do human beings have? How might these views have arisen from the views expressed in Boccaccio's story of Ser Ciappelletto?

I once read that Abdala the Muslim, when asked what was most worthy of awe and wonder in this theater of the world, answered, "There is nothing to see more wonderful than man!" Hermes Trismegistus[1] concurs with this opinion: "A great miracle, Asclepius, is man!" However, when I began to consider the reasons for these opinions, all these reasons given for the magnificence of human nature failed to convince me: that man is the intermediary between creatures, close to the gods, master of all the lower creatures, with the sharpness of his senses, the acuity of his reason, and the brilliance of his intelligence the interpreter of nature, the nodal point between eternity and time, and, as the Persians say, the intimate bond or marriage song of the world, just a little lower than angels as David tells us.[2] I concede these are magnificent reasons, but they do not seem to go to the heart of the matter, that is, those reasons which truly claim admiration. For, if these are all the reasons we can come up with, why should we not admire angels more than we do ourselves? After thinking a long time, I have figured out why man is the most fortunate of all creatures and as a result worthy of the highest admiration and earning his rank on the

---

[1]This mystical Egyptian writer, much quoted by Renaissance alchemists, probably lived in the 2nd–3rd century.
[2]Psalms 8:5.

chain of being, a rank to be envied not merely by the beasts but by the stars themselves and by the spiritual natures beyond and above this world. This miracle goes past faith and wonder. And why not? It is for this reason that man is rightfully named a magnificent miracle and a wondrous creation.

What is this rank on the chain of being? God the Father, Supreme Architect of the Universe, built this home, this universe we see all around us, a venerable temple of his godhead, through the sublime laws of his ineffable Mind. The expanse above the heavens he decorated with Intelligences, the spheres of heaven with living, eternal souls. The scabrous and dirty lower worlds he filled with animals of every kind. However, when the work was finished, the Great Artisan desired that there be some creature to think on the plan of his great work, and love its infinite beauty, and stand in awe at its immenseness. Therefore, when all was finished, as Moses and Timaeus tell us, He began to think about the creation of man. But he had no Archetype from which to fashion some new child, nor could he find in his vast treasure-houses anything which He might give to His new son, nor did the universe contain a single place from which the whole of creation might be surveyed. All was perfected, all created things stood in their proper place, the highest things in the highest places, the midmost things in the midmost places, and the lowest things in the lowest places. But God the Father would not fail, exhausted and defeated, in this last creative act. God's wisdom would not falter for lack of counsel in this need. God's love would not permit that he whose duty it was to praise God's creation should be forced to condemn himself as a creation of God.

Finally, the Great Artisan mandated that this creature who would receive nothing proper to himself shall have joint possession of whatever nature had been given to any other creature. He made man a creature of indeterminate and indifferent nature, and, placing him in the middle of the world, said to him "Adam, we give you no fixed place to live, no form that is peculiar to you, nor any function that is yours alone. According to your desires and judgment, you will have and possess whatever place to live, whatever form, and whatever functions you yourself choose. All other things have a limited and fixed nature prescribed and bounded by our laws. You, with no limit or no bound, may choose for yourself the limits and bounds of your nature. We have placed you at the world's center so that you may survey everything else in the world. We have made you neither of heavenly nor of earthly stuff, neither mortal nor immortal, so that with free choice and dignity, you may fashion yourself into whatever form you choose. To you is granted the power of degrading yourself into the lower forms of life, the beasts, and to you is granted the power, contained in your intellect and judgment, to be reborn into the higher forms, the divine."

Imagine! The great generosity of God! The happiness of man! To man it is allowed to be whatever he chooses to be! As soon as an animal is born, it brings out of its mother's womb all that it will ever possess. Spiritual beings from the beginning become what they are to be for all eternity. Man, when he entered life, the Father gave the seeds of every kind and every way of life possible. Whatever seeds each man sows and cultivates will grow and bear him their proper fruit. If these seeds are vegetative, he will be like a plant. If these seeds are sensitive, he will be like an animal. If these seeds are intellectual, he will be an angel and the son of God. And if, satisfied with no created thing, he removes himself to the center of his own unity, his spiritual soul, united with God, alone in the darkness of God, who is above all things, he will surpass every created thing. Who could not help but admire this great shape-shifter? In fact, how could one admire anything else? . . .

For the mystic philosophy of the Hebrews transforms Enoch into an angel called "Mal'akh Adonay Shebaoth," and sometimes transforms other humans into different sorts of divine beings. The Pythagoreans abuse villainous men by having them reborn as animals and, according to Empedocles, even plants. Muhammed also said frequently, "Those who deviate from the heavenly law become animals." Bark does not make a plant a plant, rather its senseless and mindless nature does. The hide does not make an animal an animal, but rather its irrational but sensitive soul. The spherical form does not make the heavens the heavens, rather their unchanging order. It is not a lack of body that makes an angel an angel, rather it is his spiritual intelligence. If you see a person totally subject to his appetites, crawling miserably on the ground, you are looking at a plant, not a man. If you see a person blinded by empty illusions and images, and made soft by their tender beguilements, completely subject to his senses, you are looking at an animal, not a man. If you see a philosopher judging things through his reason, admire and follow him: he is from heaven, not the earth. If you see a person living in deep contemplation, unaware of his body and dwelling in the inmost reaches of his mind, he is neither from heaven nor earth, he is divinity clothed in flesh.

Who would not admire man, who is called by Moses[3] and the Gospels "all flesh" and "every creature," because he fashions and transforms himself into any fleshly form and assumes the character of any creature whatsoever? For this reason, Euanthes the Persian in his description of Chaldaean theology, writes that man has no inborn, proper form, but that many things that humans resemble are outside and foreign to them, from which arises the Chaldaean saying: *"Hanorish tharah sharinas"*: "Man is multitudinous, varied, and ever changing." Why do I emphasize this? Considering that we are born with this condition, that is, that we can become whatever we choose to become, we need to understand that we must take earnest care about this, so that it will never be said to our disadvantage that we were born to a privileged position but failed to realize it and became animals and senseless beasts. Instead, the saying of Asaph the prophet should be said of us, "You are all angels of the Most High." Above all, we should not make that freedom of choice God gave us into something harmful, for it was intended to be to our advantage. Let a holy ambition enter into our souls; let us not be content with mediocrity, but rather strive after the highest and expend all our strength in achieving it.

Let us disdain earthly things, and despise the things of heaven, and, judging little of what is in the world, fly to the court beyond the world and next to God. In that court, as the mystic writings tell us, are the Seraphim, Cherubim, and Thrones[4] in the foremost places; let us not even yield place to them, the highest of the angelic orders, and not be content with a lower place, imitate them in all their glory and dignity. If we choose to, we will not be second to them in anything.

Translated by Richard Hooker

---

[3]Moses was reputed to have written the first five books of the Bible.

[4]These are the three highest orders of angels in the medieval and Renaissance theory of angelic hierarchy which is, in descending order, Seraphim, Cherubim, Thrones, Dominations, Powers, Angels, Archangels.

Petrarch: *A young lady beneath a green laurel* (mid-14th Century CE)

Francesco Petrarca was a great scholar and writer who anticipated and helped to create the Renaissance humanist movement while also influencing such writers as Geoffrey Chaucer and William Shakespeare. His most famous works are a series of poems depicting his love for a young woman named Laura whom he idealized and worshipped from afar. His many love poems are considered the very archetype of exalted romantic passion, though in later life he repented of having wasted much of his life in pursuit of a mere earthly woman. This poem is written in a particularly complex variation on a form called the sestina. *Each stanza consists of six lines which end in a word which is repeated at the end of a line in all the other stanzas, but the words occur in a different order. After the sixth stanza occurs a seventh in which all six words are used in only three lines. It is most challenging to create a moving, passionate poem within such strict rules; but the insistent repetition of the final words suggests an obsession which never swerves from its object.*

What qualities does Petrarch ascribe to Laura? Who is more vividly depicted in this poem, the lover or his beloved?

A young lady beneath a green laurel
I saw, whiter and colder than is a snow[1]
untouched by the sun for many, many years;
and her speech and her beauty and her face and all her hair
so pleased me that I carry her before my eyes
forever, wherever I am, on hill or shore.

When my thoughts will come to rest on that shore
when the green leaves are no more on the laurel,
when I have quieted my heart, dried my eyes,
then you will see burning ice and snow;[2]
to await that day, I have fewer hairs
than I would be willing to spend in years.

But because time flies and fleeing go the years
and death suddenly casts one from shore,
crowned either with brown or with white hair,[3]
I will follow the shadow of that sweet laurel
through the burning sun or through the snow,
until the last day closes these eyes.

---

[1]These images refer to Laura's "coldness" toward the poet, refusing to return his love.
[2]The laurel is an evergreen, and burning ice and snow are impossible; so Petrarch is saying he will never quiet his heart or dry his eyes: he will love her forever.
[3]Death can strike down young men as well as old ones.

Never have there been seen such beautiful eyes,
in our times or in the first years,
dissolving, melting me as the sun does the snow,
from which flows so large a tear-filled shower
which Love floods at the foot of the hard laurel
with all its diamond branches and golden hair.

I fear I first will change this face and this hair[4]
before she will with pity raise her eyes,
she, my idol sculpted in living laurel,
for it is today now seven years
since I have gone sighing from shore to shore
both night and day, both in heat or in snow.

Within fire, though without white snow,
alone with these thoughts, with whitened hair,
weeping I go over every shore,
in order to make pity run in the eyes
of one who will be born in a thousand years,[5]
if so long can live a tended laurel.

The topaz sun all aureate[6] above the snow
is outshined still by the yellow hair near those eyes
which lead my years so rapidly to shore.

Translated by Richard Hooker

_____

[4]I will grow wrinkled and gray.
[5]Petrarch expects that people a thousand years from now will read this poem and sympathize with him.
[6]Golden

Angelo Poliziano: Lament on the Death of Lorenzo di Medici (1492)

Lorenzo de' Medici ("The Magnificent") was intensely interested in the arts and scholarship. He supported many artists (including Botticelli and Michelangelo), philosophers (Marsilio Ficino and Giovanni Pico della Mirandola), musicians and authors and was a talented poet himself. The poet Angelo Poliziano and the Flemish-born composer Heinrich Isaac collaborated to produce his funeral ode. In the first stanza the poet wishes he were able to weep continuously for his late patron. The rest of the lament goes on to state that both poetry and music have fallen silent as a result of Lorenzo's death. The fact that this idea is expressed in beautiful words and music would not have struck anyone in the time as self-contradictory since extravagant praise of rulers was traditional, and not to be taken too literally. During the third stanza the tenor voice drops out symbolizing the death of Lorenzo, and only three voices remain, with the bass repeating over and over the line line from the funeral mass, "And rest in peace." A recording of the piece is available on An Evening at the Medicis *(MCA MCAD 5953, track 14).*

What references in this poem make it a good example of Renaissance classicism?

Quis dabit capiti meo	O That my head were
aquam? Quis oculis meis	waters, and my eyes
fontem lachrimarum dabit,	a fount of tears,
ut necte fleam?	that I might weep by day
ut necte fleam?	and weep by night!
Sic turtur viduus solet,	So mourns the widowed turtledove,
sic cygnus moriens solet,	so mourns the dying swan,
sic luscinia conqueri.	so mourns the nightingale.[1]
Heu miser, miser!	Ah, woe is me!
O dolor, dolor!	O grief, o grief!
Laurus impetu fulminis	Lightning has struck
illa illa iacet subito,	our laurel tree,[2]
Laurus omnium celebris	our laurel so dear
Musarum choris, nympharum choris.	to all the muses and the dances of the nymphs.
(Bass: *Et requiescamus in pace.*)	(*Bass:* And rest in peace.)
Sub cuius patula coma	Beneath whose spreading boughs
et Phœbi lyra blandius	Phœbus[3] himself more sweetly
insonat et vox dulcius;	played and sang.
nunc murta omnia,	Now all is mute
nunc surda omnia.	and there is none to hear.

Translated by John Aldington Symonds

---

[1]All three of these birds were associated with mourning. The swan was supposed to sing only before its own death.

[2]"Laurel" is a pun on "Lorenzo." The laurel wreath was the classical symbol of the arts because it was given as a prize in poetry contests.

[3]Phoebus Apollo was the classical god of poetry and music.

Leonardo da Vinci: The Painter (15th Century CE)

If there is anyone who seems to embody the Renaissance completely and totally, it is this grouchy and self-centered painter, scholar, inventor, scientist, writer, anatomist, etc. He seems to span the whole of human knowledge as it was known at the time, and combine all this knowledge into one vast, syncretic whole. For all his genius, however, he could never really finish very many projects, nor did he ever actually construct most of his inventions. Strewn through his notebooks is a small unfinished treatise on painting. The first part of the treatise signals a major shift in the European world view, one that more than anything else establishes the character of the Renaissance and its inheritance. The first part of the treatise printed here is meant to justify linear perspective; the second part explains how linear perspective is made possible. Linear perspective isn't really just a painting technology that previous generations were too stupid to invent; rather it is based on a world view, one that remaps the human landscape to privilege human beings and the uniquely human perspective (as opposed to the divine perspective). This new world view is also based on new theories of "visibility," which are expressed in the chapter "Linear Perspective."

What qualities does Leonardo claim for his own art in contrast to that of others? Why does he feel that perspective is important?

Introduction

Because I can find no useful or pleasant subject to discourse on, since the men who came before me have taken all the useful and pleasant subjects and discoursed on them at length, I find I must behave like a pauper who comes to the fair last, and can provide for himself in no other way than to take those things of trivial value that have been rejected by other buyers. I, then, will fill my shopping bag with all these despised and rejected wares, trash passed over by previous buyers, and take them and distribute them, not in the great cities, but in the poorest villages, taking whatever money might be offered.

I realize many will call my little work useless; these people, as far as I'm concerned, are like those whom Demetrius was talking about when he said that he cared no more for the wind that issued from their mouths than the wind that issued from their lower extremities. These men desire only material wealth and are utterly lacking in wisdom, which is the only true food and wealth for the mind. The soul is so much greater than the body, its possessions so much nobler than those of the body. So, whenever a person of this sort picks up any of my works to read, I half expect him to put it to his nose the way a monkey does, or ask me if it's good to eat.

I also realize that I am not a literary man, and that certain people who know too much that is good for them will blame me, saying that I'm not a man of letters. Fools! Dolts! I may refute them the way Marius did to the Roman patricians when he said that some who adorn themselves with other people's labor won't allow me to do my own labor. These folks will say that since I have no skill at literature, I will not be able to decorously express what I'm talking about. What they don't know is that the subjects I am dealing with are to be dealt with by experience[1] rather than by words, and experience is the muse of all who write

---

[1] This emphasis on experience is an absolutely crucial shift in the European world view; for instance, the notion of experiment is based on the idea of "systematized" and repeatable experience.

well. And so, as my muse, I will cite her in every case.

Although, unlike my critics, I am not able to facilely quote other writers, I will rely on an authority much greater and much more noble: on Experience, the Mistress of their Masters. These fellows waddle about puffed up and pretentious, all dressed up in the fruits, not of their own labors, but of other people's labors; these fellows will not allow me my own labors. They will scorn me as an inventor and a discoverer, but they should be blamed more, since they have invented and discovered nothing but rather go about holding forth and declaiming the ideas and works of others.

There are men who are discoverers and intermediaries and interpreters between Nature and Man, rather than boasters and declaimers of other people's work, and these must be admired and esteemed as the object in front of a mirror in comparison to the image seen in the mirror. The first is a real object in and of itself, the second is nothing. These people owe nothing to Nature; it is only good fortune that they wear a human form and, if it weren't for this good fortune, I'd classify them with the cattle and the animals.

There are many who would, with reason, blame me by pointing out that my proofs are contrary to established authority, which is, after all, held in great reverence by their inexperienced minds. They do not realize that my works arise from unadulterated and simple experience, which is the one true mistress, the one true muse. The rules of experience are all that is needed to discern the true from the false; experience is what helps all men to look temperately for the possible, rather than cloaking oneself in ignorance, which can result in no good thing, so that, in the end, one abandons oneself to despair and melancholy.

Among all the studies of natural causes, Light more than anything else delights the beholder, and among the greatest features of Mathematics is the certainty of all its demonstrations which more than anything else elevates the mind of the thinker. Therefore, perspective is to be preferred to all other discourses and systems of knowledge, for in this science the ray of light is explained using methods of demonstration which glorify both Mathematics and Physics and grace the flowers of both these magnificent sciences. But since the axioms of Perspective have been treated extensively, I will abridge them, arranging them in their natural order and the order of their mathematical demonstration. Sometimes I will deduce the effects from their causes, and sometimes I will induce the causes from the effects, while adding my own conclusions that might be inferred from these.

On the three branches of perspective.

There are three branches of perspective: first, the diminution of objects as they recede from the eye, known as Diminishing Perspective. Second, the way in which colors vary as they recede from the eye. Third, the explanation of how the objects in a picture ought to be less perfect and complete in proportion to their remoteness. The names are as follows: Linear Perspective, The Perspective of Color, The Perspective of Disappearance.

On the mistakes of those who practice without knowledge.

Those who are fond of practice without knowledge are like a sailor in a ship without a rudder or a compass who, as a result, has no certain idea where he's going. Practice must always be built from sound theoretical knowledge. The gateway to this theoretical knowledge is Perspective; without Perspective nothing can be done well or properly in the matter of painting and drawing. The painter who only relies on practice and the eye, without any intellect, is no more than a mirror which copies slavishly everything placed in front of it and which has no consciousness of the existence of these things.

Here, right here, in the eye, here forms, here colors, right here the character of every part and every thing of the universe, are concentrated to a single point. How marvelous that point is! . . . In this small space, the universe can be completely reproduced and rearranged in its entire vastness! . . .

The ten attributes of the eye as concerns painting.

Painting involves all ten attributes of sight: Darkness, Light, Solidity and Color, Form and Position, Distance and Nearness, Motion and Rest. This tiny treatise of mine will be only a brief study of these attributes of sight, for the purpose of reminding the painter of the rules and methods which should be used in his art in the project of imitating all the adornments and works of Nature. . . .

On the eye

If the eye is forced to look at an object far too close to it, that eye cannot really form a judgment of that object, for instance, when a man tries to look at his nose. As a general rule, then, Nature teaches us that no object can be seen perfectly unless it is placed at least at a distance from the eye equal to the length of the face.

The eye, which experience shows us sees all things upside-down, retains images. This is the proof: when the eye gazes at light for some time, it retains an impression, there remain in the eye images of brightness, that make less brilliant spots seem dark until the eye no longer has any trace of the image or impression of that brighter light.

Linear Perspective

Perspective is no more than a scientific demonstration in which experience shows us that every object sends its image to the eye by a pyramid of lines, and which shows that bodies of equal size will create a pyramid of larger or smaller size, according to their distance. A pyramid of lines consisting of those which start from both the surface and the edges of the objects in question and which converge from a distance into a single point. A point is that which has no dimensions and is indivisible. This point is placed in the eye and receives all the points of the pyramid of lines. . . .

If the front of a building, or a piazza or a field, is lighted by the sun and has a house opposite it, and if you make a tiny hole in the side of the house not facing the sun, all the lighted objects of that building, or piazza, or field, will send images through that small hole and be visible in that house on the wall (which should be white) opposite the hole. These images will be upside-down. If you make any more small holes you'll get precisely the same results, so that the images of the lighted objects are completely present on the wall and on every part of it. Why does this happen? This hole must admit some light into the house, and the light admitted into the house will come from the lighted objects outside. If these objects have various colors and shapes, the light rays forming the images will have various colors and shapes; hence, the images on the wall.

Translated by Jean Paul Richter

Giorgio Vasari: Michelangelo's *David* (1550 CE)

Although their patrons often still considered them merely particularly skillful servants, many artists of the Renaissance began to develop a higher opinion of themselves. In the following anecdote the great painter and sculptor Michelangelo finds a clever way to deal with his patron, a presumptuous and ignorant noble. The David did not only illustrate a story from the Bible, it was intended to act as a symbol of Florence's readiness to defend itself.

This statue, when finished, was of such a kind that many disputes took place as to how to transport it to the Piazza della Signoria. Whereupon Giuliano da San Gallo and his brother Antonio made a very strong framework of wood and suspended the figure from it with ropes, to the end that it might not hit against the wood and break to pieces, but might rather keep rocking gently; and they drew it with windlasses over flat beams laid upon the ground, and then set it in place. On the rope which held the figure suspended he made a slip-knot which was very easy to undo but tightened as the weight increased, which is a most beautiful and ingenious thing; and I have in my book a drawing of it by his own hand—an admirable, secure, and strong contrivance for suspending weights.

It happened at this time that Piero Soderini, having seen it in place, was well pleased with it, but said to Michelagnolo,[1] at a moment when he was retouching it in certain parts, that it seemed to him that the nose of the figure was too thick. Michelagnolo noticed that the Gonfalonier was beneath the Giant, and that his point of view prevented him from seeing it properly; but in order to satisfy him he climbed upon the staging, which was against the shoulders, and quickly took up a chisel in his left hand, with a little of the marble-dust that lay upon the planks of the staging, and then, beginning to strike lightly with the chisel, let fall the dust little by little, nor changed the nose a whit from what it was before. Then, looking down at the Gonfalonier, who stood watching him, he said, "Look at it now." "I like it better," said the Gonfalonier, "you have given it life." And so Michelagnolo came down, laughing to himself at having satisfied that lord, for he had compassion on those who, in order to appear full of knowledge, talk about things of which they know nothing.

When it was built up, and all was finished, he uncovered it, and it cannot be denied that this work has carried off the palm[2] from all other statues, modern or ancient, Greek or Latin; and it may be said that neither the Marforio at Rome, nor the Tiber and the Nile of the Belvedere, nor the Giants of Monte Cavallo,[3] are equal to it in any respect, with such just proportion, beauty and excellence did Michelagnolo finish it. For in it may be seen most beautiful contours of legs, with attachments of limbs and slender outlines of flanks that are divine; nor has there ever been seen a pose so easy, or any grace to equal that in this work, or feet, hands and head so well in accord, one member with another, in harmony, design, and excellence of artistry. And, of a truth, whoever has seen this work need not trouble to see any other work executed in sculpture, either in our own or in other times, by no matter what craftsman. Michelagnolo received from Piero Soderini in payment for it four hundred crowns; and it was set in place in the year 1504.

Translated by Gaston du C. de Vere

---

[1] Vasari's spelling of "Michelangelo."
[2] Won the championship.
[3] All these are comparable "giants."

Niccolò Machiavelli: *The Prince* (1532 CE)
The Way Princes Should Keep Their Word

Machiavelli's treatise on government was rejected with horror by almost all early readers, but it accurately describes the means which rulers have always used to remain in power. As a pioneering study of practical politics it has often been compared with Kautilya's Arthasastra *and the doctrines of the Chinese legalists, such as Han Fei Tzu. But what makes* The Prince *both more revolutionary and more controversial than either of these is the delight Machiavelli seems to take in scorning conventional morality. Indeed so cynical are such passages as the following that some readers have imagined that he must have been satirizing rather than advocating these ideas. His work cannot be said to have had any great impact on the world, but it strikingly marks the end of an era during which writers felt obliged to cloak their recommendations on government in a pious guise: his values are entirely secular. In describing the behavior of the successful politician Machiavelli has in mind a specific model, the ruthless Cesare Borgia (1476– 1507). Note that "prince" here means "ruler," and does not indicate merely the son of a king.*

What good qualities does Machiavelli say a prince should seem to have? Why should he only seem to have them? What attitude toward government does this passage, the Arthasastra *and Han Fei Tzu all reflect?*

Everyone understands how praiseworthy it is for a prince to remain true to his word and to live with complete integrity without any scheming. However, we've seen through experience how many princes in our time have achieved great things who have little cared about keeping their word and have shrewdly known the skill of tricking the minds of men; these princes have overcome those whose actions were founded on honesty and integrity.

It should be understood that there are two types of fighting: one with laws and the other with force. The first is most suitable for men, the second is most suitable for beasts, but it often happens that the first is not enough, which requires that we have recourse to the second. Therefore, it is necessary for a prince to know how to act both as a man and as a beast. This was signified allegorically to princes by the ancient writers: they wrote that Achilles and many other ancient princes were given to be raised and tutored by the centaur Chiron, who took custody of them and disciplined them. This can only mean, this trainer who was half beast and half man, that a prince needs to know how to use either one or the other nature, and the one without the other will never last.

Since it is necessary for the prince to use the ways of beasts, he should imitate the fox and the lion, because the lion cannot defend himself from snares and the fox cannot defend himself from wolves. Therefore, it is important to be a fox in order to understand the snares and a lion in order to terrify the wolves. Those who choose only to be a lion do not really understand. Therefore, a prudent leader will not and should not observe his promises, when such observance will work against him and when the reasons for making the promise are no longer valid. If all men were good, this precept would not be good; but since men are evil and will not keep their word with you, you shouldn't keep yours to them. Never has a prince lacked legitimate reasons to break faith. I could give you an infinite number of examples from modern times, and show you numerous peace treaties and promises that have been broken and made completely empty by the faithlessness of princes: these knew well how to use the ways of the fox, and they are the ones who succeed. But it is necessary to know how to hide this nature and to simulate a good character and to dissimulate: for the majority of men are simple and will only follow the needs of the present, so that the deceiver can always find someone he can deceive.

I'm not going to pass up a specific example from recent history. Alexander VI[1] never did or thought about anything else except deceiving people and always found some reason or other to do it. There was never a man who was better at making assurances, or more eager to offer solemn promises, or who kept them less; yet he always succeeded in his deceptions beyond his wildest dreams, because he played his role in the world so well.

Therefore, a prince doesn't need to have all the qualities mentioned earlier, but it is necessary that he appear to have them. I'll even add to this: having good qualities and always practicing them is harmful, while appearing to practice them is useful. It's good to appear to be pious, faithful, humane, honest, and religious, and it's good to be all those things; but as long as one keeps in mind that when the need arises you can and will change into the opposite. It needs to be understood that a prince, and especially a prince recently installed, cannot observe all those qualities which make men good, and it is often necessary in order to preserve the state to act contrary to faity, contrary to mercy, contrary to humaneness, and contrary to religion. And therefore he needs a spirit disposed to follow wherever the winds of fortune and the variability of affairs leads him. As I said above, it's necessary that he not depart from right but that he follow evil.

A prince must take great care never to let anything come from his mouth that is not full of the above-mentioned five qualities, and he must appear to all who see and hear him to be completely pious, completely faithful, completely honest, completely humane, and completely religious. And nothing is more important than to appear to have that last quality. Men judge more by their eyes than by their hands, because everyone can see but few can feel. Everyone can see how you appear, few can feel what you are, and these few will not dare to oppose the opinion of the multitude when it is defended by the majesty of the state. In actions of all men, especially princes, where there is no recourse to justice, the end is all that counts. A prince should only be concerned with conquering or maintaining a state, for the means will always be judged to be honorable and praiseworthy by each and every person, because the masses always follow appearances and the outcomes of affairs, and the world is nothing other than the masses. The few do not find a place wherever the masses are supported. There is a certain prince of our own time,[2] whom it would not be wise to name, who preaches nothing except peace and faith, and yet is the greatest enemy of both; and if he had observed one or the other, he already would have lost both his reputation and his state many times over.

Translated by Richard Hooker

---

[1]The worldly pope who illegitimately fathered Machiavelli's hero, Cesare Borgia.
[2]Ferdinand of Spain.

Subsaharan Africa

Bamba Suso: *The Epic of Sunjata* (13th Century CE)

Sunjata (also commonly spelled "Sundiata") was the legendary founder of the Mali Empire who defeated the earlier empire of Ghana in the early 13th Century. Scholars are agreed that Mali existed as a kingdom before this point and that most of the deeds ascribed to Sunjata are fictional, but he was undoubtedly a fierce and highly successful warrior, and is still remembered vividly today thanks to the constant retelling of his legend by traditional musician-poets called "griots." Many West Africans take great pride in tracing their heritage back to Sunjata, just as Britons are proud of the equally elusive King Arthur. Like many other great heroes such as Sargon, Krishna, and Moses, Sunjata is depicted as having to overcome in childhood great obstacles, including death threats, in order to gain his predestined status. In Sunjata's case, it is universally agreed that he was lame until he was a young man, but that he then became prodigiously powerful (able to uproot an enormous baobab tree single-handed) and evolved into a fierce warrior. The following account of his conception, birth and childhood is taken from a 1974 version recited by the most distinguished griot of Gambia, who rejects the usual image of Sunjata as victim, and makes his lameness voluntary. Rivalry between jealous co-wives in a polygamous marriage, always a feature of the Sunjata legend, is also a common feature in West African tales generally.

What signs are there before his birth that Sunjata will be an extraordinary person? Can you think of any other famous rulers or heroes who began life as outcasts or victims?

I am going to tell you the story of Sunjata,
And you must pay attention.
Sunjata's father's name was Fata Kung Makhang.
He went to Sankarang Madiba Konte.
The soothsayers had said, "If you go to Sankarang Madiba Konte
And find a wife there,
She will give birth to a child
Who will become king of the black people."
He went there.
They had told him the name of this woman;
They called her Sukulung.
Nine Sukulungs were brought forward,
And a soothsayer consulted the omens,
And then declared, "No, I do not see the woman among these ones."
They said to Sankarang Madiba Konte,
"Now, is there not another Sukulung?"
He answered, "There is, but she is ugly.
She is my daughter."
He told him, "Go and bring her here; I wish to see her."
When they had brought her,
A soothsayer consulted the omens and then told him, "This is the one."

When Fata Kung Makhang had married her in Manding.[1]
Then he and she went away.
She became pregnant, and for seven years
Sunjata's mother was pregnant with him.
She did not get a fright even once,[2]
Except for one occasion.
Her husband called her,
During the rainy season, and he happened to speak at the same time that
   thunder sounded,
So that she did not hear him speak, and he repeated the call.
Then she went in trepidation to her husband.
That was the only fright that she ever got;
For seven years she never got a fright,
Except for that one occasion.
She gave birth to Sunjata.
The king had declared,
Fata Kung Makhang had declared, "If any of my wives gives birth to a son,
I shall give my kingship to him."
Sukulung Konte eventually gave birth—
Sunjata's mother.
They sent a slave, with the instructions, "Go and tell Sunjata's father."
At that time he had built a compound out on the farm land.
When the slave came he found them eating,
And they said to him, "All right, sit down and have something to eat."
The slave sat down.
It was not long before a co-wife of Sukulung's also gave birth.
When her co-wife gave birth, they sent a griot.
When the griot arrived he said, "Greetings!"
They said to him, "Come and have something to eat before you say anything."
He said, "No!"[3]
The griot said, "Naareng Daniyang Konnate,
Your wife has given birth—a boy."
The slave was sitting; he said, "They sent me first.
It was Sukulung Konte who gave birth first."
Fata Kung Makhang declared,
"The one I heard of first,
He it is who is my son, the firstborn."
That made Sunjata angry.

---

[1]Manding is the legendary original home of the Mandinka people of West Africa, and probably did not correspond to any one village.
[2]It was believed that when the mother was frightened during her pregnancy it would make her son less brave. Thus this account explains Sunjata's extraordinary courage.
[3]Notice that the slave who is sent as the first messenger accepts a meal from Sukulung's rival co-wife, and is thus bribed to lie to make it appear that this co-wife's son was born first and is therefore the legitimate heir; but the griot who is sent as the second messenger carries out his task honestly. Griots are positively portrayed in the stories told by griots; just as the epic poet Homer depicted epic poets positively in the *Odyssey*.

For seven years he crawled on all fours,
And refused to get up.[4]
Those seven years had passed,
And the time had come for the boys who were to be circumcised to go into the circum-
cision shed.[5]
People said. "But Sunjata is crawling on all fours and has not got up;
The time to go into the circumcision shed has arrived, and all his brothers are going in."
At that time they used to smelt ore and make iron from it,
The smiths put bellowses to the ore,
And when they had smelted the ore they made it into iron,
And they forged the iron and made it into rods—
Two rods.
They put one into one of his hands,
And they put the other into his other hand,
And said that he must get up.
When he had grasped the rods, they both broke.[6]
They said, "How will Sunjata get up?"
He himself said to them, "Call my mother;
When a child has fallen down, it is his mother who picks him up."
When his mother came,
He laid his hand upon his mother's shoulder,
And he arose and stood up.
It is from that incident that the griots say,
"The Lion has arisen," they say, "The Lion of Manding has arisen,
The mighty one has arisen."

Translated by Gordon Innes

---

[4]In many versions of the story it is the mother of a rival to Sunjata who places a curse on him and causes his lameness, but in this telling, he refuses to walk out of indignation at the deception.

[5]Boys were ritually circumcised during early adolescence, a ceremony which, accompanied by a period of training, made them officially adults.

[6]Sunjata is so strong that even these iron crutches break in his hands.

Ibn Battuta (1304–1369? CE): Travels in Sub-Saharan Africa

Although Marco Polo is better known in the Western world, Ibn Battuta was a far more adventurous traveler. Starting from his home in Morocco, he journeyed through all of North Africa, went on to Syria, Arabia (including, as a pious Muslim, a hajj to Mecca), India (where he lived for eight years at the court of the Sultan in Delhi), China, South-East Asia, East Africa and—finally—joined a caravan across the Saharan Desert. As a religious and legal scholar, he expected to be warmly and generously welcomed, and he usually was. However, the ruler of the wealthy and powerful kingdom of Mali on the Niger River was not overly impressed with his visitor, and Ibn Battuta included some negative comments among the praise he had for the kingdom. He obviously misunderstood the significance of the ritual meal which he was offered, and was not willing to accommodate his notions of propriety to local customs. He was particularly shocked by the nudity of African women; but his indignation at their failure to observe Qur'anic standards of modesty did not prevent him from acquiring an attractive young slave woman to be his companion, as he did almost everywhere he went. Despite his humorless, self-important manner and occasional xenophobia, Ibn Battuta is a highly entertaining writer, and his travels make for fine reading. For this period of Malian history he is unrivaled and is therefore worth quoting at some length.

What does Ibn Battuta say are the most important virtues of the people of Mali? What does he dislike about them? What do these passages tell us about him or the culture he comes from?

From Marrakush I traveled with the suite of our master [the Sultan] to Fez, where I took leave of our master and set out for the Negrolands. I reached the town of Sijilmasa, a very fine town, with quantities of excellent dates. The city of Basra rivals it in abundance of dates, but the Sijilmasa dates are better, and the kind called *Irar* has no equal in the world. I stayed there with the learned Abu Muhammad al-Bushri, the man whose brother I met in the city of Qanjanfu in China. How strangely separated they are! He showed me the utmost honor.

At Sijilmasa I bought camels and a four months' supply of forage for them. Thereupon I set out on the 1st Muharram of the year [seven hundred and] fifty-three [18th February 1352] with a caravan including, amongst others, a number of the merchants of Sijilmasa. After twenty-five days we reached Taghaza, an unattractive village, with the curious feature that its houses and mosques are built of blocks of salt, roofed with camel skins.[1] There are no trees there, nothing but sand. In the sand is a salt mine; they dig for the salt, and find it in thick slabs, lying one on top of the other, as though they had been tool-squared and laid under the surface of the earth. A camel will carry two of these slabs. No one lives at Taghaza except the slaves of the Massufa tribe, who dig for the salt; they subsist on dates imported from Dar'a and Sijilmasa, camels' flesh, and millet imported from the Negrolands. The negroes come up from their country and take away the salt from there.

At Iwalatan [Walata] a load of salt brings eight to ten *mithqals;* in the town of Malli it sells for twenty to thirty, and sometimes as much as forty. The negroes use salt as a medium of exchange, just as gold and silver is used [elsewhere]; they cut it up into pieces and buy

[1]Taghaza was a vital stop for the caravans crossing the Sarhara, since the gold-rich Malians wanted for little that North Africa could provide, but their inland empire was distant from all sources of salt, essential for their good health.

and sell with it. The business done at Taghaza, for all its meanness, amounts to an enormous figure in terms of hundredweights of gold-dust. . . .

Thus we reached the town of Iwalatan [Walata] after a journey from Sijilmasa of two months to a day. Iwalatan is the northernmost province of the negroes, and the sultan's representative there was one Farba Husayn, *farba* meaning deputy [in their language]. When we arrived there, the merchants deposited their goods in an open square, where the blacks undertook to guard them, and went to the *farba*. He was sitting on a carpet under an archway, with his guards before him carrying lances and bows in their hands, and the headmen of the Massufa behind him. The merchants remained standing in front of him while he spoke to them through an interpreter, although they were close to him, to show his contempt for them. It was then that I repented of having come to their country, because of their lack of manners and their contempt for the whites.

I went to visit Ibn Badda, a worthy man of Sala [Sallee, Rabat], to whom I had written requesting him to hire a house for me, and who had done so. Later on the *mushrif* [inspector] of Iwalatan, whose name was Mansha Ju, invited all those who had come with the caravan to partake of his hospitality. At first I refused to attend, but my companions urged me very strongly, so I went with the rest. The repast[2] was served—some pounded millet mixed with a little honey and milk,[3] put in a half calabash shaped like a large bowl. The guests drank and retired. I said to them " Was it for this that the black invited us ?" They answered "Yes; and it is in their opinion the highest form of hospitality." This convinced me that there was no good to be hoped for from these people, and I made up my mind to travel [back to Morocco at once] with the pilgrim caravan from Iwalatan. Afterwards, however, I thought it best to go to see the capital of their king [at Malli].

My stay at Iwalatan lasted about fifty days; and I was shown honor and entertained by its inhabitants. It is an excessively hot place, and boasts a few small date-palms, in the shade of which they sow watermelons. Its water comes from underground waterbeds at that point, and there is plenty of mutton to be had. The garments of its inhabitants, most of whom belong to the Massufa tribe, are of fine Egyptian fabrics. Their women are of surpassing beauty, and are shown more respect than the men. The state of affairs amongst these people is indeed extraordinary. Their men show no signs of jealousy whatever; no one claims descent from his father, but on the contrary from his mother's brother. A person's heirs are his sister's sons, not his own sons. This is a thing which I have seen nowhere in the world except among the Indians of Malabar. But those are heathens; *these* people are Muslims, punctilious in observing the hours of prayer, studying books of law, and memorizing the Koran. Yet their women show no bashfulness before men and do not veil themselves, though they are assiduous in attending the prayers. Any man who wishes to marry one of them may do so, but they do not travel with their husbands, and even if one desired to do so her family would not allow her to go.

The women there have "friends" and "companions" amongst the men outside their own families[4], and the men in the same way have "companions" amongst the women of other families. A man may go into his house and find his wife entertaining her "companion" but he takes no objection to it. One day at Iwalatan I went into the qadi's house, after asking

[2]In this case, a ceremonial meal, ritually offered to visitors.
[3]Actually, yogurt.
[4]The phrase here translated "outside their own families" actually refers to foreign residents, of whom there were many.

his permission to enter, and found with him a young woman of remarkable beauty. When I saw her I was shocked and turned to go out, but she laughed at me, instead of being overcome by shame, and the qadi said to me " Why are you going out? She is my companion." I was amazed at their conduct, for he was a theologian and a pilgrim to boot. I was told that he had asked the sultan's permission to make the pilgrimage that year with his "companion" (whether this one or not I cannot say) but the sultan would not grant it.[5]

When I decided to make the journey to Malli, which is reached in twenty-four days from Iwalatan if the traveler pushes on rapidly, I hired a guide from the Massufa (for there is no necessity to travel in a company on account of the safety of that road), and set out with three of my companions. On the way there are many trees, and these trees are of great age and girth; a whole caravan may shelter in the shade of one of them. There are trees which have neither branches nor leaves, yet the shade cast by their trunks is sufficient to shelter a man. Some of these trees are rotted in the interior and the rain-water collects in them, so that they serve as wells and the people drink of the water inside them.[6] In others there are bees and honey, which is collected by the people. I was surprised to find inside one tree, by which I passed, a man, a weaver, who had set up his loom in it and was actually weaving.

A traveler in this country carries no provisions, whether plain food or seasonings, and neither gold nor silver. He takes nothing but pieces of salt and glass ornaments, which the people call beads, and some aromatic goods. When he comes to a village the womenfolk of the blacks bring out millet, milk, chickens, pulped lotus fruit, rice, *funi* (a grain resembling mustard seed, from which *kuskusu* and gruel are made), and pounded haricot beans. The traveler buys what of these he wants, but their rice causes sickness to whites when it is eaten, and the *funi is* preferable to it. . . .

We set out thereafter from Karsakhu and came to the river of Sansara, which is about ten miles from Malli. It is their custom that no persons except those who have obtained permission are allowed to enter the city. I had already written to the white community [there] requesting them to hire a house for me, so when I arrived at this river, I crossed by the ferry without interference. Thus I reached the city of Malli, the capital of the king of the blacks.

I stopped at the cemetery and went to the quarter occupied by the whites, where I asked for Muhammad ibn al-Faqih. I found that he had hired a house for me and went there. His son-in-law brought me candles and food, and next day Ibn al-Faqih himself came to visit me, with other prominent residents. I met the qadi of Malli, 'Abd ar-Rahman, who came to see me; he is a negro, a pilgrim, and a man of fine character. I met also the interpreter Dugha, who is one of the principal men among the blacks. All these persons sent me hospitality gifts of food and treated me with the utmost generosity—may God reward them for their kindnesses! Ten days after our arrival we ate a gruel made of a root resembling colocasia,[7] which is preferred by them to all other dishes. We all fell ill—there were six of us—and one of our number died. I for my part went to the morning prayer and fainted there. I asked a certain Egyptian for a loosening remedy and he gave me a thing called *baydar,* made of vegetable roots, which he mixed with aniseed and sugar, and stirred

---

[5]Omitted in this translation is a passage in which Ibn Battuta says that he refused the hospitality of a prominent citizen because he disapproved of his liberality in allowing his wife to socialize with a male friend (with the husband present).

[6]Probably the baobab tree.

[7]Taro.

in water. I drank it off and vomited what I had eaten, together with a large quantity of bile. God preserved me from death but I was ill for two months.

The sultan of Malli is Mansa Sulayman, *mansa,* meaning [in Mande] sultan, and Sulayman being his proper name. He is a miserly king, not a man from whom one might hope for a rich present. It happened that I spent these two months without seeing him, on account of my illness. Later on he held a banquet in commemoration of our master [the late sultan of Morocco] Abu'l-Hasan, to which the commanders, doctors, qadi and preacher were invited, and I went along with them. Reading-desks were brought in, and the Koran was read through, then they prayed for our master Abu'l-Hasan and also for Mansa Sulayman. When the ceremony was over I went forward and saluted Mansa Sulayman. The qadi, the preacher, and Ibn al-Faqih told him who I was, and he answered them in their tongue. They said to me "The sultan says to you 'Give thanks to God,'" so I said "Praise be to God and thanks under all circumstances."

When I withdrew the [sultan's] hospitality gift was sent to me. It was taken first to the qadi's house, and the qadi sent it on with his men to Ibn al-Faqih's house. Ibn al-Faqih came hurrying out of his house bare-footed, and entered my room saying "Stand up; here comes the sultan's stuff and gift to you." So I stood up thinking [since he had called it "stuff"] that it consisted of robes of honor and money, and lo! it was three cakes of bread, and a piece of beef fried in native oil, and a calabash of sour curds.[8] When I saw this I burst out laughing, and thought it a most amazing thing that they could be so foolish and make so much of such a paltry matter.

For two months after this hospitality gift was sent to me I received nothing further from the sultan, and then followed the month of Ramadan. Meanwhile I used to go frequently to the palace where I would salute him and sit alongside the qadi and the preacher. I had a conversation with Dugha the interpreter, and he said "Speak in his presence, and I shall express on your behalf what is necessary." When the sultan held an audience early in Ramadan, I rose and stood before him and said to him: "I have traveled through the countries of the world and have met their kings. Here have I been four months in your country, yet you have neither shown me hospitality, nor given me anything. What am I to say of you before [other] rulers?" The sultan replied "I have not seen you, and have not been told about you." The qadi and Ibn al-Faqih rose and replied to him, saying "He has already saluted you, and you have sent him food." Thereupon he gave orders to set apart a house for my lodging and to pay me a daily sum for my expenses. Later on, on the night of the 27th Ramadan, he distributed a sum of money which they call the *Zakah* [alms] between the qadi, the preachers, and the doctors. He gave me a portion along with them of thirty-three and a third *mithqals,* and on my departure from Malli he bestowed on me a gift of a hundred gold *mithqals.*

On certain days the sultan holds audiences in the palace yard, where there is a platform under a tree, with three steps; this they call the *pempi.* It is carpeted with silk and has cushions placed on it. [Over it] is raised the umbrella, which is a sort of pavilion made of silk, surmounted by a bird in gold, about the size of a falcon. The sultan comes out of a door in a corner of the palace, carrying a bow in his hand and a quiver on his back. On his head he has a golden skullcap, bound with a gold band which has narrow ends shaped like knives, more than a span in length. His usual dress is a velvety red tunic, made of the European fabrics called *mutanfas.* The sultan is preceded by his musicians, who carry gold and silver guimbris [two-stringed guitars], and behind him come three hundred armed

---

[8]Yogurt.

slaves. He walks in a leisurely fashion, affecting a very slow movement, and even stops from time to time. On reaching the *pempi* he stops and looks round the assembly, then ascends it in the sedate manner of a preacher ascending a mosque pulpit. As he takes his seat the drums, trumpets, and bugles are sounded. Three slaves go out at a run to summon the sovereign's deputy and the military commanders, who enter and sit down. Two saddled and bridled horses are brought, along with two goats, which they hold to serve as a protection against the evil eye. Dugha stands at the gate and the rest of the people remain in the street, under the trees.[9]

The negroes[10] are of all people the most submissive to their king and the most abject in their behavior before him. They swear by his name, saying *Mansa Sulayman ki*. If he summons any of them while he is holding an audience in his pavilion, the person summoned takes off his clothes and puts on worn garments, removes his turban and dons a dirty skullcap, and enters with his garments and trousers raised knee-high. He goes forward in an attitude of humility and dejection, and knocks the ground hard with his elbows, then stands with bowed head and bent back listening to what he says. If anyone addresses the king and receives a reply from him, he uncovers his back and throws dust over his head and back, for all the world like a bather splashing himself with water. I used to wonder how it was they did not blind themselves. If the sultan delivers any remarks during his audience, those present take off their turbans and put them down, and listen in silence to what he says. Sometimes one of them stands up before him and recalls his deeds in the sultan's service, saying "I did so-and-so on such a day" or "I killed so-and-so on such a day." Those who have knowledge of this confirm his words, which they do by plucking the cord of the bow and releasing it [with a twang], just as an archer does when shooting an arrow. If the sultan says "Truly spoken" or thanks him, he removes his clothes and "dusts." That is their idea of good manners.

Ibn Juzayy[11] adds: "I have been told that when the pilgrim Musa al-Wanjarati [the Mandingo] came to our master Abu'l-Hasan as envoy from Mansa Sulayman, one of his suite carried with him a basketful of dust when he entered the noble audience-hall, and the envoy 'dusted' whenever our master spoke a gracious word to him, just as he would do in his own country."

I was at Malli during the two festivals of the sacrifice and the fast-breaking.[12] On these days the sultan takes his seat on the *pempi* after the midafternoon prayer. The armor-bearers bring in magnificent arms—quivers of gold and silver, swords ornamented with gold and with golden scabbards, gold and silver lances, and crystal maces. At his head stand four amirs driving off the flies, having in their hands silver ornaments resembling saddle-stirrups. The commanders, qadi, and preacher sit in their usual places. The interpreter Dugha comes with his four wives and his slave-girls, who are about a hundred in number. They are wearing beautiful robes, and on their heads they have gold and silver fillets, with gold and silver balls attached. A chair is placed for Dugha to sit on. He plays on an instrument made of reeds, with some small calabashes at its lower end, and chants a poem in praise of the sultan, recalling his battles and deeds of valor. The women and girls sing along with him and play with bows. Accompanying them are about thirty youths,

---

[9]This translation condenses or omits a good deal of detail describing the richness of the Sultan's court, here and in subsequent passages.

[10]The word in the original is "Sudanese."

[11]The writer to whom Ibn Battuta dictated his account.

[12]At the end of Ramadan.

wearing red woolen tunics and white skullcaps; each of them has his drum slung from his shoulder and beats it. Afterwards come his boy pupils who play and turn wheels in the air, like the natives of Sind. They show a marvelous nimbleness and agility in these exercises and play most cleverly with swords. Dugha also makes a fine play with the sword. Thereupon the sultan orders a gift to be presented to Dugha and he is given a purse containing two hundred *mithqals* of gold dust, and is informed of the contents of the purse before all the people. The commanders rise and twang their bows in thanks to the sultan. The next day each one of them gives Dugha a gift, every man according to his rank. Every Friday after the *'asr* prayer, Dugha carries out a similar ceremony to this that we have described.

On feast-days, after Dugha has finished his display, the poets come in. Each of them is inside a figure resembling a thrush, made of feathers, and provided with a wooden head with a red beak, to look like a thrush's head. They stand in front of the sultan in this ridiculous make-up and recite their poems. I was told that their poetry is a kind of sermonizing in which they say to the sultan: "This *pempi* which you occupy was that whereon sat this king and that king, and such and such were this one's noble actions and such and such the other's. So do you too do good deeds whose memory will outlive you."[13] After that, the chief of the poets mounts the steps of the *pempi* and lays his head on the sultan's lap, then climbs to the top of the *pempi* and lays his head first on the sultan's right shoulder and then on his left, speaking all the while in their tongue, and finally he comes down again. I was told that this practice is a very old custom amongst them, prior to the introduction of Islam, and that they have kept it up.[14]

The negroes disliked Mansa Sulayman because of his avarice. His predecessor was Mansa Magha, and before him reigned Mansa Musa a generous and virtuous prince, who loved the whites and made gifts to them. It was he who gave Abu Ishaq as-Sahili four thousand *mithqals* in the course of a single day. I heard from a trustworthy source that he gave three thousand *mithqals* on one day to Mudrik ibn Faqqus, by whose grandfather his own grandfather, Saraq Jata, had been converted to Islam.

The negroes possess some admirable qualities. They are seldom unjust, and have a greater abhorrence of injustice than any other people. Their sultan shows no mercy to anyone who is guilty of the least act of it. There is complete security in their country. Neither traveler nor inhabitant in it has anything to fear from robbers or men of violence. They do not confiscate the property of any white man who dies in their country, even if it be uncounted wealth. On the contrary, they give it into the charge of some trustworthy person among the whites, until the rightful heir takes possession of it. They are careful to observe the hours of prayer, and assiduous in attending them in congregations, and in bringing up their children to them. On Fridays, if a man does not go early to the mosque, he cannot find a corner to pray in, on account of the crowd. It is a custom of theirs to send each man his boy [to the mosque] with his prayer-mat; the boy spreads it out for his master in a place befitting him [and remains on it] until he comes to the mosque. Their prayer-mats are made of the leaves of a tree resembling a date-palm, but without fruit.

Another of their good qualities is their habit of wearing clean white garments on Fri-

---

[13]This sort of recitation is the traditional role of the *griots,* common throughout West Africa, who memorize and recite on ceremonial occasions lengthy praise-songs detailing the ancestry of the ruler.

[14]Several anecdotes are here omitted by the translator, including a dispute between two wives of the Sultan.

days. Even if a man has nothing but an old worn shirt, he washes it and cleans it, and wears it to the Friday service. Yet another is their zeal for learning the Koran by heart. They put their children in chains if they show any backwardness in memorizing it, and they are not set free until they have it by heart. I visited the qadi in his house on the day of the festival. His children were chained up, so I said to him " Will you not let them loose?" He replied "I shall not do so until they learn the Koran by heart." Among their bad qualities are the following. The women servants, slave-girls, and young girls go about in front of everyone naked, without a stitch of clothing on them. Women go into the sultan's presence naked and without coverings, and his daughters also go about naked.[15] Then there is their custom of putting dust and ashes on their heads, as a mark of respect, and the grotesque ceremonies we have described when the poets recite their verses. Another reprehensible practice among many of them is the eating of carrion, dogs, and asses.

Translated by H. A. R. Gibb

----

[15]A good deal of detail on this point is omitted in this translation.

Pre-Columbian America

The Popol Vuh: The Mayan Creation Story (pre-16th Century CE)

This Mayan creation story from the Popol-Vuh, *or "The Book of the Council," was written down in the mid-16th century, but its origins are hundreds of years earlier. Note the many correspondences to the Hebrew creation story. Also notice that the human and the divine need each other. People are eventually made "right" by the Gods, but we're a work-in-progress; it takes many tries before humans are both sensible and spiritual.*

What similarities can you find between this and the Genesis creation story from the Hebrew Bible?

Preamble

This is the beginning of the ancient history of the Kiché land; we are going to record the traditions of all that the Kiché nation did, and reveal what has been hidden up till now. We are bringing this forth under Christianity, for the Popol-Vuh as our Book of the Council was called, is no longer to be seen.

The Earth

This is the story of how everything was in suspense, everything at rest, everything silent. All was motionless, hushed; and empty was the vastness of Heaven.

Here is our first document, the first account we have. There were still no men nor animals; there were no birds, fish nor crabs, no trees, stones nor caves, no ravines, grass nor woods. Only Heaven existed; the face of Earth had not yet appeared. Only the calm sea and Heaven's expanse were spread out everywhere. Nothing made a sound, nor did anything move. There was nothing which stood erect; only the water spread out peacefully, the calm and tranquil sea. There was only motionlessness and silence in the darkness of the night. Only the Creator and Fashioner, Tepeu and Gucumatz, lived in the water surrounded by radiance. They lay hidden by the green and blue feathers of great sages; in this way existed the Heart of Heaven, which means God.

Then the Word was; Tepeu and Gucumatz came and spoke to each other amid the darkness, consulting and meditating. They reached an agreement; they put their words and thoughts on life and light together in an effort to decide what to do when it should dawn. They finally resolved that man should appear, and thus they arranged for life to commence and men to be created. Tepeu and Gucumatz pronounced in unison:

"May the void be filled! May this water withdraw so Earth may arise! May it dawn on Heaven and Earth!"

This is how they planned the creation of Earth.

"Earth!" they said, and it was formed at once. Like the mist, like clouds, mountains rose from the water; through a miracle—a stroke of magic—hills and valleys were formed; at the same time cedars and pines sprang up in clusters. So Gucumatz of the green feathers was filled with joy and exclaimed:

"Welcome, Heart of Heaven, O Hurricane!"

Thus while Heaven was still in suspense, Earth was created so it could rise easily from the waters. This is how the gods accomplished their task after they had considered how to bring it to a successful conclusion.

The Animals

Then the wild animals, the guardians of the woods and spirits of the forest, were created: deer, birds, lions, jaguars, large serpents, harmless smaller snakes, and more deadly vipers. The Creators thought matters over again and came to this decision:

"Must there be only silence and stillness under the trees and beneath the vines? Someone should be guarding them."

So they spoke again, and at once deer and birds were created. They assigned them their dwellings as follows:

"You, O deer, will sleep along the river flats and in ravines; you will increase and feed in the meadows and woods, and walk on four feet."

As it was said, so it was done. Then they assigned the birds their homes; they told them what to do, and each flew to its nest. When the four-footed animals and the birds had been created, the Creator and Fashioner said to them:

"*Cry! Shout! Warble! Howl!* Each of you should speak according to your kind."

Yet it was impossible for them to speak like man—they only squealed, cackled, or brayed. Their language was meaningless, for each one cried out in a different manner. When the Creator and Fashioner saw it was impossible for them to speak, they remarked to each other:

"They cannot say the names of us, their Creator and Fashioner! That is not right."

So they announced: "You will be transformed: we have changed our minds because you do not speak. You will eat and live in the ravines and woods, for you do not call upon us, and we are going to make other creatures who will be more attentive. You must accept your fate, which is to have your flesh chewed and eaten."

Thus the Forerunners made their will known to every animal on Earth; but as these did not speak a common tongue they could not do a thing about it. In this way, the animals which exist on the face of the Earth were condemned to be killed and eaten.

The Men of Clay and Wood

Then the Creator and Fashioner wanted to try their luck again. They made another attempt to form a man who would worship them.

"Let's try again! What shall we do to be invoked and remembered on Earth? We have already tried with our first creatures, but could not get them to praise and venerate us. Let us make obedient and respectful beings. Dawn and sunrise are approaching; let us form someone to sustain and nourish us."

Thus they spoke, and then they started making fresh creations. From Earth, from plain mud, they made man's flesh—but this fell apart, for it was soft and limp and had no strength. It could not move its head, its face fell towards one side, its neck was so stiff it could not look backward. It soaked up water and would not hold together. Then the Creator and Fashioner talked things over once more.

"Let us consult an omen, since our men cannot walk nor multiply. Let us ask for some advice on this matter."

So they knocked their handiwork apart, complaining:

"What shall we do for perfect worshipers? We must find a way so the man we fashion will sustain and feed us. He must invoke and call upon us!"

Hurricane, Tepeu, and Gucumatz went off to ask the magic pair of grandparents for help, since these were soothsayers.

"Talk matters over, grandmother and grandfather: toss lots with your corn and beans, and find out if we should make a man from wood."

In order to cast a spell the old woman and old man threw lots with corn and beans:

"Get together! Speak so we can hear you! Say whether the Creator and Fashioner should make a man from wood; and whether this man will feed and nourish us. Corn! Beans! Fate! Unite! *Get together!*"

This is how the old couple talked to the corn and beans, and then they declared:

"Your figures will turn out fine if they are made of wood, and they will speak upon the face of the Earth."

"So be it!" answered the Forerunners.

Immediately the Creator and Fashioner made their figures out of wood. They resembled men, they spoke like men, and they peopled the face of Earth. These were the first men who existed in large numbers in the world.

Destruction of the Wooden Men

The wooden dolls existed and had daughters and sons; but they had no soul or understanding. They did not remember who their Creator and Fashioner were, and limped around aimlessly. At first they spoke, but their faces soon withered and their feet and hands had no consistency. They quickly forgot about the Heart of Heaven, and therefore fell into disgrace. They had no blood nor moisture nor stoutness; their cheeks were hollow, their hands and feet were shriveled, and their flesh was yellowish. They were only a sample—an attempt at making man.

Since they no longer remembered the Creator and Fashioner who had given them their being and cared for them, they were destroyed. The Heart of Heaven who is called Hurricane caused a great flood to overwhelm the wooden dolls, while a shower of pitch fell from Heaven into their eyes. It cut off their heads and gnawed their flesh; it shattered their nerves and ground their bones.

The wooden men ran around in desperation; they tried to climb up on their houses, but these collapsed and tossed them to the ground. They tried to climb the trees, and were shaken off; they wanted to crawl into the caves and were chased out of them. This was their punishment for not remembering the Heart of Heaven; the face of Earth was darkened and a black rain began to fall that lasted day and night.

Then the animals both great and small started out to eat them, and even the trees and stones struck them in the face. Their jars, dishes, and pots began to murmur and their dogs, turkeys, and grindstones rose up against them.

"On your account our faces are being worn away," said the grindstones; "day after day, at nightfall and at dawn, you make us groan—'Holee! holee! Hukee! hukee!'[1] That was our duty toward you; but now you are no longer men; we'll see how strong we are! We will grind you and reduce your flesh to dust!" the grindstones warned them.

---

[1] The sounds of corn being ground.

The dogs in turn addressed the wooden men as follows: "Why haven't you fed us? We've just looked at you from a distance, while you were eating, and you chased us away. You always had a stick handy to beat us with; this is how you treated us when we couldn't speak to you. Why shouldn't we sink our teeth into you now?"

Thus spoke the dogs, and the wooden men, attacked by their animals and utensils, perished. They say their only descendants are the monkeys in the forest; and for this reason monkeys look like men and remind us of a race who were made from wood.

Translated by Thomas Ballantine Irving

Fray Bernardino De Sahagún: Aztec Birth Rituals for Boys and Girls (1547 CE) from *General History of the Things of the New Spain*

The conquerors of Mesoamerica spoke often of the love that the Aztec people showed for their children. Since the Spanish also believed that the Aztecs were "Satanic," they were puzzled by the tenderness with which the young were treated. The Mexican fondness for formal rhetoric is evident in this excerpt. The speeches were given by the midwife as she cut the umbilical cord. One can see the masculinist bias of the Aztecs here, but also their sense that every person was valuable, both to the community and in the sacred world.

Aztec society waged ritual wars almost continuously against several of its neighbors. What evidence of this can you find in the midwife's speeches? Does the midwife's "greeting" to a female baby suggest to you that women were inferior to men in Aztec culture? Why or why not?

Here are told the words which the midwife said to the baby boy when she cut the umbilical cord. Thus she told him that it was all affliction, travail, that would befall him on earth, and that he would die in war, or would die in sacrifice to the gods. And she entrusted his umbilical cord to the distinguished warriors, those wise in war, to bury it there in the midst of the plains where warfare was practiced. So she told him he might issue forth in war in all parts. And the umbilical cord of the baby girl she only buried there by the hearth; thus she signified that the woman was to go nowhere. Her very task was the home life, life by the fire, by the grinding stone.

"My precious son, my youngest one, behold the doctrine, the example which thy mother, thy father Yoaltecutli, Yoalticitl, have established. I take, I cut [the umbilical cord] from thy side, from thy middle. Heed, hearken: thy home is not here, for thou art an eagle, thou art an ocelot; thou art a roseate spoonbill, thou art a troupial. Thou art the serpent, the bird of the lord of the near, of the nigh. Here is only the place of thy nest. Thou hast only been hatched here; thou hast only come, arrived. Thou art only come forth on earth here. Here dost thou bud, blossom, germinate. Here thou becomest the chip, the fragment [of thy mother]. Here are only thy cradle, thy cradle blanket, the resting place of thy head: only thy place of arrival. Thou belongest out there; out there thou hast been consecrated. Thou hast been sent into warfare. War is thy desert,[1] thy task. Thou shalt give drink, nourishment, food to the sun, the lord of the earth. Thy real home, thy property, thy lot is the home of the sun there in the heavens. Thou art to praise, to gladden Totonametl in manic.[2] Perhaps thou wilt receive the gift, perhaps thou wilt merit death by the obsidian knife, the flowered death by the obsidian knife.[3]

"And this which is lifted from thy side, which cometh from thy middle, I take from thee: the gift, the property of Tlaltecutli, Tonatiuh. And when war hath stirred, hath formed, it will be introduced into the hands of the eagle warriors, the ocelot warriors, the brave warriors. They go giving it to thy mother, thy father, Tonatiuh, Tlaltecutli; they go entering into the center, the middle, of the plains. And thereby thou hast been assigned, thou hast been vowed to the sun, to Tlaltecutli; thereby thou deliverest thyself to him. And thus there within the battlefield, thy name will be inscribed, will be registered in order that thy

[1]Your destiny.
[2]A title for the sun god.
[3]Death in warfare.

renown will not be forgotten, will not be lost. The precious thing removed from thy side is to be considered thy thorn, thy maguey, thy cane of tobacco, thy firm branch with which thou art to do penance, thy vow is to be fulfilled. And now let us hope for something; perhaps we shall deserve, we shall merit something. Work, my precious son; may the lord of the near, of the nigh, yet give thee life, provide for thee, array thee."

And if it were a female, the midwife said to her when she cut her umbilical cord: "My beloved maiden, my beloved noblewoman, thou hast endured fatigue! Our lord, the lord of the near, of the nigh, hath sent thee. Thou hast come to arrive at a place of weariness, a place of anguish, a place of fatigue where there is cold, there is wind. And now take heed: from thy side, from thy middle I take it, I cut it. Thy mother, thy father, Yoaltecutli, Yoalticutl, order it, request it. Thou wilt be in the heart of the home, thou wilt go nowhere, thou wilt nowhere become a wanderer, thou becomest the banked fire, the hearth stones. Here our lord planteth thee, burieth thee. And thou wilt become fatigued, thou wilt become tired; thou art to provide water, to grind maize, to drudge; thou art to sweat by the ashes, by the hearth."

Charles O. Dibble and Arthur J. O. Anderson

Aztec Poetry (c. 1490 CE)

Images of bloody human sacrifices and military imperialism dominate popular conceptions of life in Mesoamerica on the eve of the Spanish conquest. But the peoples of the Valley of Mexico were quite diverse in their tastes and talents, as shown in these excerpts from a record of a meeting that took place in the city of Huexotzinco in 1490. Huexotzinco's ruler, Tecayehuatzin, despised the militarism of his Aztec neighbors. He convened a conference of intellectuals and artists to debate what to him seemed the really important question with which states should be concerned: the utility and meaning of poetry. Poetry is here compared to adornments of feathers and gold. All three poems are translated by Miguel Leon-Portilla.

How does the second poem say that poetry can compensate at least in part for death?

I am come, oh my friends

I am come, oh my friends,
with necklaces I entwine you,
with feathers of the macaw I adorn you,
a precious bird, I dress with feathers,
I paint with gold,
I embrace mankind.
With trembling quetzal feathers,
with circlets of song,
I give myself to the community.
I will carry you with me to the palace
where we all
someday,
all must betake ourselves,
to the region of the dead.
Our life has only been loaned to us!

Let us have friends here!

Let us have friends here!
It is the time to know our faces.
Only with flowers
can our song enrapture.
We will have gone to His house,
but our word
shall live here on earth.
We will go, leaving behind
our grief, our song.
For this will be known,
the song shall remain real.
We will have gone to His house,
but our word
Shall live here on earth.

From where the eagles are resting

Tezcatlipoca, an omnipotent and omnipresent deity who gives joy and sorrow alike for inscrutable reasons is the "Giver of Life" addressed in the poem. The work is a forceful statement of the Aztec belief that their endless ritual warfare was required by the Gods. The Spanish had not yet crushed the Aztecs when this song was composed, but its defiant tone is undercut by the fear that the long-awaited end of the world might be at hand, that their empire would prove as fleeting as life itself.

The poet here equates Tenochtitlan with "the foundation of heaven." What images in the poem suggest that militarism is built into the very structure of the universe? This work seems to claim that the Mexica are unconquerable, but it also contains evidence to the contrary. In what lines can you find hints of the poet's fears for the future?

From where the eagles are resting,
from where the tigers are exalted,
the Sun is invoked.

Like a shield that descends,
so does the sun set.
In Mexico night is falling,
war rages on all sides.
Oh Giver of Life!
war comes near. . . .

Proud of itself is the city of Mexico-Tenochtitlan.
Here no one fears to die in war.
This is our glory.
This is Your Command,
oh Giver of Life!
Have this in mind, oh princes,
do not forget it.
Who could conquer Tenochtitlan?
Who could shake the foundation of heaven?

With our arrows,
with our shields,
the city exists,
Mexico-Tenochtitlan remains.

Christopher Columbus
Letter to the King concerning his first voyage (1493 CE)

Columbus's letter to the king written shortly after his return to Spain illustrates the discoverer's very idyllic view of the Caribbean peoples and of the islands they occupied. His journey, to his way of thinking, marked a return to the innocence that supposedly characterized early humanity. The writer stresses the people's fearfulness and generosity and their lack of any sophisticated religious creed. These people regarded the visitors as some variety of supernatural being, a belief that soon faded in every situation. Columbus, as was typical of Europeans of the time, expected to encounter weird beings and beasts, and, finding none on the islands he explored, related that they surely must be found just a little farther on.

What does Columbus see as the biggest differences between these people of the New World and those of Europe? What does Columbus emphasize as the primary virtues of these new people? What does Columbus hope becomes of them? How did these people perceive Columbus and his crew?

The people of this island, and of all the other islands which I have found and of which I have information, all go naked, men and women, as their mothers bore them, although some women cover a single place with the leaf of a plant or with a net of cotton which they make for the purpose. They have no iron or steel or weapons, nor are they fitted to use them, not because they are not well built men and of handsome stature, but because they are very marvelously timorous. They have no other arms than weapons made of cane, cut in seeding time, to the ends of which they fix a small sharpened stick. And they do not dare to make use of these, for many times it has happened that I have sent ashore two or three men to some town to have speech, and countless people have come out to them, and as soon as they have seen my men approaching they have fled, even a father not waiting for his son. And this, not because ill has been done to anyone; on the contrary, at every point where I have been and have been able to have speech, I have given to them of all that I had, such as cloth and many other things, without receiving anything for it; but so they are, incurably timid. It is true that, after they have been reassured and have lost their fear, they are so guileless and so generous with all they possess, that no one would believe it who has not seen it. They never refuse anything which they possess, if it be asked of them; on the contrary, they invite anyone to share it, and display as much love as if they would give their hearts, and whether the thing be of value or whether it be of small price, at once with whatever trifle of whatever kind it may be that is given to them, with that they are content. I forbade that they should be given things so worthless as fragments of broken crockery and scraps of broken glass, and ends of straps, although when they were able to get them, they fancied that they possessed the best jewel in the world. So it was found that a sailor for a strap received gold to the weight of two and a half *castellanos*, and others much more for other things which were worth much less. As for new *blancas*, for them they would give everything which they had, although it might be two or three *castellanos*[1] weight of gold or an *arroba*[2] or two of spun cotton. . . . They took even the pieces of the broken hoops of the wine barrels and, like savages, gave what they had, so that it seemed to me to be wrong

---

[1]One gold *castellano* was worth about 980 *blancas*.
[2]About 25 pounds.

and I forbade it. And I gave a thousand handsome good things, which I had brought, in order that they might conceive affection, and more than that, might become Christians and be inclined to the love and service of their highnesses[3] and of the whole Castilian nation, and strive to aid us and to give us of the things which they have in abundance and which are necessary to us. And they do not know any creed and are not idolaters; only they all believe that power and good are in the heavens, and they are very firmly convinced that I, with these ships and men, came from the heavens, and in this belief they everywhere received me, after they had overcome their fear. And this does not come because they are ignorant; on the contrary, they are of a very acute intelligence and are men who navigate all those seas, so that it is amazing how good an account they give of everything, but it is because they have never seen people clothed or ships of such a kind.

And as soon as I arrived in the Indies, in the first island which I found, I took by force some of them; in order that they might learn and give me information of that which there is in those parts, and so it was that they soon understood us, and we them, either by speech or signs, and they have been very serviceable. I still take them with me, and they are always assured that I come from Heaven, for all the intercourse which they have had with me; and they were the first to announce this wherever I went, and the others went running from house to house and to the neighboring towns, with loud cries of, "Come! Come to see the people from Heaven!" So all, men and women alike, when their minds were set at rest concerning us, came, so that not one, great or small, remained behind, and all brought something to eat and drink, which they gave with extraordinary affection. In all the island, they have very many canoes, like rowing *fustas*, some larger, some smaller, and some are larger than a *fusta* of eighteen benches. They are not so broad, because they are made of a single log of wood, but a *fusta* would not keep up with them in rowing, since their speed is a thing incredible. And in these they navigate among all those islands, which are innumerable, and carry their goods. One of these canoes I have seen with seventy and eighty men in her, and each one with his oar.

In all these islands, I saw no great diversity in the appearance of the people or in their manners and language.[4] On the contrary, they all understand one another, which is a very curious thing, on account of which I hope that their highnesses will determine upon their conversion[5] to our holy faith, towards which they are very inclined.

I have already said how I have gone one hundred and seven leagues in a straight line from west to east along the seashore of the island Juana, and as a result of that voyage, I can say that this island is larger than England and Scotland together,[6] for, beyond these one hundred and seven leagues, there remain to the westward two provinces to which I have not gone. One of these provinces they call "Avan," and there the people are born with tails; and these provinces cannot have a length of less than fifty or sixty leagues, as I could understand from those Indians whom I have and who know all the islands.

Translated by Cecil Jane

---

[3]King Ferdinand and Queen Isabella of Spain.
[4]He was later to realize that the various peoples indeed had a variety of languages.
[5]I.e., decide that they should be converted.
[6]Columbus was mistaken in thinking that Cuba was bigger even than England by itself.

Permissions

Acknowledgements for *Reading About the World Vol. I*, edited by Paul Brians, et al.

Poems from *Myths from Mesopotamia: Creation, The Flood, Gilgamesh and Others*, translated by Stephanie Dalley. Reprinted by permission of Oxford University Press, 1989.

Evil spirits, Hymn to Nanna, Excerpts from *The Treasures of Darkness* trans. by Thorkild Jacobsen, 1976, p. 2, 13, 7-8. Reprinted by permission of Yale University Press.

"Hymn to Ishtar," trans. Ferris Stephens, from *Ancient Near Eastern Texts Relating to the Old Testament*, p. 383, by James Pritchard, ed. Copyright © 1955 by Princeton University Press. Reprinted by permission of Princeton University Press.

6 Sumerian proverbs trans. Edmund Gordon from *Sumerian Proverbs: Glimpses of Everday Life in Ancient Mesopotamia*, The University Museum, University of Philadelphia, 1959.

5 Akkadian proverbs from *Babylonian Wisdom Literature*, translated by W. G. Lambert, 1963. Reprinted by permission of Oxford University Press.

Hymn to Osiris, Hymn to Sekmet-Bast, trans. Margaret Murray from *Egyptian Religious Poetry*, 1980. Reprinted by permission of John Murray Publishers, Ltd.

From *Love Songs of the New Kingdom*, translated from the Ancient Egyptian by John L. Foster and illustrated with hieroglyphs drawn by John L. Foster, pp. 13-14, 18, 30. Copyright © 1969, 1970, 1971, 1972, 1973, 1974 by John L. Foster. By permission of the University of Texas Press.

"The Two Aspects of Death" in *Voices from Ancient Egypt: An Anthology of Middle Kingdom* Writings (1991), pp. 132-133 by R.B. Parkinson. Reprinted by permission of University of Oklahoma Press.

"In Praise of Learned Scribes" trans. John Wilson, from *Ancient Near Eastern Texts Relating to the Old Testament* (1955), pp. 431-432.

"Hymn to the Aton" trans. Theophile Meek from *Ancient Near Eastern Texts Relating to the Old Testament*, p. 370 by James Pritchard, ed. Copyright © 1975 by Princeton University Press. Reprinted by permission of Princeton University Press.

The Odyssey: Box IX, lines 216-461 from *The Odyssey of Homer*, by Richmond Lattimore. Copyright © 1965, 1967 by Richmond Lattimore. Copyright Renewed. Reprinted by permission of HarperCollins Publishers, Inc.

Herodotus: "Xerxes at the Hellespont," from *The Histories*, "Pericles' Funeral Oration" and "The First Delphic Hymn," trans. © 1996 Richard Hooker.

3 Greek poems: "Spartan Soldier," "To Anaktoria," "Seizure," trans. Willis Barnstone from *Greek Lyric Poetry*, Indiana University Press, 1967. Reprinted with permission of the author.

Excerpt from *Antigone*, by Sophocles, trans. Elizabeth Wykoff (1954), pp. 171-180. Reprinted by permission of The University of Chicago Press.

Paragraphs 86, 87, 89, 100, 112, 169-174, 551, 562 from The Presocratic Philosophers, Cambridge University Press (1957), trans. G.S. Kirk and J. E. Raven and M. Schofield. Reprinted with the permission of Cambridge University Press.

Sextus Empiricus on Progatoras, excerpt from THE LOEB CLASSICAL LIBRARY. Reprinted by the permission of the publishers and the Loeb Classical Library from Sextus Empiricus: Outlines of Pyrrhonism, Vol. 1, translated by R.G. Bury, Cambridge, Mass.: Harvard University Press, 1933.

Excerpts on the Atomists from THE LOEB CLASSICAL LIBRARY. Reprinted by the permission of the publishers and the Loeb Classical Library from Diogenes Laertius: Lives of Eminent Philosophers, Vol. 2, translated by R.D. Hicks, Cambridge, Mass.: Harvard University Press, 1925.

Selections about Aristotle, Protagoras, paragraphs 14, 30 from Selections from Early Greek Philosophy, 4/e by Milton Nahm, pp. 288-289, 292-293. Copyright © 1964. Reprinted by permission of Prentice-Hall, Inc., Upper Saddle River, NJ.

Excerpt from The Nicomachean Ethics, by Aristotle (1973). Translated by David Ross, revised, J.L. Ackerill & J.O. Rumson, pp. 261-269. Reproduced by permission of Oxford University Press.

"Epitaph for the Tomb of a Roman Wife" from AUTHORS DEAD AND LIVING by F.L. Lucas, London, 1926. Reprinted by permission of Hogarth Press.

THE NATURE OF THINGS: A New Translation of Lucretius, Book I, lines 146-204. Translated by Frank O. Copley. Translation copyright © 1977 by W.W. Norton & Company, Inc. Reprinted by permission of W.W. Norton & Company, Inc.

"Daedalus & Icarus" Book 8, lines 181-235, pages 254-256, from The Metamorphoses of Ovid: A New Verse Translation, translated by Allen Mandelbaum. Copyright © 1993 by Allen Mandelbaum, reprinted by permission of Harcourt, Inc.

Propertius: "Elegies, Book I, no. 3" edited and translated by J.P. McCulloch from The Poems of Sextus Propertius, pp. 15-16. Copyright © 1972 The Regents of The University of California. Reprinted by permission.